The Mermaid and the Partridge

Studies on the Texts
of the Desert of Judah

Edited by

Florentino García Martínez

Associate editors

Peter W. Flint
Eibert J. C. Tigchelaar

VOLUME 96

The Mermaid and the Partridge

Essays from the Copenhagen Conference on
Revising Texts from Cave Four

Edited by

George J. Brooke and Jesper Høgenhaven

BRILL

LEIDEN • BOSTON
2011

This book is printed on acid-free paper.

Library of Congress Cataloging-in-Publication Data

The mermaid and the partridge : essays from the Copenhagen Conference [June 2009]
on revising texts from Cave Four / edited by George J. Brooke and Jesper Hogenhaven.
      p. cm. — (Studies on the texts of the desert of Judah, ISSN 0169-9962 ; 96)
   Includes bibliographical references and index.
   ISBN 978-90-04-19430-4 (hardback : alk. paper) 1. Dead Sea scrolls.
4Q—Congresses. I. Brooke, George J. II. Høgenhaven, Jesper.

   BM488.5.M47 2011
   296.1'55—dc22

                                                                          2010051689

ISSN 0169-9962
ISBN 978 90 04 19430 4

Copyright 2011 by Koninklijke Brill NV, Leiden, The Netherlands.
Koninklijke Brill NV incorporates the imprints Brill, Hotei Publishing,
IDC Publishers, Martinus Nijhoff Publishers and VSP.

Mixed Sources
Product group from well-managed forests
and other controlled sources
www.fsc.org   Cert no. SGS-COC-006767
©1996 Forest Stewardship Council

PRINTED BY A-D DRUK BV - ZEIST, THE NETHERLANDS

CONTENTS

LIST OF ABBREVIATIONS

AB	Anchor Bible
ABD	Anchor Bible Dictionary
ABRL	Anchor Bible Reference Library
AJEC	Ancient Judaism and early Christianity

Allegro, *Qumrân Cave 4.I*
    John M. Allegro with the collaboration of Arnold A. Anderson, *Qumrân Cave 4.I (4Q158–4Q186)* (DJDJ V; Oxford: Clarendon Press, 1968)

AnBib	Analecta biblica
ASTI	*Annual of the Swedish Theological Institute*
ASNU	Acta seminarii neotestamentici upsaliensis
ATD	Das Alte Testament Deutsch

Berrin, *Pesher Nahum Scroll*
    Shani L. Berrin (Tzoref), *The Pesher Nahum Scroll from Qumran: An Exegetical Study of 4Q169* (STDJ 53; Leiden: Brill, 2004)

BETL	Bibliotheca ephemeridum theologicarum lovaniensium
Bib	*Biblica*
BibInt	*Biblical Interpretation*

Brooke, *Exegesis at Qumran*
    George J. Brooke, *Exegesis at Qumran: 4QFlorilegium in its Jewish Context* (JSOTSup 29; Sheffield: JSOT Press, 1985)

BWANT	Beiträge zur Wissenschaft vom Alten und Neuen Testament
BZAW	Beihefte zur Zeitschrift für die alttestamentliche Wissenschaft
CBQ	*Catholic Biblical Quarterly*
CBQMS	Catholic Biblical Quarterly Monograph Series
CCAG	Catalogus Codicum Astrologorum Graecum
CNS	*Cristianesimo nella storia*
CRAI	Comptes rendus de l'Académie des inscriptions et belles-lettres
CRINT	Compendiam rerum iudaicarum ad Novum Testamentum
DJD	Discoveries in the Judaean Desert
DJDJ	Discoveries in the Judaean Desert of Jordan

Doudna, *4Q Pesher Nahum*

> Gregory L. Doudna, *4Q Pesher Nahum: A Critical Edition* (JSPSup 35; Copenhagen International Series 8; London: Sheffield Academic Press, 2001)

DSD   *Dead Sea Discoveries*

DSSEL   Dead Sea Scrolls Electronic Library

DSSR   The Dead Sea Scrolls Reader

DSSSE   Florentino García Martínez and Eibert J.C. Tigchelaar, *The Dead Sea Scrolls Study Edition* (Leiden, New York, Köln; Brill, 1997–1998)

EB   Echter Bibel

EDSS   Lawrence H. Schiffman and James C. VanderKam, eds., *Encyclopedia of the Dead Sea Scrolls* (New York: Oxford University Press, 2000

FAT   Forschungen zum Alten Testament

FOTL   Forms of the Old Testament Literature

Horgan, *Pesharim*

> Maurya P. Horgan, *Pesharim: Qumran Interpretations of Biblical Books* (CBQMS 8; Washington, DC: Catholic Biblical Association of America, 1979)

Horgan, "Pesharim"

> Maurya P. Horgan, "Pesharim," in *Hebrew, Aramaic, and Greek Texts with English Translations. Volume 6B: Pesharim, Other Commentaries, and Related Documents* (ed. James H. Charlesworth et al.; PTSDSSP; Tübingen: Mohr Siebeck; Louisville: Westminster John Knox Press, 2002), 1–193.

HTR   *Harvard Theological Review*

HUCA   *Hebrew Union College Annual*

IEJ   *Israel Exploration Journal*

JBL   *Journal of Biblical Literature*

JJS   *Journal of Jewish Studies*

JQR   *Jewish Quarterly Review*

JSJ   *Journal for the Study of Judaism*

JSOTSup   Journal for the Study of the Old Testament: Supplement Series

JSJSup   Supplements to the Journal for the Study of Judaism

JSP   *Journal for the Study of the Pseudepigrapha*

JSPSup   Journal for the Study of the Pseudepigrapha: Supplement Series

JSS   *Journal of Semitic Studies*

NT	*Novum Testamentum*
NTS	*New Testament Studies*
OrAnt	Oriens antiquus
OTF	Oriental Translation Fund
PAM	Palestine Archaeological Museum
PTSDSSP	The Princeton Theological Seminary Dead Sea Scrolls Project
RAC	Reallexikon für Antike und Christentum, ed. E. Kluser et al., Stuttgart 1950–
RB	*Revue Biblique*
RevQ	*Revue de Qumrân*
RHPR	*Revue d'histoire et de philosophie religieuses*
SBLDS	Society of Biblical Literature Dissertation Series
SBLEJL	Society of Biblical Literature Early Judaism and Its Literature
SBLMS	Society of Biblical Literature Monograph Series
SBT	Studies in Biblical Theology
SEÅ	*Svensk Exegetisk Årsbok*
SNT	Studien zum Neuen Testament
STDJ	Studies on the Texts of the Desert of Judah
Steudel, *Der Midrasch zur Eschatologie*	Annette Steudel, *Der Midrasch zur Eschatologie aus der Qumrangemeinde (4QMidrEschat$^{a.b}$): Materielle Rekonstruktion, Textbestand, Gattung und traditionsgeschichtliche Einordnung des durch 4Q174 („Florilegium") und 4Q177 („Catena A") repräsentieren Werkes aus den Qumranfunden* (STDJ 13; Leiden: Brill, 1994)
StPB	Studia post-biblica
Strugnell, "Notes en marge"	John Strugnell, "Notes en marge du volume V des «Discoveries in the Judaean Desert of Jordan»," *RevQ* 7 (1969–1970): 163–276.
SUNT	Studien zur Umwelt des Neuen Testaments
TICP	Travaux de l'instiut catholique de Paris
TSAJ	Texte und Studien zum Antiken Judentum
VT	*Vetus Testamentum*
VTSup	Vetus Testamentum Supplements
WUNT	Wissenschaftliche Untersuchungen zum Neuen Testament
ZTK	*Zeitschrift für Theologie und Kirche*

INTRODUCTION

For some years a project has been under way to carry out a thorough-going revision of volume V in the series Discoveries in the Judaean Desert (of Jordan).[1] Recently this project has itself been revised. Those originally assigned the task have invited several other scholars to join them in working on the rich range of complex texts. The new expanded team includes many of those who have written monographs or extensive studies on the respective manuscripts for which they have now assumed responsibility.

The new team was invited by the Department of Biblical Exegesis of the Faculty of Theology at the University of Copenhagen to meet in Copenhagen in June 2009. The papers in this volume represent some of the ongoing work of the expanded team, but the major purpose of the meeting was to allow for detailed discussion of how the project should be brought to fruition in a timely and consistent manner. In particular a number of issues related to how the process of the revision of a principal edition of texts should be undertaken were discussed. However, the meeting also offered the opportunity for the presentation of some working papers on topics that were of particular concern to the individual contributors to the revision. It is a selection of those papers which is published here.

The title of this volume refers to the subject matter and to the setting for the discussions it reflects. The manuscripts published in DJD V were all found in cave 4 at Qumran. This cave, which of all the Qumran caves contained the greatest number of scroll remains, has also been called the "Cave of the Wounded Partridge," reflecting the tradition that a partridge had led local Bedouin to an early discovery of the cave years before its rediscovery in 1952. The Mermaid from Hans Christian Andersen's fairy-tale, represented by a statue by the Danish sculptor Edvard Eriksen situated on the Copenhagen waterfront, is the most well-known symbol of that city.

Not every manuscript that appears in DJD V is the subject of a study here. To begin with, not every member of the new team was able

---

[1] John M. Allegro with the collaboration of Arnold A. Anderson, *Qumrân Cave 4.I (4Q158–4Q186)* (DJDJ V; Oxford: Clarendon Press, 1968).

to attend the Copenhagen meeting. Two of those unable to be present, Devorah Dimant and Eibert Tigchelaar, have recently published studies elsewhere on the manuscripts for which they are responsible.[2] In addition Mladen Popović had to withdraw at the last minute; in his case the full and long form of his new edition of 4Q186 is included here, since it is likely that in the re-edition of DJD V this will be shortened considerably because of issues of space.[3] Furthermore, Jutta Jokiranta, who is taking responsibility for the revised edition of *Pesher Psalms* (4Q171), only spoke informally at the conference about the implications of the acrostic structure of Psalm 37 for the better understanding of parts of the extant commentary and how that fitted with what she has written about elsewhere concerning the construction of identity in the community responsible for the composition of *Pesher Psalms*, both in terms of collective designations as well as individual ones, such as is reflected in the role of the Teacher as a prototypical image of the group.[4] Finally and regrettably, Annette Steudel's contribution could not be included in this volume. She addressed directly the challenge on where the debate had reached concerning her views on 4Q174 and 4Q177. She remains inclined to see 4Q174 and 4Q177 as two copies of the same composition because of their distinctive shared terminology, formulae and method, and because of the character of their dualism which seems to belong to a particular phase in the history of the

---

[2] See Devorah Dimant, "On Righteous and Sinners: 4Q181 Reconsidered," in *Manières de penser dans l'Antiquité méditerranéenne et orientale: Mélanges offerts à Francis Schmidt par ses élèves, ses collègues et ses amis* (ed. Christophe Batsch and Mădălina Vârtejanu-Joubert; JSJSup 134; Leiden: Brill, 2009), 61–85. See also Eibert J. C. Tigchelaar, "Lady Folly and Her House in Three Qumran Manuscripts: On the Relation between *4Q425 15, 5Q16,* and *4Q184 1,*" *RevQ* 23/91 (2008): 371–81; idem, "Constructing, Deconstructing and Reconstructing Fragmentary Manuscripts. Illustrated by a Study of 4Q184 (4QWiles of the Wicked Woman)," in *Rediscovering the Dead Sea Scrolls: An Assessment of Old and New Approaches and Methods* (ed. Maxine L. Grossman; Studies in the Dead Sea Scrolls and Related Literature; Grand Rapids: Eerdmans, 2010), 26–47.

[3] His earlier detailed work, predominantly concerned with 4Q186, is well known: Mladen Popović, *Reading the Human Body: Physiognomies and Astrology in the Dead Sea Scrolls and Hellenistic-Early Roman Period Judaism* (STDJ 67; Leiden: Brill, 2007).

[4] See Jutta Jokiranta, "Identity on a Continuum: Constructing and Expressing Sectarian Social Identity in Qumran *Serakhim* and *Pesharim*," (Ph.D. diss., University of Helsinki, 2005), 115–23; eadem, "Qumran—The Prototypical Teacher in the Qumran Pesharim: A Social Identity Approach," in *Ancient Israel: The Old Testament in Its Context* (ed. Philip F. Esler; Minneapolis: Fortress Press, 2006), 254–63; eadem, "Social Identity Approach: Identity-Constructing Elements in the Psalms Pesher," in *Defining Identities: We, You, and the Other in the Dead Sea Scrolls. Proceedings of the Fifth Meeting of the IOQS in Groningen* (ed. Florentino García Martínez and Mladen Popović; STDJ 70; Leiden: Boston, 2008), 85–109, esp. 93–108.

sect (after the composition of the *Damascus Document*, the *Rule of the Community* and *MMT*, but before *Pesher Habakkuk*).

The well-known extensive review of DJD V by John Strugnell[5] began by welcoming the new volume produced by Allegro and Anderson. Strugnell pointed out just how very diverse the compositions were in the group that had been assigned to Allegro, and he described the volume as containing the majority of the "textes exégétiques de la bibliothèque qumrânienne." He also plainly stated that there would have to be much more work done before there was a perfect understanding of these difficult texts and his lengthy review was a first attempt at offering something of a more fulsome edition of the texts than Allegro and Anderson had provided in order to bring the volume into line with the earlier ones in the series. Some of the many issues that have been faced subsequently by students of these texts are the subjects of the studies in this volume. Indeed, most of the studies here take up Strugnell's challenge and try to expound some of the issues that the editors of the respective manuscripts have been facing forty years after the first principal edition. The revised DJD V will not be able to offer comprehensive commentaries because on several of these manuscripts there have been more than one monograph and many other shorter studies. Rather in the light of all the comment and suggestion so far, the new editors will attempt to offer a balanced summary of the *status quaestionis*, with some clear indication of preferred choices of reading and understanding. The opportunity afforded by this volume allows readers of the forthcoming revised principal edition to see how several of the contributors have been thinking about their specific assignments as they approached the task of producing new editions of these intriguing texts.

Molly Zahn presents some of her fresh reflections on 4Q158. In the first place she reconsiders its contents, nomenclature and status. She notes how nearly all the text that survives on the fragments can be related to Exodus in some way and so she wonders whether 4Q158 only originally covered the book of Exodus. She reaffirms her opinion that the concerns and approaches of 4Q158 differ from those of 4Q364–367 and so she endorses the view that it should not simply be viewed as another copy of the composition on those other manuscripts; 4QReworked Pentateuch A as a designation shows that it is a composition of a slightly different sort. The overarching hermeneutical

---

[5] John Strugnell, "Notes en marge."

project reflected in 4Q158 is its attempt to create or strengthen connections between two different pentateuchal texts. Most often these connections are between parts of Exodus, as divine commands are matched by explicit statements of fulfilment; sometimes the passages being coordinated are close together, but sometimes they are much further apart, such as between Exodus 6 and 24 in frg. 4. Sometimes other books seem to have been involved: in frags. 1–2 there appears to be a juxtaposition of Exodus 4 and Genesis 32. Overall, Zahn urges readers of texts like 4Q158 to reconsider how text and interpretation belong together in the early stages of the transmission of the authoritative text.

Moshe Bernstein has been reconsidering 4Q159 for several years.[6] In his contribution he notes how not every part of the composition has to do with legal matters, so, as with many of the fragmentary manuscripts from Qumran it is actually very difficult to decide upon a suitable title for the work. Once an appropriate order for the various fragments is determined, then further questions can be asked about the composition, especially questions concerning why the particulars discussed in the composition were selected and not others. Bernstein is especially sensitive to the fact that not necessarily all the subjects in the composition were the topics of disputes with other contemporary Jewish groups. This aspect seems to separate the text from 4Q513–514, with which it has often been associated. In the end Bernstein suggests that more attention ought to be paid to the wide variety of forms employed in the Qumran material when "legal" issues were treated, and that, for the purpose of analyzing the presentation and development of "legal" issues, the differences between the manuscripts may be more important than their similarities.

Alex Jassen offers a fresh analysis of 4Q161, *Pesher Isaiah A*, an analysis that takes seriously the full range of suggestions by earlier scholars to shed some new light on the ideological similarities of this Isaiah commentary and that espoused in some parts of the *War Rule* and 4Q285. Jassen pays attention to the structure of the commentary, especially its use of re-citation in some places to mark what he understands to be "brief digressions;" such re-citation seems to be undertaken

---

[6] See, e.g., Moshe J. Bernstein, "4Q159 Fragment 5 and the 'Desert Theology' of the Qumran Sect," in *Emanuel: Studies in Hebrew Bible, Septuagint, and Dead Sea Scrolls in Honor of Emanuel Tov* (ed. Shalom M. Paul, Robert A. Kraft, Lawrence H. Schiffman, and Weston W. Fields; VTSup 94; Leiden: Brill, 2003), 43–56.

to assert key points, especially about the character of the superiority of the priests to the Davidic messiah who is subordinated to them. Since the detailed readings of the manuscript fragments have not been scrutinised closely, as has been the case with some more prominent sectarian compositions, he also offers some suggestions for adjusted readings, using both scriptural and sectarian passages to support his suggestions, thus providing a larger framework for the exegesis of the pesher than the other fragments alone. In making various proposals for new readings and restorations, Jassen also revisits the exegetical strategy behind the composition and therein also lies his concern to understand the similarities and differences with other sectarian literature in particular, such as the *War Rule* and 4Q285. Characteristic of 4Q161 is that the scriptural lemmata are usually made up of several verses of Isaiah and the comments are comparatively brief. Within what survives Jassen demonstrates that the pesher presents its own portrait of the eschatological war. That does not preclude the possibility that actual contemporary military campaigns are in mind, such as the assault by Ptolemy Lathyrus (understood as a repetition of the Assyrian campaign—the referent of Isaiah), but the primary focus is the future war against the Kittim, a war in which the royal messiah, dressed in a priestly fashion, takes over the priestly role during the actual battle while not in the end challenging their authority. This fresh reading of 4Q161 aligns it more closely with the priestly perspectives of other sectarian militaristic compositions and sets its messianism in a wider framework.

Roman Vielhauer has worked closely both with the scriptural book of Hosea and with the two distinct Hosea pesharim that come from Cave 4.[7] In his contribution to this study he neatly combines both aspects of his expertise to delve into the question concerning how the Book of Hosea was read, received and understood at Qumran. Vielhauer convincingly shows that whereas in the scriptural book divine judgement was directed against the whole of Israel, in the Qumran pesharim that same judgement is given specificity so that it was directed against just one particular sacrilegious group. Then, by considering the other explicit uses of Hosea in the sectarian literature, especially the

---

[7] Roman Vielhauer, *Das Werden des Buch Hosea: Eine redaktionsgeschichtliche Untersuchung* (BZAW 349; Berlin: de Gruyter, 2007); idem, "Materielle Rekonstruktion und historische Einordnung der beiden Pescharim zum Hoseabuch (4QpHos^a und 4QpHos^b)," *RevQ* 20/77 (2001): 39–91.

Damascus Document, he notes how the same exegetical move is commonly made with the prophet's words being applied with specificity to one group or another. With the analysis of some other references to Hosea in sectarian compositions Vielhauer convincingly demonstrates how Hosea is consistently understood as being concerned with a differentiation within Israel between the righteous and sinners. In addition he concludes that the Qumran group developed their approach to Hosea, not only on the basis of their own experiences but particularly probably on their viewing the scriptural book through the lens of its final verse: "For the ways of the Lord are straight, and the righteous walk in them, but the sinners stumble in them."

Trine Bjørnung Hasselbalch bravely attempts to say something in greater detail than has been done heretofore about fragments 1 and 4 as they have been assigned to the collection of unidentified fragments labelled as 4Q172. For fragment 1 she proposes that although its contents permit little to be said, its partially extant formulaic data provide evidence of formal traits that belong either to legal or exegetical contexts; given that one phrase survives, בעת רעב, which echoes other exegetical passages rather than legal ones, it seems likely that the association of the fragment with exegetical literature is entirely justified. For fragment 4 there is enough vocabulary to permit the suggestion that the contents are a complex interweaving of parts of Hos 7:2–6 and Zeph 3:4. There are no introductory formulae of any sort, so Hasselbalch likens the handling of scripture to similar juxtapositions in the reworkings of Jeremiah and Ezekiel in 4Q383–391. These suggestions have broader implications, for they seem to indicate that it may well be incorrect to differentiate, as some scholars have done, between the exegetical treatments of Isaiah and the Twelve on the one hand from those of Jeremiah and Ezekiel on the other, for whom no explicit pesher type commentary is extant.

Another study dealing with a small piece is offered by Søren Holst. It has become widely recognized that 4Q173 fragment 5 is probably not to be assigned with the other fragments that are labelled as 4Q173. This single fragment is now identified as 4Q173a and continues to provoke interest.[8] Holst discloses how the fragment might be able to

---

[8] See, e.g., David Hamidović, "Le retour au temple de Jérusalem (4Q173a olim 4Q173 5)?" *RevQ* 24/94 (2009): 283–6; Émile Puech, "4Q173a: note épigraphique," *RevQ* 24/94 (2009): 287–90.

disclose much more than its few surviving letters at first suggest. With due care and caution he notes how several details in the presentation of the composition on the manuscript, such as the representation of the divine name, can be juxtaposed with ideas implied in the few extant words to disclose the sectarian preferences for scriptural language to express their particular kind of temple ideology. Significantly his essay goes beyond the straightforward identification of scriptural allusions and citations towards an attempt at outlining why it was those scriptures that were chosen for reuse rather than others. Intriguingly, if Vielhauer is correct in his appeal to Hos 14:10 as the lens through which the Qumran sectarians read Hosea, then it could be that a similar attention to "stumbling" in 4Q173 5 deserves wider contextual interpretation.

George J. Brooke considers whether it is appropriate to change the name of 4Q174 and the similar compositions in some related manuscripts. There are obvious problems in renaming any work, problems mostly related to the confusion that can be introduced for those working in the field, but especially for those working on the edges of this specialist discipline who do not appreciate that ongoing research is causing several different kinds of redefinition and adjustment, as the recent release of revised lists by Emanuel Tov attests.[9] Brooke argues that for both emic and etic reasons it is time to change both the titles assigned to 4Q174: *Florilegium*, which was originally intended to define the selection of scriptural passages commented upon rather than the composition as a whole, and *Eschatological Midrash*, whose second element is capable of a multitude of misconstruals, are to be replaced by the title *Eschatological Commentary*. The first part of the new title is retained in part to reflect some continuity with previous understandings of the work and in part because it also genuinely covers all the extant parts of the composition which are indeed tied together through the common phrase אחרית הימים, "the latter days." The second part allows for some distance to be created between what is present in this sectarian work and the later rabbinic midrashim as well

---

[9] See Emanuel Tov, *Revised Lists of the Texts from the Judaean Desert* (Leiden: Brill, 2010). Since the publication of the database in 2002 (Emanuel Tov [ed.], *The Texts from the Judaean Desert: Indices and an Introduction to the* Discoveries in the Judaean Desert *Series* [DJD XXXIX; Oxford: Clarendon Press, 2002], 27–114), Tov states that "changes were inserted in some twenty-five percent of the lines of the database" (p. vii).

as connecting the composition both with other sectarian compilations, such as the *Commentary on Genesis A* (4Q252), and with more or less contemporary Greek and Latin commentary literature in a broader cultural context.

Jesper Høgenhaven adds to his recent work on 4Q176.[10] He argues that the name *Tanḥumim* should be retained, although it does not cover all the contents of the composition; he also wonders what should be done with the explicit subtitle in I, 15. He pays particular attention to various issues that lie behind the reconstruction of the manuscript, especially discussing the two scribal hands that feature variously. He also considers the kind of exegesis that is present in the principal surviving parts of the composition, noting astutely that no explicit exegetical formulae survive and that while some parts follow passages of Isaiah in its scriptural order, there is also a pastiche of other scriptural passages, not least from the Psalms, showing that this is creative rewriting of the tradition not unlike that to be found in some treatises. He addresses directly a set of literary questions that disclose something of the character of such a text: Who is the implied speaker? What is he saying and is it entirely controlled by scriptural tradition? Who is the implied audience he addresses? What is not quoted (such as the servant song passages or passages about idolatry) that one might have expected? These observations on the scribal features of the text, the suitable classification of its relation to earlier scriptural tradition, and its literary purposes all disclose just how much of value will be found in the new edition of this text.

Shani Tzoref, who in the revision of DJD V is actually responsible for 4Q169 (*Pesher Nahum*),[11] presented an analysis of the scriptural background of 4Q177, *Eschatological Commentary B*, work she has undertaken with Mark Laughlin. Through noting how 4Q177 offers comments on a selection of Psalms with supplementary scriptural passages informing the commentary, Laughlin and Tzoref attempt to outline what might be at stake in the selection process. They note, to begin with, how the chosen Psalms all stand as individual laments or as pleas to God for salvation from enemies; even Psalm 16 shares

---

[10] Jesper Høgenhaven, "The Literary Character of 4QTanhumim," *DSD* 14 (2007): 99–123.

[11] See Shani Berrin (Tzoref), *The Pesher Nahum Scroll from Qumran: An Exegetical Study of 4Q169* (STDJ 53; Leiden: Brill, 2004).

the same form and content as these laments, although it is sometimes understood by modern scholars slightly differently. Against such an overall perspective, Laughlin and Tzoref continue by identifying the major aspect of the structure of three columns of 4Q177 as corresponding with the seven elements of the individual lament as these are generally identified: address, complaint, expression of trust, reasoned justification, oracle of salvation, vow, and praise. They develop their approach to the text on the basis that the compiler of the composition in 4Q177 paid attention both to the whole original context of each psalm, even though only part is cited explicitly, and also to ways in which the individualism of the scriptural laments could be read collectively of the experience of the community. Ps 5:3 provides the address, Psalms 11 and 12 provide the complaint and expression of trust, Psalm 13 in particular is used to give reasons for divine intervention, and Psalms 16 and 17 are the basis for a vow to offer praise. The subordinate citations are used, so it seems, to support this compositional structuring of the commentary and in effect take the prayers of leaders and adopt them for the community. The use of the Psalms and subordinate citations together are systematically and generically interwoven. This is not a commentary in a straightforward way but prayer and its scripturalisation.

Amongst the manuscripts in DJD V the most difficult to read are probably 4Q163, *pap Pesher Isaiah C*, and 4Q185, a sapiential text. Mika Pajunen presents a detailed analysis of his fresh close reading of the fragments assigned to 4Q185. In particular he sets his work alongside the study by Hermann Lichtenberger.[12] Pajunen pays special attention to all the data on the manuscript, notably supralinear letter shapes and various scribal markings, most of which were absent from Lichtenberger's edition, even though Hartmut Stegemann had checked Lichtenberger's readings on the original manuscript in 1977. Consideration of the full data seems to help with the overall reading of the surviving text in surprising ways, not least in making the parallelism of the wisdom composition all the clearer.

---

[12] Hermann Lichtenberger, "Eine weisheitliche Mahnrede in den Qumranfunden (4Q185)," in *Qumrân: Sa piété, sa théologie et son milieu* (ed. M. Delcor; BETL 46; Paris–Gembloux: Duculot; Leuven: University Press, 1978), 151–62.

Two papers are also included by scholars associated with Copenhagen's Institute for Biblical Exegesis, but who are not part of the newly extended editorial team for the revision of DJD V. Gregory L. Doudna reconsidered some of his historical conclusions concerning *Pesher Nahum* (4Q169).[13] Doudna reads *Pesher Nahum* 3–4 I, 8–12 as having a twofold reference: in the first place there is a general statement that indicates that anybody hung up is accursed, and in addition such a curse is applied specifically to a ruler. On the basis that the sobriquets in *Pesher Nahum* should not be considered solely as veiled allusions to figures in the distant past, but as references to contemporary people and events, Doudna proposes that the curse was made actual in relation to the defeat of Antigonus Mattathias at the hands of the Romans. According to Dio Cassius he was hung up alive on a cross and tortured in the process of being executed. With this possibility in mind Doudna sets about filling in some of the other identifications, offering an impressionistic set of possibilities of intriguing potential. Doudna daringly suggests that the "Lion of Wrath" of *Pesher Nahum* is Mark Anthony himself, the gentile responsible for the crucifixion. With the Ephraimites of the pesher identified as the "seekers-after-smooth-things," as Pharisees of non Judahite origin, Doudna wonders whether it is time to align the followers of the Teacher of Righteousness (Hycanus II) with the Sadducees in some form as has been hinted at by several scholars for the communities behind the sectarian Dead Sea Scrolls of an earlier period. The overall implication of these identifications is that the group behind the sectarian scrolls should only be considered as out of influence in Jerusalem from 40 BCE onwards.

Mogens Müller offers a short paper on the typologies of scriptural commentary in the pesharim and in the New Testament, a study with wide-ranging implications. He challenges the widely held assumption that the dominant form of exegesis in the New Testament is proof-texting. Rather he has noticed that for Paul and the early Gospels experiences are read out of and back into scripture with little attention to the plain meaning of the text, like the *method* discernible in the continuous pesharim. However, at a later stage in group development the plain meaning reasserts itself, as continuous commentaries (with the *form* of the continuous pesharim) develop with the scriptural text

---

[13] Gregory L. Doudna, *4Q Pesher Nahum: A Critical Edition* (JSPSup 35; Copenhagen International Series 8; London: Sheffield Academic Press, 2001).

in control in their structure. These slightly later developments in interpretative practices also need to be put alongside how the scriptural texts that are being commented upon are moving from an authoritative status within the group to something more akin to canonical status. The phenomenology of scriptural interpretation has not received much attention; Müller's essay has taken some bold steps forward with this agenda, an agenda which has much relevance especially for the so-called "continuous pesharim" in DJD V.

Overall the studies in this volume reinforce the value of undertaking the revision of DJD V. The rich variety of compositions in DJD V is expounded all the more fruitfully through the employment of a range of interpretative strategies. First, there are several instances in this volume, such as with 4Q185, where the importance of the right reading of even small fragments and their suitable placement in manuscripts is apparent. Second, attention has to be paid not just to the content of the fragments, but their layout and other features: scribal information can assist in the appropriate appreciation of a number of literary issues. Third, although the exegesis in many of the compositions assigned to DJD V is of several different kinds, it is apparent in several texts, such as 4Q158 and 4Q177, that the way they reflect authoritative scriptural traditions is basic to their construction; as a result the right discernment of how such exegetical conclusions were reached and why is fundamental to the correct modern understanding of most of these compositions. Fourth, the reconsideration of the reading and reconstruction of these texts enables fresh literary questions to be posed. These questions include such matters as the reconsideration of the genres of several of the compositions, reconsiderations that encourage editors to consider renaming some of the texts on these fragmentary manuscripts. But the fresh literary perspectives also produce new understandings of the structures of these intricate compositions, their purposes and their likely settings in the life of the communities where they were produced and transmitted.

The three days spent in Copenhagen were charged full of enthusiasm for this revitalized project. The warm welcome provided by the Faculty of Theology provided a convivial setting for genuine progress on the new editions of these complex fragmentary manuscripts. The hospitality of the Dean of the Faculty of Theology, Steffen Kjeldgaard-Pedersen, and the Institute for Biblical Exegesis provided through a generous grant from the H. P. Hjerl Hansen Foundation was much appreciated by all the participants and has contributed substantially

towards the completion of this long-awaited work. We are also grateful to Florentino García Martínez for accepting this set of studies into
the distinguished series Studies on the Texts of the Desert of Judah.

Jesper Høgenhaven, Copenhagen
George J. Brooke, Manchester

BUILDING TEXTUAL BRIDGES:
TOWARDS AN UNDERSTANDING OF 4Q158
(4QREWORKED PENTATEUCH A)[1]

MOLLY M. ZAHN
Lawrence, Kansas

John Allegro published 4Q158 in DJD V under the title "Biblical Paraphrase: Genesis, Exodus."[2] Allegro gave no defense or explanation of
this title, and provided little indication of how he thought the fifteen
fragments grouped under this siglum should be understood. For much
of the forty years since that initial publication, scant attention was
paid to 4Q158, and thus little progress was made towards answering
basic questions about the nature of this text.[3] This began to change
when 4Q158 was identified by Emanuel Tov as a fifth copy of the composition represented by 4Q364–367, a composition which eventually
received the name 4QReworked Pentateuch (4QRP).[4] Over the past
fifteen years, 4Q158 (now labeled 4QReworked Pentateuch[a]) and the
other 4QRP manuscripts have come to play a central role in discussions concerning the interpretation and transmission of the scriptural
text in the Second Temple period, especially as pertains to the phenomenon known as "rewritten Scripture."[5] Despite the increased attention,

---

[1] I would like to extend my thanks to Moshe Bernstein and George Brooke for
inviting me to be involved in the re-edition of the DJD V materials, as well as to Jesper Høgenhaven for organizing the Copenhagen symposium at which this paper was
originally delivered. I am especially grateful to Professor Bernstein for the numerous
conversations over the past several years that continue to deepen my understanding
of 4Q158 and the other Reworked Pentateuch texts.

[2] Allegro, *Qumrân Cave 4.I*, 1–6.

[3] Exceptional are the substantive discussions of 4Q158 in two of the major reviews
of DJD V; see Strugnell, "Notes en marge"; Raphael Weiss, "פרסום חדש ממגילות
המלח ים," in *Studies in the Text and Language of the Bible* (Jerusalem: Magnes,
1981), 319–34.

[4] Emanuel Tov, "The Textual Status of 4Q364–367 (4QPP)," in *The Madrid Qum-
ran Congress: Proceedings of the International Congress on the Dead Sea Scrolls, Madrid
18–21 March 1991* (ed. Julio Trebolle Barrera and Luis Vegas Montaner; STDJ 11;
Leiden: Brill, 1992), 1.43–82, at pp. 46–8. For the *editio princeps* of 4Q364–367, see
Emanuel Tov and Sidnie White, "4QReworked Pentateuch," in DJD XIII (Oxford:
Clarendon, 1994), 187–351.

[5] See the literature cited in the notes throughout this essay.

however, much remains to be understood about 4Q158. This short contribution presents one preliminary result of my ongoing investigation of 4Q158 and the ways its editor or editors read, interpreted, and reconfigured the pentateuchal text.[6] I will demonstrate that especially prominent in 4Q158 are a series of alterations that aim to create or strengthen connections between two passages that are regarded as in some way parallel. These changes give 4Q158 a distinct profile, and point to the significant implications of even this relatively fragmentary manuscript for our understanding of the various ways in which the Pentateuch was transmitted and transformed in the Second Temple period. Before moving to the texts themselves, however, some introductory points are in order.

CONTENTS, NOMENCLATURE, AND STATUS

4Q158 is preserved in 15 numbered fragments which range in size from approximately 10 cm long by 7 cm wide to less than a square centimeter. All fifteen fragments were published by Allegro, although John Strugnell subsequently identified two further fragments that could be associated with frag. 14.[7] In some cases, several fragments can be grouped through reconstruction. Thus, fragments 7, 8, and 9 represent a continuous section of text, as do fragments 1 and 2 and fragments 10, 11, and 12. Nearly all of the fragments can be linked with specific portions of the Pentateuch, although the degree of agreement with the pentateuchal text as we know it from elsewhere varies a great deal. Some fragments, like frag. 5 and frags. 10–12, appear to have contained nothing other than the familiar pentateuchal text, with only very minor unique readings. Others clearly reflect particular verses, but contain additional material, juxtapose texts in unexpected ways, or present other types of major difference from known versions of the Pentateuch. Finally, there are fragments that do not closely correspond with the wording of any particular pentateuchal passage, but which seem to be a paraphrase or restating of a specific text, as is the

---

[6] There is little to suggest that all the differences between 4Q158 and known versions of the Pentateuch were introduced by a single individual: they may have resulted from the work of a series of editors/scribes.

[7] A transcription and photograph (PAM 44.191) were published in Strugnell, "Notes en marge," 175 + Plate 1. The fragments in question are also visible on PAM 42.619 and 44.180.

case for frag. 3 and frag. 14. The majority of the fragments contain material from Exodus; the only other biblical book represented is Genesis, in frags. 1–2 and frag. 3. It may be the case that 4Q158 in fact only originally covered the book of Exodus, since the Genesis material in frags. 1–2 is juxtaposed with Exodus material and Exodus seems to be the original narrative context of the fragment.[8] Frag. 3 does not show explicit connections to Exodus, but may have been located there as well.

As mentioned above, 4Q158 has already undergone one change in nomenclature, from 4QBiblical Paraphrase to 4QReworked Pentateuch[a]. It has become clear, however, that another change is necessary. While Tov and Crawford argued in their edition of 4Q364–367 that those four manuscripts, along with 4Q158, represented copies of a single composition, that conclusion has been challenged. There is very little physical overlap between any of the manuscripts, and thus almost no concrete evidence for a single composition. The alleged similarity in the way all five manuscripts rework the pentateuchal text, which Tov and Crawford cited as the main evidence for a single composition, is not obvious, and has been questioned by Moshe Bernstein and Michael Segal.[9] George Brooke approached the problem from the perspective of the material evidence of the manuscripts, and has demonstrated convincingly that, even where more than one of the 4QRP MSS treat the same pentateuchal text, they can almost never be reconstructed as having the same text.[10] In recent work I have been able to confirm earlier suggestions of the texts' hermeneutical independence from one another, showing that each of the 4QRP manuscripts has its own set of concerns and particular approaches in its reworking of

---

[8] Michael Segal, "Biblical Exegesis in 4Q158: Techniques and Genre," *Textus* 19 (1998): 45–62, at p. 48. On the juxtaposition of Genesis and Exodus material in frag. 1–2, see further below.

[9] Moshe J. Bernstein, "Pentateuchal Interpretation at Qumran," in *The Dead Sea Scrolls after Fifty Years* (ed. Peter W. Flint and James C. VanderKam; Leiden: Brill, 1998), 1.128–59, at p. 134; Moshe J. Bernstein, "'Rewritten Bible': A Generic Category Which Has Outlived its Usefulness?," *Textus* 22 (2005): 169–96, at p. 196; Michael Segal, "4QReworked Pentateuch or 4QPentateuch?," in *The Dead Sea Scrolls: Fifty Years After Their Discovery* (ed. Lawrence H. Schiffman, Emanuel Tov, and James C. VanderKam; Jerusalem: Israel Exploration Society/Shrine of the Book, Israel Museum, 2000), 391–9, at pp. 396–7.

[10] George J. Brooke, "4Q158: Reworked Pentateuch[a] or Reworked Pentateuch A?," *DSD* 8 (2001): 219–41.

the pentateuchal text.[11] Thus, although the five manuscripts do use similar techniques and sometimes have similar approaches to the scriptural text, they should not be regarded as copies of the same composition. A more appropriate title for 4Q158 is therefore 4QReworked Pentateuch A.

Yet another change in nomenclature—in effect—has recently been suggested by various scholars. Here the issue is not how the 4QRP manuscripts relate to one another, but their compositional status. Because of their sometimes major departures from the text of the Pentateuch as we know it, Tov and Crawford assumed that the 4QRP manuscripts represented an extra-biblical, interpretative composition belonging to the category of "rewritten Scripture." More recently, a number of scholars have argued that this assumption is not valid and that the 4QRP manuscripts most likely represent nothing more than expanded copies of the Pentateuch—thus, perhaps, a better name for them would simply be 4QPentateuch. The main argument of these scholars is that the differences between the 4QRP manuscripts and the text of the Pentateuch as known from elsewhere are the same *types of differences* as occur *within* the transmission history of the biblical text itself.[12] That is, since we know the text of the Hebrew Scriptures was still in a state of flux in the late Second Temple period, why should we rule out the possibility that the 4QRP manuscripts simply represent hitherto unknown expanded editions of the Pentateuch? In the last few years Tov himself has embraced this position wholeheartedly.[13]

---

[11] Molly M. Zahn, *Rethinking Rewritten Scripture: Composition and Exegesis in the 4QReworked Pentateuch Manuscripts* (STDJ 95; Leiden: Brill, 2011).

[12] Eugene Ulrich, "The Dead Sea Scrolls and the Biblical Text," in *The Dead Sea Scrolls after Fifty Years* (ed. Peter W. Flint and James C. VanderKam; Leiden: Brill, 1998), 1.79–100, at p. 88; Eugene Ulrich, "The Text of the Hebrew Scriptures at the Time of Hillel and Jesus," in *Congress Volume Basel 2001* (ed. André Lemaire; VTSup 92; Leiden: Brill, 2002), 85–108, at pp. 102–3; James C. VanderKam, "Questions of Canon Viewed through the Dead Sea Scrolls," in *The Canon Debate* (ed. Lee M. McDonald and James A. Sanders; Peabody, Mass.: Hendrikson, 2002), 91–109, at pp. 96–100. See also Armin Lange, "The Status of the Biblical Texts in the Qumran Corpus and the Canonical Process," in *The Bible as Book: The Hebrew Bible and the Judean Desert Discoveries* (ed. Edward D. Herbert and Emanuel Tov; London: British Library, 2002), 21–30, at p. 27. Michael Segal has espoused a variant form of this position, arguing that 4Q364–367 most likely represent pentateuchal manuscripts, while 4Q158 constitutes rewritten Scripture. See Segal, "4QReworked Pentateuch," 394–5.

[13] See for example Emanuel Tov, "Three Strange Books of the LXX: 1 Kings, Esther, and Daniel Compared with Similar Rewritten Compositions from Qumran and Elsewhere," in *Die Septuaginta-Texte, Kontexte, Lebenswelten* (ed. Martin Karrer and Wolfgang Kraus; Tübingen: Mohr Siebeck, 2008), 369–93, at p. 392.

Crawford has also moved in this direction, though somewhat more cautiously.[14] Others, notably Moshe Bernstein, remain skeptical.[15] I am not convinced that we have enough information to settle the question definitively.[16] One thing, however, is clear. No matter whether we regard 4Q158 as a copy of the Pentateuch or a portion thereof, or as something else entirely, the contents of this manuscript raise questions pertaining precisely to the intersection between the transmission of the pentateuchal text, the theological reflection on and interpretation of the text, and the ways in which interpretation was legitimated or authorized. The set of examples that I will discuss here will, I believe, demonstrate this point.

STRENGTHENED INTRAPENTATEUCHAL CONNECTIONS IN 4Q158

As mentioned above, besides sections which correspond closely with known versions of the Pentateuch, 4Q158 presents a variety of types of textual alteration, including additions of various sizes, new sequences, and paraphrase and other modifications. I speak confidently of "alteration" because, although each unique reading must be evaluated individually, it is clear that the vast majority, if not all, of the significant variants preserved in 4Q158 represent a later form of the text than that attested in MT, the Samaritan (= SP), and other versions. That is, it is of course possible that 4Q158 at times preserves an earlier reading than other known witnesses, but most often the nature of the variant makes clear that one or more editors have revised the text for a particular exegetical reason that is usually identifiable. These exegetical

---

[14] Sidnie White Crawford, *Rewriting Scripture in Second Temple Times* (Grand Rapids: Eerdmans, 2008), 56–7. Note that Crawford's discussion of the status of the 4QRP MSS in this book focuses exclusively on 4Q364 and 4Q365. However, her arguments here are not substantially different than those made in an earlier article regarding 4QRP as a whole; Sidnie White Crawford, "The 'Rewritten' Bible at Qumran: A Look at Three Texts," *ErIsr* 26 (1999): 1–8 (Eng.). A similar position is found in Daniel K. Falk, *The Parabiblical Texts: Strategies for Extending the Scriptures in the Dead Sea Scrolls* (Companion to the Qumran Scrolls 8; London: T&T Clark, 2007), 111.

[15] See, most recently, Moshe J. Bernstein, "What Has Happened to the Laws? The Treatment of Legal Material in 4QReworked Pentateuch," *DSD* 15 (2008): 24–49, at pp. 48–9. Agreeing with Bernstein's position is Torleif Elgvin, "Sixty Years of Qumran Research: Implications for Biblical Studies," *SEÅ* 73 (2008): 7–28, at p. 16.

[16] See my discussion of the problem in Molly M. Zahn, "The Problem of Characterizing the 4QReworked Pentateuch Manuscripts: Bible, Rewritten Bible, or None of the Above?," *DSD* 15 (2008): 315–39.

motivations range from filling perceived gaps in the scriptural text to clarifying halakhah.[17] Yet, although many types of changes are preserved in 4Q158, most of the largest share a particular hermeneutical theme. Put broadly, these changes function in some way to create or strengthen connections between two different pentateuchal texts.

One particular manifestation of this hermeneutical theme or tendency is famous from the Samaritan Pentateuch itself and is now also attested in the pre-Samaritan texts from Qumran:[18] the desire to ensure that every divine command is matched precisely by a narrative of its fulfillment, and that every recollection (such as Moses' recollection of the wilderness wandering on the plains of Moab) corresponds with the events as originally described. Thus, for example, an editor systematically expanded the plague narratives of Exodus to make sure that no doubt could remain that Moses and Aaron scrupulously carried out God's commands exactly as they were instructed.[19] As we shall see, 4Q158 sometimes demonstrates precisely the same concern with making sure commands are fulfilled. Yet while in the Samaritan text tradition this type of change occurs in very specific situations, the editor or editors responsible for 4Q158 show a concern to coordinate distant texts in a much greater variety of ways, seemingly for a much greater variety of purposes. Connections are made, not just between incidents that are formally parallel, such as command and fulfillment, but also between more loosely connected texts. Interestingly, in all but one of the instances of this type of change in 4Q158, all the texts involved come from Exodus. That is, the concern to coordinate disparate passages in various ways did not generally extend beyond the borders

---

[17] A full study is available in Zahn, *Rethinking Rewritten Scripture*.

[18] I regard the pre-Samaritan texts as "new literary editions" of an earlier text-type represented for the most part by MT. While I do not assume that every variant from MT in SP or the pre-SP MSS is later than the corresponding MT reading, the major differences between the two text-types are clearly the result of exegetical expansion of a text that must have been similar to MT on the part of editors in the pre-SP text tradition. For the idea of "multiple literary editions" of biblical books, see Eugene Ulrich, *The Dead Sea Scrolls and the Origins of the Bible* (Grand Rapids: Eerdmans, 1999), 99–120.

[19] For an astute analysis of the nature of this category of changes in the Samaritan Pentateuch, see Michael Segal, "The Text of the Hebrew Bible In Light of the Dead Sea Scrolls," *Materia Giudaica* 12 (2007): 5–20, at pp. 11–7. See also my discussion of the evidence of SP specifically as relates to the 4QRP MSS in Zahn, *Rethinking Rewritten Scripture*, chapter 4.

of the book of Exodus.[20] This may constitute additional evidence that 4Q158 did not originally cover the entire Torah but focused on Exodus alone.

In what follows, I will present examples of these "coordinating" changes in 4Q158 by proceeding along a spectrum from cases closer to what we find in the Samaritan text tradition to those more distant.

1. 4Q158 7, 4–5

In one case, in frag. 7, we see a move that is precisely analogous to the practice of the pre-Samaritan texts: a divine command that is not explicitly carried out in other known versions is given a record of its exact fulfillment. Aside from a significant rearrangement attested in lines 1–3, frag. 7 follows the text of Exod 20:21b–21:4 as known from sp and the pre-Samaritan Qumran text 4QpaleoExod[m]. In other words, 4Q158 is here based upon a *Vorlage* that corresponds with the pre-Samaritan tradition. Thus, starting in frag. 7, 3, 4Q158 contains the material from Deut 5:30–31 that in the Samaritan text tradition was spliced into the Sinai pericope in Exodus 20 along with other material from Deuteronomy 5 and 18. In this section (Exod 20:21b sp = Deut 5:30–31 = 4Q158 7, 3–4), God commands Moses to instruct the people to return to their tents, and then to "stand before" him to receive "the whole commandment."[21] Now, in the Samaritan-type text that constituted a *Vorlage* for 4Q158, God's command is never fulfilled. From the end of Deut 5:31, sp moves directly back to Exod 20:22, which also contains divine speech to Moses, and from there to the Covenant Code. Moses is supposed to dismiss the people so that he alone receives God's ordinances (משפטים)—in order to mediate them to all Israel later—but according to sp God launches into the משפטים without giving Moses a chance to instruct the Israelites to return to their tents. In 4Q158 this problem has been solved through the moderate addition in lines 4–5 (double-underlined in the Appendix).

---

[20] The only non-Exodus text involved is Genesis 32 (see Example 6 below). In Example 1, material is involved that in the MT and LXX is located in Deuteronomy. As I discuss in the next section, however, this material had been integrated into Exodus already in the pre-Samaritan version of Exodus, and it is clear that 4Q158 used this version, or a text very like it, as a *Vorlage*. Therefore, while this example may appear to involve Deuteronomy, it in fact pertains exclusively to Exodus in the particular version that the editor responsible for 4Q158 was using.

[21] For the text of frag. 7, 1–7, see the Appendix, Text 1.

The beginning of line 5 makes clear that God now stops talking long enough for Moses to go and fulfill his command. The people dutifully head off for their tents, and Moses returns so that God can continue.

As mentioned above, here 4Q158 contains precisely the same type of editorial intervention as is common in the Samaritan text tradition: it supplies the "missing" record of the fulfillment of a divine command. It is notable, however, that the "problem" of the missing fulfillment is actually *created* by the pre-SP editor who inserted the Deuteronomy 5 material into Exodus 20. In other words, the lack of mention of the fulfillment of the command constitutes a problem only in the pre-SP version of Exodus. In Deuteronomy (both in SP and in other versions), God's command is quoted in the context of Moses' recollection, on the plains of Moab, of the events at Horeb. This recollection is interwoven with Moses' "present-day" adjurations to the Israelites. Immediately after recounting God's command ("Go, tell them…"), for example, Moses stops recalling God's words and speaks directly to the Israelites ("Make sure that you do just as YHWH your God has commanded you…"; Deut 5:32). In other words, God's command in the context of Deuteronomy is part of a "flashback" that does not extend to the fulfillment of that command. Thus, in this insertion we see the editor responsible for 4Q158 responding specifically to a "problem" that, ironically, was itself caused by an earlier revision of the text of Exodus.

2. *4Q158 4, 2*

In other cases, 4Q158 preserves changes that show a concern with the same types of passages as SP, namely commands, recollections, and similar speech events, but intervenes in cases that seem to have fallen outside the purview of the editors in the Samaritan tradition. It should be stressed that in SP these interventions occur in very specific situations—basically, where God tells someone to do something and there is no record that they in fact later did that thing, or where someone says that they did or said something at an earlier point in time, but there is no earlier record that they did or said that particular thing.[22] In 4Q158 we sometimes see a similar interest in these sorts of speech events that refer forward or backward in time, but with looser

---

[22] See Segal, "Text of the Hebrew Bible," 16–7.

parameters. Here it is not the case that a notice of the fulfillment of a command or the appropriate precedent for a recollection is *absent*; instead an editor intervenes to strengthen or make more explicit the connections between two related passages.

For example, the context of frag. 4 is clearly the covenant ceremony at Mt. Sinai as described in Exodus 24: according to lines 3–5, the *maṣṣebot* are erected for the twelve tribes, sacrifice is offered, half the blood collected in bowls, and the other half sprinkled on the altar.[23] In line 2, however, there is material that points directly to Exod 3:12, where God says to Moses, בהוציאך את העם ממצרים תעבדון את האלהים על ההר הזה, "When you lead the people out from Egypt, you shall worship God upon this mountain." Obviously this prediction (which seems to be interpreted as a command in 4Q158; see the words צוה לכה in line 1) is fulfilled through the Israelites' sacrificial worship at Sinai. In most versions, however, there is no explicit notice that the ceremony described in Exodus 24 actually fulfills God's earlier words. The connection is left to the reader or hearer to deduce. In 4Q158, this connection is not left to chance; instead, an editor has inserted some sort of explicit reference back to Exod 3:12, surely with the purpose of noting that God's command upon that occasion is now being fulfilled.

3. *4Q158 1, 15–19*

A similar concern with coordination of speech events can be seen in frag. 1.[24] Lines 14–15 contain the text of Exod 4:28, according to which "Moses related to Aaron all the words of YHWH with which he sent him and all the signs that he commanded him." The extant portion of line 16 then reads...יהוה לי לאמור בהוציאכה את, "...YHWH to me, saying, 'When you lead out the...'" Although the context is fragmentary and becomes increasingly so, it seems clear that an editor was not satisfied with the simple indirect report that Moses reported God's words to Aaron, but felt compelled to add a "transcript" of Moses' speech, such that Moses now directly tells Aaron of the promise God makes in Exod 3:12. As in the previous example, there is no speech or description "missing": the text as found in other versions simply refers indirectly to Moses' speech to Aaron without providing the precise

---

[23] For the text of frag. 4, see the Appendix, Text 2.
[24] For the text of frag. 1, see the Appendix, Text 3.

contents of the speech. The additional material in 4Q158 strength-
ens the cross-reference to "all the words of YHWH" by including,
it appears, a recapitulation in Moses' own voice of his conversation
with God.[25]

4. *4Q158 14*

Another interesting example along the same lines can be found in frag.
14.[26] This fragment was originally considered by Tov to contain no
biblical material, and it is true that several of the preserved phrases do
not strike the ear as particularly biblical.[27] However, frag. 14 in fact has
connections with two distinct biblical texts. The first of these is Exod
6:3–8, where, after revealing the divine name to Moses, God promises that he will deliver Israel from Egypt, take Israel as his people,
and give them the land as their inheritance. Reminiscences of these
themes appear in lines 5, 6, and 7 of frag. 14: וגאלתים at the end of
line 5, ועשיתי לי לעם in line 6, and ארץ לבטח in line 7. The second
passage in view here must be the Song of the Sea in Exodus 15: besides
the mention of Egypt and "redeeming," the words מצולות, לבב ים,
and תהום in lines 7 and 8 create an unmistakable connection to that
poetic description of God's deliverance of Israel from Egypt. (Compare
בלב ים, Exod 15:8; מצולת, Exod 15:5; תהמת, Exod 15:5, 8.)[28]

Now, how does this fit in with the dynamics of coordinating parallel passages that I have been discussing? As Michael Segal pointed out
already some years ago, it seems most likely that frag. 14 represents a

---

[25] The remains in the badly damaged lines 17–19 contain further allusions to the
topics of Moses' discussion with God in Exod 3:4–4:17, and thus probably represent
the continuation of Moses' speech. However, they do not appear merely to reproduce
the pentateuchal text. Instead, it seems that these lines may have contained a para-
phrased version of Moses' encounter with God.

[26] For the text of frag. 14, see the Appendix, Text 4.

[27] See for example וכול הרוחות in line 2, לברכה להארץ in line 3, and תהי צרה
in line 5.

[28] It is interesting to note that, despite the obvious correspondences to Exodus 15,
the lexical parallels to the Hebrew text of MT and SP are not exact: לבב instead of
לב, מצולות תהום instead of מצולת in the absolute state, and תהום instead of the
plural תהומות. (I am grateful to Prof. Moshe Bernstein for this observation.) This
may simply suggest that the editor responsible for 4Q158 used a *Vorlage* that differed
slightly from known versions of Exodus 15. On the other hand, the differences may
point to a conclusion more clearly implied by the material elsewhere in this fragment
that is not obviously pentateuchal; namely, that the purpose of the new material in
frag. 14 cannot be only or solely an attempt to integrate Exodus 6 and Exodus 15 (see
further below).

rewriting or paraphrase of the divine promise in Exodus 6 to deliver the people from Egypt and bring them into the land. This paraphrase incorporates into Exodus 6 language that directly points to Exodus 15.[29] In this way, an editor has made God's promise in Exodus 6 more explicit, anticipating not just *that* he will deliver the Israelites from Egypt, but precisely *how* he will do so—by defeating the Egyptians at the Sea. In other words, Exodus 6 constitutes a promise, and Exodus 15 describes how God fulfilled at least the first portion of that promise. While these texts are related conceptually in our familiar versions of Exodus—if one thinks about it—they do not share very much specific language. In 4Q158 this is changed, so that the prediction in Exodus 6 now corresponds more closely to the fulfillment in Exodus 15. While the slight differences in vocabulary and the non-biblical phrases make clear that more must be going on here than simply the coordination of two scriptural texts, it seems that part of the editors' goal at this point was to effect a textual strengthening of the connection between promise and fulfillment, just as in the previous examples.

5. 4Q158 4, 6–7

In the previous three cases, one could argue that there is still a formal or metatextual relationship between the two texts that are connected: even if (prior to the editing in 4Q158) the texts share little *language*, they are related in that one episode recounts the fulfillment of a promise or command made in the other. At the farthest end of the spectrum, however, are cases that involve texts with an even looser relationship to one another.

For example, in frag. 4, the clear connection with Exodus 24 mentioned earlier disappears after line 5. In line 6 we get the phrase אשר הראיתי אל אברהם ואל..., "which I showed to Abraham and to..." and presumably we can fill in "Isaac and to Jacob."[30] In line 7 there is a reference, similar to that in frag. 14, to God's promise to become the God of the Israelites. The *hiph'il* of ראה in line 6, coupled with mention of the patriarchs, points us back again to Exodus 6, where in v. 3 God

---

[29] Segal, "Biblical Exegesis," 54–5.

[30] In fact, the word after ואל has been erased, and a trace of the tail of ק is visible in the middle of the word below the erased area. It appears that the scribe initially wrote אל אברהם ואל יעקוב, but then, realizing that he had forgotten יצחק, erased יעקוב and continued after the erasure.

says that he "appeared" or "revealed himself" (וארא, *niph'al*) to Abraham and his offspring as El Shaddai. In Exodus 6 we also find God's promise to become the God of the descendants of Abraham (v. 7). Frag. 4, therefore, seems to make some sort of connection between Exodus 24 and God's self-revelation to the patriarchs in Exodus 6.[31]

The key term linking these two texts, though it is not preserved in the extant portion of frag. 4, must be ברית, "covenant." Covenant language occurs early on in Exodus 6: right after God announces that he appeared to Abraham, Isaac, and Jacob as El Shaddai but did not reveal his true name to them, God continues by saying וגם הקמתי את ברית אתם, "and I also established my *covenant* with them" (Exod 6:4). In 4Q158 frag. 4, the last action from the covenant ceremony of Exodus 24 that is preserved for us is Moses taking half the blood and sprinkling it upon the altar (line 5 = Exod 24:6). As the reconstruction shows, the next thing Moses does according to Exodus 24 is to take the ספר הברית, "book of the covenant," and read it to the people (Exod 24:7). The text of frag. 4 shifts from third-person verbs in lines 4–5 (זרק, ויעל) to a first-person verb in line 6: היראתי, "I showed." Surely the "I" here, who shows or reveals something to Abraham, must be God. The shift of speaker indicates that what we have in lines 6 and following in frag. 4 must represent the *contents* of the ספר הברית, which Moses is now reading out loud to the people.[32] And whatever else these contents might be, they seem to open with a connection being made between God's self-revelation to the patriarchs and establishment of a covenant with them, and the covenant now being ratified at Sinai, as Strugnell and Segal have suggested.[33] As it is in other versions of Exodus, the promises to the patriarchs are not mentioned in the context of Sinai, and the ברית here ratified is not associated with God's earlier covenant-making. In 4Q158, it may be the case that the two covenants are identified, just as *Jubilees* envisions a single covenant periodically renewed.[34] Whether or not this is true, the two covenants are clearly

---

[31] See Strugnell, "Notes en marge," 170; Segal, "Biblical Exegesis," 49–50. As Segal and Strugnell both note, there is also allusion here to God's covenant with Abraham in Genesis 17, which has thematic and lexical correspondences with Exod 6:3–8. For further discussion, see Zahn, *Rethinking Rewritten Scripture*, 48–54.

[32] Strugnell, "Notes en marge," 170.

[33] See the two previous notes.

[34] See especially *Jubilees* 6:10–12, where Noah's eternal covenant is associated with the eternal covenant made at Sinai. For analysis of the attitude towards covenant in *Jubilees*, see John C. Endres, *Biblical Interpretation in the Book of Jubilees* (CBQMS 18;

brought into textual and conceptual proximity: through his reconfiguration of the passage the editor expresses the hermeneutical and theological conclusion that the covenant at Sinai is a direct continuation of God's earlier involvement with the people of Israel—a point that is made, to be sure, in the book of Deuteronomy, but not elsewhere explicated within the account of the Sinai covenant itself.[35] Here, two events that are not directly related at all in other versions of Exodus are brought together: the link here strengthened by an editor in 4Q158 is now topical or thematic, rather than involving any kind of formal or metatextual connection as in the previous examples.

6. 4Q158 1–2

Finally, a similar thematic connection seems to lie behind one of the most striking changes to the pentateuchal text preserved in 4Q158. Frags. 1–2 juxtapose the story of Jacob wrestling with the mysterious "man" in Genesis 32 with the episode from Exodus 4 of Moses' encounter with Aaron in the wilderness (Exod 4:27–28). The reason for this otherwise unattested juxtaposition is not immediately evident. The only plausible interpretation to date is that of Strugnell, who tentatively suggested that the two pericopes may have been brought together because of the parallel between Jacob's wrestling match and the episode immediately preceding Moses' reunification with Aaron, namely the "bridegroom of blood" pericope in Exod 4:24–26.[36] It is also possible that other parallels, such as the fact that both Jacob and Moses are on their way to meet their brother when the encounter with a potentially hostile divine being occurs, further influenced the association of these passages.[37] It is not necessary to reconstruct the editor's precise train of thought, however, to conclude that these two passages

Washington, D.C.: Catholic Biblical Association, 1987), 226–8; Betsy Halpern Amaru, *Rewriting the Bible: Land and Covenant in Post-Biblical Jewish Literature* (Valley Forge, Penn.: Trinity Press International, 1994), 25–30.

[35] The theme of the land promised to the ancestors is of course very prominent in Deuteronomy; special mention can be made of the connection of this theme with the requirement of obedience to God's commands in e.g. Deut 6:10–15; 7:12–13; 8:18–19.

[36] Strugnell, "Notes en marge," 169. The parallel was already noted by Rashbam in his commentary to Gen 32:29. See Moshe Greenberg, *Understanding Exodus* (New York: Behrman House, 1969), 111.

[37] A number of commentators have observed various parallels between Exod 4:24–26, along with its immediate context, and Genesis 32. For an example, with literature, see Bernard P. Robinson, "Zipporah to the Rescue: A Contextual Study of

have been juxtaposed because of the topical and thematic similarities between them. Once again, there is no inherent textual connection between the two—they are simply two similar stories whose points of correspondence are highlighted in 4Q158 by positioning them in proximity to one another.

Conclusions

4Q158 thus demonstrates the efforts of an editor, or multiple editors, to make explicit within the text formal and conceptual connections that were not made or were left to the reader to infer in other versions of the pentateuchal text. This concern is, in my mind, one of the major distinguishing characteristics of 4Q158. This type of connection-building, which often in 4Q158 involves major reconfiguration of the text, is not found to anywhere near the same degree in the other four 4QRP manuscripts. In that it is narrative in focus it is also not strictly comparable with the *Temple Scroll*. I suspect that further investigation might reveal parallels in *Jubilees* or perhaps the *Genesis Apocryphon*. In its hermeneutical approach, this concern to create or strengthen connections between various biblical events certainly seems to anticipate rabbinic aggadic midrash and the pentateuchal Targumim.[38] Here, in a way not as clearly expressed in the other 4QRP manuscripts, we see the signs of the Torah being read as a whole, in light of itself, in a broader way than the very targeted interventions of the pre-Samaritan tradition. This way of reading clearly constitutes an advanced stage in the development of an attitude towards the scriptural text that is more familiar from later works.

What do we make of all this, and does it have any bearing on the continuing debate over whether 4Q158 and the other 4QRP manuscripts should be considered copies of the Pentateuch or something else? To the latter question I am inclined to say "no." While I believe I

Exodus IV 24–6," *VT* 36 (1986): 447–61, at pp. 451–2. I am grateful to Leeroy Malacinski for this reference.

[38] On the creation of intertextual connections in rabbinic writings, see Alexander Samely, *The Interpretation of Speech in the Pentateuch Targums: A Study of Method and Presentation in Targumic Exegesis* (TSAJ 27; Tübingen: Mohr, 1992), 65–7; Alexander Samely, *Forms of Rabbinic Literature and Thought* (Oxford: Oxford University Press, 2007), 182–4; Marc Hirshman, "Aggadic Midrash," in *The Literature of the Sages: Second Part* (ed. Shmuel Safrai, et al.; CRINT II.3a; Assen: Royal Van Gorcum, 2006), 107–32.

understand and even agree with Prof. Bernstein's statement some time ago that 4Q158 is "more exegetical" than the other 4QRP manuscripts,[39] I would not agree that the more markedly hermeneutical approach visible in this text would somehow require us to regard it as something other than a copy of the Pentateuch (or a portion thereof). After all, there is something of this attitude already present in the pre-Samaritan versions of the Pentateuch and in the other 4QRP manuscripts, even if it is not developed to the same extent. Ultimately, I would still follow Michael Segal and argue that for a rewritten work to be clearly identified as *not* a copy of the Pentateuch it needs to change some constitutive literary feature of the original, such as its narrative voice or setting. (As, for instance, in the book of *Jubilees* the voicing is changed so that the Angel of the Presence is the speaker instead of the anonymous narrator of Genesis.)[40] Despite its differences from the known text of Genesis and Exodus, 4Q158 does not preserve any of these diagnostic features. Therefore, until we develop a better way to think about these problems of classification, I believe the possibility must be taken seriously that 4Q158 represents a copy of the Pentateuch, or at least of Exodus and maybe Genesis as well.

In the end, however, the debate over what we should call this text should not obscure its significance. Whether it was intended, or accepted, as a pentateuchal manuscript or not, 4Q158 helps fill out the picture of how the scriptures were read and interpreted in the late Second Temple period. Its connections with the text and the interpretative strategies of the Samaritan Pentateuch on the one hand, and with *Jubilees* and later rabbinic interpretation on the other, show how we must continue to work to overcome the disciplinary and conceptual boundaries between study of the formation and transmission of the scriptural text and study of the various modes of interpretation of that same text. 4Q158 invites us to continue working to join these two discourses.

---

[39] Bernstein, "Pentateuchal Interpretation at Qumran," 1.134.
[40] Michael Segal, "Between Bible and Rewritten Bible," in *Biblical Interpretation at Qumran* (ed. M. Henze; Grand Rapids: Eerdmans, 2005), 10–29. See further Zahn, "4QReworked Pentateuch Manuscripts."

APPENDIX: TRANSCRIPTION AND TRANSLATION OF FRAGMENTS DISCUSSED[41]

Text 1. Fragment 7, 1–7 (Exod 20:12–17, 21b–25 SP)
Single underline: see Deut 5:30–31
Double underline: unique to 4Q158

1 את אב[יכה ואת א]מכה למ[ען] יאריכ[ון ימיך על האדמה אשר יהוה אל]היכה נתן לכה לא תרצח
  ולוא תנאף
2 ולוא תגנוב ולוא תענה ברעכה עד שוא לוא תחמוד אשת רעכה לוא תחמוד בית רעכה שדהו ו[עבדו]
  ואמתו
3 ושורו וחמורו וכל אשר לרעכה ויהי כשמוע כל העם את הקולות ואת הלפידם ואת קול השופר ואת ההר עשן ו[ירא]
  העם
4 וינועו ויעמדו מרחק ויאמרו אל מושה דבר אתה עמנו ונשמעה ואל ידבר עמנו אלוהים פן נמות
  ויאמר אלי
5 יהוה שמעתי את קול דברי העם הזה אשר דברו אליכה היטיבו כל אשר דברו
  מי יתן והיה לבבם זה להם
6 ליראה אותי ולשמור את כל מצותי כל הימים למען ייטב להם ולבניהם לעולם לך אמור להם שובו לכם
  לאהליכמה
7 ואתה פה עמוד עמדי ואדברה אליכה את כל המצוה והחקים והמשפטים אשר תלמדם ו[עשו] בארץ
  אשר אנוכי

1. your [father] and your mother[so that your days might be long upon the soil that YHWH your God is giving to you. You shall not murder. You shall not commit adultery. You shall not steal. You shall not give]
2. false testimony [against] your [neighbor]. You shall not covet [your] nei[ghbor's] wife. [You shall not covet your neighbor's house, nor his male or female slave, nor his ox, nor his donkey, nor anything that belongs to your neighbor.]
3. And YHWH said to Moses, "Go, tell them: Return t[o your tents! But you stay here with me, and I will tell you the whole commandment, the statutes]

---

[41] The following transcriptions are preliminary and presented in the order discussed above. For the final versions, please see the forthcoming new edition of the DJD V materials. In the transcription, a question mark (?) indicates ink traces that cannot be identified. Question marks in the reconstructed portions indicate uncertainties in the reconstruction.

4. and the ordinances that you will teach them so that they might do them in the land which[I am giving to them to inherit."
So Moses went and said to the people, "Return to your tents!"]

5. So each of the people returned to his tents, while Moses remained before [YHWH. YHWH spoke to Moses, saying "Say to the children of Israel: You yourselves]

6. have seen that it was from heaven that I spoke to you. You shall not make[in my presence gods of silver, and gods of gold you shall not make for yourselves. You shall make for me an earthen altar, and you shall sacrifice]

7. upon it your burnt offerings and your offerings of well-being; your sheep [and your cattle. In every place where I cause my name to be remembered I will come to you and bless you. And if an altar of stones]

Text 2. *Fragment 4 Col ii*

(? + Exod 3:12 + Exod 24:4–7 + paraphrase of Exod 6:3–8)

Single Underline: Exod 3:12
Double Underline: Exod 24:4–7
Dotted Underline: cf. Exod 6:3–8

]הזה לכ[	1
םכמ םירצמ תא וה‸צוה ?? הזה הזבגה תא וה‸זה הוהי ... רשע םינ	2
??? לארשי ינב לכ רשא תא הזבג לארשי ‸‸‸בעת יכ‸‸ כמ לע רשע‸‸ םסכב	3
םער םורח זא חבזמ הנבי (?) דלמ הזבג ה‸‸‸א זבזמ םיממה ‸‸‸מ ‸‸ לע [וה]זהב תא	4
??? םעה ‸‸‸א אל[‸‸‸] סבכ בבלב הוהמ ‸‸‸‸‸[‸‸‸]‸‸ לע בבל הזה ‸‸ חתי ‸‸‸‸‸	5
]??ימ‸‸ לאו םורבא לא יתארנ רשא תאו	6
]? םיהלאל םלוכל םלוה‸‸ה‸הל[‸‸]‸‸ה םאו	7
]? הוהי ?[ ]ל[ ]ש ה[ ]םולש ךל[ע]	8
]הו[	9

1. [ ]commanded you [When you bring out]
2. the people from Egypt you shall worship [God upon this mountain ??? He built an altar under the mountain and twelve stone pillars]

MOLLY M. ZAHN

3. according to the number of the twelve tribes[of Israel. And he sent the young men of Israel (?)   ???   ]
4. and he offered up the burnt offering upon the alta[r, and he offered bulls as sacrifices of well-being to YHWH (?). And Moses took half of the blood and put it]
5. in bowls, and half of the blood he sprinkled upon the [altar. And he took the book of the covenant and read it in the hearing of the people. . . ???]
6. which I showed to Abraham and to ??q??[Isaac and to Jacob . . .   ]
7. with them to be[come] a God to them and to their se[e]d ?[   ]
8. [f]oreve[r   ]t ʿ[ ]l[   ]? YHWH ?[   ]
9. [   ]wh[   ]

Text 3. Fragment 1–2 (Gen 32:25–33 + Exod 4:27–28 + additions)

Single underline: Gen 32:25–33
Double Underline: Exod 4:27–28
Dotted Underline: cf Exod 3:12

1	]לך ?[
2	]ו ישׂראל[
3	]?[
4	כל עקבו ותקע כף ירך יעקב אל לו ?כי נגע בכף ירך יעקב ויאמר שׁלח כי עלה השׁחר ו]ימ[ר לוא אשׁלח]ך כי[אם ברכ]ת[ני]ויאמר א[ליו מה שׁמך ויאמר
5	אם ירא]נ[י אלוהים ויאמר לוא יעקב יאמר עוד שׁמך כי אם ישׂראל כי שׂרית עם אלהים ועם אנשׁים ותוכל וישׁאל יעקב ויאמר הגידה נא שׁמך ?ל[? הזה]ויאמר[למה זה תשׁאל לשׁמי
6	ויברך אתו שׁם ויקרא יעקב שׁם המקום פניאל כי רא]י[תי אלהים פנים אל פנים ותנצל נפשׁי]ויזרח[
7	לו השׁמשׁ כאשׁר עבר את פנואל והוא צלע על ירכו על כן לוא יאכלו בני ישׂראל את גיד הנשׁה אשׁר על כף הירך עד ה]יום הזה כי נ[גע
8	בכף ירך יעקב בגיד הנשׁה]וי[אמר יהוה אל אהרון לך לקראת מ]שׁה ה[מדברה וי]ל[ך ויפגשׁהו בהר האלהים וישׁק ל[ו]
9	]ויג[ד מ]שׁ[ה לאהרון
10	]את[כל דברי יהוה אשׁר שׁלחו ואת כל האתת אשׁר צוהו וילך משׁה ואהרון ויאספו
11	]את[כל זקני בני ישׂראל וידבר אהרון את כל הדברים אשׁר דבר יהוה אל משׁה ויעשׂ האתת לעיני
12	העם ויאמן העם וישׁמעו כי פקד יהוה את בני ישׂראל וכי ראה את ענים ויקדו וישׁתחוו ?[
13	???? וכי אהיה עמך וזה לך האות כי אנכי שׁלחתיך בהוציאך את העם ממצרים תעבדון א]ת[האלהים על ההר הזה
14	*כל אם הדבר אשׁר צוה יהוה לעשׂת אתם ?[ ] יהוה למשׁה לאמר לך אל פרעה*

ויאמר יהוה

זה החזה אשר יצוה ??? אתכם אשר המזוזת כל ראו את ... ישלח אשר ויהי   יהוה   15
את ... הפלאת את המזבח מהבצרת הזה ... אל הזה יהוה   יהוה   16
ויקרא לה   17
להם יהוה   18
ויאמן ישראל   19

1. [
2. [   ]?[
3. [   ] And J[ac[ob]re[mained a]lone there, and [a man] wrestled[with him until the dawn came. And he saw that he could not prevail over him, so he struck him on the hollow of his hip socket, and Jacob['s hip socket was]
4. [wrenched out of joint] when he wrestled with him.[And]he said to [him, "Release me, for dawn has come!" And he said to him, "I will not release you unless]
5. [you give a blessing (?)] to me." He said to him, "What is your name?" And he said [to him, "Jacob." He said, "No longer shall you be called Jacob, but rather Israel, because you have striven with God
6. [and]wi[th]humans and you have prevailed."][a]cob asked [and]sai[d, "Te]l[l me, wh]at is your name?" But he said, "Why do you ask my name?"]
7. [And he bless]ed him there, and he said to him, "May YH[WH] make you fruitful [and....]you[....
8. [kno]wledge and understanding, and may he deliver you from all violence and ?[....
9. until this day and until eternal generations[....
10. And he went on his way after having blessed him there. And [Jacob] ca[lled the name of the place Peni'el, because "I have seen God face to face, and yet my life has been saved."]
11. And the sun [rose] upon him as he passed by Penue[l, and he was limping because of his hip...
12. on that day, and he said, "Do not ea[t....
13. upon the two sockets of the hip until to[day, because he struck Jacob on the hip socket, on the tendon of the sciatic nerve... YHWH spoke]
14. to Aaron, saying "Go to mee[t]M[oses in the wilderness." So he went, and he met him on the mountain of God, and he kissed him. And Moses related to Aaron al]l
15. the words of YHWH with which he had sent him and al[l the signs with which he had commanded him. ??? And Moses said to Aaron, "This is the sign that]
16. YHWH [commanded] me, saying "...When you bring[the people out from Egypt, you shall worship God upon this moun-tain...]

]s so that[
]you have striven and p[
]?[

17. to go as passers-by (??), and see, they are thirt[y(?) …]
18. YHWH God[ ]h[ ]to[…]
19. drew off(?) [ ]to[ ]?[ ]

Text 4. Fragment 14 (Col. i)⁴²

Bold Underline: See Exodus 15
Dotted Underline: See Exodus 6
Double Underline: See both

#	(right column)	Hebrew	(left column)
1	]ה		[
2	]ר וכל הרוחות		[
3	]לברכה לארץ		[ ]?[
4	]זות [ ] ובארץ מצרים		[ ]??[ ] the nations[
5	]בכל (?) יד מצרים ואגאלם		יהי צרה ?[ ]בקר אברא ?[
6	] מצרים ו[ ]'		מידם ועשיתי אתם לי לעם עד הדור
7	]לב ים במצולות		בניכה ?[לב]טח ישבו l[
8	]? ישכון		תהום ?[
9	]?wly?		בו[ ]l[

Translation

1. […]h
2. […]?r and all the winds/spirits
3. [ ]?[…]for a blessing for the earth/land
4. [ ]??[ ] the nations[…]this [ ] and in the land of Egypt
5. There will be distress and ?[ ] I will create *bqr*?[…]with all (?) the power of Egypt, and I will redeem them
6. from their hand, and I will make (them) my people until the generation[… …] Egypt and the [ ]'
7. of your sons ?[la]nd in security l[…] the heart of the sea in the depths
8. of the Deep ?[…]? who will dwell
9. in it[ ]l[…]?wly?

---

⁴² For layout purposes, the two halves of this fragment are here positioned closer to one another than they would have been originally. If frag. 14 is consistent with other fragments in 4Q158, the total line length would have been close to 100 letter spaces.

4Q159: NOMENCLATURE, TEXT, EXEGESIS, GENRE[1]

Moshe J. Bernstein

The text discussed in this essay, 4Q159—*Ordinances^a*, is the second in the series of texts published by Allegro in DJD V, and is the only one in that collection, other than 4Q158 (and, much more distantly, 4Q180–181) that is related to the Pentateuch.[2] In many ways, the issues and difficulties that the fragments of this manuscript present to us characterize, in microcosm, many of the obstacles that re-editing this whole group of 29 texts entails. None of these documents is a manuscript of a previously known work, and the task of reconstruction is therefore often a speculative and hazardous one. Of course when dealing with works closely related to the Bible, such as 4Q158[3] and the pesharim, our knowledge of the biblical text is obviously a very valuable tool in reconstruction. In the case of 4Q159, on the other hand, the decision how much to base the reconstruction on the biblical text is dependent on what sort of work the editor thinks that it is.

The task of the editor, then, once the fragments that belong to a single text have been identified, would appear to begin with the establishment of the best possible text. But in order to reconstruct the text correctly, we have to first decide what kind of text it is, i.e., to what "genre" does it belong?[4] We do not yet have to name it, to call it by its proper designation, but we do have to have a sense for what it is. One of the key questions in determining genre, in the case of almost all the texts in DJD V, is to clarify the nature of their relationship, if any, to the Hebrew Bible (or, if you prefer, to what becomes the Hebrew

---

[1] My thanks to Professor Steven Fraade for commenting on an early version of this essay, and to Dr Shani Tzoref for reading a later one.

[2] Fragment 1 was first published by John M. Allegro in "An Unpublished Fragment of Essene Halakhah (4QOrdinances)," *JSS* 6 (1961): 71–3, followed by the publication of all the fragments in Allegro, *Qumrân Cave 4.I*, 6–9. The whole document was republished by Lawrence H. Schiffman, "Ordinances and Rules," in *The Dead Sea Scrolls: Hebrew, Aramaic and Greek Texts with English Translations. Volume 1. Rule of the Community and Related Documents* (ed. J. H. Charlesworth; PTSDSSP; Tübingen: J.C.B. Mohr, 1994), 145–57.

[3] Since I do not believe that 4Q158 is to be identified with the other so-called "Reworked Pentateuch" manuscripts (4Q364–367), the possible identification of the others as "biblical" has no implications for our generic classification of 4Q158.

[4] I am employing the term "genre" fairly loosely, as a heuristic device.

Bible). The degree that our reconstruction stays close to or deviates from the biblical text depends on how we perceive that relationship. So the generic identification and textual reconstruction can easily lead us into a circular trap. How can we determine genre without reconstructing the text? How can we reconstruct a text without having some idea of the genre?

The question of nomenclature is related, although not quite as critical. The names that were assigned to Qumran texts in the early years of Qumran scholarship often gave an exaggerated sense of the scope and contents of a work.[5] Even though one might argue that scholars should know better than to be misled by the titles created in modernity, we all know that names can be very influential upon the ways in which later scholarship will approach a text. Finally, as we have learned over the past sixty years, not every text found in the Qumran caves is a "Qumran text," and, although the neat division of the texts into "sectarian" and "non-sectarian" can certainly be misleading at times, we need to evaluate each text in terms of relationship to the "library" found in the caves and the group that may have produced many of these documents.

Only some of the foregoing is exaggerated; all these elements of attacking a new Qumran text are related to one another, and we thus run the risk of circular reasoning at every turn. This may be true even when the "new" text has been in the public domain for fifty years, because these methodological issues do not automatically disappear even with the passage of half a century, and often are ignored when the sands of time cover them over. It is possible that it is the very fact that this text as a whole does not easily lend itself to comprehensive analysis, in terms of either its structure or its content, that has hitherto precluded almost all attempts at full or overarching handling.[6] Because 4Q159 has received limited thorough treatment in the past, some of my analysis will read as if the text really was a "new" one.

---

[5] I have discussed this matter with reference to narrative texts in "The Contours of Genesis Interpretation at Qumran: Contents, Contexts and Nomenclature," in *Studies in Ancient Midrash* (ed. James L. Kugel; Cambridge, MA: Harvard Center for Jewish Studies/Harvard University Press, 2001), 57–85.

[6] The only broad treatments are two essays by Francis D. Weinert, "4Q159: Legislation for an Essene Community outside of Qumran?" *JSJ* 5 (1974): 179–207, and "A Note on 4Q159 and a New Theory of Essene Origins," *RevQ* 9/34 (1976–78): 223–30; and one by Charlotte Hempel, "4QOrd^a(4Q159) and the Laws of the Damascus Document," in *The Dead Sea Scrolls Fifty Years After Their Discovery: Proceedings of the International Congress in Jerusalem* (ed. Emanuel Tov et al.; Jerusalem: Israel Exploration Society, 2000), 372–6.

The remains of this manuscript consisted originally of nine fragments, but two (6 and 9) now appear to be missing. They can be combined into three major groups: 1+9, 2–4+8, and 5.[7] One of the first
tasks of the editor of a text like 4Q159 is to try to determine whether
a reasonable sequence can be postulated for the fragments and then
to explain it. In the earliest days of Qumran scholarship, when no
obvious sequence of fragments presented itself immediately to the editors, fragments were often numbered, more or less, based on their size,
and, in the case of texts like 4Q159, the result of that tendency was to
ignore possible internal clues in the text to both the order and perhaps
the source of its contents.

I therefore propose to re-arrange the material following a sequence
of the fragments that I believe is likely based on their contents, and
not based on the numeration of the fragments by the original editors.
The contents are as follows:

> *Fragments 2–4+8 (to be referred to henceforth as frag. 2)*
> Laws of Israelite sold to non-Jew (Lev 25:47, 53, 42)[8] (lines 1–3)
> Court of [ten] Israelites and two priests for capital cases (no explicit
>   biblical source, but apparently related to Deut 17) (lines 4–6)
> Prohibition of transvestism (Deut 22:5) (lines 6–7) followed by *vacat*
> Husband's claim of non-virginity of bride and its consequences (Deut
>   22:13–21) (lines 8–10)
> *Fragment 1+9 (to be referred to henceforth as frag. 1)*
> A reference to "atonement for all their iniquities" (lines 1–2)
> Laws of leaving for the poor in the granary and field (Deut 23:25–26;
>   24:19–21) (lines 3–5)
> Money of valuation/half-sheqel (Exod 30:12–13; 38:25–26) (lines 6–7)
>   "Digression" detailing the collection of the half-sheqel in the wilder-
>   ness (lines 7–12)
> Two lines about *ephah = bath* and three *'esronim* (cf. Ezek 45:11) (lines
>   13–14) followed by *vacat*
> Two lines with reference to Moses and burning (Golden Calf?) (Exod
>   32:20?) (lines 16–17)
> *Fragment 5*
> A passage containing a reference to Exod 33:7 with two occurrences of
>   the term פשר

---

[7] Fragment 8 is restored in 2–4 10, following an oral suggestion by Elisha Qimron,
and fragment 9 in 1 II, 4 following Strugnell.

[8] I suspect that the author originally intended to follow the biblical verse order,
employing a paraphrase of Lev 25:55, but unconsciously slipped into the text of 25:42
which closely resembles it.

My ordering of the fragments is based on the following observations: frag. 2 contains material from Deut 22 and frag. 1 from Deut 23;
frag. 1 concludes with material related to Exod 32, and frag. 5 appears
to be connected to Exod 33.[9] Our tentative suggestion, therefore, and
I stress the term "tentative," is that the fragments should be ordered 2,
1, 5.[10] If my suggestion for the "re-organization" of 4Q159 is accepted,
placing frag. 2 before frag. 1, then we may further observe that many
of the laws are based on Deuteronomy, and, furthermore, that we have
laws related to 22:5, 22:13–21, and 23:25–26 in that order. According
to my hypothesis, then, the first, almost completely missing, column of
frag. 1 (and perhaps one or more columns that preceded it) would then
have contained regulations linked in some way to Deut 22:22 through
23:24. We have thus arranged the material based on its relationship to
material in the Hebrew Bible, even though there is no further internal
evidence within the document for such an arrangement.

I make this suggestion knowing full well that there are questions
which immediately arise for which I have no ready answer, such as
what explains the opening lines of frag. 2 which are linked to Lev 25,

---

[9] A number of scholars have suggested, since the earliest days of the study of
4Q159, that frag. 5 does not belong to the same manuscript as the others, hence avoid-
ing the generic conundrum that it generates. Thus, for example, Joseph A. Fitzmyer
in his review of Allegro, *CBQ* 31 (1969): 237, "The fifth fragment of this text (4Q159)
is so different in content from the rest that one wonders if it rightly belongs to this
group of fragments." Francis D. Weinert, "Legislation for an Essene Community,"
203–4, comments, "The total absence of any such [pesher] formulae in all the rest
of 4Q159 makes the conclusion unavoidable that fragment 5 is not derived from the
same text as 4Q159." Lawrence H. Schiffman, "Ordinances and Rules," 145, writes
"Fragment 5 was misidentified and does not belong with this manuscript. It is in fact
a *pesher*, probably to Leviticus 16:1." When I consulted Dr Ada Yardeni in the fall
of 2001 for her paleographic evaluation of the fragments, she indicated, after a brief
examination of photographs of the fragments of 4Q159, that she felt that all the fragments had been written by a single hand. Frag. 5 thus qualifies to be part of 4Q159
from a paleographic standpoint, and can only be excluded from belonging to this
manuscript with the admittedly not unreasonable claim that this scribe wrote more
than one manuscript which survived at Qumran. In my view, it is those juxtaposed
chapters in Exodus which furnish the key to understanding the connection of frag.
5 to the other fragments. I have reconstructed frag. 5 based on the assumption that
it belongs together with the other fragments of 4Q159 and interpreted it in relationship to the other fragments in "4Q159 Fragment 5 and the 'Desert Theology' of the
Qumran Sect," in *Emanuel: Studies in Hebrew Bible, Septuagint and Dead Sea Scrolls
in Honor of Emanuel Tov* (ed. Shalom M. Paul et al.; VTSup 94; Leiden: Brill, 2003),
43–56.

[10] Hempel, "4QOrd[a] (4Q159) and the Laws of the Damascus Document," 374–5,
noted the sequence of Deuteronomy material in frag. 2, but did not draw the same
inference regarding the sequence of the fragments that I do.

and on what is the transition to the Deuteronomy material based?[11] And even assuming that the law that follows about courts in 2 4–6 is related to Deut 17, why is there no material from Deut 17 through Deut 22 treated in the text?

This arrangement of the fragments, furthermore, is also based on the premise that 4Q159 would have followed the order of the biblical material on which it appears to be based, and that the text functions as the "restatement" or "rewriting" (to choose somewhat neutral terms) of a variety of laws deriving from, or related to, the Bible, with the biblical order governing the order in the manuscript. While this is quite plausible as a working hypothesis, we have to remember that it is, after all, just a hypothesis. This assumption then leads to a series of further questions, since at first glance, and perhaps at second and third as well, there does not seem to be any rhyme or reason for these particular laws being selected, rewritten and placed in proximity to one another (beyond their order in Deuteronomy). In the forms that they take in 4Q159, furthermore, they may be abbreviated, or expanded; clarified, or merely restated; they may even really be "new," in their not really resembling a particular pentateuchal text in any but the most superficial fashion. The divergent nature of the relationship of the different laws to the Bible thus also appears to complicate our analysis.

Since my goal is not to present a full preliminary edition and commentary on the text in this paper, but to employ this document as a model for the sorts of difficulties confronted in revising DJD V, I have chosen to present here the textual analysis of one passage in 4Q159 that I have not discussed elsewhere, consisting of the two relatively readable laws in frag. 1 II. In order, however, to contextualize them in the document appropriately, I need to say a few words about the laws in frag. 2.[12] Those three relatively complete laws in frag. 2 differ radically from each other in their style and in their relationship to

---

[11] If we accept my working hypothesis that Deuteronomy serves as the framework for the laws in this text, it is just possible that this Lev 25 material on the Israelite slave was introduced following textual material (that is now missing) based on Deut 15:12–18 that deals with the same topic, but this suggestion must be regarded as extremely tenuous in the absence of some further evidence to confirm the theory.

[12] A relatively full discussion of the three "complete" laws in frag. 2 is to be found in my essay "The Re-Presentation of 'Biblical' Legal Material at Qumran: Three Cases from 4Q159 (4QOrdinances^a)," in *Shoshanat Yaakov: Ancient Jewish and Iranian Studies in Honor of Professor Yaakov Elman* (ed. Steven Fine and Samuel Secunda; Leiden: Brill, forthcoming).

the Hebrew Bible. The first is a "non-biblical law," calling for a court
of twelve, including at least two priests, to hear capital cases. It is,
however, apparently modeled on the biblical law in Deut 17, although
partly through the employment of a non-pentateuchal text. The second, dealing with transvestism, is much more recognizable as a biblical law that has been rewritten very minimally, with some variation
from MT, and slight expansion as compared with the biblical original.
The third, the law of the bride accused of pre-marital sexual activity,
is a biblical regulation that has been summarized and compressed in
its presentation in 4Q159, with many details in the biblical text being
omitted, while a number of non-biblical particulars have been added.
Taken together they exemplify many of the phenomena that perplex
the student of this text: they are not juxtaposed in the Pentateuch; they
are characterized by very different modes and degrees of rewriting;
they have nothing in common topically; and they are not uniquely
"Qumranic" in nature.

With that background, we turn to frag. 1, col. II. Its first two lines
clearly continue a topic from the previous column (a column which
itself survives in only a few letters at its leftmost edge), with only a few
letters on the first line of column II, and with the second concluding
[ם]פשעיה לכול ולכפר ו[צ]מ אֹת אֹל[. Suffice it to say that none of
the earlier attempts at reconstruction are sufficiently convincing for
me to translate them, explain them or even to suggest a context for
them.

Frag. 1 II, 3–5 then continues[13]

3   י[עשה 14 איש ממנה גורן וגת הבא לגור[ן] ולגת   [

4   אֹשֹׁר בישראל אשר אין לו יאוכלנה וכנס לו ולב[יתו   [

5   השדה יֹאכֹל בפיהו ואל ביתו לוא יביא להניחו]   [

3. [should] a man make of it a threshing-floor or winepress, whoever
   comes to the threshing floor[or the winepress   ]
4. [anyone] in Israel who has nothing may eat it and gather it in for
   himself, and for his ho[usehold   ]
5. [in] the field may eat with his mouth, but may not bring it into his
   house to store it up[   ]

---

[13] The text and translation are based on my provisional edition, appearing in
Emanuel Tov, ed., *The Dead Sea Scrolls Electronic Library* (rev. ed.; Leiden: Brill;
Provo, UT: Brigham Young University, 2006). Both are the end results of scholarship
that began almost a half-century ago with Allegro and his many critics.
[14] The restoration ועשה is also conceivable.

We should probably restore at the beginning of line 3 (and perhaps at the end of line 2) something along the lines of "should they harvest their produce and someone makes…" or "when they gather in the produce of the land and someone makes…." The antecedent of ממנה in line 3 must be a feminine noun such as תבואה or ארץ that stood in the now missing text.[15]

The conclusion of line 4 (the end of the first law, or of the first part of a single law) is probably to be completed וכנס לו ולב[יתו, "he shall gather in for himself and his household;" the leavings of the threshing-floor/winepress may either be eaten there or be taken home (as might be indicated by the employment of the same preposition ל), as opposed to those taken in the field (line 5) which may only be eaten on the spot, but not taken home (and where the structure with preposition ואל seems to be contrastive). This reading and interpretation diverges from a number of earlier translations and commentaries which furnish a negative following ולב[יתו, along the lines of "he may gather in for himself, but [not take] for his household," thus prohibiting the taking of food home and making this case parallel to the next one.[16] The latter is clearly an interpretation of Deut 23:25 ואל כליך לא תתן, understanding the purpose of placing the grain into one's vessels as being to transport it home to store up for later use.

As we have just observed, this material presents either one law with two parts, or perhaps two laws, that appear to be related to laws in Deut 23:25–26 כי תבא בכרם רעך ואכלת ענבים כנפשך שבעך ואל

---

[15] The fragmentary nature of the text precludes any more certainty about the nature of the restoration.

[16] Florentino García Martínez, *The Dead Sea Scrolls Translated* (tr. W. G. E. Watson; 2nd ed.; Leiden: Brill; Grand Rapids: Eerdmans, 1996), 86, translates with a negative after the equivalent of ולב[יתו, as do Weinert, "Essene Origins," 225, and Schiffman, "Ordinances and Rules," 150–1, although Schiffman's interpretation, p. 151 n. 7, actually contradicts the reading which he furnishes; Michael O. Wise et al., *The Dead Sea Scrolls: A New Translation* (New York: HarperSanFrancisco, 1996), 205, add the negative, but with a question-mark; and explain the one in ll. 3–4. Allegro and Geza Vermes, *The Complete Dead Sea Scrolls in English* (rev. ed.; London: Penguin, 2004), 529, render as we do, while Jean Carmignac, *Les textes de Qumrân: traduits et annotés* (Paris: Letouzey et Ané, 1963), 2.297, does not restore the line, but offers both possibilities in his note. Aharon Shemesh, in a forthcoming book (part of which he was kind enough to share with me), suggests that there are two laws in the passage, the first dealing with the tithe of the poor, thus explaining why it is given at the גורן וגת, and the second, like the biblical law, dealing with the individual entering the field who is permitted to eat only on the spot. His evidence for his first law being the tithe of the poor does not appear particularly compelling to me.

כליך לא תתן: כי תבא בקמת רעך וקטפת מלילת בידך וחרמש לא תניף
על קמת רעך:

> When you enter your neighbor's vineyard, you may eat grapes until your
> appetite is satisfied, but you may not put any into your vessel. When
> you enter your neighbor's standing grain, you may pluck stalks with
> your hand, but you may not wave a sickle over your neighbor's stand-
> ing grain.

The relationship of the Qumran laws to the law in Deuteronomy appears
to be primarily stylistic modeling, since they differ from the original
in both language and content. And even that modeling appears to be
rather weak, so that 4Q159, for example, does not employ the terms
כרם and קמה, "vineyard" and "standing grain" of Deuteronomy, but
first refers to גורן וגת, "threshing floor and winepress" and then to
שדה, "field."

This is the kind of feature that it makes our characterization of
4Q159 particularly difficult; on the one hand, the law in the Qumran
text resembles the biblical law, but, on the other, quite clearly diverges
from it. The biblical text permits someone to eat of the grapes in a
neighbor's vineyard, but not to collect them into a vessel; and to break
off ears of grain in a neighbor's field, by hand but not with an implement. In the first law in 4Q159, there is no stricture against taking
home from the threshing floor or winepress, while in the second law
there appears to be a distinction made between the threshing floor/
winepress and the field in terms of the permissibility of taking some of
the food back to one's home, although the biblical distinction between
hand and implement does not appear in the surviving text.[17]

More significantly, we must ask who are the subjects of the law in
4Q159 who are permitted to enter private property and collect food?
Whereas later rabbinic interpretation on the whole interprets this text

---

[17] 4QDeut^a, 4QDeut^f, 4QDeut^i, 4QDeut^k2 show no substantive variants from MT.
Jacob Liver, "The Half-Shekel Offering in Biblical and Post-biblical Literature," *HTR*
56 (1963): 193, agrees that l. 5 is based on Deuteronomy, but claims that Allegro "is
not correct in viewing ll. 3–4 as an expansion of that same biblical law." He asks,
193–4, "Why should the ruling be lenient for produce already on the threshing floor
and in the wine-vat, after the labor of the harvest and vintage, and more severe for
produce in the field?" The question is a good one, but need not be answered only by
his hypothesis that once the produce had been brought in to the threshing floor and
winepress, that which remained in the field was available to the poor. In fact, the formula "whoever comes to the threshing floor" appears to fly in the face of his claim.
It is more likely that what is being made available to the poor is whatever is left over
after the threshing floor or winepress has been cleared out.

of Deuteronomy as pertaining to what is allowed to workers while they harvest in someone else's field,[18] our text adopts a straightforward reading of the biblical text that implies that it does not pertain to employees but to the poor.[19] There is no explicit biblical regulation providing for the poor going into the threshing-floor or winepress to collect the leavings there, although Deut 24:19–21 teaches of practices that must be observed in the *field* and the *vineyard* during the grain-harvest or other time of collection כי תקצר קצירך בשדך ושכחת עמר בשדה לא תשוב לקחתו לגר ליתום ולאלמנה יהיה למען יברכך ה' א-להיך בכל מעשה ידיך: כי תחבט זיתך לא תפאר אחריך לגר ליתום ולאלמנה יהיה: כי תבצר כרמך לא תעולל אחריך לגר ליתום ולאלמנה יהיה.

> When you reap your harvest in your field, and have forgotten a sheaf in the field, you may not go back to get it; it shall belong to the stranger, the fatherless, and the widow; so that the Lord your God may bless you in all your handiwork. When you beat your olive-tree, you may not go over the boughs again; it shall belong to the stranger, the fatherless, and the widow. When you gather the grapes of your vineyard, you may not glean it after yourself; it shall belong to the stranger, the fatherless, and the widow.

---

[18] For rabbinic treatments of these verses, see Joseph Heinemann, "The Status of the Labourer in Jewish Law and Society of the Tannaitic Period," *HUCA* 35 (1954): 263–325, esp. 310–6 (pre-Qumran discoveries) and Meir Ayali, "When You Come into Your Neighbor's Vineyard…," *Heqer Veiyyun: Studies in Judaism* [Hebrew] (ed. Yaacov Bahat, Mordechai Ben-Asher and Terry Fenton; Haifa: University of Haifa, 1976), 25–38 (for which latter reference I thank Professor Alexander Rofé). The overwhelming majority of rabbinic texts asserts that these verses deal only with the rights of workers, and emphasizes that even they are to be limited in the amount that, and the circumstances under which, they may eat. The view of Issi ben Aqavya in *y. Maʿaśrot* 2:4 (cited in *b. B. Meṣiʿa* 92a as Issi ben Yehuda), however, differs from that "standard" rabbinic position and insists that "this verse deals with all other individuals" and not just workers. The reference to not waving the sickle, according to Issi, indicates that the right of all individuals to eat is only "at the time of the waving of the sickle," i.e., during the harvest. The version in the Babylonian Talmud in *B. Meṣiʿa* reads, "Rav said, 'I found a secret scroll in the house of R. Hiyya in which it was written that Issi ben Yehuda says "'Should one enter one's neighbor's vineyard' speaks of the entry of anyone'" (בכל אדם הכתוב מדבר). Rav said further, 'Issi would not allow anyone to live.'"

[19] Ayali, "When You Come into Your Neighbor's Vineyard…," 28, points out, that the language of the biblical verse, "should you enter…you may eat," might very well be understood to deal with one who enters the field with permission. He subsequently writes that "one should not discount the possibility that regarding the leftovers (ספיחים) of the Sadducees and Boethusians this interpretation [permitting entry into the fields by the poor] remained the only legitimate interpretation" (p. 37). It is perhaps symptomatic of the state of the knowledge of Qumran material among those who studied rabbinic halakhah in the 1970s that he did not bring our text to bear on his analysis and on that suggestion.

It is possible that the author of this document inferred from the pen-tateuchal references to כרם and קמה in Deut 23 that different (and more lenient) rules apply in places other than כרם and קמה, such as the threshing-floor and winepress. שדה in the Qumran text would then represent the biblical כרם and קמה where the restrictions on how much may be taken are more severe, while at the גורן וגת, the inferential addition of the author of 4Q159, the restrictions on how much may be taken are more lenient. From a compositional perspective, however, it remains a bit strange that he leads off with גורן וגת and only then proceeds to שדה, a sequence inverted from the one that we should have expected.[20] His reading, like that of the rabbis, may be intended to limit the sense of the biblical verse, which itself seems to place no such limitations on who may take from the produce, and which perhaps implies that passersby may do so, despite the obvious problem involved in permitting incursions into and consumption of private property.[21]

If that be the case, then the author of 4Q159 and the rabbis both felt that the simple sense of the biblical text required modification of some sort to protect the interest of the landowner, but they adopt two differ-

---

[20] The term כהן המחזר\המסבב על הגרנות exists in rabbinic literature (b. Ketub. 105b; Tanḥ. Vayeḥi 10) to describe a priest who goes from threshing floor to threshing floor to collect priestly emoluments and עניים המחזרין בין הגרנות (t. Pe'ah 2:18 [ed. Lieberman, p. 49]) refers to the poor who go to the threshing floors to collect the poor tithe.

[21] Josephus, Ant. 4.8.21 (234), on the other hand, is often thought to maintain the most liberal interpretation, writing that passersby are permitted to eat from the field or from what the vintagers are taking to the winepress. Ayali, "When You Come into Your Neighbor's Vineyard...," 32, although he is careful to avoid the assertion that Josephus's reading indicates that this was the "rabbinic" reading in his day, claims "that the simple sense of the text was understood in his generation as pointing to a liberal law, allowing any passerby to turn aside to eat in a vineyard, and the regulation that limits this permission was not yet widespread when Josephus still lived in Eretz Yisrael." A careful reading of Josephus's law however, indicates that he, too, may have limited the biblical text in a way that protected the rights of the landowner. Josephus speaks only of "those walking on the road," not of those who enter into a field, and of those who meet the vintagers on the way to the winepress, not of those entering the vineyard. Josephus presents each of the two biblical cases in such a fashion as to minimize the circumstances which allow for unchecked entry into private property and consumption of its produce. Ayali suggests as further evidence that the rabbinic law, limiting the right to workers, was not in effect in the first century the fact that Jesus and his disciples are faulted only for plucking grain on the Sabbath (Matt 12:1–8 and parallels), and not for plucking from a field as passersby. That inference is somewhat weak, considering the relative severity of the violation of the Sabbath compared to entry into the fields and eating from the produce.

ent sorts of restrictive modification. The rabbis limit Deut 23:25–26 to workers at the time of the harvest, while the author of 4Q159 adopts the standard of אשר אין לו, "not having anything," an extremely impoverished state, for one entering a private domain, wine-press or threshing-floor, and collecting charity to take home. The surviving text of 4Q159 does not allow us any insight into the way in which it protected the landowner's rights in the second instance. It would appear that for entry into fields and consuming food on the spot such a low level of poverty is not demanded by 4Q159 as is required for entry to the threshing-floor or winepress.[22]

The next segment of frag. 1 is composed of two parts, one legal and brief (6–7c), and one that I must call "historical" and rather lengthier (7d–12). This passage is the only one in this portion of the text which has indubitably "Qumranic overtones."

[ע[ל]דבר]כסף הערכים אשר נתנו איש ⁵פר נפשו מחצית[השקל] 6
תרומה לי-הוה[]

רק ⁰[פעם] אחת יתננו כול ימיו עשרים גרה השקל ב[שקל הקודש] 7
ויהי כסף הכפורים[]

לשש מא[ו]ת האלף מאת ככר לשלישית מחצית הככר[ולחמש] 8
המאות חמשה מנים[]

ולחמשים מחצית המ[נ[ה ̇ [עשרים ו[ḥ̇משה שקל הכול[בשקל] 9
הקודש [

המנה ש̇[ ] [ל[ ]ל[ ]וש לעשרת המנים[] 10
חמ[שה [כס]ף מעשר ה[מנה] 11
שק[ל הקודש מחצ]ית] 12
הא̇פה והבת תכון א [חד] 13
ש[לושת העשרונים ⁰[ ] 14
va[cat   ] 15

6. [Rega]rding [the matter of the] money of valuation which they gave, each one as the ransom for his life, half [a sheqel as an offering to the Lord;]

7. only one [time] in his days shall he give it. The sheqel is twenty *gerah* by the sa[nctuary sheqel. And the atonement money was]

8. for the six h[u]ndred thousand, one hundred talents; for the third (?), half a talent, [and for the five hundred, five minas]

9. and for the fifty, half a m[in]a, [twenty-]five sheqel. Al[l by the sanctuary sheqel   ]

10. the mina. š[ ]*l*[ ]*wš* for the ten minas[   ]

11. [fi]ve [silv]er pieces, a tenth of a m[ina   ]

---

[22] Rabbinic literature (e.g., *m. Pe'ah* 8:7–9) also discusses the level of poverty to be demanded of those seeking to take advantage of differing modes of charity.

12. [   ]sanctuary [sheq]el, ha[lf   ]
13. [   ]the *ephah* and the *bath* are [on]e measure [   ]
14. [   ] the [th]ree tenths [   ]
15. [   ]*vacat* [   ]

The opening lines of the text are clearly modeled on Exod 30:12–13,

כי תשא את ראש בני ישראל לפקדיהם ונתנו איש כפר נפשו לה' בפקד
אתם ולא יהיה בהם נגף בפקד אתם: זה יתנו כל העבר על הפקדים
מחצית השקל בשקל הקדש עשרים גרה השקל מחצית השקל תרומה
לה':

> When you take a census of the Israelites, each shall give his life's ransom
> to the Lord when they are counted, so that there be no plague among
> them when they are counted. This shall they give, all who pass among
> the counted, a half-sheqel by the holy sheqel; the sheqel is twenty *gerah*,
> half a sheqel as an offering to the Lord.

Even though the term ערכים is usually applied to the valuations of Lev
27:1ff., where its root ערך appears frequently, its usage here seems to
refer rather to the half sheqel offering whose nature was the subject
of debate among Jewish groups during the Second Temple era.[23] A
similar expression וכסף הערכים לפדוי נפשם, "valuation money for
the redemption of their souls," appears in a broken context in 4Q270
2 II, 9 in a list of donations which are assigned to the priests. It is very
possible, if not likely, that 4Q270 is also referring to the half-sheqel
donation rather than the passage in Leviticus because of the idiom
"redemption of their souls," which resembles כפר נפשו, "ransom of
his soul" in Exodus, both of which presumably refer to the souls of the
payers.[24] The text in Lev 27 makes no reference to any sort of redemption or ransom.

According to the explicit ruling in 4Q159, the half-sheqel tax was to
be paid but once in the lifetime of an individual.[25] Qimron reads 11QT
XXXIX, 7–10 as referring to the same regulation:

---

[23] *Contra* Liver, "The Half-Shekel Offering in Biblical and Post-biblical Literature,"
195, who believes that "the valuation money is treated independently in the end of
l. 5 and the beginning of l. 6; then the subject of the half-shekel offering is treated,
beginning with the biblical text, introduced by the word אשר," but the text of 4Q270
which was unknown to him makes his comment indefensible.

[24] The text of Exodus reads further לכפר על נפשתיכם, "to atone for your souls,"
in 30:15 and 16.

[25] Although there has been considerable discussion of the innovation of the annual
half-sheqel assessment (cf. David Flusser, "מחצית השקל באוונגליון ואצל כת מדבר
יהודה," *Tarbiz* 31 [1962]: 150–6 [= "The Half-shekel in the Gospels and the Qum-

לוא תבוא בה אשה וילד עד יום אשר ישלים חוק על[ומיו ונתן פדיו]ן נפשו
לי-הוה מחצית השקל לזכרון במושבותיהמה עשרים גרה השקל *vacat*
וכאשר ישאו ממנו את מחצית הש[ק]ל [ישב]ע לי אחר יבואו מבן עשרים
[שנ]ה ולמעלה

No woman or child may enter it until the day that he completes the
portion of his yo[uth and gives the redempti]on of his soul to the Lord
a half-sheqel as a memorial in their settlements, twenty *gerah* being
the worth of the sheqel. *Vacat* And when they take from him the half-
sheq[el he shall swea]r to me; afterward they may enter from twenty
[yea]rs and upward.[26]

The implication is that this fee was to be paid only once by an individual, upon his reaching maturity.[27] That payment of the half-sheqel
tax was known to have been disputed in antiquity even before this
passage was published. *Megillat Taʿanit* records a controversy between
the Pharisees and Boethusians regarding the source out of which the
daily sacrifice in the Temple was to be brought.[28] This has been linked
in modern scholarship with the dispute about the annual payment of
the half-sheqel, as has Matt 17:25–27.[29] What is further interesting is
the fact that whereas the most reasonable reconstructions of both the

ran Community," *Judaism of the Second Temple Period Vol. I: Qumran and Apoc-
alypticism* (Grand Rapids: Eerdmans; Jerusalem: Magnes, 2007), 327–33]; Moshe Beer,
"הכיתות ומחצית השקל," *Tarbiz* 31 [1962]: 298–9; Liver, "The Half-Shekel Offering in
Biblical and Post-biblical Literature," 173–98), there is no reason to assume, as does
Liver, "The Half-Shekel Offering in Biblical and Post-biblical Literature," 195, that
the annual half sheqel "is an obligation that was fixed after the sect had sequestered
itself from the community and the temple." The traditionalist outlook of the Qumran
group might very well have opposed such halakhic novelty even before they distanced
themselves geographically.

[26] Elisha Qimron, *The Temple Scroll: A Critical Edition with Extensive Reconstructions* (Beer Sheva: Ben-Gurion University of the Negev Press; Jerusalem: Israel Exploration Society, 1996), 56. He notes there, "My reading of this column differs from Yadin's
in many details (see *Leshonenu* 42 [1978], 144–5 vs. Yadin's English edition)."

[27] Liver, "The Half-Shekel Offering in Biblical and Post-biblical Literature," 197,
who did not know the *Temple Scroll*, intuited well in writing, "Perhaps the sect understood the Pentateuchal ordinance of the life-ransom as referring exclusively to a first
census when a man reached adulthood, at which time his name was recorded for
the first time in the census registers, and not to the annual ceremony of entering the
covenant and reviewing the registers, which was apparently not considered a 'census'
for those whose names already appeared in the registers."

[28] Cf. Vered Noam, *Megillat Taʿanit: Versions, Interpretation, History with a Critical Edition* [Hebrew] (Jerusalem: Yad Ben Zvi Press, 2003), 165–73, esp. 173, and *b.
Menaḥ.* 65a. For other possible Qumran allusions to this dispute, cf. Albert I. Baumgarten, "Rabbinic Literature as a Source for the History of Jewish Sectarianism in the
Second Temple Period," *DSD* 2 (1995): 20–1, and the literature cited there.

[29] For the NT material, see Flusser, "Half-Shekel."

Temple Scroll and 4Q159 have the donation being given "to the Lord,"
4Q270, if indeed it is dealing with the same payment, has it on the list
of emoluments which are given to the sons of Aaron, a position consistent with other gifts 'לה, "to the Lord" in Qumran exegesis.[30]

After the series of laws related to Deuteronomy, we have been
perhaps a bit surprised to find this law deriving from Exodus in our
text, but that is a minor astonishment when compared with what follows. The text moves from the two-line expression of the law to a
very detailed specification of the amount of this tax which had been
collected in the desert according to Exod 38:25–26 וכסף פקודי העדה
מאת ככר ואלף ושבע מאות וחמשה ושבעים שקל בשקל הקדש: בקע
לגלגלת מחצית השקל בשקל הקדש לכל העבר על הפקדים מבן עשרים
שנה ומעלה לשש מאות אלף ושלשת אלפים וחמש מאות וחמשים:
"one hundred talents and 1,775 sheqels." It does not take too much
in the way of restoration or higher mathematics to realize that 4Q159
furnishes the same amount in Second Temple currency. This historical recollection places a "wilderness" perspective on the passage, even
though it is not a narrative located in past time, and contributes to our
need to view the document as not purely legal in genre.[31] But why did
the author feel the need to engage in this historical bookkeeping in this
document? Can it tell us anything about the nature of the document
as a whole? I admit that I have no answers, for the present, to either
of those questions.

Lines 13–14 in 4Q159 are even more difficult to understand than
the preceding few fragmentary lines which appear merely to present
the totals for the census tax in several forms, because they do not seem
at all connected with any pentateuchal law. The passage in Ezek 45:11
האיפה והבת תכן אחד יהיה which is apparently cited here (as well as
in 4Q513 1–2 I, 4 and 4Q271 2 2) as האֹפה והבת תכון א]חד[deals in
its original context with the need for exact and just measures for contributions to communal offerings in the Temple. The context in 4Q513

---

[30] It is very possible that the sect derived this principle by an analogical ruling based
on Lev 23:20 קדש יהיו לה' לכהן, "they shall be holy for the Lord, for the priest,"
inferring that anything which is declared by the Pentateuch to be 'לה is assigned to
the priests.

[31] Schiffman, "Ordinances and Rules," 153 n. 21, thinks that the amounts are now
broken down according to mustering units: 1000, 100, 50, 10, with each subtotal then
being furnished. Although that description is correct, it does not explain why these
extensive details find their place in a text which seems to be characterized by brevity.

deals with impurity, containing the words מהמה הטמאה twice,[32] and that in 4Q271 with priestly(?) gifts, neither of which seems to be relevant to our passage in 4Q159. Even granted the fragmentary context of our lines, we cannot see how any connection with either of those topics would have been made.

The attempt to identify 4Q159 and 4Q513–514 as different manuscripts of the same work should therefore be considered an excellent example of the scholarly tendency to seek to link Qumran texts with one another rather than to dichotomize them and analyze them individually. The two possible overlaps between 4Q159 and 4Q513 appear to have been weighted far more heavily by scholars than the overall implications of the style and contents of the two manuscripts.[33] A careful reading of those two texts seems to indicate that they are not at all the same sort of legal document. We have described the contents of 4Q159 sufficiently to demonstrate that, whatever we name it and to whatever genre we assign it, a work such as 4Q513 whose contents appear to be so heavily oriented toward purity and the Temple does not resemble it at all.[34]

---

[32] Joseph M. Baumgarten, "Halakhic Polemics in New Fragments from Qumran Cave 4," in *Biblical Archaeology Today: Proceedings of the International Congress on Biblical Archaeology, Jerusalem, April 1984* (ed. Janet Amitai; Jerusalem: Israel Exploration Society/Israel Academy of Sciences and Humanities in cooperation with the American Schools of Oriental Research, 1985), 391, perhaps overstates when he writes "The first step toward understanding the intent of the text is to note that both here [4Q513] and in Ezekiel the measures are used to separate the priestly *terumah.*" The thrusts of the two passages appear to be somewhat different.

[33] Even Maurice Baillet's restoration of 4Q513 1–2 I, 2–5 to be the same text as 4Q159 is somewhat problematic. He restores line 2 on the basis of 4Q159 1 II, 12, but needs to insist on a very large gap between שק[ל הקודש and מחצית in 4Q513 in order to justify the restoration. His completion of lines 4–5 with האיפה וה[בת תכון אחד [עשרה עשרנים כאיפת ה[דגן בת היין והסאה [שלושת העש[רנים ושלישת ה[עשרון is less open to question, although it is far from certain. The text of 4Q513 continues with further remarks on quantities and impurity for which there is certainly no place in the reconstruction of 4Q159. There remains a nagging suspicion that Baillet restored 4Q513 on the basis of 4Q159, and then proceeded to identify them as copies of the same manuscript on the basis of his restoration! The other alleged overlap between 4Q513 17 2–3 שר[כים א]ם הער[ ] בפיהו ושנת[and lines 5–6 of 4Q159 יאכל בפיהו...[ע/ל] דבר [כסף הערכים אשר is also doubtful since the reading in line 2 is simply not the same as the one in 4Q159, and the one in line 3 is very tenuously restored.

[34] The apparent reference in frags. 3–4 to "waving a sheaf" appears to refer to the well-known calendrical dispute between the Sadducees and Pharisees regarding the day for bringing the ʿomer offering. The text accompanying it indicates that it is the debate over calendar that is at issue.

This must lead at least to the consideration of the likely possibility that these "overlaps" are coincidental and that there is no more reason to identify 4Q159 and 4Q513 as two manuscripts of the same work than there is to identify it as another manuscript of 4QD because of the overlap with 4Q271. The issue of the reason for the appearance of this passage in 4Q159, parallel to those in 4QD and 4Q513, should remain an open question at this point. The more significant question, one for which I unfortunately have no constructive suggestion, is what impelled the author of 4Q159 to introduce this material at this point in his text?

If frag. 1 II were to have broken off immediately after the list of values and volumes, my question would not be as strong or my dilemma so profound. We might have surmised that the text continued in such a fashion as to make some coherent sense. But alas, the following text does survive, and it sharpens the question. 4Q159 returns from the mathematical data to narrative material from Exodus 32 after a *vacat*, thus following reasonably after the census material from Exodus 30 (and then continuing in frag. 5 according to my reconstruction with material from Exodus 33).[35] This suggested "coherence" of texts from the book of Exodus, if I have understood it correctly, makes the intervening lines stand out even more as strange, and undermine further, in my view, any identification of this text with 4Q513.

This last section of 4Q159 1 II can thus serve us well as the transition from the close analysis of the two laws that we have presented to the larger issues that the interpretation of this manuscript raises. In the midst of a document that appears to be composed of legal material, albeit one whose organizational principle or selectivity is not clear, the text moves to legal material which does not follow consequently in the slightest fashion on that which preceded it, and from there digresses to a series of texts that are fundamentally narrative in nature. All this without any obvious, or even covert, rationale. This simultaneously calls into question our implicit and tentative identification of this as a "legal" document, demolishes our limited observations about its apparent sequential connection to Deuteronomy, and presents further serious obstacles to its interpretation. All at once, significant doubts regarding our initial thoughts on nomenclature, genre, and relationship to the Pentateuch have been raised.

---

[35] Cf. n. 9 above.

And we are therefore compelled to return to the larger concerns that we raised in our prefatory remarks to this paper. Although throughout our treatment to this point we avoided as much as possible the circularity of reasoning with which we were concerned by paying little attention to genre or nomenclature in our restoration of the text, we have no choice but to confront those issues now. These two questions are inevitably connected, and we shall begin by asking what we shall call this text, the question in microcosm, before asking to what genre it belongs, the macrocosmic one.

The original editor named this document "Ordinances," an admittedly strange name for a Jewish legal document.[36] There is no term within the text itself that would seem to attract such nomenclature, and Strugnell's first critical remark regarding Allegro's edition of 4Q159 is "mieux vaut ne plus utiliser ce titre moderne."[37] But we can perhaps sympathize with Allegro's inability to do a better job of naming the document, even as we disagree with his choice of terms. There is simply no obvious terminology that can be employed to describe a text such as 4Q159 that contains laws of diverse sorts (as well as material that is not, strictly speaking, legal). There is no convenient adjectival modifier for "ordinances," or for "laws" or "statutes" or "commandments" or "regulations," for that matter, that would limit the noun in such as way as to describe our text more appropriately.

The dilemma of naming and classifying legal texts from Qumran can perhaps best be demonstrated by the way in which they are categorized in DJD XXXIX. The overall unit is called "Texts Concerned with Religious Law," furnishing a broad generic rubric, with sub-categories "community rules," "eschatological rules," "purity rule," "other rules," "halakhic midrash," "parabiblical texts concerned with religious law," and "unclassified texts concerned with religious law."[38] Texts such as the *Community Rule, Damascus Document* and *War Rule* are placed under specific headings, while 4Q159 and 4Q513–514 are placed

---

[36] It received its superscript "a" because it was seen as linked (on grounds that are somewhat insubstantial, in my view) with 4Q513 and 4Q514, "Ordinances[b] and [c]" that were later published by Maurice Baillet in DJD VII.

[37] Strugnell, "Notes en marge," 175.

[38] Armin Lange and Ulrike Mittmann-Richert, "Annotated List of Texts from the Judaean Desert Classified by Content and Genre," in *The Texts from the Judaean Desert—Indices and an Introduction to the Discoveries in the Judaean Desert Series* (ed. Emanuel Tov; DJD XXXIX; Oxford: Clarendon, 2002), 132–3. 4QMMT has its own subcategory "epistolary treatise concerned with religious law."

under the "other rules" rubric together with *Halakhah A* (4Q251) and *Miscellaneous Rules* (4Q265).[39] Note that the latter two "titles" are as unspecific and unenlightening as *Ordinances*. "Religious Law" is also excessively broad as an overarching heading since it might very well include everything from pentateuchal laws to later enhancement of those laws to sectarian legislation for the present or the future. We might have expected the significant issue of the possible connection of Qumran laws to the Pentateuch to have been marked in some of the names, but, other than the terms "midrash" and "parabiblical," there is no indication in the title of any of these documents regarding the text's relationship to the Pentateuch, whether exegetical or otherwise. We make these points not to suggest that the classification of these documents was a simple or trivial task that should have been carried out more effectively, but rather to emphasize its difficulty. It is therefore a desideratum, in the ongoing re-study of all legal material from Qumran, that more specific and descriptive categories should be sought for many of these texts.

Even if we attempt to describe 4Q159 rather than name it or classify it, we find that our task is not much easier. Our suggested "freeing" it from its connection with 4Q513–514 unfortunately does not offer much immediate assistance in this direction beyond removing some potential constraints on our analysis. The one significant observation is of a negative nature: 4Q159, with the exception of the half-sheqel passage, does not appear to be focused on issues that divided the Qumran group from their halakhic opponents.[40] In that regard, it differs radically from another somewhat anomalous "legal" text from Qumran, *MMT*, whose stance and orientation are quite explicitly polemical. It is striking, furthermore, that none of the surviving fragments of 4Q159

---

[39] It is worth noting, if only for the purpose of contrast, that Vermes, *Complete Dead Sea Scrolls*, while placing 4Q251, 4Q265 and 4QMMT under "Rules," locates 4Q159 and 4Q513–514 "Ordinances or Commentaries on Biblical Law," under the rubric "Bible Interpretation."

[40] The demand in 2 4–6 that a particular court consist of both priests and Israelites is typical of Qumran legislation (e.g., CD X, 4–6 and 11QT LVII, 11–14), but is unlikely to be polemic since the rabbis in commenting on the same verse in Deuteronomy also recommend that courts include both priests and Levites (cf. *Sifre Deut.* 153 to Deut 17:9 [ed. Finkelstein, p. 206]). The number twelve demanded for that court, however, might be characteristic of Qumran, since there are several texts in the Dead Sea Scrolls that refer to bodies of twelve or its multiples for various functions (cf. 11QT LVII, 11–14; 1QS VIII, 1; 4QpIsa^d 1 3–5; and my comments in the Elman Festschrift, n. 12).

deals with the purity laws or festal regulations which play such a significant role in the remains of 4Q513 and other Qumran legal texts.[41]
We might succeed in describing what 4Q159 is not by comparing it to
two other Qumran texts that are often employed as divergent exem-
plars of legal material, CD/4QD and the *Temple Scroll* (11QT), and
concluding that it is unlike either of them.[42] Such an approach would
still fail to furnish us with a positive orientation towards the document. It is not just that it differs from other Qumran legal texts, but
that its own compositional techniques are so enigmatic and unclear.
We have to realize that the fundamental problem with 4Q159 is not
what we name it or to what genre it belongs, but rather "what is it?"
There is very little about this text which is straightforward or obvious,
neither its selection of laws, nor its relationship to the Bible, nor the
diverse ways in which the laws are rewritten.

Weinert suggests that "determination of the genre of 4Q159, then,
will depend on the function that this legislation was meant to perform."[43]
I agree with very little of Weinert's subsequent analysis, but I think
that he is one of the few to have asked one of the right questions. He
may be too confident, however, when he employs the term "legislation" and implies that it had a "function...to perform." We have to
be very careful when we suggest that legal texts from Qumran were
intended to "function" in some fashion. His concluding remarks, furthermore, go too far, in my view, when he suggests that "4Q159 is

---

[41] Weinert, "Essene Origins," 228, takes this point too far, claiming that "what
4Q159 lacks compounds the case against a Qumran origin. [e.g.] none of the polemic
against alternate Jewish religious groupings that emerges at an early stage in other
Qumran literature..." The occurrence of the term פשר in frag. 5 would also point
strongly to a Qumran origin, and the use of וענשו in 2 9 in place of the biblical וענשו
(Deut 22:19) recalls the employment of this term 48 times in 1/4QS, CD, 4QD and
4Q265.

[42] It has been suggested by Aharon Shemesh and Cana Werman, "Halakhah at
Qumran: Genre and Authority," *DSD* 10 (2003): 104–29, that those two works represent the two fundamental halakhic genres at Qumran, but it appears to me that
a narrow, binary, classification of Qumran legal texts is far too constricting. And I
certainly cannot concur with their fundamentally unproven claim that the halakhot
in the Ordinance texts belong "to the same genre as the Damascus Document" (115),
or even with Joseph M. Baumgarten's weaker formulation of the same assertion ("The
Laws of the *Damascus Document* in Current Research," in *The Damascus Document
Reconsidered* [ed. Magen Broshi; Jerusalem: Israel Exploration Society], 56). We need
to stress the differences among the legal works from Qumran in order to understand
them fully rather than lump them together on the basis of superficial similarities, thus
blurring the significant distinctions among them.

[43] "Legislation for an Essene Community," 181.

an exposition of biblical legislation taken almost exclusively from the Pentateuch and it is faithful for the most part to the sense of the laws that it cites."[44] I am not sure what he means by "exposition," but it is clear to me based on my analysis of the three laws that I discuss in the Elman *Festschrift* and the two that we have seen in this essay, that we cannot speak of the laws in the surviving fragments of 4Q159 as "faithful to the sense" of the pentateuchal laws on which they are modeled. I have wondered on occasion whether we can describe 4Q159 as a kind of legal commentary, rather than a law code, but I am left with the feeling that changing the name in this way does not really help us understand more about its contents.

It is quite striking that the two most distinguished scholars of Qumran halakhah, Joseph M. Baumgarten and Lawrence H. Schiffman, have each independently alluded, en passant of another text, to the fact that 4Q159 does not "fit" our standard categories. Baumgarten writes, regarding 4Q159 and 4Q265, another text that is not easy to categorize, "The genre of these miscellaneous legal and narrative texts should now be added to the heterogeneous classifications of Qumran compositions, although their functional purpose has yet to be clarified."[45] Note that Baumgarten refers to these texts as "legal and narrative," since neither is purely legal, and points to the need for the clarification of their purpose, while not suggesting one or drawing any further conclusions. Schiffman, also discussing 4Q265, states, "In any case, this text can be considered in light of other Qumran texts that appear to be anthologies. Especially to be compared is 4QOrdinances, which seems to be a legal anthology of some kind. All this points to the complex literary history of the larger Dead Sea Scroll texts, an area of research begun only recently and already bearing important results."[46]

Charlotte Hempel has observed that "five of the seven stipulations preserved in 4Q159 contain material also dealt with in the recently published legal material from 4QD."[47] I am not sure that the parallels are striking enough for us to build connections between the two documents upon them, as Hempel herself is careful to note. She suggests that "redactor/compiler responsible for the Laws of the DD in their present form drew upon a collection of traditional legal material not

---

[44] Ibid. 204.

[45] Joseph M. Baumgarten, "4Q265. Miscellaneous Rules," in *Qumran Cave 4.XXV: Halakhic Texts* (ed. J. M. Baumgarten et al.; DJD XXXV; Oxford: Clarendon, 1999), 60.

[46] Lawrence H. Schiffman, "Serekh-Damascus," *EDSS*, 2, 868a.

[47] Hempel, "4QOrdᵃ(4Q159) and the Laws of the Damascus Document," 373.

dissimilar to 4QOrdinances[a]." If she is correct, that would give us some insight into the conceptual lineage of the 4QD material, but would not necessarily offer direct help in solving the generic and related questions that we have raised regarding 4Q159.

If we consider for a moment the language employed by the three scholars whom I just cited, it becomes clear that there is a great deal that we do not know about the genres of Qumran "legal" texts and their literary histories. Baumgarten speaks of "miscellaneous legal and narrative texts" and "heterogeneous classifications," stressing the unusual combination of legal and non-legal material and the generic uncertainty; Schiffman of "legal anthology," a term which clearly carries no definable generic implications; and Hempel of "collection of traditional legal material," employing an even less formal term than Schiffman's "anthology," one that does not imply a reason for bringing the material together. Taken together, they underline the fact that we need to rethink the way that we approach the study of the "legal" corpus in the Dead Sea Scrolls, and we need to reflect on an underlying issue that is more encompassing than the superficial ones of nomenclature and genre to which we have alluded throughout this essay, because those focus on one text at a time.

The larger matter, which I do not think has been the subject of very much discussion, is the picture, so far as we are able to sketch it, of the development of post-biblical legal writing furnished by the Qumran scrolls. It would seem reasonable to assume that the efforts to "rewrite" or "rearrange" biblical law took on various forms, and what we see at Qumran represents some of the evidence of those attempts. We should not allow the convenient dichotomy between the 11QT-type and the CD/4QD-type to create a binary constraint that forces us to allocate all Qumran legal texts to one category or the other. It is much more likely that in the process of developing ways to (re)write biblical law in the post-biblical period, a variety of "genres," or literary forms, were experimented with before the one(s) that worked best was/were determined. It is too simplistic to presume that there were only two sorts.

I therefore suggest that we begin to employ the term "pluriformity," which has been employed frequently in recent discussions of the biblical text in antiquity, particularly at Qumran, when speaking of the Dead Sea manuscripts containing legal material.[48] What I have

---

[48] In this section, I reiterate a number of points made in the essay on 4Q159 in the Elman *Festschrift*. For "pluriformity" in discussions of the biblical text, cf., e.g., Eugene

observed, over and over, regarding 4Q159 is that it does not behave the way we "expect" legal material from Qumran to behave, that is to say, like the "paradigmatic" legal texts, the *Temple Scroll* and the *Damascus Document*. This indicates to me that we should treat it, and probably all the other "minor" legal texts from Qumran, like 4Q251 and 4Q265, 4Q513 and 4Q514, as independent entities, analyzing separately for each one the list of laws that they present, the language with which they formulate them, the ways in which they are arranged, and the type of exegesis employed to derive them. For the purposes of that analysis, which, on the whole, has not been carried out, the differences among the manuscripts may be more important than their similarities. Once the differences have been established, we may begin to look for points of commonality between and among the documents, with an eye toward establishing conceptual and historical links whenever that might be possible.

The question of the possible applicability or observance, and the function or role or social context of each of those "legal" texts is, needless to say, also very significant, but its investigation should probably be deferred until the literary and exegetical issues that we are raising here are worked out. The internal analysis of these documents, as fraught with ambiguity as it may be, is still considerably more concrete than any attempt to locate them in social or historical context. And when the texts contain both legal and non-legal material, as CD/4QD and 4Q159 do, there are further questions that must be asked regarding the nature and context of such texts.[49]

C. Ulrich, "Pluriformity in the Biblical Text, Text Groups, and Questions of Canon," in *The Madrid Qumran Congress: Proceedings of the International Congress on the Dead Sea Scrolls, March 1991* (ed. Julio Trebolle Barrera and Luis Vegas Montaner; Leiden: Brill, 1992), 1.23–41; Adam S. van der Woude, "Pluriformity and Uniformity: Reflections on the Transmission of the Text of the Old Testament," in *Sacred History and Sacred Texts in Early Judaism: A Symposium in Honour of Adam S. van der Woude* (ed. Jan N. Bremmer and Florentino García Martínez; Kampen: Kok Pharos, 1992), 151–69; Magne Sæbø, "From Pluriformity to Uniformity: The Emergence of the Massoretic [sic] Text," in *On the Way to Canon: Creative Tradition History in the Old Testament* (Sheffield: Sheffield Academic Press, 1998), 36–46.

[49] CD is probably the paradigmatic example of this sort of text, and it has been bifurcated for a very long time into "Admonition" and "Laws," a division that does not do much to help us understand the fundamental nature of the document. For a recent attempt to understand the relationship of the two so-called sections of CD, see Stephen Fraade, "Law, History and Narrative in the Damascus Document," *Meghillot: Studies in the Dead Sea Scrolls* 5–6 (2007): 35–55. Fraade further pointed out in commenting on an early draft of this paper that "the need to categorize 'legal'

If we adopt such an approach, separating texts from one another rather than linking them generically, we shall suffer the temporary inconvenience of having more pigeonholes than we really want for our Qumran legal texts, but that is a small price to pay for the ability to describe more accurately the mosaic of legal texts that comprise such a significant portion of the corpus of Qumran documents. Whether we are studying Qumran legal exegesis, or the practice of halakhah at Qumran, or the development of post-biblical legal compositions, our future conclusions based on a more accurate description of the Qumran legal corpus will be based on much firmer foundations.

---

and 'non-legal'" is the problem of the 21st century scholar, not that of the Qumran authors.

RE-READING 4QPESHER ISAIAH A (4Q161) FORTY YEARS AFTER DJD V

ALEX P. JASSEN

University of Minnesota

INTRODUCTION

Pesher Isaiah A (4Q161) is the most often cited of the pesharim on Isaiah.[1] It has gained this prominence in scholarly literature based on the appearance of the messianic interpretation of Isa 11:1–5 in the final lines of the extant text.[2] The ubiquity of references to the pesher,

---

[1] Six pesharim on Isaiah are extant, one from Cave 3 (3Q4) and five from Cave 4 (4Q161–65). The Cave 4 manuscripts were identified by Allegro with the sigla 4QpIsa^a–e. In current practice, the use of a superscript lowercase letter indicates that the editor considers this manuscript to be one of several copies of a single text from antiquity. Several indicators suggest that the pesharim on Isaiah likely do not represent a single composition, though it is not clear how many distinct pesharim are represented by the six manuscripts. No textual overlap exists among the six manuscripts. Indeed, the opposite feature is present. 4Q161 and 4Q163 6–7 II, 11–22 each contain distinct pesher interpretations of Isa 10:22–24, which would suggest the existence of at least two distinct compositions. Several formal characteristics also distinguish the manuscripts. While most of the pesharim interpret the text of Isaiah continuously, 4Q163 moves freely throughout the book of Isaiah, while also utilizing lemmata from other scriptural books. These distinctions were already noted in Cecil Roth, "The Subject Matter of Qumran Exegesis," *VT* 19 (1960): 56. See more recent discussion in George J. Brooke, "Isaiah in the Pesharim and Other Qumran Texts," in *Writing and Reading the Scroll of Isaiah: Studies of an Interpretive Tradition* (ed. Craig C. Boyles and Craig A. Evans; VTSup 70; 2 vols.; Leiden: Brill, 1997), 2:618–9. Based on these formal and literary features, the editors of the Isaiah pesharim in the revised DJD V (Moshe J. Bernstein and myself) have recommended modifying the sigla to 4QpIsa A–E.

[2] For analysis of the manuscript in the context of its messianic allusions, see, for example: John M. Allegro, "Further Messianic References in Qumran Literature," *JBL* 75 (1956): 177–82 (esp. 181–2); Adam S. van der Woude, *Die messianischen Vorstellungen der Gemeinde von Qumran* (Assen: Van Gorcum, 1957), 75–82; Jacob Liver, "The Doctrine of Two Messiahs in Sectarian Literature in the Time of the Second Commonwealth," *HTR* 52 (1959): 158, 160–1; Hebrew reprint in *Studies in the Bible and Judean Desert Scrolls* (Jerusalem: Bialik, 1971), 155–85; Lawrence H. Schiffman, "Messianic Figures and Ideas in the Qumran Scrollls," in *The Messiah: Developments in Earliest Judaism and Christianity* (ed. James H. Charlesworth; Minneapolis: Fortress, 1992), 124; James C. VanderKam, "Messianism in the Scrolls," in *The Community of the Renewed Covenant: The Notre Dame Symposium on the Dead Sea Scrolls* (ed. Eugene Ulrich and James C. VanderKam; Notre Dame: University of Notre Dame Press, 1994), 216, 219, 231–2; Florentino García Martínez, "Messianic Hopes," in idem

however, should not lead us to think that this text has been fully studied. Indeed, if we subtract the treatments of the messianic interpretation of Isa 11:1–5, the rest of the pesher has received less attention
than it deserves. The purpose of this article is to present some insights
that have emerged from my study of this text in preparing the revised
DJD V edition.

4Q161 is represented by 10 fragments, which preserve the existence
of three columns.[3] Paleographical analysis of the manuscript identifies the text as a rustic semi-formal hand, suggesting a date for the
copying of the manuscript between 30 BCE–30 CE.[4] The extant fragments contain scriptural citations and interpretations for Isa 10:22
and 10:24–11:5, though it is almost certain that additional scriptural verses were interpreted.[5] The primary focus of the pesher is the

---

and Julio Trebolle Barrera, *The People of the Dead Sea Scrolls: Their Writings, Beliefs,
and Practices* (Leiden: Brill, 1995), 164–5; Kenneth E. Pomykala, *The Davidic Dynasty
Tradition in Early Judaism: Its History and Significance for Messianism* (SBLEJL 7;
Atlanta: Scholars Press, 1995), 197–203; John J. Collins, *The Scepter and the Star: Jewish Messianism in Light of the Dead Sea Scrolls* (ABRL; New York: Doubleday, 1995),
57–8; Martin G. Abegg Jr., "The Messiah at Qumran: Are We Still Seeing Double?" *DSD*
2 (1995): 136; Richard J. Bauckham, "The Messianic Interpretation of Isaiah 10:34 in
the Dead Sea Scrolls, 2 Baruch and the Preaching of John the Baptist," *DSD* 2 (1995):
202–16; Johannes Zimmermann, *Messianische Texte aus Qumran: Königliche, priester-
liche und prophetische Messiasvorstellungen in den Schriftfunden von Qumran* (WUNT
2/104. Tübingen: Mohr Siebeck, 1998), 59–71; Gerbern S. Oegema, *The Anointed and
His People: Messianic Expectations from the Maccabees to Bar Kokhba* (JSPSup 27;
Sheffield: Sheffield Academic Press, 1998), 90; Kenneth Atkinson, "On the Herodian
Origin of Militant Davidic Messianism at Qumran: New Light from *Psalm of Solomon*
17," *JBL* 118 (1999): 447–9; Moshe J. Bernstein, "Pesher Isaiah," *EDSS*, 2:652; Geza
G. Xeravits, *King, Priest, Prophet: Positive Eschatological Protagonists in the Qumran
Library* (STDJ 47; Leiden: Brill, 2003), 51–5; Serge Ruzer, "Who is Unhappy with the
Davidic Messiah? Notes on Biblical Exegesis in 4Q161, 4Q174, and the Book of Acts,"
CNS 24/2 (2003): 232–4; Casey D. Elledge, "The Prince of the Congregation: Qumran
'Messianism' in the Context of *Milḥâmâ*," in *Qumran Studies: New Approaches, New
Questions* (ed. Michael T. Davis and Brent A. Strawn; Grand Rapids: Eerdmans, 2007),
189–91; Joseph Blenkinsopp, *Opening the Sealed Book: Interpretations of the Book of
Isaiah in Late Antiquity* (Grand Rapids: Eerdmans, 2006), 114–21; Joseph A. Fitzmyer,
The One Who is to Come (Grand Rapids: Eerdmans, 2007), 99.

   [3] Frags. 1, 6, and 10 all preserve evidence of a bottom margin, thus ensuring the
existence of at least three columns. Allegro does not discuss the bottom margins and
thus the *editio princeps* lacks column numbering. See further, Horgan, *Pesharim*, 71;
Zimmermann, *Messianische Texte*, 65–6.

   [4] See Strugnell, "Notes en marge," 183; Horgan, *Pesharim*, 71; Brooke, "Isaiah in
the Pesharim," 620.

   [5] Below, I argue that Isa 10:20–23 likely serves as the initial lemma in frags. 2–6
(the extant citation of Isa 10:22 therefore representing a re-citation). Allegro, *Qumrân
Cave 4.I*, 11 understands frag. 1 as a citation of Isa 10:21 with pesher interpretation
of vv. 20–21. Due to the highly fragmentary nature of frag. 1, Allegro's suggestion

eschatological war that will be waged against the Kittim under the leadership of the messianic Prince of the Congregation. The expectation of this war and its specific elements are exegetically woven into several central themes from Isaiah. As in other pesher texts, the scriptural passages from Isaiah are recast as alluding to the unfolding events of the "end of days." The reference to the "remnant" of Israel from Isa 10:22 is identified as an allusion to the sectarian community that survives while the rest of Israel is destroyed in the end-time;[6] the march of the Assyrian enemy toward Jerusalem from Isa 10:28–32 prefigures the arrival of the Kittim;[7] the encounter with the Assyrians in Isa 10:33–34 provides the details for the eschatological battle against the Kittim; the Davidic figure in Isa 11:1–5 is understood as the messianic descendent of David who leads the campaign against the eschatological enemies.

The preliminary edition of 4Q161 was published by John Allegro in 1956, followed by the DJD V *editio princeps* in 1968.[8] Since its initial publication, the text has received extensive analysis, including John Strugnell's review of DJD V, substantial commentaries by Adam S. van der Woude, Jean Carmignac, Joseph D. Amoussine, and Maurya Horgan, and many other analyses in articles and monographs.[9] The

---

has found few adherents (cf. Pomykala, *Davidic Dynasty*, 198; Blenkinsopp, *Opening*, 114–6). See further discussion in Horgan, *Pesharim*, 72. Frags. 8–10 break off in the midst of an interpretation of Isa 11:1–5 and it is therefore unclear how much additional scriptural material was interpreted in this text.

[6] The remnant theme in 4Q161 and its relationship to the larger Dead Sea Scrolls corpus is treated in Joel Willitts, "The Remnant of Israel in 4QpIsaiah[a] (4Q161) and the Dead Sea Scrolls," *JJS* 57 (2006): 11–25.

[7] It is not clear which exact campaign is referred to in Isaiah, though an Assyrian advance is almost certain based on the surrounding context (e.g., the mention of Assyria in v. 24). The singular verbs in vv. 28–32 are generally understood as referring to the king of Assyria, either Sennacherib or Sargon II (see further discussion in Marvin Sweeney, "Sargon's Threat against Jerusalem in Isaiah 10,27–32," *Bib* 75 [1994]: 459–69). From the perspective of the later interpretation in the pesher, the precise identity of the aggressor is not important.

[8] Allegro, "Further Messianic References," 177–82 + pls. II–III; idem, *Qumrân Cave 4.I*, 11–15 + pls. IV–V.

[9] Van der Woude, *Messianischen Vorstellungen*, 175–82; Jean Carmignac, "Notes sur les Peshârîm," *RevQ* 3/12 (1961–1962): 511–5; idem, *Les Textes de Qumrân traduits et annotés, vol. 2* (Paris: Letouzey et Ané, 1963), 68–72; Strugnell, "Notes en marge," 183–7 + pl. I. Joseph D. Amoussine, "A propos de l'interprétation de 4Q161 (fragments 5–6, 8)," *RevQ* 8/31 (1972–1975): 381–92; idem (Amusin) "The Reflection of Historical Events of the First Century BC in Qumran Commentaries," *HUCA* 48 (1977): 123–34; Horgan, *Pesharim*, 70–87; eadem, "Pesharim," 83–97. Less detailed commentaries can be found in Xeravits, *King, Priest, Prophet*, 51–5; Zimmermann, *Messianische Texte*, 59–71. With the exception of Horgan, none of these commentaries covers the entire preserved text of 4Q161. Isolated textual comments can be found

preparation of a new *editio princeps* for 4Q161 therefore involves rereading the text in light of both 50 years of scholarship as well as our
much fuller understanding of the Dead Sea Scrolls corpus, early Jewish
biblical interpretation, and the development of eschatology in Second
Temple Judaism. To be sure, the wealth of earlier scholarship on this
text has more easily facilitated this process. Thus, for example, while
scholars debate many specific readings, we have a relatively good sense
of how to read the manuscript itself. Yet, the bulk of these analyses
were conducted before the full availability of the scrolls corpus in the
1990s and the renewed attention to the forms and techniques of biblical interpretation in the scrolls that followed. Moreover, scholarship
on 4Q161 has tended to examine specific issues within the text (e.g.,
reconstruction of specific words or clauses, messianism, historical allusions), often to the detriment of analysis of the text as a whole.

In my reading of this text and its scholarly literature, I have found
several areas that are in need of a much fuller discussion: (1) There
is a significant debate between Allegro and Horgan—and now also
Moshe Bernstein—on how to arrange and understand the fragmentary
remains—in particular, column length, reconstruction of lemmata,
evidence for lemma re-citation, and the use of citation and re-citation
formulas. These issues are at the heart of the exegetical technique of
the pesher and its relationship to other pesharim.[10] (2) As has been
the case with many of the less prominent pesharim, the text as reconstructed and understood by Strugnell or Horgan seems to have become
canonical, with little interest in revisiting long-held understandings of
the text or even passages that were thought to be impossible to reconstruct with any degree of certainty. (3) Perhaps the largest lacuna in
the scholarship on 4Q161 is the lack of attention to its exegetical tech-

---

in Yigael Yadin, "Some Notes on the Commentaries on Genesis xlix and Isaiah from
Qumran Cave 4," *IEJ* 7 (1957): 67–8; idem, "Recent Developments in Dead Sea Scrolls
Research," in *Studies in the Dead Sea Scrolls: Lectures Delivered at the Third Annual
Conference (1957) in Memory of E. L. Sukenik* (ed. Jacob Liver; Jerusalem: Kiryat Sep-
her, 1957), 49–52 [Hebrew]; Joseph A. Fitzmyer, "Review of Allegro, *Qumrân Cave
4.1*," *CBQ* 31 (1969): 237. See also Timothy H. Lim, *Pesharim* (Companion to the
Qumran Scrolls 3; London: Sheffield Academic Press, 2002), 28. As noted above (n. 2),
most non-commentary analyses of 4Q161 focus on its messianic content, thus often
generally disregarding the remainder of the text.

[10] See Horgan, *Pesharim*, 71–3; Moshe J. Bernstein, "Introductory Formulas for
Citation and Re-citation of Biblical Verses in the Qumran Pesharim: Observations on
a Pesher Technique," *DSD* 1 (1994): 36–9. As observed by Bernstein, questions surrounding these formal characteristics are critical to determining how many distinct
pesharim on Isaiah are represented in the six extant manuscripts (see above, n. 1).

nique, which is only episodically treated and rarely in a sophisticated way.[11] (4) The messianic references and allusions to the eschatological war against the Kittim are commonly discussed.[12] Yet, the scholarship has not fully located these features more broadly within the Qumran corpus, particularly in light of our newly available texts—such as *Sefer ha-Milḥamah* (4Q285=11Q14)—and our better understanding of the Qumran war texts.[13]

This article is intended as a snapshot of my larger understanding of the text and its relationship to other literature in the scrolls corpus and early Jewish exegetical and eschatological literature. I begin by working through some of my observations on the first six lines of frags. 2–6. My discussion highlights 1) my attempts to provide a better reading of the text at places; 2) elements of exegetical technique in 4Q161; and 3) issues raised by Horgan and Bernstein on the reconstruction of the lemmata. I then turn to two specific examples where the text of 4Q161 can inform other texts in the Qumran corpus and be informed by them—both examples focus on exegetical technique and the relationship between 4Q161 and the war texts.

FORMAL STRUCTURE, CITATION AND PESHER FORMULAE, AND EXEGETICAL TECHNIQUE

The joining of frags. 2–6 is aided by the preservation of fragmentary lemmata from Isa 10:22, 24–32.[14] The nature of the lemma citations throughout these fragments, however, is neither consistent nor entirely

---

[11] Aspects of the exegetical technique of the pesher are treated in Judah M. Rosenthal, "Biblical Exegesis of 4QpIs," *JQR* 60 (1969–1970): 27–30; Bauckham, "Messianic Interpretation," 204–6; Willitts, "Remnant," 11–25; Blenkinsopp, *Opening*, 114–21.

[12] See bibliography above, n. 2.

[13] Another area that is lacking in the *editio princeps* is treatment of textual variants in the lemmata within the larger context of the text of Isaiah in antiquity. This issue is now addressed fully in George J. Brooke, "The Qumran Pesharim and the Text of Isaiah in the Cave 4 Manuscripts," in *Biblical Hebrew, Biblical Texts: Essays in Memory of Michael P. Weitzman* (ed. A. Rapoport-Albert and G. Greenberg; JSOTSup 333; Sheffield: Sheffield Academic Press, 2001), 304–20.

[14] Allegro treats frags. 2–4 and 5–6 separately, while Horgan arranges them together as representative of column 2 (see Horgan, *Pesharim*, 71–3). Allegro and Horgan also differ in the line numbering for 4Q161. Allegro merely begins the line numbering with the extant text, while Horgan reconstructs column lengths of 29 lines and thus renumbers each line accordingly (ibid., 72–3). Below I argue that Horgan's reconstruction of the opening lines of frags. 2–6 is incorrect and thus her line numbering system should be abandoned at least for this specific portion of the text. For convenience, I refer to

clear. Isa 10:28–32 is relatively well preserved, and is followed by a
four line pesher.[15] Isa 10:24–27 is poorly preserved, and is followed
by at least three lines of pesher.[16] The situation for the initial lemma
and pesher is less clear. Frags. 2–6 begin with one and a half lines
of indiscernible text followed by what is generally reconstructed as
וא[שר אמר, then a citation of Isa 10:22 followed by a fragmentary two
line pesher. ואשר אמר, as observed by Horgan, functions in *Pesher
Habakkuk* as a re-citation formula to introduce a pesher on a lemma
that has already been cited.[17] She therefore surmises that the beginning
of the column cited Isa 10:22–23 in full—what she reconstructs as lines
1–3 followed by a line *vacat*.[18] Thus, Horgan reconstructs frags. 2–6 as
follows (lemma of v. 22 marked with single-underlining):

[כיא אם היה עמכה ישראל כחול הים שאר]	1
[ישוב בו כליון חרוץ ושוטף צדקה כיא כלה ונחרצה אדוני]	2
[יהוה צבאות עושה בקרב כול הארץ *vac* [	3
[*vacat*]	4
[כ̇י̇א̇] [בי בני] [	5
[ע̇מ̇ו̇] וא[ש̇ר אמר אם ה̇י̇]ה עמכה] [	6
[ישראל כחול הים שאר ישוב בו] כ[ליון חר]וץ ושוטף צד]קה]	7
[לות בי]°[ ]ג̇ה ורבים יוב]דו]	8
[ ]°[ה]ארץ באמת ולוא ימ]לטו למט] [	9
[ ] [לכן...[19]	10

---

the text of 4Q161 throughout with both sets of column and line numbers (though I
adopt Horgan's alignment of frags. 8–10 as col. III for Allegro as well).

[15] Following Allegro, the lemma and pesher are found in 5–6 4–13. Following Horgan, 2–6 II, 21–29.

[16] The lemma is preserved in A 2–4 6–10=H 2–6 II, 10–16, though it is extant only
on frags. 2–4. The pesher on this lemma appears in frag. 5. Three lines of pesher are
extant, though the first line contains three indistinguishable letters (see Horgan, *Pesharim*, 78). It is not clear how close together these fragment pieces should be aligned and
thus how much pesher material was originally found for this lemma. It is likely for this
reason that Allegro treats frags. 5–6 as a separate unit (see n. 14). Horgan suggests the
existence of a line *vacat* between the lemma and pesher (her l. 16), consistent with the
appearance of line *vacats* elsewhere in the text (see below, n. 17). Because she argues
more generally for 29 line columns in this text, she does not suggest the existence of
further pesher content here.

[17] On this formula, see Horgan, *Pesharim*, 243; Bernstein, "Introductory Formulas,"
passim.

[18] Line *vacats* appear in 4Q161 in several places, following either the lemma or
pesher: H 2–6 II, 20 (though not numbered by Allegro, this appears following 5–6 3);
8–10 III, A 10=H 14. A third line *vacat* seems to be present in 8–10 III, H 21, though
it is not marked by Allegro. See further Horgan, *Pesharim*, 72.

[19] Following a brief *vacat*, לכן represents the beginning of the next lemma (Isa
10:24–27).

The reconstruction of the column length and the role of the lemmata in the text is a much larger and separate issue, but I offer here some general observations as they help us understand the particular issue in this column. In particular, I draw attention to Moshe Bernstein's criticism of Horgan here.[20] As he observes, prior to the citation formula, the word עמו is preserved on Horgan's l. 6 (marked with double-underlining).[21] This word can be deciphered either as "with him" or "his people." Though we must bear in mind the fragmentary nature of the manuscript, it is likely that this word is an exegetical link to עמכה ישראל in Isa 10:22 and thus should be read as "his nation."[22] Yet, as noted by Bernstein, lemmata which have already been interpreted are generally not re-cited a second time in the pesharim.

The second issue raised by Bernstein is the presence of הארץ in Horgan's l. 9 (marked with double-underlining), also presumably an exegetical link to a lemma, but in this case, Isa 10:23 (כי כלה ונחרצה אדני יהוה צבאות עשה בקרב כל־הארץ). If this understanding is correct, then the pesher has moved from a re-citation and pesher of v. 22 to a pesher on v. 23, without a new (re-)citation of v. 23. Ultimately, however, Bernstein leaves the issue unresolved.[23]

The solution to this issue can be found in the pesher on Isa 11:1–5 in frags. 8–10, which contains the only clear example of a re-citation in this text—that is the re-citation of Isa 11:3b also introduced with ואשר אמר (A ll. 21–22=H ll. 26–27):[24]

---

[20] Bernstein, "Introductory Formulas," 36–9.

[21] Bernstein, "Introductory Formulas," 38. The upper portion of frag. 2 that contains this word is not found in Allegro's *editio princeps*, but was added later by Strugnell (see "Notes en marge," 184 + pl. I).

[22] Bernstein, "Introductory Formulas," 38. Willitts, "Remnant," 14, restores the text as [רשעי] עמו, based on the similar formula in 1QpHab V, 3. Though this is possible based on the context of both passages, עמו is a very common locution in the scrolls. The fragmentary nature of this line precludes making any definitive reconstruction here.

[23] This inconsistency was previously observed by Strugnell. He therefore restores the citation formula as כאש[ר אמר ("Notes en marge," 184). He identifies this citation formula as equivalent to כיא הוא אשר אמר, which appears when the lemma is cited *after* its pesher interpretation (see Horgan, *Pesharim*, 243). Thus, the pesher that follows the citation would not be related to v. 22. Rather, עמו is part of the pesher on v. 22, which is then cited post-pesher. This solution, however, does not resolve the problem of ארץ in l. 5, since v. 23 is still absent (see further Bernstein, "Introductory Formulas," 39).

[24] The text presented here follows Horgan, though there are only two places where her reconstruction differs from Allegro's (see following notes).

צמח] דויד 25 העומד באח[רית הימים [	]	17=22
או]יבו ואל יסומכנו ב[רוח ג]בורה 26 [ ]	]	18=23
כ]סא כבוד נזר ק[ודש]ובגדי ריקמ[ו]ת[27]	]	19=24
[ ] בידו ובכול הג[ואי]ם ימשול ומגוג	]	20=25
כו]ל העמים תשפוט חרבו ואשר אמר לוא	]	21=26
[למראה עיניו ישפוט]ולוא למשמע אוזניו יוכיח פשרו אשר	]	22=27
[וכאשר יורוהו כן ישפוט ועל פיהם	]	23=28
[עמו יצא אחד מכוהני השם ובידו בגדי	]	24=29

4Q161 8–10 III, A 11–16=H 15–20 cites Isa 11:1–5 in full, followed by a nearly five line pesher, prior to the recitation of 11:3b—marked here by single-underlining. What has not been noticed, however, is that the re-citation and associated pesher should be understood as a digression from the general pesher on Isa 11:1–5. Namely, the re-citation interrupts the general pesher in order to express the view that the victorious Davidic messiah must now take orders from the priests, an idea illustrated well by the re-cited lemma.[28] But, if we look at the extant pesher on the next and final line (A l. 24=H l. 29), the subject matter has clearly shifted. The priests are still in the picture, but the pesher has turned its attention to a matter of clothing—as marked by the double-underlining. I will have more to say about the clothing below, but for now it suffices to say that the clothing in A l. 24=H l. 29 is exegetically related to Isa 11:5, which describes how the Davidic figure will be girded in righteousness and faithfulness (והיה צדק אזור מתניו והאמונה אזור חלציו). This same verse seems to be the exegetical link for the description of the messiah's clothing in A l. 19=H l. 24—also marked by double-underlining.

---

[25] The lacuna is generally restored as דויד [צמח, "Branch of David" (Allegro, *Qumran Cave 4.I*, 14; Horgan, *Pesharim*, 85). This specific title is likely exegetically linked to the plant imagery in Isa 11:1 (נצר ,חטר). Its restoration here is certain based on the other uses in the scrolls: 4Q174 1 I, 11 (also with העומד); 4Q252 1 I, 3–4 (עד צמח הצדק משיח בוא); and most importantly 4Q285 7 3, 4, which interprets Isa 11:1 as an allusion to the דויד צמח (who is also identified with the Prince of the Congregation; see below). See further, Pomykala, *Davidic Dynasty*, 201 and more generally on the title, Xeravits, *King, Priest, Prophet*, 154–9.

[26] The reconstruction ב[רוח ג]בורה (A 18=H 23) is proposed by Strugnell based on an earlier suggestion of Patrick Skehan ("Notes en marge," 184; Horgan, *Pesharim*, 85). Allegro restores the equally plausible: ב[ה[תורה.

[27] Horgan deciphers the final word as [ריקמו]ת, rather than [רוקמו]ת, as found in Allegro and Strugnell. Carmignac, "Notes," 512, restores רוקמה. On the meaning of this phrase, see below, n. 117.

[28] See Blenkinsopp, *Opening*, 120–1.

The end result of all of this is that the re-citation of v. 3b and its pesher unit seem to be a brief digression from the more general pesher unit on vv. 1–5—to make the very specific point of subordinating the authority of the messiah to the priests. The introduction of the priests as expressed through the pesher on v. 3b marks a transition point in the larger pesher unit, since it now turns its attention more directly to the priests. The garments are a focal point of the entire pesher unit, though they are only explicitly identified with the priests after the re-citation of v. 3b.[29] However, what is important is that the pesher has moved out of the exegesis of v. 3b and seemingly back into the larger pesher on vv. 1–5, more specifically as an exegetical comment on the clothing imagery of v. 5. Unfortunately, our text runs out right where we could find more concrete evidence for the formal characteristics of this pesher. The continuation of the text may have included more re-citations or merely continued the general pesher on vv. 1–5 and then moved right to a new lemma.

This understanding of the re-citation can work equally well in the opening of frags. 2–6 and thus resolve the two issues raised by Bernstein. If the citation of Isa 10:22 is understood as a digressive re-citation, then the presence of עמו in l. 2 (=H l. 6) would be explained as due to the fact that it is part of a larger general pesher on the lemma. Similarly, the presence of ארץ in l. 5 (=H l. 9) indicates that the digressive re-citation has ended and the pesher has returned to a more general pesher on the lemma. The brief nature of the digressive pesher would correspond with the length of the pesher on the re-cited Isa 11:3b in frags. 8–10.

This suggestion also resolves another difficulty with Horgan's understanding that was not raised by Bernstein. Horgan restores Isa 10:22–23 as the lemma in ll. 1–3 and then a general pesher of only one and a half lines before the re-citation of 10:22. This model is inconsistent with her observation that the lemmata and pesher units in 4Q161 are relatively long.[30] The one unequivocal example of a lemma + pesher + re-citation in frags. 8–10 has a lemma of five verses followed by a pesher of nearly five lines prior to the re-citation. Indeed, the other extant lemmata in the text are long, either four (10:24–27) or five verses (10:28–32).[31] Thus, we might suggest starting the lemma in

---

[29] See below pp. 83–90 for further discussion of the garments and their relationship to the priests.

[30] See Horgan, *Pesharim*, 72. This feature is similarly noted in Lim, *Pesharim*, 28.

[31] To be sure, 8–10 III, A 1–9=H 5–13 preserves lemmata for only 10:33–34, though the formal characteristics of the lemma and pesher units are not entirely clear.

the opening lines of frags. 2–6 at Isa 10:20, which likewise represents the beginning of the literary unit regarding the "remnant" in Isaiah. Based on purely formal considerations, it is plausible that the first five and a half lines of frags. 2–6 contain a general pesher on at least Isa 10:22–23—but possibly also vv. 20–21—as well as a re-citation and digressive pesher on Isa 10:22. Based on the comparative data of frags. 8–10 and lemma re-citations in *Pesher Habakkuk*, we should expect at least a few additional lines of a general pesher prior to the re-citation of v. 22. Thus, I find it best to reject Horgan's tidy reconstruction of Isa 10:22–23 as the purported ll. 1–3. Ultimately, we can only guess as to the length of the initial pesher and thus it is impossible to know where to locate the lemma. Accordingly, I suggest returning to Allegro's original line numbering, whereby Horgan's l. 5 is once again identified as l. 1 of frags. 2–6.

RECONSTRUCTING THE TEXT AND EXEGETICAL TECHNIQUE OF
4Q161 A 2–4 4–5=H 2–6 II 8–9[32]

] 4	[לות בי]°[[גה ורבים יוב]דו	
] 5	ים[לטו למט] [ארץ באמת]°[ ]	

Let me now add some sense of the exegetical technique in the first pesher unit that bolsters my understanding of its formal characteristics and builds upon some newly suggested reconstructions. I begin with the lacunae in l. 4, for which Allegro, Strugnell, and Horgan have no suggestions. If we assume that ll. 2–3 are a re-citation of Isa 10:22, then at least l. 4 would contain a pesher interpretation of the passage.[33] The lemma and the extant text at the end of l. 4 (ורבים יוב]דו) suggest

---

[32] The preserved portions of ll. 4–5 are presented here based on the readings found in Allegro, Strugnell, and Horgan (see especially Horgan, "Pesharim," 86). The reconstructions at the end of l. 4 and the beginning of l. 5 are generally agreed upon, though I note other possibilities in the course of the discussion below (as well as for the other lacunae).

[33] As noted by Horgan, *Pesharim*, 74, a pesher introduction formula should likely be restored at the beginning of the line. She suggests פשרו. Another common formula פשרו אשר appears following the re-citation of Isa 11:3b in 8–10 III, A 22=H 27 and may have appeared here if 4Q161 is consistent in its citation formulae. The longer form, however, leaves less room for reconstruction in the lacuna (though it is possible that the first word should be restored at the end of l. 3). Florentino García Martínez and Eibert J. C. Tigchelaar, DSSSE 1.314, suggest פשרו על.

that this pesher refers to the destruction of the wider segment of
Israel.[34]

Florentino García Martínez and Eibert J.C. Tigchelaar suggest
reconstructing the first word as לכ[לות, "to destroy," the *pi'el* infinitive
construct from the root כלה.[35] I agree that the reconstruction כ[לות is
very likely—with either the *qal* meaning of "end, perish," or more likely
the *pi'el* "destroy, destruction"—but the lack of context recommends
against reconstructing the prefix ל. In addition to working with the
preserved letters, this reconstruction adds a direct exegetical link to the
word כליון in the lemma (Isa 10:22) and corresponds with the scriptural
imagery of destruction. It is possible to make a tentative suggestion
regarding the preceding prefix/word. While the prepositions ב, ל, or
ב are common before כלות in all its various meanings, the preposition
עד ("until") is commonly found in biblical literature and the Dead Sea
Scrolls before כלות when it refers to impending violent destruction.[36]

The use of עד + כלות in Jer 44:27 is particularly helpful in providing
a larger literary and exegetical context. In this verse, the Judean exiles
in Egypt will be destroyed by the sword and famine (ותמו כל־איש
יהודה אשר בארץ־מצרים בחרב וברעב עד־כלותם).[37] These agents of
destruction (along with "plague") appear at several places in the pesharim in reference to the expected destruction (אבד√) of the "many"
(רבים), the precise phrase found at the end of l. 4.[38] In all likelihood
one or more of these agents of destruction should therefore be restored
in the lacuna at the end of l. 4.

Moreover, Jer 44:27–28 employs imagery similar to the "remnant"
theme in Isa 10:20–23. Jeremiah 44 contains a scathing critique of
the wayward actions of the Judean exiles, such that they are initially
informed that no remnant (שארית) shall survive from among them
(vv. 7, 12–14), a prediction that is reinforced in v. 27. The very next
verse, however, affirms that a small remnant of "survivors of the

---

[34] Strugnell, "Notes en marge," 184, notes that the final word on l. 4 could be
restored יומ[ן. The combination of אבד√ and רבים in several other Qumran texts (see
below, n. 38), however, recommends against this reading.

[35] García Martínez and Tigchelaar, DSSSE 1., 314.

[36] See 1 Sam 15:18; 2 Sam 22:38; Jer 9:15; 44:27; 49:37; Ezek 4:8; Ps 18:38; 2 Chr
18:10. With one exception (Jer 44:27), all forms are *pi'el*; 1QS IV, 13–14; 1QM III, 9;
VIII, 1; XI, 10–11. To be sure, these examples all contain possessive suffixes (except
1QM XI, 10–11).

[37] See also Jer 49:37, where the agent of destruction is the sword.

[38] 1QpHab VI, 10; 4Q171 1–10 I, 26; 1–10 II, 1; 1–10 III, 2–4; cf. 1QpHab II, 13 as
restored by Horgan, *Pesharim*, 26. This constellation of disasters seems to draw upon
Jer 32:24; 44:13.

sword" will indeed return to Judah (פליטי חרב ישבון מן־ארץ מצרים ארץ יהודה).[39] Like Jeremiah 44, the pesharim that employ these three agents of destruction apply them to the annihilation of wider segments of the Jewish population. 4Q161 2–6 II, 4 (H 8)—following the biblical lemma from Isa 10:22—employs similar imagery as found in Jeremiah and the other pesharim in order to identify the end-time as a period in which the general population of Israel, in particular the community's immediate opponents, would be destroyed through a variety of means.

The next word on l. 4 preserves an initial *bet* and *yod* prior to a short lacuna.[40] The *bet* has a range of possible meanings, but I am suggesting that it should be understood as a *bet* of time or place.[41] In particular, I call attention to 1QHᵃ VII, 30 (XV, 17), which refers to a "day of slaughter" (יום הרגה) that will befall the wicked (ורשעים בראתה ל[קץ ח]רונכה ומרחם הקדשתם ליום הרגה), which I suggest restoring in the second lacuna.[42] This language draws from Jer 12:3, in which the wicked are imagined as slaughtered on this day like sheep (ואתה יהוה ידעתני תראני ובחנת לבי אתך התקם כצאן לטבחה והק דשם ליום הרגה).[43] The pesher may have in view the same anticipated day of slaughter, during which, as in Isaiah, the wider population of wicked Israel will be destroyed. The restoration of יום here adds another

---

[39] Contrary to commentators who argue that v. 28a is a gloss, since v. 27 asserts that *all* the Judeans exiles were killed (see William McKane, *A Critical and Exegetical Commentary on Jeremiah* [2 vols.; London: T. & T. Clark, 1996], 2.1081). The point of v. 28a is there will indeed be a small remnant that will survive the devastation articulated in v. 27 (see R. David Kimḥi ad. loc.). It is possible that the "remnant (שארית) of Judah" in v. 28b similarly refers to the exiles who return to Judah. While MT identifies them as the remnant "who came to live in Egypt" (and thus presumably the annihilated exiles in Egypt from v. 27), this phrase is lacking in the LXX.

[40] A slight trace of the bottom right portion of the third letter is visible, but not enough to identify the letter. Strugnell, "Notes en marge," 184, suggests restoring an *'aleph* here, but this is unlikely (see Horgan, *Pesharim*, 78).

[41] For the *bet* of time or place following the infinitive construct כלות (*pi'el*), see David J.A. Clines, ed., *Dictionary of Classical Hebrew, Volume IV* (Sheffield: Sheffield Academic Press, 1998), 417b. See especially the use with יום in Gen 2:2; Num 7:1; Neh 3:34; 2 Chr 29:17 (though these are all with the meaning "to complete").

[42] This restoration can similarly be found in García Martínez and Tigchelaar, DSSSE 1.314. Another plausible restoration is the prepositional agent ביד, with the lacuna containing a more specific reference to the human agents of destruction (cf. 1QpHab V, 3).

[43] See the similar expression ביום הרג רב in Isa 30:25. התקם כצאן לטבחה is lacking in the LXX (it is present in 4QJerᵃ), though this is likely a scribal error resulting from homeoarchton (Jack Lundbom, *Jeremiah 1–20* [AB 21A; New York: Doubleday, 1999], 645).

exegetical link with the biblical lemma. Isa 10:20, which was likely cited at some point prior to the extant pesher, locates the entire scene as "on that day" (ביום ההוא), which the pesher thereby understands as the "day of slaughter" (ביום הרגה).[44] יום would also serve as the link to Jer 12:3. It is also possible that the reference to כליותיהם in Jer 12:2 (אתה בפיהם ורחוק מכליותיהם) קרוב corresponds with כליון in Isaiah and thus also to the proposed כ[לות in the pesher. The emphasis on the destruction of the wicked among Israel continues in the end of the line with the description of the annihilation of the "many," which as noted, is employed in the pesharim to refer to the destruction of other Jews.

The other element in the lemma, as continued from the preceding verses, is the assertion that a remnant shall rise up from among the devastation to continue as Israel. This imagery works well with the community's own self-understanding as the true Israel. In l. 5, I suggest following Horgan's reconstruction ימלטו (niph'al).[45] My larger understanding of this line, however, suggests that the subject has switched from the bad guys to the community and therefore I reject her reconstruction of ולוא in the lacuna.[46] The suggestion to follow Horgan's restoration is guided by the use of מלט in the Damascus Document to refer to the division between the wicked destined for destruction and righteous who "escape" (CD VII, 14; VII, 21–VIII, 1; XIX, 9–10).[47] CD XIX, 9–10 identifies those that survive in the time

---

[44] That that pesher therefore has in mind a specific day might suggest restoring the definite יום ההרגה. It is more likely, however, that the pesher draws upon the established phrase from Jeremiah without modification. As in the Hodayot, the indefinite expression is understood with a definite sense.

[45] The extant letters suggest that the complete word (in whatever form) comes from a root with a lamed second radical and ṭet third radical, for which the best options are מלט, פלט, and שלט. In BH, שלט (hiph'il) + ל + infinitive construct means "to grant someone the power to do something" (Qoh 5:18; 6:2), though the verb does not appear in Qumran Hebrew. פלט "to escape" (qal), though infrequent in BH, could also work here and would thus correspond to the root in the lemma (v. 20). The related passages in the Damascus Document (see below), however, favor מלט. The final waw could represent (1) the suffix of a finite verb (e.g., 3rd or 2nd masc. pl. imperfect or 3rd masc. pl. perfect); (2) a 3rd masc. sg. object suffix on a verb; (3) a 3rd masc., sg. possessive suffix on a infinitive construct or noun.

[46] Horgan presumably understands the subject of the verb as the רבים from the previous line and thus her restoration of the negation. Horgan's reconstruction is likewise found in Zimmermann, Messianische Texte, 60.

[47] The specific form of the מלט, however, is uncertain (see above n. 45, for the range of possibilities). It could also be an infinitive construct with the suffix referring in the singular to the community. This form would likely have a temporal preposition

of visitation as the "poor of the flock" who escape (והשומרים אותו
הם עני הצאן אלה ימלטו בקץ הפקדה). The expression "poor of the
flock" draws from Zech 11:7 (וארעה את־צאן ההרגה לכן עני הצאן).[48]
In Zechariah, this flock is identified as designated for slaughter like the
flock in Jer 12:3 (התקם כצאן לטבחה והקדשם ליום הרגה).[49] In CD,
as in 4Q161, this flock *escapes* the slaughter.[50] In contrast, in CD XIX,
10–13, it is the "rest" (נשארים) who are handed over to the sword
(חרב). The emphasis on a select few who survive and the allusions
to the destruction of wider Israel work well with the biblical lemma
in 4Q161, which has likewise been re-oriented to the eschatological
scenario.

The next word in l. 5 preserves *lamed, mem,* and *ṭet*, which Allegro
initially restored as מטה, "rod," no doubt on account of the importance
of this word in the lemma that follows (Isa 10:24).[51] I reconstruct this
word as למט]עת, "planting," with the *lamed* functioning as a *lamed* of
purpose.[52] Plant imagery is well attested in Qumran literature as a self-

---

[48] as well (e.g., בהמלטו, "when it escaped…" or עד המלטו, "until its escape…"). I follow
Horgan's restoration of the 3rd masc. pl. imperfect since it corresponds to the verbal
form in the preceding line (יוב]דו) and the related examples in CD VII, 14; XIX, 10
(VII, 21 has the perfect). See also García Martínez and Tigchelaar, DSSSE 1.314, who
reconstruct והם ימ]לטו.

[48] For Zech 11:7, instead of עני הצאן, כי, LXX has εἰς τὴν Χαναανῖτιν (also v. 5),
which means either "in/at Canaan" or "to the Canaanites" or "for the merchants" (see
discussion in Carol L. Meyers and Eric M. Meyers, *Zechariah 9–14* [AB 25C; New
York: Doubleday, 1993], 261–2).

[49] Note also that Zech 11:1–2 contains several keywords (יער, אדרים, לבנון) found
in Isa 10:34.

[50] See also ועני] in 4Q161 8–10 III, A 3=H 7.

[51] Allegro, *Qumran Cave 4.I*, 12. The initial *lamed* is found on the fragment that
Strugnell attached to frag. 2 (see "Notes en marge," 184 and PAM 44.191). Note that
1QM V, 1 could be reconstructed as referring to the "s[taff] of the Prince of all the
Community" (ועל מ]טה נשיא כול העדה). The emphasis on the Prince elsewhere in
4Q161 suggests that this may be in view here as well (perhaps: למט]הו, "to/for/with/
by means of his staff")

[52] On the *lamed* of purpose, see Bruce K. Waltke and Michael P. O'Connor, *Introduction to Biblical Hebrew Syntax* (Winona Lake: Eisenrauns, 1999), §112.10d (p. 209).
למטע represents another possible restoration (García Martínez and Tigchelaar suggest
למטעם). While only מטע appears in BH, both forms are frequent in Qumran Hebrew
with the identical meaning. מטעת is employed both for the absolute (CD I, 7=4Q266 2
I, 12; 4Q270 2 II, 6; 4Q313 2 1) and construct forms (1QS VIII, 5; XI, 8; 1QHᵃ XIV, 18
(VI, 15); XVI, 7, 11 (VIII, 6, 10); 4Q394 3–10 IV, 12=4Q396 III, 2=4Q397 II, 4; 4Q418
81 + 81a 13). My preference for the longer form is guided by the length of the lacuna,
which recommends the presence of an additional letter and the use of the longer form
in the parallel passages in the *Rule of the Community*.

referential designation for the Qumran community.[53] Most importantly, this term is employed twice in the Rule of the Community with a *lamed* of purpose. In 1QS VIII, 5; XI, 8, the community is established למטעת עולם, "as an eternal planting." Together with the suggestion for the previous word, the pesher would refer to the community that "will escape to become a planting."[54]

If my reconstruction of the first part of the line is correct, then the next clause should likely be restored with Allegro as ב[ארץ באמת, "in the land truthfully."[55] The truthful plant imagery seems to draw from Jer 32:41b (ונטעתים בארץ הזאת באמת) and Isa 60:21 (ועמך כלם צדיקים לעולם יירשו ארץ נצר מטעו [מטעי] מעשה ידי להתפאר). Similar language and imagery is employed elsewhere in the Dead Sea Scrolls and Second Temple literature.[56] The keyword in this proposed pesher may be נצר, which is shared by Isa 11:1 and 60:21. The appearance of this word and general plant imagery in a later lemma (frags. 8–10 III, A 11=H 15) may have provided the trigger for the employment of this entire motif in the present pesher. The further identification of the planting as "righteous" (צדיקים) in Isa 60:21 may have provided another exegetical link with צדקה in the lemma (Isa 10:22) and therefore with the wider *righteous* (Heb. √צדק=Aram. √קשט) plant imagery in biblical and Second Temple literature.[57] The

---

[53] See Patrick A. Tiller, "The Eternal Planting in the Dead Sea Scrolls," *DSD* 4 (1997): 312–35; Paul Swarup, *The Self-Understanding of the Dead Sea Scrolls Community: An Eternal Planting, A House of Holiness* (Library of Second Temple Studies 59; London T. & T. Clark, 2006).

[54] See also the plant imagery associated with the slaughtered in Jer 12:2–3.

[55] Allegro, *Qumran Cave 4.I*, 12; García Martínez and Tigchelaar, DSSSE 1.314. Horgan restores ה[ארץ, though with no explanation (followed in Zimmermann, *Messianische Texte*, 60).

[56] *Jub.* 21:24 refers to a "plant of truth in [Ge'ez: all] the earth" (מטעת ה[אמת באראץ]; 4Q219 II, 29–31). See also *Jub.* 16:26; 36:6. *1 Enoch* repeatedly refers to the "plant of righteousness," which refers to the survivors of the generation of the Watchers (10:16; 4Q204 1 V, 4: ותתחזא נ[צבת קושטא), Abraham (93:5), and the special segment of Israel (93:10; 4Q212 1 IV, 12–13: א[ל]מ[על קשט נ[צבת). In all three passages, the righteous/truthful planting is the remnant that survives a wider period of devastation and wickedness. The truthful planting is also found in 1QH[a] XVI, 11 (VIII, 10); 1QS VIII, 5. 1QH[a] XIV, 18 (VI, 15); XVI, 10 refer specifically to the "shoot" (נצר) of the plant.

[57] See Blenkinsopp, *Opening*, 116 n 49. As noted by Swarup, *Self-Understanding*, 60–2, both Isa 5:7 and 61:3 use the root צדק to refer to the planting. He likewise identifies this linguistic combination in *Jub.* 21:24. To be sure, the Ge'ez translation contains the equivalent of Hebrew צדקה (*takla ṣedq*). The Hebrew original (4Q219 II, 30), however, clearly has אמת (see text in previous note), which corresponds to the adjective elsewhere applied in Second Temple literature to the planting (e.g., 1QH[a] XVI, 11 (VIII, 10); 1QS VIII, 5). It is therefore likely that the other occurrences of

use of the righteous/truthful planting motif works well with the general sense of the pesher on Isa 10:22–23 (possibly also vv. 20–21). The biblical lemma refers to the destruction of the wider segment of Israel and the formation of a small remnant that will survive.[58] Similarly, the truthful or righteous planting is identified as a specially selected individual or group that is reconstituted after the destruction of the surrounding wicked generations and thus is equal to the "true Israel."[59] In this pesher, the community draws upon its self-identification as the truthful planting to align itself with the remnant of Israel in Isaiah.

Based on the foregoing discussion, I am proposing the following reconstruction and translation for 4Q161 A 2–4 A 1–6=H 2–6 II 5–9:

[כֹֿיאֿ] [°ֿי בני] [ ] 1
[עמֿוֿ] ואֿ[שֿר אמר אם היֿ]ה עמכה] [ ] 2
[ישראל כחול הים שאר ישוב בו] כֿ[ליון חר]וֿץ ושוטף צד[קה] 3
[פשרו עד כֿ]לֿות ביוֿ[ם הר]גֿה ורבים יוב[דו 4
[ים]ֿלֿטו למטֿ[עֿת ב]ֿארץ באמת °[ ] 5

1. [...] for [   ] °y sons of [...]
2. [...] his people [and re]garding that which it says: "*Even if [your people,*
3. *O Israel], Should b[e as the sands of the sea, Only a remnant of it shall return. De]struction is decr]eed; and it overflows with righteous[ness]*" (Isa 10:22)
4. [its interpretation (is that)...until des]truction on the d[ay of slau]ghter; and many shall peri[sh
5. [...they will es]cape to be as a truthful plan[ting in the] land °[...

READING 4Q161 WITH THE WAR TEXTS: TWO EXAMPLES

As previously noted, the allusions to the eschatological war with the Kittim have prompted scholars to examine 4Q161 within the larger

---

takla ṣedq in the Geʿez text (16:26; 36:6) likewise reflect an original מטעת אמת. The *1 Enoch* passages are more equivocal. The preserved Aramaic original for 10:16 and 93:10 has the root קשט, which can correspond either to the Hebrew צדק (e.g., *Tg. Onq.* to Lev 19:36; Deut 16:18, 20; 25:15; *Tg. Neof.* to Deut 1:16; 16:18, 20) or אמת (e.g., *Tg. Onq.* to Gen 24:27, 29; Exod 18:21; *Tg. Neof.* to Gen 24:27; 32:11). Indeed, the Greek translation for 10:16 (followed by the Geʿez) renders this as "righteousness" (δικαιοσύνης) and truth" (ἀλειθείας) (see Matthew Black, *Apocalypsis Henochi Graece* [Leiden: Brill, 1970], 26).

[58] This interpretation of Isa 10:22–23 should be compared to Dan 11:36, which applies the language of v. 23 to refer to the future destruction of Antiochus. See Blenkinsopp, *Opening*, 116.

[59] See Swarup, *Self-Understanding*, esp. 193–5.

context of the war texts among the scrolls corpus.[60] Yet, most of these discussions are brief, with the explanation provided that the fragmentary nature of 4Q161 precludes more thorough treatment.[61] Notwithstanding these reservations, a more full-scale analysis of the relationship of 4Q161 to the war texts—which are now fully available and more properly understood—remains a desideratum. I offer here treatment of two issues—one example from *Sefer ha-Milḥamah* and one from the *War Scroll*—that seek to move the discussion beyond merely noting parallel language and themes. The two issues focus on specific difficulties that have arisen in the interpretation of 4Q161. My goal is to demonstrate how the interpretation of the passages in 4Q161 can be illuminated by the related war texts at the same time as 4Q161 can shed new light on our understanding of these texts. As in the previous sections, my attention is simultaneously directed at bringing into sharper focus the reconstruction of the text of 4Q161 and its exegetical technique.

1. *Who Ascends from Akko and Why?*
(4Q161 A 5–6 10–13= H 2–6 II, 26–29)

The third lemma unit in 4Q161 contains Isa 10:28–32, which narrates the march of the Assyrian enemy toward Jerusalem. Four fragmentary lines of pesher are preserved:

---

[60] On the war texts in general, see Jean Duhaime, *The War Texts: 1QM and Related Manuscripts* (London: T. and T. Clark, 2004). Duhaime does not discuss 4Q161.

[61] The one notable exception is the discussion of 4Q161 and Sefer ha-Milḥamah (4Q285=11Q14): Geza Vermes, "The Oxford Forum for Qumran Research: Seminar on the Rule of War from Qumran Cave 4 (4Q285)," *JJS* 43 (1992): 85–90; Bauckham, "Messianic Interpretation"; Atkinson, "Militant Davidic Messianism," 447–52; Brooke, "Isaiah in the Pesharim," 621–3; Jonathan Norton, "Observations on the Official Material Reconstructions of *Sefer Ha-Milḥamah* (11Q14 and 4Q285)," *RevQ* 21/81 (2003): 10–22. For more limited comments highlighting parallel language and themes (in particular the expression מדבר העמים, "wilderness of nations" in A 5–6 2–3= H 2–6 II, 18–19 and 1QM I, 3), see Allegro, "Further Messianic References," 181; van der Woude, *Messianischen Vorstellungen*, 179–80; Yadin, "Commentaries," 67–8; idem, "Recent Developments," 50; idem, *The Scroll of the War of the Sons of Light Against the Sons of Darkness* (trans. B. and Ch. Rabin; Oxford: Oxford University Press, 1962), 257; Millar Burrows, *More Light on the Dead Sea Scrolls* (New York: Viking, 1958), 351; André Dupont-Sommer, *The Essene Writings from Qumran* (trans. Geza Vermes; Cleveland: Meredian, 1962), 274; Horgan, *Pesharim*, 78–9, 83; Pomykala, *Davidic Dynasty*, 198–9; Collins, *Scepter*, 57; Bruce W. Longenecker, "The Wilderness and Revolutionary Ferment in First-Century Palestine: A Response to D. R. Schwartz and J. Marcus," *JSJ* 29 (1998): 331–2; Willitts, "Remnant," 19; Blenkinsopp, *Opening*, 116–7.

[פשר ה]פתגם⁶² לאחרית הימים לבוא]°	10=26
[ ]רֹה⁶³ בעלותו מבקעת עכֹו ללחם בֹ]°°	11=27
[ ]דה ואין כמוה⁶⁴ ובכול ערי ה]°⁶⁵	12=28
ועד גבול ירושלים]	13=28

The interpretation of the phrase בעלותו מבקעת עכו, "when he ascends from Akko," has long been the subject of dispute. Three related issues are involved in determining the proper interpretation: (1) Who is the subject of the suffix on עלותו? (2) Do the events described here refer to events in the past from the perspective of the author (i.e., a historical allusion) or are they imagined as unfolding in a still future time (i.e., the eschatological war)? (3) How should the final word be restored—namely, who is the object of fighting here?

Allegro initially suggested that the subject of "ascends" is the messiah on his triumphant march to Jerusalem, in particular noting that the enemies in this section of the text are otherwise identified in the plural.⁶⁶ Millar Burrows countered that the sense of the lemma—where the Assyrian army led by the king is on its march toward Jerusalem—recommends identifying the pesher as referring to the eschatological foe, whom he identified as either the "Antichrist," Gog, or Magog, understood as a cipher for the Roman enemy.⁶⁷ Notwithstanding Allegro's subsequent defense of his position, nearly all later scholarship

---

⁶² The partially reconstructed citation formula פשר ה]פתגם was first suggested by Strugnell, "Notes en marge," 184, and has since been followed in all presentations of the text.

⁶³ Allegro's reconstruction (*Qumran Cave 4.I*, 12) of חר[דה (based on its appearance in Isa 10:29) is possible. The first extant letter was initially restored in idem, "Further Messianic References," 178, as a *reš*, which is preferred by Horgan, *Pesharim*, 81.

⁶⁴ Allegro identified the ink dot following כמוה as possibly a *waw*, thus producing the masculine suffix. See, however, Strugnell, "Notes en marge," 184; Amoussine, "L'Interprétation," 383; Horgan, *Pesharim*, 82.

⁶⁵ The final ink trace is possibly a *šin* or *mem* (Horgan, *Pesharim*, 82).

⁶⁶ Allegro, "Further Messianic References," 181 and idem, "Addendum to Professor Millar Burrow's [*sic*] Note on the Ascent from Accho in 4QpIsaᵃ," *VT* 7 (1957): 183. The argument regarding the plural vs. singular subject is found in the latter article. The suggestion in the preliminary edition is based on the assumption that Akko—understood as the port of Ptolemais (see below)—would be the closest port of entry to the site of Armageddon.

⁶⁷ Millar Burrows, "The Ascent from Acco in 4Q p Isaᵃ," *VT* 7 (1957): 104–5. The more specific identification of the enemy as the Romans is asserted in idem, *More Light*, 321–2. I have framed the initial debate as a dialogue between Allegro and Burrows on account of their exchange in *Vetus Testamentum*. A similar criticism of Allegro, however, was independently made by Yadin in a publication that also appeared in 1957 ("Recent Developments," 52).

has followed Burrows' basic assessment that the subject is the enemy of Israel, not the messiah.[68] A related re-interpretation of the text was proposed by Joseph Amoussine, who contends that the passage does not have in view a future eschatological enemy, but rather is a historical allusion to a contemporary enemy of Israel, whom he identifies as Ptolemy Lathyrus.[69] As noted by Amoussine, Josephus describes Ptolemy Lathyrus conquering Ptolemais and then embarking on a campaign to subdue all of Judea (*War* 1.4.2 (86); *Ant.* 13.12–3 (324–56)). Amoussine further argues that the enemy mentioned in frags. 8–10 is likewise Ptolemy Lathyrus and thus the Kittim in 4Q161 are the Greeks.

The lines of the debate drawn by Burrows and Amoussine escape simple resolution. As noted by George Brooke, the solution rests partially on whether one maintains that the Kittim mentioned later in 4Q161 need not be identified with the Romans, as they are in the other Pesharim.[70] At the same time, Brooke further observes that we need to reorient the way we read 4Q161, particularly in light of the

---

[68] See van der Woude, *Messianischen Vorstellungen*, 180; Dupont-Sommer, *Essene Writings*, 274; Carmignac, *Les Textes*, 71; Rosenthal, "Biblical Exegesis," 27–8; Horgan, *Pesharim*, 81; Pomykala, *Davidic Dynasty*, 199; Atkinson, "Militant Davidic Messianism," 449; see also Brooke, "Isaiah in the Pesharim," 621. Bauckham, "Messianic Interpretation," 204–5 and Blenkinsopp, *Opening*, 118, follow Allegro's interpretation, though with little new argument. Willitts's defense of Allegro based on the literary context of Isaiah is unconvincing ("Remnant," 17–8).

[69] Amoussine, "L'Interprétation," 383–7 = idem, "Historical Events," 126–32. This interpretation is similarly embraced in Brooke, "Isaiah in the Pesharim," 623; James H. Charlesworth, *The Pesharim and Qumran History: Chaos of Consensus?* (Grand Rapids: Eerdmans, 2002), 101–3; Hanan Eshel, "Alexander Jannaeus and His War against Ptolemy Lathyrus," in *The Dead Sea Scrolls and the Hasmonean State* (Grand Rapids: Eerdmans; Jerusalem: Yad Ben-Zvi, 2008), 91–100 (see also idem and Esther Eshel, "4Q448, Psalm 154 (Syriac), Sirach 48:20, and 4QpIsa[a]," *JBL* 119 [2000]: 653–4). This passage is similarly understood as a historical allusion in Cecil Roth, *Historical Background of the Dead Sea Scrolls* (New York: W. W. Norton, 1965), 36, who opines that the text refers to the Roman forces during the Jewish revolt in the first century CE (who arrive in Ptolemais).

[70] Brooke, "Isaiah in the Pesharim," 621. On the identification of the Kittim in the Pesharim, see Brooke, "The Kittim in the Qumran Pesharim," in *Images of Empire* (ed. Loveday Alexander; JSOTSup 122; Sheffield: Sheffield Academic Press, 1993), 135–59; Hanan Eshel, "The Kittim in the War Scroll and in the Pesharim," in *Historical Perspectives from the Hasmoneans to Bar Kokhba in Light of the Dead Sea Scrolls: Proceedings of the Fourth International Symposium of the Orion Center for the Study of the Dead Sea Scrolls and Associated Literature, 27–31 January, 1999* (ed. David M. Goodblatt, Avital Pinnick, and Daniel R. Schwartz; STDJ 37; Leiden: Brill, 2001), 29–44; Lim, *Pesharim*, 65–6.

evidence provided by 4Q285.[71] 4Q285 7, notes Brooke, indicates that the figure of the militant Prince of the Congregation is identified as the messianic Branch of David (צמח דויד), who plays a central role in the defeat of the Kittim in the eschatological war.[72] Accordingly, 4Q161, which mentions these elements across its various pesher units, "should not be read disjointedly, pericope by pericope, but each interpretation should be read in light of the other."[73] Following Brooke's advice, I am suggesting that the thoroughly eschatological orientation of frags. 8–10 should not stand in isolation, but rather, guide our understanding of the other pesher units. Indeed, if we read the text of 4Q161 backwards (i.e., from best preserved to least preserved units), it seems clear that the pesher is presenting its own portrait of the eschatological war, which is exegetically woven into the lemmata from Isaiah. Moreover, this portrait finds important points of contact with other descriptions of the war. The close connections between 4Q161 and 4Q285 indicate that these two texts should be read in dialogue with one another.[74]

4Q161 8–10 III, A 17=H 22 applies a messianic interpretation of Isa 11:1–5 to "the Branch of] David who stands in the en[d of days]."[75] The remainder of the text seems to refer to the further subjugation of the nations by the messiah. In the aftermath of the battle, the messiah will judge the nations based on the direction provided by the priests (A l. 24=H l. 29: [וכאשר יורוהו כן ישפוט ועל פיהם).[76] The judgment

---

[71] The bibliography on 4Q285 is extensive. I make reference to the relevant studies in the course of my discussion. The text and numbering system for the fragments follows Philip S. Alexander and Geza Vermes, "4Q285. Sefer ha-Milḥamah," in *Qumran Cave 4.XXVI: Cryptic Texts and Miscellanea, Part 1* (ed. Stephen J. Pfann et al.; DJD XXXVI; Oxford: Clarendon, 2000), 228–46. See also Philip S. Alexander, "A Reconstruction and Reading of 4Q285 (*Sefer ha-Milḥamah*)," *RevQ* 19/75 (2000): 333–48.

[72] On the militant messiah in 4Q285, see further Collins, *Scepter*, 58–60; Vermes, "Oxford Forum," 88–9.

[73] Brooke, "Isaiah in the Pesharim," 623.

[74] See bibliography above, n. 61.

[75] On this reconstruction, see above, n. 25. Isa 11:1–5 was a popular text for messianic interpretation and amplification elsewhere in the Dead Sea Scrolls (1QSb V; 4Q285 7) and Second Temple Judaism (e.g., *Pss. Sol.* 17:21–25; 18:6–8; 4 Ezra 13:9–11; See Collins, *Scepter*, 53, 57–60, 65; Darrell D. Hannah, "Isaiah within Judaism of the Second Temple Period," in *Isaiah in the New Testament* [ed. Steve Moyise and Maarten J. J. Menken; London: T. & T. Clark, 2005], 11–22). It is also popular in the New Testament and early Christianity (e.g., Matt 2:23; John 1:29–34 with parallels; Rev 19:11; Justin Martyr, *Dial.* 86.4); and is widespread in later rabbinic literature (see references in Collins, ibid., 72 n. 67).

[76] This understanding assumes that the plural subject of יורוהו is the priests mentioned in the following line. See further treatment in Allegro, "Further Messianic References," 182; van der Woude, *Messianischen Vorstellungen*, 181; Dupont-Sommer,

here presumably refers to the earlier mention of the messiah's sword judging all the nations (A l. 21=H l. 26: כו]ל העמים תשפוט חרבו). A similar description of priestly authority in the aftermath of the battle is present in 4Q285 7 5–6, where the priest is depicted issuing commands, perhaps instructions on how to dispose of the corpses of the Kittim mentioned later in l. 6 or more general instructions to the messiah (as in 4Q161).[77] The previous pesher unit on Isa 10:33–34 in 4Q161 8–10 III, A 1–9=H 1–14 describes the eschatological battle against the Kittim. The location of this pesher unit and its exegetical basis must be understood in dialogue with 4Q285 7 1–4, which recounts the final destruction of the Kittim at the hands of the Prince of the Congregation.[78] As demonstrated by Richard Bauckhaum, 4Q161 and 4Q285 share nearly identical interpretations of Isa 10:34b (ולבנון באדיר יפול) as a reference to the destruction of the enemy—most likely the Kittim, led by their king (see below)—by the militant messiah.[79]

The eschatological orientation of frags. 8–10, more specifically as a vision of the battle against the Kittim, should similarly be applied in the earlier portions of the text. The fragmentary reference to "their return from the wilderness of the nat[ions" in the pesher on Isa 10:24–27 (A 5–6 2=H 2–6 II, 18) likely refers to the initial mustering of the armies of the Sons of Light, as it does in the opening lines of the War Scroll (1QM I, 2–3).[80] The fragmentary reference to the Prince of the Congregation in the following line (A l. 3=H l. 19) likely refers to his central role in directing the military campaign against the

---

Essene Writing, 275 n. 1; Yadin, "Notes," 515; VanderKam, "Messianism," 231–2; Markus Bockmuehl, "A 'Slain Messiah' in 4Q Serekh Milhamah (4Q285)?" Tyndale Bulletin 43 (1992): 166–7; García Martínez, "Messianic Hopes," 164; Pomykala, 202; Collins, Scepter, 76; Atkinson, "Militant Davidic Messianism," 448; Ruzer, "Davidic Messiah," 233–4; Willitts, "Remnant," 23; Blenkinsopp, Opening, 121; Joseph L. Angel, Otherworldly and Eschatological Priesthood in the Dead Sea Scrolls (STDJ 86; Leiden: Brill, 2010), 185–6.

[77] On this understanding of 4Q285, see Bockmuehl, "Slain Messiah," 166–7; Abegg, "Messianic Hope," 82; Zimmermann, Messianische Texte, 88; Alexander, "Reconstruction," 345; Alexander and Vermes, "4Q285," 241; Xeravits, King, Priest, Prophet, 66; Angel, Otherworldly, 199–200.

[78] For the various issues involved in interpreting the expression והמיתו in l. 4, see Alexander and Vermes, "4Q285," 240 and nearly every other treatment of 4Q285.

[79] Bauckham, "Messianic Interpretation," 202–6. See also Vermes, "Oxford Forum," 88–9; Robert P. Gordon, "The Interpretation of 'Lebanon' and 4Q285," JJS 43 (1992): 92–94; Norton, "Observations," 12–3.

[80] On this shared language, see bibliography above, n. 61. The phrase is drawn from Ezek 20:35.

Kittim, as in 4Q285. Moreover, 4Q285 7 4–5 demonstrates that the Prince of the Congregation in 4Q161 A 5–6 3=H 2–6 II, 19 should be identified with the Branch of David in 4Q161 8–10 III, A 17=H 22. In light of the surrounding literary context, the pesher on Isa 10:28–32 in A ll. 10–14=H ll. 26–29 should likewise be understood in this eschatological setting. Indeed, the opening of the pesher identifies the interpretation that follows as applying to the "end of days to come," just as the interpretation of Isa 11:1–5 in frags. 8–10.[81] The pesher unit in ll. 10–14=H ll. 26–29 therefore likely describes the approach of the enemy in anticipation of the eschatological battle that is described in the following pesher units.[82]

With this understanding of the literary structure, let me focus more narrowly on the pesher on Isa 10:28–32. In addition to solving the issue of the subject of בעלותו, we can consider the significance of the wider pesher unit, its exegetical links to the lemma, and the relationship to 4Q285. First, Allegro's primary argument in favor of making the messiah the subject of בעלותו was the fact that the enemy is not described in the singular until much later in the text: "when he flees (בברחו) from before Is[rael]" (4Q161 8–10 III, A 9=H 13). 4Q285 provides us with an important piece of new information because it refers throughout to the enemy in the singular (4 8, 10; 7 4)[83] and in the plural (4 7, 8).[84] This same contrast can be detected in 4Q161, where 8–10 III, A 2–8=H 6–12 refers to the Kittim as the enemy in the plural, while 8–10 III, A 9=H 13 turns its attention to a singular enemy.

---

[81] The end of the expression in 8–10 III, A 17=H 22 is lost in the lacuna and thus it is unclear if לבוא would have also been employed. On the future orientation of the "end of days" in 4Q161, see further Annette Steudel, "'The End of Days' in the Qumran Texts," *RevQ* 16/62 (1993): 230.

[82] My interpretation does not preclude the possibility that the assault of Ptolemy Lathyrus is also in view. Though the primary focus is the future eschatological war against the Kittim, it is likely that the pesherist looked to the contemporary conflict with Ptolemy Lathyrus as a repetition of the Assyrian campaign, thus also prefiguring the future arrival of the Kittim in the end-time.

[83] On the identification of the subject of ויעמד עליהם in 4 8 as the enemy, see Philip S. Alexander, "The Evil Empire: The Qumran Eschatological War Cycle and the Origins of Jewish Opposition to Rome," in *Emanuel: Studies in the Hebrew Bible, Septuagint and Dead Sea Scrolls in Honor of Emanuel Tov* (ed. Shalom M. Paul et al.; VTSup 94; Leiden: Brill, 2003), 24.

[84] The subject of ושבו in 4 9 seems to be the victorious Israelites (see Alexander, "Evil Empire," 24).

More significantly, 4Q285 seems to identify the singular eschatological foe as the king of the Kittim (4 5), a suggestion based on the similar appearance of the king in 1QM XV, 2, but more importantly because 4Q285 is drawing upon the royal imagery of Gog in Ezekiel 39.[85] Like 4Q285, 4Q161 has its own royal imagery as found in the figure of Assyrian king (i.e., Sennacherib or Sargon II) from the lemma. Moreover, there is a fragmentary reference to Magog in 8–10 III, A 20=H 25. There may be some exegetical connection between the fact that Lebanon in Isa 10:34—the eschatological foe—will *fall*, and the similar use of the idea of the enemy falling in Ezek 39:3–4 (וחציץ מיד ימינך אפיל, "I will make your arrows *drop* from you right hand"; על הרי ישראל תפול, "upon the hills of Israel, *you shall fall*"), the scriptural basis in 4Q285 4 3–4.[86]

Thus, Pesher Isaiah merges the historical Assyrian king from the lemma together with the eschatological Gog/Magog and the king of the Kittim. As such, it is reasonable to suggest that the singular enemy in 4Q161 is similarly the king of the Kittim, who "flees (בברחו) from befo[re Is]rael" (8–10 III, A 9=H 13).[87] This corresponds with the chase scene that is narrated in 4Q285 4 6–8.[88] In both texts, the simultaneous identification of a singular enemy (the king of the Kittim) and a plural enemy (the Kittim) is based on the exegetical traditions regarding

---

[85] Alexander and Vermes, "4Q285," 235, restore מלך ה[כתיים in 4 5. The identification of the enemy as the king of the Kittim in found in Vermes, "Oxford Forum," 89; Gordon, "Interpretation," 93; Markus Bockmuehl, "Slain Messiah," 165 n. 28; Abegg, "Messianic Hope," 87–8; Bauckham, "Messianic Interpretation," 206; Collins, *Scepter*, 59; Alexander, "Reconstruction," 344; idem, "Evil Empire," 24; Norton, "Observations," 13. Aside from 1QM XV, 2, the only other certain reference to the king of the Kittim is the non-sectarian 4Q247 6. See also Milik's reconstruction מל[כי כתיאים for 1Q16 (1QpPs[a]) 9–10 1–2 (the plural is preferred since it appears in the lemma—Ps 68:30; see Dominique Barthélemy and Józef T. Milik, *Qumran Cave 1* [DJD I; Oxford: Clarendon, 1955], 82). Gordon, ibid., further notes that "Lebanon" (the scriptural peg for the enemy) is commonly applied in the Targum to a king (see further evidence collected in Geza Vermes, *Scripture and Tradition: Haggadic Studies* [StPB 4; Leiden: Brill, 1961], 27).

[86] See also 1QM XI, 11–12, which views the destruction of the Kittim as prefigured by the *fall* of the Assyrians in Isa 31:8 עד גבורת ידכה בכתיים לאמור ונפל אשור (בחרב לוא איש וחרב לוא אדם תואכלנו).

[87] See van der Woude, *Messianischen Vorstellungen*, 180; Bauckham, "Messianic Interpretation," 206.

[88] Note as well the similar language used to describe the escape of the singular enemy in 4Q161 (בברחו מלפ[ני יש[ראל) and the suggested reconstruction for the plural enemy in 4Q285 (וינוס[ו מפני ישראל).

"Lebanon" from Isa 10:34, whereby it can refer to a king (sg.) or the nations (pl.).[89]

Several additional observations are pertinent to the interpretation of 4Q161 and its relationship to 4Q285 4. *Pesher Isaiah* refers to the eschatological foe ascending from Akko, which in Hellenistic-Roman times was understood as the port of Ptolemais.[90] This may be a purely technical reference to the fact that one goes up from a port. It may be an allusion to the movement up toward Jerusalem, as suggested by Yadin's reconstruction for the end of the line (ללחם בי[רושלים).[91] However, if we look to 4Q285 4 4, we see that the scriptural source for the war imagery there, Ezek 39:3, refers to the battle taking place upon the "hills of Israel" (על הרי ישראל תפול). Thus, the movement of the enemy from Akko may be southward toward the hill country of Israel, where a battle will take place, not unlike the identification of the location of the war as Har Megiddo (i.e., Armageddon) in Rev 16:16.[92]

Another question that presents itself is why the plain of Akko as the starting point for this march? If the goal is Jerusalem—as suggested both by the lemma and the fragmentary reference to Jerusalem in A l.13=H. l. 29—why start in the north at Akko? The choice of Akko is based on a careful exegetical re-alignment of the lemma. In the lemma, the Assyrians assault from the northeast and move southward through several towns until they reach the "mountain (גבעה) of Jerusalem" (Isa 10:32). The pesher has identified the Assyrians as the Kittim—that is, the Romans. Thus, the enemy must arrive by sea and also come from the west. Ptolemais (Akko) therefore provides a western port of entry for the boats of the Kittim. The southward march of the Kittim from the northwest toward the גבול ("border," "mountain") of Jerusalem—now lost in the fragmentary A l. 12=H l. 28—mimics the similar southward

---

[89] See Vermes, *Scripture and Tradition*, 27–9. The movement in 4Q161 between a singular and plural enemy may also be exegetically linked to the shift between singular and plural verbs to describe the march of the enemy in Isa 10:28–32. See also the reference to enemy as the "nations" in 4Q161 8–10 III, A 20=H 25, which does not seem to be identical with the earlier mention of the Kittim. This term is likely an interpretation of Magog as in Rev 20:8 (cf. 1QM XI, 16; 4Q523).

[90] See Emil Schürer, *The History of the Jewish People in the Age of Jesus Christ (175 BC–AD 135), Volume 2* (revised and edited by Geza Vermes and Fergus Millar; Edinburgh: T. & T. Clark, 1979): 121–5.

[91] Yadin, "Recent Developments," 52. Note that Isa 10:32 locates Jerusalem upon a hill.

[92] See also *Tg. Jon.* to Gen 49:11, which describes how the messiah will destroy all the kings and will "redden the mountains" with their blood.

march of the Assyrians in the northeast.[93] The specific choice of Ptolemais was likely guided by the memory of Ptolemais as a common port for Roman entry into Israel, particularly for hostile reasons as with Herod's entry in 40 BCE.[94] There is likely also an exegetical link between the lemma and Ptolemais. The only clear reference to Akko in the Hebrew Bible is Judg 1:31, which notes that the tribe of Asher did not conquer the city: אשר לא הוריש את ישבי עכו, "Asher did not dispossess the inhabitants of Akko." The pesher is drawing upon the clear phonetic and consonantal similarities between אשר (Asher) and אשור (Asshur), to re-orient Akko with the Assyrians of the lemma and thus Ptolemais with the Kittim. While Asher did not conquer Akko, 4Q161 asserts that Assyria (= Kittim) did.[95]

In light of the understanding presented here, it makes sense to re-revisit the different reconstructions for the end of the line: ללחם ב°°[, "to fight against…"[96] While both of the final two letters traces are difficult to decipher with certainty, Allegro restored the first letter as a *yod* based on the clear presence of the upper stroke.[97] Subsequent

---

[93] גבול likely has a double meaning here of "boundary" and its less common meaning of "mountain." On the latter meaning, see especially Ps 78:54 and Mitchell Dahood, "Biblical Geography," *Greg* 43 (1962): 74.

[94] See Josephus *War* 1.15.3 (290); *Ant.* 14.15.1 (394). Ptolemais had a long history of hostility to Jews in the Hellenistic and Roman periods (see Schürer, *History*, 123–25). I am not suggesting that Herod's entry in 40 BCE should be used as a *terminus a quo* for the dating of 4Q161. Rather, it is merely illustrative of the association of Ptolemais with hostile Roman incursion, which would have left a lasting impression on Jews in the first century BCE (cf. Atkinson, "Militant Davidic Messianism," 449). My interpretation of the exegetical technique could also work with understanding the enemy as Ptolemy Lathyrus and the Kittim as Greeks. Indeed, this historical incursion may also have been in the mind of the pesherist and shaped the similar expectations of the entry of the eschatological Kittim in the end-time battle.

[95] This exegesis is similar to the phenomenon of "converse translation" in the Targum and ancient versions, whereby the translation yields a sense exactly the opposite of the source text. See Michael Klein, "Converse Translation: A Targumic Technique," *Bib* 57 (1976): 515–37; Robert P. Gordon, "'Converse Translations' in the Targum and Beyond," in *Hebrew Bible and Ancient Versions: Selected Essays of Robert P. Gordon* (Society for Old Testament Study; Aldershot: Ashgate, 2006): 263–77; Repr. from *JSP* 19 (1999): 3–21. This example might be properly labeled "converse exegesis."

[96] The preposition *bet* following לחם (*niph'al*) is most often employed in a combative sense (see, e.g., 1QM I, 2). The *bet* could possibly also mean that place/time of the battle or the instrument of the battle.

[97] Allegro, "Further Messianic References," 184, restored only the *bet*. Aided by an additional piece of frag. 5, he restored בי °[in the *editio princeps* (*Qumran Cave 4.I*, 12). The space after the *yod* is certainly an error, since a subsequent ink trace is clearly visible. To be sure, this upper stroke could plausibly belong to a *waw* or a *pe* (*apud* Strugnell).

scholars have offered several plausible restorations: (1) ביש[ראל,
"against Israel"[98] (2) ביר[ושלים, "against Jerusalem"[99] (3) ביה[ודה,
"against Judah."[100] Strugnell suggested that the object of fighting is
Philistia (בפל[שת), with the visible ink trace representing the upper
stroke of a *pe*—a reading followed by Horgan and Hanan Eshel.[101]
Amoussine, however, noted that it not clear why the battle would
move so quickly from the north to the southern region of Philistia.[102]
Moreover, the object of fighting based on the larger sense of the passage
is clearly Israel. Thus, I think it best to follow those who reconstruct
ללחם ביש[ראל, "to fight against Israel."[103] The designation "Israel"
refers to the people of Israel as well as the geographical region. As
suggested above, the fighting was likely envisioned as unfolding in the
hill country of Israel, as is part of the setting presumed for 4Q285
based on Ezek 39:3 (על־הרי ישראל).[104]

Even without 4Q285, Burrows was clearly right to look to the sense
of the lemma for understanding the identity of the individual in the
pesher. But the evidence of 4Q285 as well as a closer examination
of the relationship between the pesher and the lemma allows us to
see a bit more of the context. The pesher here identifies the march
of the eschatological foe—likely the king of the Kittim with his

---

[98] Van der Woude, *Messianischen Vorstellungen*, 176; Fitzmyer, "Review of Allegro,
Qumrân Cave 4.I," 237; Dupont-Sommer, *Essene Writings*, 274 n. 2. This suggestion is
also found in Strugnell, "Notes en marge," 184.

[99] Yadin, "Recent Developments," 52.

[100] Amoussine, "L'Interprétation," 383.

[101] Strugnell, "Notes en marge," 184; Horgan, *Pesharim*, 81–2; Eshel, "Alexander
Jannaeus," 97–8.

[102] Amoussine, "L'Interprétation," 383. His suggestion (ביה[ודה) works well for
the understanding of the passage as a historical allusion to Ptolemy Lathyrus, since
Josephus reports that he departed Ptolemais to subdue all of Judea. Eshel, "Alexander Jannaeus," 98, suggests that Strugnell's reading can be understood in light of the
request of the inhabitants of Gaza that Ptolemy Lathyrus free the region from the rule
of Alexander Jannaus (*Ant.* 13.12.4 (334)).

[103] Judah and Jerusalem are also unlikely since both would refer to specific loca-
tions in the south. The reference to "all the cities" in the following line suggests that
the eschatological foe is following a modified itinerary from Isaiah towards Judah and
Jerusalem, which is only reached in the final line. Moreover, though the ink trace is
minimal, it preserves a slight curvature that is inconsistent with the clean angle of the
upper right portion of the *reš* elsewhere in the manuscript.

[104] The locution √לחם + בישראל appears seven times in the HB. In five uses, the
subject of the root לחם is a foreign king (Num 21:1, 23; Josh 24:9; 2 Kgs 6:8). The
Philistines are the subject in 1 Sam 28:1; 31:1=1 Chr 10:1 (though Achish is mentioned
in 1 Sam 28:1). The possible royal associations of this phrase works well with the
lemma and the identity of the eschatological foe as the king of the Kittim.

armies—towards Jerusalem in a way that re-orients the march of the Assyrian king in the lemma. This account finds important thematic and exegetical points of contact with the description of the battle in 4Q285, particularly frag. 4.[105]

2. *The Garments (of Warfare) (4Q161 8–10 III, A 17–24= H 22–29)*

Let me now turn to the often cited final passage in Pesher Isaiah, the messianic pesher on Isa 11:1–5.[106] My analysis here focuses on the throne of glory and the intriguing set of garments in A l. 19=H l. 24 (כ[סא כבוד] [נזר ק]ודש [ובגדי ריקמו]ת]), the latter of which also seem to be in view in the fragmentary reference to clothing in A l. 24=H l. 29 (ובידו בגדי]). Based on the context, the garments in A l. 19=H l. 24 almost certainly would have been worn by the messianic Branch of David, the Prince of the Congregation. A l. 24=H l. 29 suggests that it is the priest who gives the messiah the clothes.[107] As noted above, the identification of the messiah's clothing is exegetically linked to Isa 11:5, which describes the Davidic figure girded in righteousness and faithfulness.

The combination of these three specific elements is likely based on an exegetical reuse of Ezek 26:16, which describes the response of the "islands" (איים) to the downfall of Tyre (v. 15). The "princes of the sea (נשיאי הים)" (1) step off their thrones (כסאותם); (2) following the LXX, take off their crowns (μίτρας); (3) remove their robes and strip off their embroidered garments (בגדי רקמתם). Instead, "they cloth themselves with trembling (חרדות), and shall sit on the ground; they shall tremble (וחרדו) every moment." The "princes of the sea" would surely have been understood by the sectarians as the Kittim, and the royal imagery works well with the suggested enemy in 4Q161. In 4Q161, the Prince of the Congregation appropriates the exact three

---

[105] Unfortunately, the fragmentary nature of both manuscripts makes further observations speculative. It is worth noting, however, that 4Q285 4 presents a maritime setting for the battle: "[the Pr]ince of the Congregation [will pursue them] towards the [Great] Sea[" (l. 6). The battle against the Kittim is conceptualized as moving from the land to the sea (see further, Alexander, "Reconstruction," 344). Are the Kittim being driven down from the hills—as in Ezek 39:3—the proposed location of the battle in 4Q161? Moreover, the pursuit of the Kittim to the Great Sea (e.g., the Mediterranean Sea) is likely intended to hint at their place of entrance to Israel. Could 4Q285 also have in mind specifically their port of entry—i.e., Ptolemais?

[106] For the text, see above.

[107] As first noted by Allegro, "Further Messianic References," 182. See also Burrows, *More Light*, 322; Dupont-Sommer, *Essene Writings*, 275 n. 1; Atkinson, "Militant Davidic Messianism," 448; Xeravits, *King, Priest, Prophet*, 215.

things that the "princes of the sea" shed in fear. The keyword may be
the "trembling" that the princes of the sea clothe themselves in, which
appears in an earlier lemma in the pesher (Isa 10:29).[108]

The significance of the messiah's garments or their relationship to
the priest who confers them upon the messiah has not been properly
understood. Moreover, Carmignac (followed by others) noted the
parallels between this passage and a similar description of the priestly
"garments of warfare" in 1QM VII, 9–12, though this parallel has also
not been analyzed closely:[109]

9   ובסדר מערכות המלחמה לקראת אויב מערכה לקראת מערכה
    ויצאו מן השער התיכון אל בין המערכות שבעה
10 כוהנים מבני אהרון לובשים בגדי שש לבן כתונת בד ומכנסי בד
    וחוגרים[110] באבנט בד שש משוזר תכלת
11 וארגמן ותולעת שני וצורת ריקמה מעשה חושב ופרי מגבעות[111]
    בראשיהם בגדי מלחמה ואל המקדש לוא
12 יביאום[112]

9. When they array the battle lines against the enemy, line against
   line, then shall march out, from the middle gate towards the space
   between the lines, seven
10. priests from the Sons of Aaron, dressed with garments of white
    byssus, a linen tunic and linen breeches, girded with a linen <u>girdle</u>,
    twisted byssus in violet,
11. both purple and scarlet, <u>with a many-colored design</u>, a skillful work,
    (wearing) <u>turban head-dresses</u> on their heads. (These are) war gar-
    ments; into the sanctuary they shall not
12. bring them.

[108] See Allegro's restoration of this word in A 5–6 11=H 2–6 II, 27 (see above,
n. 63). It could also be restored in the following line.

[109] As far as I can tell, Carmignac, Les Textes, 73, was the first to note the parallel.
See also Yigael Yadin, The Temple Scroll (3 vols.; Jerusalem: Israel Exploration Society, the Shrine of the Book, 1983), 1.270; Blenkinsopp, Opening, 120 n. 59. Text and
translation of 1QM^a following Jean Duhaime, PTSDSSP, 2.111–13. Part of this passage overlaps with 4Q491 (4QMa) 1–3 18. See Maurice Baillet, "4Q491. La Règle de
la Guerre (i)," in Qumrân Grotte 4.III (4Q482–4Q520) (DJD VII; Oxford: Clarendon,
1982), 14; Duhaime, PTSDSSP 2.144; and idem, "Étude comparative de 4QMa fgg.
1–3 et 1QM^a," RevQ 14/55 (1990): 469–70. Several linguistic elements in 1QM IX are
treated in Avi Hurvitz, "The Garments of Aaron and His Sons According to 1Q War
VII, 9–10," in Studies in Bible and the Ancient Near East (ed. Y. Avishur and J. J. Blau;
Jerusalem: Rubenstein, 1978), 139–44 [Hebrew].

[110] Lacking in 4Q491.

[111] See Exod 29:9; 39:28; Lev 8:13.

[112] Based on the arrangement of the extant text, Baillet, "La Règle," 14, restores
4Q491: ואל המקדש לוא יביאום [כ]יא [אלה בגדי מל]חמה (see also Duhaime,
PTSDSSP 2.144). As noted by Duhaime, 4Q491 yields a better syntax for this clause
("Étude comparative," 470).

As first glance, the imagery in 4Q161 8–10 III, A 19=H 24 seems to work well with the royal messiah. He presumably sits upon the throne of glory and wears a crown, exactly what we would expect for a royal figure. But, upon closer examination of the three terms in this line, we note that each term shares both royal and priestly imagery.[113] Thus, the phrase "throne of glory" (כסא כבוד)—which appears only four times in the HB—is indeed an allusion to the Davidic monarchy as in Isa 22:23, as is כסא more generally.[114] In two other uses in the HB, however, the throne of glory refers to the temple or ark (Jer 14:21; 17:12), and כסא more generally has this and other cultic meanings as well.[115] Similarly, נזר is commonly employed to refer to the royal crown, though the specific language here of a נזר קודש is a clear allusion to the priestly headdress.[116] The final term, [בגדי ריקמו[ת, was translated by Allegro as "garments of variegated stuff."[117] This expression, too, has important

---

[113] Nearly all treatments of this passage only note the royal associations. See, e.g., Pomykala, *Davidic Dynasty*, 201: "ln. 19 affirms that he will possess a throne of glory, a holy crown, and embroidered garments, all appurtenances indicative of royal status and power." See also Abegg, "Messiah at Qumran," 136.

[114] See also 1 Sam 2:8; 4Q405 23 I, 3. On כסא and royalty more generally, see Heinz-Josef Fabry, "כסא," in G. Johannes Botterweck and Helmer Ringgren (eds.), *Theological Dictionary of the Old Testament* (8 vols.; Grand Rapids: Eerdmans), 7.245–53. See also *1 En.* 45:3; Matt 19:28; 25:31.

[115] See Fabry, "כסא," 253–7. See also *Pss. Sol.* 2:20; 11Q17 X, 7.

[116] For נזר as a royal crown, see 2 Sam 1:10; 2 Kgs 11:12=2 Chr 23:11; Pss 89:40; 132:18. See further G. Mayer, "נזר," in Botterweck and Ringgren, *Theological Dictionary of the Old Testament* 9.310. For the priestly diadem נזר הקודש, see Exod 29:6; 39:30; Lev 8:9; cf. Lev 21:12.

[117] The root רקם here indicates that the clothing is variegated, whether a work of embroidery or woven. See Ludwig Koehler and Walter Baumgartner, *The Hebrew and Aramaic Lexicon of the Old Testament* (2 vols.; Leiden: Brill, 2001), 2:1290–1. This root is elsewhere employed in the scrolls in 4Q270 7 I, 14—כי אין לאמ[ו]ת רוקמה [בתוך [העדה—a *crux interpretatum* of scrolls scholarship. Recently, John F. Elwolde has argued that רוקמה in 4Q270 has the meaning of "authority" ("*RWQMH* in the Damascus Document and Ps 139:15," in *Diggers at the Well: Proceedings of the Third International Symposium on the Hebrew of the Dead Sea Scrolls and Ben Sira* [ed. Takamitsu Muaraoka and John F. Elwolde; STDJ 36; Leiden: Brill, 2000], 65–83) This interpretation is based in part on its biblical uses for expensive clothing, which are thus signs of authority (in particular Ezek 16:18; 26:16; see following note). Moreover, he argues that this meaning was known to the scribe of the Psalms Scroll, based on his rendering of Ps 139:15 (11QPs^a XX, 6–7). For further defense of Elwolde's interpretation and a summary of earlier treatments, see George J. Brooke, "Between Qumran and Corinth: Embroidered Allusions to Women's Authority," in *The Dead Sea Scrolls and the New Testament* (Minneapolis: Fortress, 2005), 196–214. It is not clear if Elwolde's interpretation of 4Q270 has any bearing on the related expression in 4Q161. It is possible that that identification of the garments as works of variegated stuff is likewise intended to confer additional authority on the messiah (or the priests; see below).

royal connotations.[118] The language employed here, however, is also rich in priestly imagery, since the root רקם is employed to describe the priest's girdle (אבנט), the only such garment identified as a work of embroidery (מעשב רקם).[119]

In all three expressions, 4Q161 has merged priestly/cultic and royal imagery. Moreover, contrary to what most commentators have noted, it is the priestly imagery that seems to be more dominant. What do we make of the merging of priestly and royal imagery in this text? These features work well with the general sense of the passage that the authority of the Prince is subject to that of the priests, as in other sectarian literature (e.g., 1QSa, 4Q174, 4Q285).[120] But it doesn't explain why the messiah seems to be wearing priestly garments and is otherwise associated with priestly/cultic language and imagery. The answer I think can be found in the parallel passage in the *War Scroll*.

1QM VII, 2–3 begins by identifying the minimum age for military service—25—which is the same as the age indicated in the 1QSa I, 12–13, both of which rely upon the age for levitical service in Num 8:24.[121] 1QM VII, 3–7 continues by describing the expectation of physical and ritual purity in the war camp, which corresponds with similar expectations in the present community in the *Damascus Document* (CD XV, 15–17 with 4Q266 8 I, 6–9),[122] the eschatological community in the *Rule of the Congregation* (1QSa II, 2–8), and the future temple

---

[118] See especially Ezek 26:16. In Ps 45:15, the maiden is brought before the king לרקמות (Elwolde, "*RWQMH*," 70, suggests the meaning of "by acts of authority"). See also Judg 5:30.

[119] For the girdle, see Exod 28:39; 39:29. See also the similar description of the "screen" (מסך) in the Tabernacle (Exod 26:36; 27:16; 36:37; 38:18). In Ezek 16:18, the embroidered clothing of Jerusalem seems also to have a cultic sense. Similar language and imagery is also employed in the *Songs of the Sabbath Sacrifice* (e.g., 4Q402 2 3; 4Q403 1 II, 1; 4Q405 20 II + 21 + 22 10–11). See Carol A. Newsom, "Shirot 'Olat HaShabbat," in *Qumran Cave 4.VI: Poetical and Liturgical Texts, Part 1* (ed. Esther Eshel et al.; DJD XI; Oxford: Clarendon, 1998), 225–6. See also 4Q179 1 II, 12.

[120] See above, n. 76. On priestly authority in the other texts, see Collins, *Scepter*, 75–7. Note that in 2 Kgs 11:12, the royal crown in given to Joash at the behest of Jehoiada the high priest.

[121] See Lawrence H. Schiffman, *The Eschatological Community of the Dead Sea Scrolls* (SBLMS 38; Atlanta: Scholars Press, 1989), 86. Moreover, 1QSa identifies the military service as עבדת העדה ("service of the congregation"), a slight modification of several different biblical expressions denoting service for/in the tabernacle/temple. See evidence collected in Alex P. Jassen, "The Dead Sea Scrolls and Violence: Sectarian Formation and Eschatological Imagination," *BibInt* 17 (2009): 36–7.

[122] CD is extremely fragmentary here, though the correct reading is ensured by 4Q266. See Joseph M. Baumgarten, *Qumran Cave 4.XIII: The Damascus Document (4Q266–273)* (DJD XVIII; Oxford: Clarendon, 1996), 63–4.

in 4QFlorilegium (4Q174 1–2 + 21 I, 4).[123] This builds up to 1QM VII, 9–12 which describes the priests clothed in priestly garments blowing the trumpets as the war camp moves forward in battle. The text harmonizes several biblical descriptions of the priestly garments in order to create a unique priestly wardrobe that is at once cultic, but at the same time distinctly used for warfare.[124] Notwithstanding their clearly cultic aspect, these "garments of war" are not allowed to enter the temple.[125] Among the modifications to the biblical description of the priestly garments, the girdle (אבנט) is "a many-colored design" (צורת ריקמה) as in Exod 28:39 and 39:29, but is also "a skillful work" (מעשה חושב), which is not mentioned in the biblical account of the girdle.[126] This exact combination appears elsewhere in the *War Scroll*'s description of the sword (ויד הכידן קרן ברורה מעשה חושב צורת ריקמה בזהב ובכסף ואבני חפץ).[127] In making this unique combination of terms, the *War Scroll* further reinforces the martial character of these unique priestly vestments. The *War Scroll* is not merely assigning the priests martial responsibilities, as is well known from the *War Scroll* and other sectarian literature.[128] Rather, the priestly vestments are now both ritual garments and military attire, and thus the identity of the priests is simultaneously cultic and martial.[129]

---

[123] These exclusions are based on an exegetical application of Deut 23:2–3, with the presence of angels provided as a further explanation for the exclusion of physically and ritually impure individuals. See further Jassen, "Dead Sea Scrolls and Violence," 35–6.

[124] As Yadin, *Scroll of the War*, 219, observes, 1QM harmonizes the descriptions of the priestly vestments in Exod 28; 39:27–31; Lev 16:3–4; Ezek 47:17–19.

[125] Yadin, *Scroll of the War*, 220, notes that there is no parallel for the expression בגדי מלחמה. The language here seems to be an exegetical reformulation of Lev 16:3–4, where Aaron is instructed not to enter the holy precinct (בזאת יבוא אהרן אל הקדש) unless he is carrying the appropriate sacrifices (v. 3) and wearing the holy vestments (v. 4: בגדי קדש). 1QM seems to understand זאת in v. 3 specifically as referring to the holy vestments. While the בגדי קדש *are* to be brought into the holy precinct (v. 3: בזאת יבוא אהרן אל הקדש), the בגדי מלחמה *are not* to be brought into the temple (1QM: ואל המקדש לוא יביאום).

[126] Yadin, *Scroll of the War*, 220.

[127] 1QM V, 14. This parallel was noted by Yadin, *Scroll of the War*, 220. On the sword, see ibid., 129–31.

[128] See Angel, *Otherworldly*, 196–202.

[129] Compare the reuse of Isa 11:5 in Eph 6:14 (linguistic overlap marked by single-underlining): "gird your <u>loins</u> (ὀσφὺν) with <u>truth</u> (ἀλήθεια); and put on the <u>breastplate</u> of <u>righteousness</u> (δικαιοσύνης)." Isa 11:5 is not interpreted messianically here, but rather refers to the church community who must prepare themselves for the imminent battle against forces of evil (see v. 13). In the reformulation of Isa 11:5, the priestly imagery of the breastplate is introduced as part of the armor necessary to fight off evil.

In an argument developed in a earlier study of 1QM VII, 9–12, I suggest that the conflation of priestly and martial imagery—in the age of military service, the expectation of ritual and physical purity, and the description of the garments—serves to transpose the ritualized order of the temple service onto the equally ritualized order of the eschatological battle. Thus, the priestly regiment becomes equivalent to a "temple in movement," fully clothed for warfare. In doing so, the *War Scroll* merges the sectarian self-identification as the spiritualized temple, the stewards of the permanent eschatological temple, and the militaristic community ordained to ensure the sanctity of all these sacred spaces.[130]

But, what becomes clear later in the *War Scroll* (1QM IX, 7–9) is that the priests themselves seem to stand at a distance during the actual battle, so as not to contract corpse impurity. Thus, while the priests are conceptualized as a "temple in movement" in this battle, ultimately they do not actually carry out the martial aspect of the battle.[131] While the *War Scroll* does not spell out here who takes charge of the battle while the priests are at a safe distance, elsewhere we learn that the *War Scroll* envisions the divine warrior and the angelic hosts leading the charge in the battle.[132]

The merging of priestly and royal imagery in 4Q161 suggests that, at least from the perceptive of the pesher's vision of the battle, it is the royal messiah who takes over the priestly role during the actual battle. He likely wears the same priestly garments that the priests wear while they blow the trumpets in order to reinforce the same martial and cultic imagery expressed in 1QM VII. The Prince acts as a surrogate for the priests while on the actual battlefield. Just as the priests conceptualize their war activity as a manifestation of temple ritual, so too the Prince's martial activity is infused with cultic significance. By having the Prince wear the priestly garments on the battlefield, the priests are likewise able to affirm their authority even from afar.[133] Once the battle is over,

---

[130] Jassen, "Dead Sea Scrolls and Violence," 35–8.

[131] Thus, Angel, *Otherworldly*, 198, characterizes the priestly role in the war as "thoroughly ceremonial."

[132] See, e.g., 1QM I, 8–10; XI, 1–3, 9–10. See further Philip R. Davies, "The Biblical and Qumranic Concept of War," in *The Bible and the Dead Sea Scrolls, Volume One, Scripture and the Scrolls* (ed. James H. Charlesworth; Waco: Baylor University Press, 2006), 228.

[133] Thus, the limitations on the messiah's authority are exegetically linked to Isa 11:3 and Ruzer, "Davidic Messiah," 233–4, notes that the Targum to Isa 11:5 similarly curbs the authority of the messiah by translating "girded with righteousness (צדק)"

then the priests re-assert their authority, by directing the post-battle activities of the Prince—an idea similarly expressed in 4Q285 (see above). It is likely that the fragmentary reference to "garments" in the hands of the priest in A l. 24=H l. 29 should be restored as "garments of warfare" (בגדי] מלחמה), perhaps even a reference to the fact that the garments are now returned to their priestly domain.

In contrast to the ideal priestly war manual reflected in the *War Scroll*, 4Q161 and 4Q285 identify the royal messiah as the primary militant protagonist in the eschatological war. At the same time, the priests retain an important role in both texts. Since the initial introduction of 4Q285 by Józef T. Milik, scholars have noted the literary and thematic correspondences between the *War Scroll* and 4Q285.[134] Indeed, Milik suggested that it represents the missing end of the *War Scroll*.[135] This intriguing suggestion is problematic on account of the central role in 4Q285 of the Prince of the Congregation, who is essentially absent in the *War Scroll*.[136] In light of the otherwise close connections between the two texts, Kenneth Pomykala proposes that 4Q285 is a different recension of the *War Scroll* that highlights the role of the Prince.[137] This suggestion is highly speculative and ultimately unlikely on account of several important differences between the two texts.[138]

In contrast, Jonathan Norton suggests that 4Q285 is a "messianic reworking" of the *War Scroll*.[139] As in 4Q161, the Prince is an important figure in 4Q285, but also is directed at various stages in the war by the priests. Thus, 4Q161 and 4Q285 appropriate central themes and language from the *War Scroll*, but introduce the Prince as the primary militant protagonist in the eschatological war. My discussion of the garments in 4Q161 and 1QM reinforces this assessment of the relationship between these texts. 4Q161 (and likely also 4Q285) seems to be responding to the tactical problem created by the lack of

as "surrounded by just ones (צדיקיא)." Ruzer suggests that the messiah's entourage is intended to deny the messiah absolute power.

[134] See especially the linguistic correspondences noted in Abegg, "Messianic Hope," 82–3; Norton, "Observations," 17–23.

[135] Józef T. Milk, "Milkî-ṣedeq et Milkî-reša' dans les ancient écrits juifs et chré-tiens," *JJS* 23 (1972): 143.

[136] The Prince of the Congregation appears in 1QM XV, 2. He also seems to be referred to in 4Q496 10 3–4. See further Alexander and Vermes, "4Q285," 231; Duhaime, *War Texts*, 33.

[137] Pomykala, *Davidic Dynasty*, 210.

[138] Alexander, "Reconstruction," 348; idem, "Evil Empire," 29–30; Duhaime, *War Texts*, 33.

[139] Norton, "Observations," 17.

human commander during the battle envisioned in the *War Scroll*. The description of the garments in 4Q161 suggests that 4Q161 does not merely incorporate the Prince into the eschatological battle scenario. Rather, he is introduced as the military commander, while simultaneously infused with the priestly/cultic significance that is so characteristic of the *War Scroll*.

CONCLUSION

4Q161 has been read and reread many times since its initial publication over 50 years ago. But, like many of the texts published in the early days of Dead Sea Scrolls scholarship, it deserves a new rereading. This new rereading is warranted based on the significant advances in our general knowledge of the Dead Sea Scrolls corpus as well as early Jewish biblical interpretation and the history of messianic speculation in the scrolls and Second Temple Judaism. Notwithstanding the often fragmentary character of 4Q161, there is much that we can learn from this text. In this study, I have treated various aspects of the text that focus on the four specific issues in need of more extensive analysis, as I outlined in the introduction. At the same time, I have sought to provide a general sense of the text as a whole and its relationship to other exegetical and eschatological literature in the Dead Sea Scrolls and Second Temple Judaism.

READING HOSEA AT QUMRAN*

ROMAN VIELHAUER
Göttingen

How was the Book of Hosea understood at Qumran? Or, put differently: can we detect in the Qumran literature a consistent perspective of reading for a discrete prophetic book? And if so, how does it relate to the authors' overall understanding of the book itself? These questions will be addressed in the following study. In this regard I will confine myself to those explicit Hosea quotations marked as such by quotation or interpretation formulas. They are encountered in the two *pesharim* on the Book of Hosea, the *Damascus Document*, and 4Q177—a work, originally designated as "Catena A", in the forthcoming new DJD V edition renamed as *Eschatological Commentary B*. One further quotation might be found in *Pesher Isaiah C*.

1. THE PESHARIM ON THE BOOK OF HOSEA

Two Qumran *pesharim* are attested for the Book of Hosea: 4Q166 known as 4QpHos[a] and 4Q167 known as 4QpHos[b]. A material reconstruction of both manuscripts has shown that we have to distinguish between two formally very distinct works, the first of which merely draws on select passages of Hosea while the latter quotes and comments on the entire book.[1] Regarding the designation of the two *pesharim* it might hence be advisable to use capital instead of superscript letters. In the following I will draw on my own edition of the texts.[2]

* My thanks to Franziska Ede for preparing the English translation.
[1] See Roman Vielhauer, "Materielle Rekonstruktion und historische Einordnung der beiden Pescharim zum Hoseabuch (4QpHos[a] und 4QpHos[b])," *RevQ* 20/77 (2001): 39–91.
[2] Cf. Vielhauer, "Materielle Rekonstruktion". First edition of the entire text by John M. Allegro, *Qumrân Cave 4.I*, 31–6, pl. X–XI; corrections and additions: John Strugnell, "Notes en marge" cf. further the editions by Horgan, *Pesharim*, 138–58 (textbook, 38–45); eadem, "Pesharim," in PTSDSSP 6B, 113–17, 119–31; for 4QpHos B see also Gregory L. Doudna, "4QPesher Hosea[b]: Reconstruction of Fragments 4, 5, 18, and 24," *DSD* 10 (2003): 338–58.

a) *4QpHos A*

4QpHos A consists of a single fragment with remains of two columns and according to palaeographic evidence might be dated to the late Herodian period. In contrast to the fragmentary preservation of the first column, the second column can be reconstructed almost entirely. This *pesher* is concerned with Hosea 2, a judgement discourse, portraying Israel as God's spouse, an unfaithful adulteress.[3]

4Q166 (4QpHos A) II, 1–19

[לוא ידעה כיא] אנוכי נתתי לה הדגֹ[ן] והתירוש]	1
[והיצהר וכסף]הֹרביתי וזהב{°°ה} עשוֹ[ן] לבעל פשרו]	2
אשר [אכלו וי]שבעו וישכחו את אל המאֹ[כילם ואת כול]	3
מצוותיו השליכו אחרי גום אשר שלח אליהֹם[ביד]	4
עבדיו הנביאיֹם ולמתעיהם שמעו ויכבדום] [	5
וכאלים יפחדו מהם בעורונם *vacat*] [	6
vacat	7
לכן אשוב ולקחתי דגני בעתו ותירושי[במועדו]	8
והצלתי צמרי ופושתי מלכסות את[ערותה]	9
ועתה אגלה את נבלותה לעיני מאה[ביה ואיש]	10
לוא יצילנה מידי *vacat*	11
פשרו אשר הכם ברעב ובערום להיות לקלו[ן]	12
וחרפה לעיני הגואים אשר נשענו עליהם והמה	13
לוא יושיעום מצרותיהם והשבתי כול משושה	14
חֹ[ג]ה חד[שה ושבתה וכול מועדיה פשרו אשֹר	15
[את ימי ה]עֹדות יוליכו במועדי הגואים ו[כול] *vacat*	16
[שמחתם]נהפכה להם לאבל והשמותי [גפנה]	17
[ותאנתה] אשר אמרה אתנם הם לי [אשר נתנו]	18
[לי מאהב]י ושמתים ליער ואכלתם חֹ[ית השדה]	19

1. [*"She did not know that*] *I myself had given her the grain*[*and the new wine*]
2. [*and the oil, and*] (*that*) *I had supplied* [*silver*] *and gold* (*which*) *they made*[*into Baal.*" (Hos 2:10) Its interpretation is]
3. that [they ate and] were satisfied, and they forgot God who had f[ed them; and all]
4. his ordinances they cast behind them, which he had sent to them[by the hand of]
5. his servants the prophets. But to those who led them astray they listened, and they honoured them[
6. and, like divine beings, they dread them in their blindness. *vacat* [
7. *vacat*

---

[3] The English translation follows Horgan, "Pesharim," 117, with slight modifications.

8. *"Therefore, I again shall take back my grain in its time and my wine[*
   in its season,]
9. *and I shall withdraw my wool and my flax from covering [her naked-*
   ness.]
10. *And now I shall uncover her private parts in the sight of [her] lov[ers*
    and]
11. *no [one] will withdraw her from my hand."* (Hos 2:11–12) *vacat*
12. Its interpretation is that he smote them with famine and with naked-
    ness so that they became a disgra[ce]
13. and a reproach in the sight of the nations on whom they had leaned,
    but they
14. will not save them from their afflictions. *"And I shall put an end to*
    all her joy,
15. *[her] pilgr[image,] her [new m]oon, and her sabbath, and all her*
    appointed times." (Hos 2:13) Its interpretation is that
16. they used to conduct [the days of the] testimony according to the
    feasts of the nations. *vacat* And [all]
17. [their joy] has been turned for them into mourning. *"And I shall*
    make desolate [her vine]
18. *[and her fig tree] of which she said, They (are) my hire [that] my*
    [lovers have given me.]
19. *And I shall make them a forest, and the w[ild beast of the field] will*
    devour them." (Hos 2:14)

Three *pesher* interpretations have been preserved: the first one, lines
2–7, an interpretation of Hos 2:10, is dominated by a depiction of
delinquencies. Drawing on phrases in Deuteronomy 8, Neh 9:26, and
2 Kgs 17:13 Israel's adultery is construed as their abandoning God,
expressed accordingly in their rejection of the commandments transmitted through the prophets and their godlike veneration of those
"who led them astray." It is especially this latter reproach which sur-
passes substantially our biblical evidence. The second interpretation
in lines 12–14 addresses the divine punishment. In relative agreement
with Hos 2:11–12 this penalty consists of "hunger and nakedness"—a
condition, which might not be countermanded by any former allies,
represented by the lovers in the biblical text. The last *pesher* interpretation is found in lines 15–17. It combines the penalty of Hos
2:13 with a further delinquency. This issue, as Moshe Bernstein[4] has
rightly pointed out, concerns the use of a calendrical system leaning

---

[4] See Moshe J. Bernstein, "'Walking in the Festivals of the Gentiles': 4QpHosea[a]
2.15–17 and *Jubilees* 6.34–38," *JSP* 9 (1991): 21–34.

on a pagan arrangement. It harkens back to a phrase in *Jubilees*
(Jub. 6:35).

Following Joseph Amoussine,[5] the events alluded to in 4QpHos A
are generally dated to the year 65 BCE, when the Nabatean king Are-
tas III was incited by Hyrcanus II to besiege Jerusalem as a means to
decide the latter's fratricidal war with Aristobulus II in his own favour.
Josephus' portrayal in *Antiquities* 14.2.1–3 (19–33) usually serves as
evidence in this regard. According to this evidence Hyrcanus II would
have relied heavily on the Pharisees—"those who led them astray"
(מתעיהם) in line 5 of the *pesher*—as far as domestic policies are concerned. As far as the siege of Jerusalem is concerned, his bet would
have been placed on the Nabatean military, which had to withdraw
because of Roman intervention—cf. lines 12–14. Moreover, the siege
coincided with passover—cf. lines 15–17. As the besiegers rejected let-
ting the sacrificial animals pass, divine punishment is thought to have
caused a famine—cf. line 12.

However, this interpretation is problematic for two reasons. First,
the identification of "those who led astray" in line 5 with the Pharisees
is opposed by the fact that the Pharisees seem to be the object of divine
veneration in line 6. Second, the reference to the passover of the year
65 BCE in lines 15–17 is difficult, as this passage is not primarily concerned with an actual perpetration—i.e. the withholding of sacrificial
animals—on an actual holiday, but with polemicising against a calendrical system, leaning on a pagan, in this case Seleucid, arrangement.

Thence, I would like to suggest a different interpretation of
4QpHos A.[6] In my view, the crucial key to the understanding of this
pesher is the interpretation of lines 5–6, especially the identification of
"those who led them astray" (מתעיהם) in line 5. While the wording
תעה (Hiphil) might initially evoke the idea of inner-Judean adversaries within the congregation, the characterization of such in line
6 as objects of divine veneration denies this construal. The peculiar
reproach, that Jews would have venerated a group of people in a godlike manner, is reminiscent of events related to the Seleucid king Antiochus IV Epiphanes (175–164 BCE), who favoured the introduction
of a godlike veneration of the monarch in Jerusalem. As well as his

---

    [5] See Joseph D. Amoussine, "Observatiunculae Qumraneae," *RevQ* 7/28 (1971):
545–52; idem, "The Reflection of Historical Events of the First Century BC in Qumran
Commentaries," *HUCA* 48 (1977): 146–50.
    [6] See Vielhauer, "Materielle Rekonstruktion," 78–80.

successors, Antiochus was met with such veneration by hellenophile Jews, who saw their political centre in the Acra, until their dissipation in 141 BCE.[7] Thus, "those who led them astray" (מתעיהם) might most easily be identified with the Seleucid kings from Antiochus IV Epiphanes to Demetrius II Nicator. At least in Dan 11:32 Antiochus IV is explicitly referred to as the enticer (יחניף בחלקות) of a covenant-breaking group within Israel.

The remaining text might easily be integrated into that historical context. This is, for one, true for the indictments mentioned, since the abrogation of the Torah, lines 3–5, as well as the reformation of the cult, broken down as the use of the Seleucid calendar, line 16, and a participation in the godlike veneration of the monarch, lines 5–6, both address the quintessence of the religio-political measures connected with the construction of the Acra as a heathen-Jewish *polis* (Dan 7:25; 1 Macc 1:44–51).[8] Moreover, the judgement stated in lines 12–14—hunger and nakedness—and lines 15–17—supersession of the cult—can readily be linked to the Maccabean actions taken against the inhabitants of the Acra: in 143 BCE Simon had built a wall around the Acra to cut off the inhabitants' food supply (1 Macc 12:36; Josephus, *Antiquities* 13.5.11 (181–83)). Even though supported by the Seleucid troops under General Tryphon, who—hindered by the sudden onset of winter—had to withdraw empty-handed (1 Macc 13:21–22; Josephus, *Antiquities* 13.6.5 (203–07); cf. 4QpHos A II, 13–14), the Acra was forced to surrender due to famine in 141 BCE (1 Macc 13:49–50; Josephus, *Antiquities* 13.6.6 (208–09)). Hence, the conquest of the Acra might as well have put an end to the Hellenistic cult in Jerusalem.

---

[7] For the historical background cf. Elias Bickermann, *Der Gott der Makkabäer: Untersuchungen über Sinn und Ursprung der makkabäischen Erhebung* (Berlin: Schocken Verlag, 1937); Martin Hengel, *Judentum und Hellenismus: Studien zu ihrer Begegnung unter besonderer Berücksichtigung Palästinas bis zur Mitte des 2. Jh.s v. Chr.* (WUNT 10; Tübingen: Mohr Siebeck, 1988), 486–554; Vielhauer, "Materielle Rekonstruktion," 79–80.

[8] See Hengel, *Judentum und Hellenismus*, 532–7. For the introduction of the Seleucid calendar in Jerusalem by extremely Hellenophile Jews, cf. James C. VanderKam, "2 Maccabees 6,7a and Calendrical Change in Jerusalem," *JSJ* 12 (1981): 52–74; idem, "Calendrical Texts and the Origins of the Dead Sea Scrolls Community," in *Methods of Investigation of the Dead Sea Scrolls and the Kirbeth Qumran Site: Present Realities and Future Prospects* (ed. Michael O. Wise et al.; Annals of the New York Academy of Sciences 722; New York: New York Academy of Sciences, 1994), 371–86, drawing on Dan 7:25; 1 Macc 1:59; 2 Macc 6:7a.

Should these observations be right, we might conclude that unlike Hosea 2 the *pesher* 4QpHos A comprehends both indictment and judgement as referring to merely one sacrilegious group within Israel—i.e. the hellenophile Jews of the Acra—as opposed to Israel as a whole. It was exactly those Jewish circles, whose religio-political measures triggered schisms in Judaism which eventually resulted in the emergence of groups like the Qumran community.

b) *4QpHos B*

40 fragments of this *pesher* have been preserved. According to material reconstruction, more than half of those fragments can be attributed to five sequential columns, located in the middle of the book. Attested are the text and partly the comments on Hos 2:2 as well as Hosea 5, 6 and 8, maybe even 7. This manuscript can be dated to the late Herodian period.

Only fragment 2 includes noteworthy remains of comments:

4Q167 (4QpHos B) 2 1–4

1]   ולוא יגהה מכ[ם מזור *vacat* פ[שר   [
2]   [° כפיר החרון כי אנוכי כשׁח[ל לא[פ[רי]ם] וככפיר לבית]
3]יהודה פשרו   [ל [ה]כוֹהן האחרון אשר ישלח ידו להכות באפרים
4]   *vacat*   דו[

1. ["nor can he heal you]r sore" (5:13). *vacat* The in[terpretation
2. [   ] the Lion of Wrath. *"For I am like a young l[ion to E]ph[rai]m [and like a lion to the house]*
3. [*of Judah*" (5:14). Its interpretation   ]*l* the last priest; he will stretch out his hand to smite Ephraim
4. [   ]*dw vacat*

The interpretation concerns two verses of Hosea 5, in which God is portrayed as a lion fighting his people of Ephraim and Judah. The *pesher* connects the biblical menace of judgement with two apparently contemporary persons: the "Lion of Wrath" and the "Last Priest." Due to a parallel in 4QpNah 3–4 I, 5–6 the "Lion of Wrath" is generally identified with the Hasmonean king Alexander Jannaeus.[9] The correlation of this "Lion of Wrath" with the "Last Priest"—perhaps a des-

---

[9] See John M. Allegro, "Further Light on the History of the Qumran Sect," *JBL* 75 (1956): 92, and recently Shani L. Berrin (Tzoref), *Pesher Nahum Scroll*, 105–07. Gregory L. Doudna, *4Q Pesher Nahum*, 572–3, however, thinks of a gentile ruler.

ignation for the contemporary High Priest[10]—remains uncertain. The only certain fact is that one of the two "stretches out his hand to smite Ephraim," line 3. John Allegro assumed both figures to be identical.[11] Hartmut Stegemann and Gregory Doudna, on the other hand, suggest that the two should be distinguished. Stegemann understands the "Last Priest" to be the subject of hitting.[12] Doudna, however, takes both "Ephraim" and the "Last Priest" to be the object of the "Lion of Wrath's" judgement.[13] Owing to the fragmentary character of the text, a definite solution seems unlikely. Yet, a comparison with other Qumran texts suggests that "Ephraim" might be seen as referring to a group opposed to the Qumran community (cf. 4QpNah 3–4 II, 2, 8; III, 5; 4QpPs A 1–10 II, 18), which might even be connected with the supporters of the "Man of the Lie."[14] Thence, one might conclude that 4QpHos B, like 4QpHos A, limits the judgement, which was targeted at the entirety of Israel in the biblical book of Hosea, to just one sacrilegious group within Israel, even though caution is in order, as the manuscript breaks off immediately following the word "Ephraim."

2. The Damascus Document (CD)

The so-called *Damascus Document*[15] includes four explicit Hosea quotations, all of which are part of the paraenetic parts of the work (the

---

[10] For the "Last Priest," see Hartmut Stegemann, "Die Entstehung der Qumrangemeinde" (Ph.D. diss., Rheinische Friedrich-Wilhelms-Universität Bonn, 1971), 115–20.

[11] Allegro, "Further Light," 93.

[12] Stegemann, "Die Entstehung der Qumrangemeinde," 123–4; idem, *Die Essener, Qumran, Johannes der Täufer und Jesus* (4th ed.; Freiburg: Herder, 1994), 182. More precisely, he historically identifies the "Last Priest" with Aristobulus II (67–63 bce), who upon the death of his Pharisee-friendly mother Salome (cf. Josephus, Antiquities 13.16 (405–33)) is said to have deprived the Pharisees, known as "Ephraim," of their political influence.

[13] Doudna, *4Q Pesher Nahum*, 557–73.

[14] See Stegemann, "Die Entstehung der Qumrangemeinde," 69–82. For the use of the term "Ephraim" in the Dead Sea Scrolls, see recently Berrin (Tzoref), *Pesher Nahum Scroll*, 109–18.

[15] For introductory questions, see the overview by Charlotte Hempel, *The Damascus Texts* (Companion to the Qumran Scrolls 1; Sheffield: Sheffield Academic Press, 2000), as well as Devorah Dimant, "Qumran Sectarian Literature," in *Jewish Writings of the Second Temple Period: Apocrypha, Pseudepigrapha, Qumran Sectarian Writings, Philo, Josephus* (ed. M. E. Stone; CRINT 2.2; Assen/Philadelphia: Fortress Press, 1984), 483–550. For an overview of the use of scripture, see Jonathan G. Campbell, *The Use of Scripture in the Damascus Document* (BZAW 228; Berlin: de Gruyter, 1995), and

"admonition": CD I–VIII/XIX–XX). The basis for the following interpretation will be the Cairo Geniza text.[16]

a) *CD I, 11–17*

CD I, 11–17 quotes and interprets Hos 4:16a:

ויקם להם מורה צדק להדריכם בדרך לבו *vacat* ויודע 11
לדורות אחרונים את אשר עשה בדור אחרון בעדת בוגדים 12
הם סרי דרך היא העת אשר היה כתוב עליה כפרה סוריה 13
כן סרר ישראל בעמוד איש הלצון אשר הטיף לישראל 14
מימי כזב ויתעם בתוהו לא דרך להשח גבהות עולם ולסור 15
מנתיבות צדק ולסיע גבול אשר גבלו ראשנים בנחלתם למען 16
הדבק בהם את אלות בריתו להסגירם לחרב נקמת נקם 17

11.   [...]   *vac* And he informed
12. the latter generations that which he did in the last generation among
     the congregation of traitors,
13. who are those who depart from the Way; that is the time of which
     it was written, "*As a wayward cow,*
14. *so did Israel stray*" (Hos 4:16)—when the man of mockery arose,
     who sprinkled upon Israel
15. waters of falsehood and led them astray in a chaos without a way,
     bringing low the eternal heights and departing
16. from paths of righteousness and moving the border marked out by
     the first ones in their inheritance so as
17. to apply to them the curses of his covenant, surrendering them to
     the avenging sword of the covenant's vengeance.

Hos 4:16 compares Israel to a wayward cow, replacing her God by
idols. Within the *Damascus Document* quotation and interpretation
are part of a historical portrayal comprising the time from the Babylonian exile to the emergence of a certain "Teacher of Righteousness" (CD I, 1–II, 1).[17] This teacher is opposed by the "congregation of

---

recently Liora Goldman, "Biblical exegesis and pesher interpretation in the Damascus
Document" (Ph.D. diss., University of Haifa, 2007).

[16] Text according to Martin Abegg in DSSEL; cf. also Samuel Schechter, *Fragments
of a Zadokite Work* (Documents of Jewish Sectaries 1; Cambridge: Cambridge University Press, 1910); Magen Broshi, ed., *The Damascus Document Reconsidered* (Jerusalem:
Israel Exploration Society; The Shrine of the Book, Israel Museum, 1992). Translations according to Joseph M. Baumgarten and Daniel R. Schwartz, "The Damascus
Document," in PTSDSSP 2, 13 (CD I), and Florentino García Martínez and Eibert
J. C. Tigchelaar, DSSSE 1.550–81 (CD IV, VIII, XIX, XX).

[17] For details regarding the interpretation, cf. Stegemann, "Die Entstehung der
Qumrangemeinde," 131–45.

traitors," the date of origin of which is alluded to in Hos 4:16a. Twice, the group's behaviour is referred to as going astray (סור, line 13), an action which the "Man of Mockery"[18] enticed them to take (lines 14–15). The root סור onomatopoetically draws on Hosea's סרר (wayward). Again, the reproach targeted at the entirety of Israel in the book of Hosea is now addressed to a sacrilegious group in her midst.

b) *CD IV, 19–20*

A further Hosea quotation is found in the famous subsequence CD IV, 12–V, 19 concerning "the three nets of Belial"—fornication, wealth and polluting the sanctuary—, in which the contemporary Israel is ensnared. Here CD IV, 19–20 draws on Hos 5:11—a verse addressing Ephraim's delinquencies and his fate in a fratricidal war with Judah[19]—while providing antitheses:

CD IV, 19- 20

19 בזה *vacat* בוני החי׳ץ אשר הלכו אחרי צו הצו הוא מטיף
20 אשר אמר הטף יטיפון...

19. [...] *vac* The builders of the wall who "*go after Zaw*" (Hos 5:11)— Zaw is the preacher
20. of whom he said: "Assuredly they will preach." (Mic 2:6) [...]

In CD IV, 19–20 as in Ezek 13:10 the supporters of an adverse group are described as "the builders of the wall" (cf. CD VIII, 12/XIX, 24–25) and with reference to Hos 5:11b broken down as those "who go after Zaw". The word "Zaw," which is uncertain even within the book

---

[18] For the "Man of Mockery" (איש הלצון), cf. CD XX, 11; Isa 28:14; Prov 29:8. In other texts, he is referred to as the "Man of the Lie" (איש הכזב: CD XX, 15; 1QpHab II, 2; V, 11) or the "Spouter (or Preacher) of the Lie" (מטיף הכזב: CD VIII, 13; XIX, 26; 1QpHab X, 9). For the figure, see Timothy H. Lim, "Liar," *EDSS* 1.493–494.

[19] For basic remarks on the fratricidal war in Hos 5:8–11, cf. Albrecht Alt, "Hosea 5,8–6,6: Ein Krieg und seine Folgen in prophetischer Beleuchtung," in *Kleine Schriften zur Geschichte des Volkes Israel 2* (3rd ed.; Munich: C. H. Beck, 1964), 163–87; repr. from *NKZ* 30 (1919); further Francis I. Andersen and David N. Freedman, *Hosea* (AB 24; Garden City: Doubleday, 1980), 399–410; James L. Mays, *Hosea* (OTL; Philadelphia: Westminster Press, 1969), 85–98; Jörg Jeremias, *Der Prophet Hosea* (ATD 24,1; Göttingen: Vandenhoeck & Ruprecht, 1983), 78–89; Reinhard G. Kratz, "Erkenntnis Gottes im Hoseabuch," *ZTK* 94 (1997): 7–11; Andrew A. Macintosh, *A Critical and Exegetical Commentary on Hosea* (ICC; Edinburgh: T&T Clark, 1997), 193–213; Roman Vielhauer, *Das Werden des Buches Hosea: Eine redaktionsgeschichtliche Untersuchung* (BZAW 349; Berlin: de Gruyter, 2007), 45–62.

Hosea,[20] applies to the "Man of Mockery," the founder of the oppos-
ing group, whose agency—like in CD I, 14 and alluding to Mic 2:6—is
specified as "preaching" (נטף Hiphil). Just as is the case in CD I, the
Hosea text is associated with a conflict with the congregation of the
"Man of Mockery." It is noteworthy, however, that even the original
Hosea phrase is found in the context of a fratricidal war.

c) *CD VIII, 1–5 par. XIX, 13–17*

A further Hosea quotation is encountered in connection with an
extensive judgement scene addressing opponents of the congregation.
This quotation is attested in both recensions of the Geniza text. The
quotation is taken from Hos 5:10, a causal announcement of judgement against the "princes of Judah", belonging to the above context
of a fratricidal war between Ephraim and Judah.

CD VIII, 1–5

1   והנסוגים הסגירו לחרב וכן משפט כל באי בריתו אשר

2   לא יחזיקו באלה לפוקדם לכלה ביד בליעל הוא היום

3   אשר יפקד אל היו שרי יהודה אשר תשפוך עליהם העברה

4   כי יחלו למרפא ‹וידבק מום› כל מורדים מאשר לא סרו מדרך

5   בוגדים...

1.   [...]   Thus will be the judgement of all those entering
   his covenant but who
2. do not remain steadfast in them; they shall be visited for destruction
   at the hand of Belial. This is the day
3. when God will make a visitation. *"The princes of Judah are those upon
   whom the rage will be vented"* (Hos 5:10),
4. for they hope to be healed but <the defect sticks (to them)>; all are
   rebels because they have not left the path of
5. traitors [...]

CD XIX, 13–17

13   והנשארים הסגרו לחרב נוקמת נקם ברית וכן משפט לכל באי

14   בריתו אשר לא יחזיקו באלה החקים לפקדם לכלה ביד בליעל

15   הוא היום אשר יפקד אל כאשר דבר היו שרי יהודה כמשיגי

16   גבול עליהם אשפך כמים עברה כי באו {באו} בברית תשובה

17   ולא סרו מדרך בוגדים...

---

[20] Cf. Vielhauer, *Das Werden des Buches Hosea*, 47–8.

13. [. . .] Thus will be the judgement of all those entering

14. his covenant, but who do not remain steadfast in these precepts; they shall be visited for destruction at the hand of Belial.

15. This is the day when God will make a visitation, as he said: *"The princes of Judah will be like those who move*

16. *the boundary, upon them I will pour out fury like water"* (Hos 5:10). For they entered the covenant of conversion,

17. but have not left the path of traitors [. . .]

Recension A offers a loose quotation of Hos 5:10 combined with Deut 13:18 or Job 31:7. Instead of such a further allusion, recension B renders the quotation explicitly, by completing it and identifying the "princes of Judah" more clearly: "they entered the covenant of conversion, but have not left the path of traitors." Elsewise, "covenant of conversion" is not attested elsewhere in the Hebrew Bible or in Qumran. Yet, it is highly probable that we are facing a self-designation of the Qumran community.[21] The "princes of Judah" seems to be an enigmatic designation for a group, which once belonged to the Qumran community, but has since apostasized, not leaving the path of traitors.[22] The use of שר "prince" is onomatopoetically reminiscent of סור "go astray."[23] A comparison with further Qumran texts (cf. e.g. 1QpHab V, 9–12) suggests that this group should be identified with the supporters of the "Man of the Lie." Thus, we might conclude that, again, the quotation was chosen wisely, as both quotation and interpretation allude to a fratricidal war.

d) *CD XX, 13–20*

Finally, a quotation of Hos 3:4 is found in CD XX, 13–20:

13 ולא יהיה להם {ו} ולמשפחותיהם חלק בבית התורה ומיום

14 האסף יורה היחיד <היחד> עד תם כל אנשי המלחמה אשר שבו

15 עם איש הכזב כשנים ארבעים *vacat* ובקץ ההוא יחרה

16 אף אל בישראל כאשר אמר אין מלך ואין שר ואין שופט וא[י]ן

17 מוכיח בצדק { } ושבי פשע יעקֹב שמרו ברית אל אז ידברו איש

---

[21] This is at least indicated by the return/covenant phrasings in CD XV, 9; XVI, 1–2; cf. Maxine Grossman, *Reading for History in the Damascus Document: A Methodological Study* (STDJ 45; Leiden: Brill, 2002), 163–4.

[22] Cf. André Dupont-Sommer, *Die essenischen Schriften vom Toten Meer* (trans. W. W. Müller; Tübingen: Mohr Siebeck, 1960), 148.

[23] For the pun on סור, cf. CD I, 13, and VII, 12–13.

18 אל רעהו להׁצּדׁיק אׁיׁש את אׁחיו לתמוך צעדם בדרך אל ויקשב
19 אל אל דׁבׁריהם וישמע ויכתב סׁפׁרׁוכ רון [לפניו] ליראי אל וׁלחושבי
20 שמׁו עד יגלה { } ישע וצדקה ויראׁי אׁל...

13.   [...]   And from the day
14. of the gathering in of the unique teacher, until the end of all the men of war who turned back
15. with the Man of the Lie, there shall be about forty years. *vac* And in this age the wrath
16. of God will be kindled against Israel, as he said: "*There shall be no king, no prince, no judge, no-one [who]*
17. *reproaches in justice*" (Hos 3:4). But those who revert from the sin of Jacob, have kept the covenant of God. "They shall then speak", each
18. to his fellow, acting just with one's brother, so that their steps become steady in the path of God, and God "will pay attention" to
19. their words. "And he will listen; and it will be written in a book of remembrance [before hi]m for those who fear God and think on
20. his name" (Mal 3:16), until salvation and justice are revealed to those who fear God. [...]

This passage describes a time span of "about forty years" (cf. Deut 2:14 as well as 1QM II; 4QpPs A 1–10 II, 7–8) from the death of the "unique teacher" to the final annihilation of all those who support the "Man of the Lie" (line 14) and to the advent of salvation for the God-fearing (line 20). The quotation of Hos 3:4, predicting for Israel a period devoid of all political and cultic institutions, is here related to the teacher-less time of the Qumran community. In this regard, the teacher reference is owing to a secondary act of interpretation by the *Damascus Document*, which reads "no-one who reproaches in justice" instead of the original "no Ephod and no Teraphim."[24] Again, a quotation addressed to the whole of Israel in Hosea is limited to a group within her midst, this time, however, not aiming at an adverse group, but at the Qumran community itself.

---

[24] For "reproaching" (יכח hi.) as an action taken by the "Teacher of Righteousness" (מורה הצדק), see 1QpHab V, 9–12. Further the targum reads "teacher" (מחוי) at the end of Hos 3:4.

3. ESCHATOLOGICAL COMMENTARY B

Following the reconstruction of Annette Steudel,[25] two manuscripts of the so-called *Eschatological Commentary* or, as Steudel put it, *Midrash on Eschatology* have been preserved. 4Q174 (*Eschatological Commentary A*) provides us with text stemming from the beginning of the work, 4Q177 (*Eschatological Commentary B*) with fragments of its middle.[26] According to palaeographic evidence 4Q174 needs to be dated to the last third of the 1st century BCE, 4Q177 somewhat later. The work itself was most likely composed between 71 and 63 BCE. Thematically speaking, we have to deal with a commentary, concerned with אחרית הימים, i.e. the last inauspicious epoch of salvation time.[27] The work can be divided into a brief introductory part, drawing on both the blessing of the tribes in Deuteronomy 33 and the Nathan's prophecy in 2 Samuel 7, and a main section, which grapples with eschatological issues while alluding to Psalms and, to a lesser extent, other biblical books. In this regard, col. X (4Q177 1–4 13–14) likewise quotes and interprets Hos 5:8a, an appeal to sound the trumpet, found, once more, within the context of Ephraim's and Judah's fratricidal war:[28]

4Q177 (4QEschatological Commentary B) 1–4:, 13–14 (=X, 13–14)

13   [ ] [°°] [ל]ו[ל] ולזרעו [עד] עולם ויקום משמה ללכתֹ° מֹן אֹרֹם]
[תקעו שופר בגבעה השופר הואה ספר

14   [התורה חצוצרה ברמה הח]צֹוֹ[צרה הי]אה ספר התורה שנית
אשרֹ מאסו בֹ]וֹל א[ֹנֹשֹיֹ עצתו וידברו עליו סרה וישלֹח

13.   [...]   "*Blow Shophar in Gibeah*" (Hos 5:8a). The "Shophar", that is the book of

---

[25] Annette Steudel, *Der Midrasch zur Eschatologie. Editio princeps* of the entire text: Allegro, *Qumrân Cave 4.I*, 53–57, pl. XIX–XX (4Q174), and 67–74, pl. XXIV–XXV (4Q177); corrections and additions: Strugnell, "Notes en marge," 220–25, 236–48; cf. further the edition by Jacob Milgrom with Lidija Novakovic, "Catena A (4Q177 = 4QCatᵃ)" in PTSDSSP 6B, 286–303.

[26] Further attestations might be encountered in 4Q178 (*Eschatological Commentary D*), 4Q182 (*Eschatological Commentary C*) and 4Q183 (*Eschatological Commentary E*), cf. Steudel, *Der Midrasch zur Eschatologie*, 152–7.

[27] For the אחרית הימים, see Annette Steudel, "אחרית הימים in the Texts from Qumran," *RevQ* 16/62 (1993): 225–46.

[28] For the respective text and its interpretation, cf. Steudel, *Der Midrasch zur Eschatologie*, 106–9.

14. [the Torah. *"(Blow) Chazozrah in Ramah"* (Hos 5:8a). The "Cha-] zo[zrah", that i]s the book of the Torah again which a[ll the me]n of his council have spurned and they have spoken rebelliously against him. […]

Due to the merely fragmentary preservation of the column, the integration of both quotation and its interpretation cannot be determined for certain. The quotation itself consists of two parts. First, only the first sentence of Hos 5:8a is cited: "Blow Shophar in Gibeah!" The following brief interpretation identifies "Shophar" with a book, presumably the Torah. Very few, but explicit remains of letters found in line 14 render the reading of "Chazozrah" as part of an interpretation highly likely. The preceding lacuna might well have contained a quotation of the second part of Hos 5:8a—the part which addresses the "Chazozrah". As is the case with the first part of the Hosea quotation, a single element is being interpreted, namely now "Chazozrah" as compared to "Shophar". Like "Shophar" the term "Chazozrah" is identified with the Torah: "The Chazozrah, that is the book of the Torah again[29] which all the men of his council have spurned and they have spoken rebelliously against him" (line 14). Against the background of the remaining Qumran texts, this interpretation gains in clarity: The "Men of his Council" are best identified as the supporters of the "Man of the Lie", who—disagreeing on the interpretation of the Torah— broke with the "Teacher of Righteousness" and his followers (cf. e.g. 1QpHab V, 9–12). Again, the Hosea quotation is connected with a schism within Israel. Its relation to the fratricidal war is already suggested by the biblical context.

---

[29] Yigael Yadin, *The Temple Scroll* (vol. 1; Jerusalem: Israel Exploration Society; The Institute of Archaeology of the Hebrew University of Jerusalem; The Shrine of the Book, 1983), 396–7, however, follows Allegro, *Qumrân Cave 4.I*, 68, by translating היאה ספר התורה שנית as "(the trumpet) is the Book of the Second Law" and considers התורה שנית a possible designation for the Temple Scroll. Aside from the fact, that a "Book of the Second Law" is not attested elsewhere in the Qumran scrolls, Yadin further has to reckon with a haplography of ה (השנית instead of שנית), so that the translation "that is the book of the Law again" first suggested by Strugnell, "Notes en marge," 241, and taken up by Hartmut Stegemann, "The origins of the Temple Scroll," in *Congress Volume Jerusalem 1986* (ed. John A. Emerton; VTSup 40; Leiden: Brill, 1988), 243, and Steudel, *Der Midrasch zur Eschatologie*, 109, remains most likely.

4. Pesher Isaiah C

Pesher Isaiah C, 4Q163, is usually considered to comprise 61 fragments.[30] Due to the usage of papyrus as writing material, the fragments are but poorly preserved. According to palaeographic evidence, two different handwritings can be discerned, a semi-formal Hasmonean and a more cursive one.[31] The work represents the oldest preserved *pesher* manuscript we know (first third of the 1st century BCE). It deals with selected passages of the Book of Isaiah, quotations of which are preserved for chapters 8–10, 14, 19, and 29–31. In addition, further prophetic books are considered in the commentary parts, amongst them the Book of Hosea with one reference.

Regardless of its fragmentary preservation, a quotation of Hos 6:9a can be detected with relative certainty in fragment 23, col. ii, line 14. Yet, the formulaic embedding of the quotation into its context is lost. Since all non-Isaianic references are marked by citation formulas, we might expect the same to be true for our Hosea quote. Thus, it seems justified to include 4QpIsa C into our overview of explicit Hosea quotations found in Qumran texts.

Hos 6:9 describes the priests of the Northern kingdom as a community of thieves and sneaky murderers. In 4QpIsa C, the quotation is found within the context of an interpretation of Isa 30:15–18:[32]

4Q163 (4QpIsa C) 23 II, 3–14a

3	‏[כי]א כ[ו]ה אמר יהוה קדוש ישראל בשובה ונ[ח]ת[ ] תושעון[
4	‏[בה]שקט ובטח תהיה גבורתכמה ולוא אביתמה ות[ואמרו]
5	‏לוֹא כיא על סוס ננוס על כן תנוסון ועל קל נרכב על בֿן‎
6	‏יקֿלו רודפיכמה אלף אחד מפני גערת אחד מפני גערת
7	‏חמשה תנוסון עד אם נותרתמה כתרן על רואש הר
8	‏וכנס על גבעה לכן יחכה אדוני לחנֿ[נכ]מה ולכן ירום
9	‏לרחמכמה כיא אלוהי משפט יהוה אשרי כול חוכי לו
10	‏פשר הדבר לאחרית הימים על עדת ד[ורשי] החלקות
11	‏אשֿר בירוֹשלימֿ°°° הֿ[°
12	‏בתורה ולוא יהֿ[ ] °°[
13	‏לב כיא לדושֿ°[

---

[30] *Editio princeps* of the entire text: Allegro, *Qumrân Cave 4.I*, 17–27, pl. VII–VIII; corrections and additions: Strugnell, "Notes en marge," 188–95; cf. further the editions by Horgan, *Pesharim*, 94–124 (textbook, 20–33); eadem, "Pesharim," 47–81.

[31] Cf. Strugnell, "Notes en marge," 188–9.

[32] The text and its translation follow Horgan, "Pesharim," 70–73 (the numbering of lines 14 and 14a are taken from Allegro, *Qumrân Cave 4.I*, 24).

[כיחכה איש גדוד]ים חבר כוהנים   14
[התורה מאסו]   14a

3. ["Fo]r th[u]s says YHWH, the Holy One of Israel: 'With return and r[es]t [you will be saved.]

4. [In] quiet and in trust will be your strength.' But you were not willing, and you [said,]

5. 'No! For on horseback we will flee.' Therefore, you shall flee! 'And on swift (steeds) we will ride.' Therefore

6. swift shall your pursuers be! A thousand before the threat of one, before the threat of

7. five you shall flee, until you are left like a flagstaff on a mountain-top,

8. and a standard on a hill. Therefore the Lord waits to be gracious to you, and therefore rises up

9. to be merciful on you, for YHWH is the God of justice. Happy (shall be) all who wait for him!" (Isa 30:15–18)

10. The interpretation of the passage (with regard) to the latter days concerns the congregation of the S[eekers-after-]Smooth-Things

11. who are in Jerusalem h [ ]

12. in the Torah, and not yh[ ] [ ]

13. heart, for to trample [ ]

14. "As the raider[s] lie in wait for a man, [a band of priests" (Hos 6:9)]

14a. they have rejected the Torah. [ ]

Among scholars, it is highly disputed whether the quotation, line 14, or its interpretation, line 14a, need to be considered secondary. In this passage the line spacing is reduced considerably. Maurya Horgan advocates that the quotation was added "as a gloss on the commentary, perhaps inspired by the verb ḥkh, 'to wait for,' in both Isa 30:18 and Hos 6:9a."[33] With reference to the indent, John Allegro and John Strugnell, however, assume line 14a to be a later addition.[34] Regardless of the decision favoured, the following might be suggested as to the Hosea quotation within the context of the Isaiah *pesher*: in lines 10–13 the quotation Isa 30:15–18 is interpreted as relating to אחרית הימים and "the congregation of the Seekers-after-Smooth-Things" (line 10) "who are in Jerusalem" (line 11). Considering other Qumran texts, this group might be identified with the supporters of the "Man of the

---

[33] Horgan, *Pesharim*, 120. In this regard the *pesher* adjusts the orthographically difficult verbal form of the Hosean text (כחכי) to the Isaian text (כיחכי); cf. Russel Fuller, "Textual Traditions in the Book of Hosea and the Minor Prophets," in *The Madrid Qumran Congress* (vol. 1; ed. Julio Trebolle Barrera and Luis Vegas Montaner; STDJ 11,1; Leiden: Brill, 1992), 252.

[34] Allegro, *Qumrân Cave 4.I*, 24; Strugnell, "Notes en marge," 193.

Lie" (cf. e.g. CD I, 13–21; 4QpIsa B II, 6–7, 10). This fits well with the reproach of line 14a: the abrogation of the Torah (cf. 1QpHab I, 11; V, 9–12; 4QpIsa B II, 6–7, 10). Again, a Hosea quotation is used in connection with a dispute between the Qumran community and their opponents—an interpretation, which is even suggested by the quotation (Hos 6:9) itself, seeing as it addresses a sacrilegious group within Israel, namely the priests.

CONCLUSIONS

This overview of explicit Hosea quotations present in the Qumran manuscripts shows an amazingly coherent pattern on how the book of Hosea was read at Qumran. Constitutive for the comprehension of the book seems to be a differentiation within Israel, separating the righteous from the sinners.

The bulk of quotations addresses the sinners. They are once probably identified as the hellenophile Jews living in the Acra (4QpHos A). Elsewhere they mostly represent the supporters of the "Man of the Lie" (4QpHos B; CD I, 11–17; IV, 19–20; VIII, 1–5/XIX, 13–17; 4QEschatological Commentary B; 4QpIsa C). One quotation addresses the Qumran community itself, i.e. the righteous ones (CD XX, 13–20).

In detail, the Qumranic interpretation of Hosea shows a bifocal perspective: first, certain Qumran texts refer solely to Hosean passages that are either dealing with the fratricidal war between Ephraim and Judah or are concerned with a distinction within Israel by accusing one group only. In this context we might mention the three references to Hos 5:8–11 (Hos 5:8a in 4QEschatological Commentary B; Hos 5:10 in CD VIII, 1–5/XIX, 13–17; Hos 5:11b in CD IV, 19–20), which deals with the fratricidal war, or Hos 6:9 (in 4QpIsa C), which addresses the delinquencies especially of the priests. Second, passages referring to the entirety of Israel in the Book of Hosea are limited to a single group within her midst (Hos 2:10–13 in 4QpHos A; Hos 3:4 in CD XX, 13–20; Hos 4:16 in CD I, 11–17, Hos 5:14 in 4QpHos B).

If we have thus rightly described the Qumran perspective on Hosea as one distinguishing between the righteous and the sinners, the question arises: How did the authors reach this conclusion? On the one hand, this reading is already suggested by the special historical situation of the Qumran community, namely one of serious conflict between opposing groups. On the other hand—and this is in my view the decisive fact—such an interpretation is inherent in the Book of

Hosea itself. That is especially likely because the final verse of the book, Hos 14:10, already includes a separation of the righteous and the sinners as the hermeneutical key to the understanding of the entire book—a fact which has repeatedly been pointed out by various biblical scholars:[35]

Hosea 14:10

מִי חָכָם וְיָבֵן אֵלֶּה נָבוֹן וְיֵדָעֵם 10
כִּי־יְשָׁרִים דַּרְכֵי יְהוָֹה
וְצַדִּקִים יֵלְכוּ בָם
וּפֹשְׁעִים יִכָּשְׁלוּ בָם:

10. Whoever is wise, let him understand these things;
whoever is discerning, let him know them.
For the ways of the LORD are straight,
and the righteous walk in them,
but the sinners stumble in them.

From that key the Qumran exegetes might have interpreted the overall understanding of the book purported by Hos 14:10[36] while transferring it to their own, presently grievous situation. Unlike the final verse of Hosea, however, the Qumran exegetes do not understand the comprehension of the scriptures as a result of their own efforts alone. As other Qumran texts show, the understanding of the scriptural text is presented as if it was part of a special revelation, offered to the Teacher of Righteousness by God himself (cf. e.g. 1QpHab II, 7–10; VII, 1–8). This supposed divine revelation warrants the interpretation's authenticity and enables the Qumran exegetes to understand the prophetic book as a testimony for their own time given by the one and ever consistent God.

---

[35] E.g. Gerald T. Sheppard, *Wisdom as a Hermeneutical Construct: A Study in the Sapientializing of the Old Testament* (BZAW 151; Berlin: de Gruyter, 1980), 129–36; Mays, *Hosea*, 190; Jeremias, *Das Buch Hosea*, 174; Kratz, "Erkenntnis Gottes im Hoseabuch," 17–8; Ehud Ben Zvi, *Hosea* (FOTL; Grand Rapids: Eerdmans, 2005), 313–7; Vielhauer, *Das Werden des Buches Hosea*, 201–3.

[36] In this regard it can hardly be a coincidence, that Hos 14:10 is generally considered one of the latest additions to the Book of Hosea among biblical scholars (cf. e.g. Sheppard, *Wisdom as a Hermeneutical Construct*, 129–36; Jeremias, *Das Buch Hosea*, 174; Kratz, "Erkenntnis Gottes im Hoseabuch," 17–8; Vielhauer, *Das Werden des Buches Hosea*, 201–3). The Qumran interpretation starts off where the inner-biblical interpretation came to its (provisional) end. Hence it seems legitimate to say, that both inner- and extra-biblical interpretation show a certain correlated continuity (cf. Vielhauer, *Das Werden des Buches Hosea*, 207–23).

TWO APPROACHES TO THE STUDY OF GENRE IN 4Q172

Trine B. Hasselbalch
University of Copenhagen

4Q172 consists of fourteen fragments; these were named by John Allegro in the *editio princeps* as "Commentaries on unidentified texts."[1] The fragments were lumped together under this heading based on their material appearance and handwriting, which Allegro found to be similar to the pesher documents of 4Q161, 4Q166, 4Q171 and 4Q167, believing some of the fragments might originate in that group of texts. John Strugnell subsequently pointed out that this particular handwriting was widespread in cave 4, and that the text could have originated from other, non-pesherite material.[2] Maurya Horgan has stated that "there is too little preserved on any of the fragments to determine the character or content of the texts."[3] Of course, the inclusion of them in her book about the pesharim, is due to her assumption that at least some of the fragments might belong in a pesher text. I will attempt to show that something more *can* be said about the content and character of two of the larger fragments, 1 and 4.

The two fragments invite very diverse kinds of investigations. The selection of vocabulary in Fragment 1, for instance, has little to offer for an analysis of contents, even if it is one of the more "copious" fragments. Nevertheless, there is sufficient material for a more thorough analysis of formal traits. Fragment 4, on the other hand, contains vocabulary that suggests connections with specific scriptural sources and perhaps even interpretative traditions, but it does not lend itself easily to decisive formal analysis and cannot on formal grounds be defined as pesher or any other genre.

---

[1] John M. Allegro, *Qumran Cave 4 I*, 50–1 + plate XVIII. Supplementary commentaries are offered in John Strugnell, "Notes en marge," 218–9.

[2] Strugnell, "Notes en marge," 218.

[3] Maurya P. Horgan, *Pesharim*, 264.

Fragment 1: Consideration of Genre Based on Form[4]

Frag. 1

[כול ר°[1
[בעת רעב ואשרֹ]   2
[רֹו היאֹה הצֹדֹקֹ]   3
[ספו את צד]   4
]°°[5

Based primarily on רעב "hunger" in line 2, Horgan suggested that fragment 1 might be "connected with" 4QpPsᵃ, in which the word occurs
three times (1–10 II, 1; III, 2, 4). The only secure formal trace of the
genre pesher, however, is found in frag. 14, which Allegro reluctantly
placed in 4Q172. In frag. 1 it is possible to reconstruct the formulaic
expressions פשרו in line 3 and ואשר אמר in line 2.[5] The basis for
such a proposal for line 2 is ואשר. In the Dead Sea Scrolls the relative
pronoun אשר with a copula is practically always followed by a verb
in the 3rd pers. sg. masc. In about half of the cases the verb that follows is אמר, and the phrase ואשר אמר is without exception found in
exegetical texts, most of which are pesharim.[6] But how about the other
cases containing verbs other than אמר? Do they seriously throw doubt
on the solution suggested, that line 2 (and 3) contains remains from
lost exegetical formulas?

Most instances of ואשר followed by a verb other than אמר occur in
legal texts, typically in the protasis of casuistic rules fixing the punishment for various violations, e.g., "and whoever lies knowingly, shall
be punished for six months."[7] Negated clauses introduced by ואשר
express prohibitions. Besides legal texts, there are only a few instances
of ואשר followed by verbs other than אמר. Two of these are found

---

[4] The transcriptions below of frags. 1 and 4 result from discussions with Jesper
Høgenhaven and Søren Holst. Up to this point our assessments have been based on
the study of photographs.

[5] In light of this there are possibly traces of such a formula also in line 1.

[6] 4Q159 (4QOrdinances) 5 3; 4Q183 (4QHistorical Work) 1 II, 9; 4Q217 (4Qpap-
Jubileesᵇ) 5 2; the one instance found in 4Q159 is located in frag. 5 with a pesher-like
character not found in the rest of the document. In the various manuscripts of the
Damascus Document (4Q266 6 I, 8; 8 II, 8; 4Q270 6 II, 19; 4Q271 3 4; 4 II, 7; 4Q272 1
I, 17) the phrase ואשר אמר introduces scriptural quotations from the Torah, namely
Leviticus.

[7] 1QS V, 14, 15, 16; VI, 25–26; VII, 3–4 (quoted), 5, 8, 9, 10, 13, and parallel texts
in 4Q256; 4Q258; 4Q259; 4Q261; 4Q266. Furthermore, it also occurs in the regulative
contexts of 4Q267; 4Q270; 4Q271; 4Q274; 4Q416; CD XIV, 21.

within the section of 1QM X, 1–8, in the introductions of scriptural citations. Even if the syntactical environment of ואשר is different and much less formal here than in the pesharim and the exegetical texts referred to previously, the function of ואשר is likewise to introduce scriptural quotations.[8] Finally, in only four cases ואשר occurs in syntactical environments differing significantly from the ones treated up to this point and in texts of differing genres.[9]

The distribution of the phrase ואשר in the Dead Sea Scrolls makes legal texts (casuistic definitions of punishment; prohibitions) and exegetical texts, particularly pesharim, by far the most probable types of context for this phrase. The total number of instances is distributed evenly between the two types. Therefore, the occurrence of ואשר in line 2 supports the impression that this piece of text could belong to an exegetical/pesherite context, but it suggests at the same time a legal context as equally probable. In either case ואשר is most probably part of an impersonal and more or less formulaic passage.

However, the occurrence of the prepositional phrase בעת רעב points to an interpretative context as more likely than a legal one (and the argument hinges not on the fact that רעב also occurs in other pesharim). Common sense paired with an investigation of the distribution of the prepositional phrase בעת followed by a nomen rectum in the Dead Sea Scrolls shows that it is common in texts with a historical or eschatological focus (particularly in didactic and narrative texts), but is not used once in casuistic (timeless) rulings.[10] In sum, the occurrence of בעת רעב in line 2 corroborates Horgan's cautious suggestion

---

[8] In both cases and contrary to what we find in introductory formulae in exegetical texts, the verb following ואשר has a personal subject. It appears relatively clearly from the context that Moses must be the subject of ואשר הגיד לנו in line 1, introducing a quotation from Deut 20:2–5. In the introduction in line 6 to the next scriptural quotation, Num 10:9, God (addressed in the 2nd pers.) is the subject, the one who speaks throughout the subsequent scriptural quotation, but it is perfectly clear that it is Moses who mediates his message: ואשר ד[בר]תה ביד מושה לאמור. In both cases the verbs are personal because the author of 1QM not only refers to authoritative scriptural passages, but also recalls the historical context of their origins. This, however, does not weaken the point that ואשר, as in exegetical literature serves to mark the introduction of a scriptural quotation.

[9] In three cases the subject of the verb is seemingly personal, and the initial אשר functions either as a conjunction, (4Q423 5 1; 4Q504 1–2 VI, 6) or as a relative pronoun referring to the object (4Q419 1 2). In 4Q416 2 IV 6 אשר is the indefinite subject in an instruction not identical but similar to the casuistic rulings mentioned above.

[10] There are, for instance, no occurrences in casuistic rulings in 1QS, but several in general instructions to the maskilim, particularly in column IX.

that ואשר אמר "might possibly be restored,"[11] and the combination
of these expressions renders an exegetical context, presumably pesher,
the most probable context type or genre.

FRAGMENT 4: CONSIDERATION OF GENRE BASED ON SCRIPTURAL CONNECTIONS

Frag. 4

[כן ויזנ֯ו֯ כֹעֹם]	1
[העול ברחו]	2
[פחז עמורה]	3
[בוערת וגם כ∘]	4
[לבבם	5
[∘איתיב ב∘]	6

Strugnell suggested that line 4 of this fragment, because of the participle
בוערת, could be related to Hos 7:2–6. On the other hand, he refuted
on material grounds that frag. 4 could be part of 4QpHos B; against
Allegro, Strugnell did not see any evidence that any of the fragments
of 4Q172 might belong to 4QpHos B.[12] Even so, an investigation of
possible scriptural links shows that Hosea, as well as Zephaniah, could
be quoted in this fragment. A closer look at the context of 4Q172 4 4
suggests inspiration from the book of Hosea. The phrase לבבם in line
5 has its counterpart in Hos 7:2 (לִלְבָבָם) and 7:6 (לִבָּם). These are the
only scriptural instances of לבב with a 3. pers. plural pronominal suffix. Elsewhere in the Dead Sea Scrolls לבבם is employed in a negative
characterization of evil people (1QHᵃ XIV 25(22)), a usage that agrees
with Hosea, particularly 7:2: "but they do not consider that I remember their wickedness." The verb בער in line 4 and the subject phrase
לבבם occur in relative proximity in Hosea, within vv. 7:2–4 (as well
as 7:4–6). In favour of seeing lines 4 and 5 as reflecting Hos 7:2–6 is
the occurrence in line 1 of the verb ויזנו, "and they commit adultery."[13]
This verb is frequently used in Hosea, particularly in ch. 4, and the
theme of committing adultery runs through the book from the very

---

[11] Horgan, *Pesharim*, 264. Indirectly, the restoration of פשרו in line 3 is supported as well.

[12] Strugnell, "Notes en marge," 218.

[13] The proposed reading roughly corresponds to that of Strugnell ([כן ויזנו עמם]) against that of Allegro ([בהיותו עמם]), who is followed by Horgan. See PAM 40.579.

beginning (1:2). Even if the verb זנה is not used in ch. 7, the theme of adultery is present in the very context we are discussing through the participle מְנָאֲפִים ("adulterers/committing adultery") in Hos 7:4.

Before I go on to discuss more closely this connection between 4Q172 4 and Hosea 7, I will deal with the possible relation of line 3 to the book of Zephaniah, which may shed some light on the general idea pictured fragmentarily in the words of frag. 4. The words of line 3, פחז עמורה "the lewdness of Gomorrah," offer a negative characterization of Gomorrah. The root פחז is rare in the Hebrew Bible (the only instances being Zeph 3:4; Judg 9:4; Gen 49:4). In Zeph 3:4 פחז is used to describe the prophets of a defiled city, Jerusalem, so it seems, which has "listened to no voice; it has accepted no correction. It has not trusted in the Lord; it has not drawn near to its God" (Zeph 3:2). Only in Zeph 3:4 does פחז occur in the same, admittedly large, context as עמורה (Zeph 2:9): "Moab shall become as Sodom and the Ammonites as Gomorrah." Here Gomorrah and its twin city Sodom are displayed as archetypical cities of haughtiness, which will eventually fall. The various cities and peoples mentioned throughout Zephaniah 2 are all, so it seems, typologically comparable to Sodom and Gomorrah. Because of the unique combination in Zephaniah of Gomorrah and the rare word פחז, that scriptural text is most probably the source of פחז עמורה in 4Q172 4 3.

As we return to consider the relation between 4Q172 4 and Hosea, we should keep in mind the biblical picture of the fall of Gomorrah. The city is hit by a downpour of sulphur and fire (Gen 19:24; Amos 4:11). Thus it is likely that the burning in 4Q172 4 3 refers to the burning of Gomorrah *or* a city of its kind. Gomorrah occurs also in *Commentary on Genesis A* (4Q252 III, 2–3) in what seems to be an interpretation of the haggling scene in Genesis 18.[14] Is it also possible that the phrase, עמו[רה וגם העיר הזואת "Gom[orrah and also this city," in the *Commentary on Genesis A* refers to Gomorrah as the typological, negative role model for another city? Moreover, could "Gomorrah" in 4Q172 4 be a reference to such a negative role model for Ephraim, which in Hosea is repeatedly characterized by its adulterous behaviour (Hos 4:17ff; 5:3; 6:10; 7:8ff; 8:9)? Ephraim in the Dead

---

[14] George J. Brooke, "4Q Commentary on Genesis A," *Qumran Cave 4 XVII, Parabiblical Texts, Part 3* (ed. J. C. VanderKam, DJD XXII; Oxford: Clarendon Press, 1996), 185–207.

Sea Scrolls is depicted as a city in 4Q169 3–4 II, 7; and this fact favours such an interpretation, even though "Ephraim" in the text of Hosea is not a designation for a city as such, but for the idolizing northern kingdom. It is definitely conceivable that the author of 4Q172 4, with reference to the text of Zephaniah, unfolds a similar image of Ephraim as a city sharing the qualities of Gomorrah.

In the light of the proposed relationship between 4Q172 4 and Hosea, it is tempting to speculate about how the particular wording in line 4, which Strugnell saw as a possible rendering of Hos 7:2–6, might reflect the text of Hosea. Is it conceivable that בוערת in line 4 mirrors the scriptural phrase כְּמוֹ תַנּוּר בֹּעֵרָה ("[they are] like a heated oven") in Hos 7:4 whereas וגם כ] ("and also like") represents the parallel expression כְּאֵשׁ לֶהָבָה ("like a flaming oven") in 7:6? The speculative character of such a suggestion cannot be denied. What seems clear is that if the text of Hosea is used here, and I believe this is the case, it is not followed precisely and with punctiliousness. Rather, frag. 4 could be some sort of paraphrasing interpretation of Hosea or a part of it, utilising a reference to Zephaniah for its own interpretative purposes.

There are no traces of formulae by which we can define frag. 4 as a pesher text. Analysis of verbal forms and pronominal suffixes might support the notion that the text is a pesher. Two verbs in the 3rd masc. plur. could easily have had a negatively characterized subject, typical for the pesharim—"they *commit adultery*" in line 1 and in line 2, "men of iniquity *choose*," which seems to be a plausible reading.[15] Finally, לבבם in line 6 is elsewhere utilised in a negative characterization of evil people (1QHª XIV 25(22)). If frag. 4 is some sort of rewriting of Hosea material, however, these plural forms simply reflect or repeat the use of verbs and pronominal suffixes in the text of Hosea. The forms of ויזנו and לבבם are found in the text of Hosea directly, whereas בוערת could be reflected in the similarly feminine singular form בֹּעֵרָה (Hos 7:4). In either case, it is obvious that none of the words discussed are part of direct quotations from Hosea; they appear in a different order and have been squeezed into a smaller portion of text, a portion into which an allusion to Zephaniah is added.

---

[15] In the Dead Sea Scrolls עוּל is only found as the regens of a construct compound as in "men of iniquity" and "sons of iniquity."

How can we characterize this little piece of text, then? The group of texts labelled 4Q383–391 might be the right place to look for something similar. Their editor, Devorah Dimant, finally decided to divide these documents into two groups and named them, due primarily to their style and content, *Jeremiah Apocryphon* and *Pseudo-Ezekiel*.[16] With Strugnell she has distinguished several interpretative methods at work in the text of 4Q385 4, a larger fragment from the Pesudo-Ezekiel corpus.[17] Even if 4Q172 4 does not hold the amount of text we would need to make secure conclusions, it is reasonable to suggest that the following of those interpretative methods are employed in 4Q172 4, as well:

- Omission of repetitious or redundant details (because words seem to have been transferred from a larger portion of biblical text to the smaller portion contained in the fragment)
- Substitution of biblical terms (בוערת instead of בְּעֵרָה)
- Slight rewriting of the biblical version; shortening, simplification (word order differs from the biblical text; the immediate context of the biblical words employed differs as well)
- Use of parallel or related biblical texts (inserted allusion to Zephaniah)

I do not see any apparent sign of small interpretative additions, which is a further interpretative method mentioned by Dimant and Strugnell.

Monica Brady, who is critical of Dimant's content-based distinctions within the 4Q383–391 material, advocates seeing this whole group of texts as constituents of a larger exegetical work reworking and alluding to various scriptural works in order to convey a message of its own.[18] The scriptural texts employed are not only from the books of Jeremiah and Ezekiel, but also from the pentateuch and other prophetic books, which are concerned with the theme of exile from the land as punishment for unfaithfulness to the covenant. She bases her

---

[16] Devorah Dimant, *Qumran Cave 4. XXI: Parabiblical Texts, Part 4: Pseudo-Prophetic Texts* (DJD XXX; Oxford: Clarendon Press, 2001).

[17] Dimant and Strugnell worked the list out in relation to their joint work on 4Q385 4. They characterize the text as a non-pesherite, yet "intentional" and "explicit" abridgement of the Merkabah vision in Ezek 1. Devorah Dimant and John Strugnell, "The Merkabah Vision in *Second Ezekiel* (4Q385 4)," *RevQ* 14/55 (1990): 331–48.

[18] Monica Brady, "Biblical Interpretation in the 'Pseudo-Ezekiel' fragments (4Q383–391) from Cave Four," in *Biblical Interpretation at Qumran* (ed. Matthias Henze; Grand Rapids/Cambridge: Eerdmans, 2005), 88–109.

proposal primarily on the observation that the previously mentioned exegetical techniques are at play throughout the documents, some-times several of them within single larger fragments. Brady explicitly declares that those texts are not any of the following: copies of biblical books, commentaries, pesharim, complete reworkings of Jeremiah or Ezekiel or any other book in its entirety.[19]

I am not suggesting here that 4Q172 4 is part of this particular "larger exegetical work," even if in both corpuses the scribal hands can be characterized as "early Herodian." However, the text's dense fusing of elements from Hosea and Zephaniah suggests that it could be part of such a non-pesherite exegetical work, possibly including widespread scriptural passages.

The Texts of Hosea and Zephaniah Working Together

I will mention one of Brady's examples that I find particularly illus-trative in relation to the allusion to Zephaniah in 4Q172 4. In 4Q385 a 17 II, 4–9, which follows Nah 3:8–10 rather closely, the addressee is Amon, regardless of the fact that in the text of Nahum Niniveh is the addressee. Brady suggests that this shift in addressee is a way of adapting the text to the exegetical purpose of the writer. She is not very specific on this point, but in her overall interpretation of the group of texts under consideration, she sees the theme of exile as particularly important and resonant with the situation of the Dead Sea community as they lived "in the desert, away from other Jews."[20] The implication is that the author of this non-sectarian composition accentuated this exilic theme by directing the prophecy of Nahum against Amon and the Egyptians, repeating, as it were, the prophecy against the Egyptians by Jeremiah (Jer 46:25). Clearly, such specific conclusions cannot be made in the discussion of 4Q172 4. It is conceivable, however, that the fusing of elements from Hosea and Zephaniah is a similar exegeti-cal adaptation, melting together connotations to the whoring Ephraim with the idea of sinful Gomorrah and the scriptural knowledge of a group of faithless prophets in yet another city, Jerusalem. Perhaps, in the minds of the audience, the negative qualities of Ephraim and

---

[19] Ibid. 104–5.
[20] Ibid. 108.

the fate of Gomorrah were transferred to a particular group of people within the contemporary Jewish society in Jerusalem.

In Zephaniah the prophets of the defiled city are called not only פחזים, but also אנשי בגדות "faithless persons." In the sectarian Dead Sea Scrolls, similar characterisations are employed to describe adversaries. It is likely that the inspiration for those characterisations was found in scriptural texts like Zephaniah, which already contained a negative identification of an inner Jewish group, rather than scriptures using similar epithets in a generic, less polemical way.[21] With regard to the combination in 4Q172 4 of texts from Hosea and Zephaniah, it is worthwhile recalling that both of them make plenty of room for both positive and negative social entities within "Israel" and could therefore easily lend themselves to function as representations of Jewish society as polarized and divided according to a dualistic worldview.

Summary

Using two different strategies, we have been able to establish firmer opinions about the contents and literary character of frags. 1 and 4. It appears from the occurrence of ואשר that the meagre material of frag. 1 is the remains of formal language from exegetical literature or casuistic rulings. The casuistic rulings can be rejected. It seems safe to say that frag. 1 must have belonged in an exegetical context, very probably a pesher.

The technique used in frag. 4 is different, due to the character of what is extant. Though the fragment lacks formal traits, it has significant words, which point to the books of Hosea and Zephaniah as likely literary sources. The constellation of significant words in frag. 4 seems to reflect an exegetical praxis recognized also in larger fragments from 4Q383–391. Thus, the investigation leaves the impression that frag. 4 is part of an exegetical text reworking scriptural texts rather freely, and not a pesher or running commentary on one single scriptural text.

---

[21] Scriptural counterparts to אַנְשֵׁי בִגְדֹות, which have their counterparts in the sectarian Dead Sea Scrolls as well, occur in less polemic settings: Prov 29:27 (אִישׁ עֹול); מאִישׁ מרמה 43:1 (אִישׁ דמים ומרמה); Pss 5:7 (אִישׁ דמים ומרמה); Job 15:16 (אִישׁ שתה כמים עֹולה); 55:24 (אנשי דמים ומרמה) (ועֹולה). In these contexts, there are no hints those negatively defined should be found in a specific social entity, such as a particular professional group (prophets) or a particular city (the city of God, i.e. Jerusalem).

Because of the sparseness of the material, the suggestions made here cannot be conclusive, not least because they suggest two different genres in a single manuscript. Yet, the very different types of concordance work employed on the two fragments do contribute further to the determination of "the character or content of the texts," which Horgan thought impossible.

4Q173A: A PART OF AN ESCHATOLOGICAL MIDRASH?

SØREN HOLST
University of Copenhagen

What does one do with an individual unassigned Qumran fragment preserving a total of six lines with no more than two consecutive words in any of them? The subject of the present article[1] is one such tiny fragment, originally published by Allegro as frag. 5 of the Cave 4 *Pesher Psalms B*. That manuscript interprets passages of Pss 127 and 129 and (in this fragment) 118. Due to the handwriting as well as other material qualities of the fragment, however, Strugnell already described it as "at least half a century later, not necessarily belonging to the *pesher* genre, and seemingly unique among the Cave 4 fragments,"[2] while Skehan characterised it as "a stray bit."[3] Allegro himself, too, may have been toying with the idea that the fragment was to be understood independently of 4QpPs[b], since in several of Allegro's own photographs (now available as images 28.D5–D9 on the microfiche reproductions of the *Allegro Qumran Photograph Collection*) it occurs together with 4QParaphrase of Gen and Exod (4Q422) frag. 10a,[4] and until recently, subsequent publications have followed suit, in one case giving the name

---

[1] To an even greater extent than is so often the case in Qumran scholarship, the present piece of work is a collaborative effort, originating in the weekly seminar of the Qumran Initiative of the University of Copenhagen where Trine Bjørnung Hasselbalch, Jesper Høgenhaven and not least Bodil Ejrnæs contributed most of the ideas here presented. The fact that Bodil has recently felt compelled to resign from her position has been a severe blow to the working environment of our department.

[2] "plus récent d'au moins un demi siècle...n'est pas nécessairement du genre littéraire *pešer*...semble une pièce unique parmi les fragments de *4 Q*" (Strugnell, "Notes en marge," 219).

[3] Patrick W. Skehan, "The Divine Name at Qumran, in the Masada Scroll, and in the Septuagint," *Bulletin of the International Organization for Septuagint and Cognate studies* 13 (1980): 14–44 (27).

[4] *The Allegro Qumran Photograph Collection* (ed. George J. Brooke with the collaboration of Helen K. Bond) Leiden/New York: E.J. Brill, 1996, cf. George J. Brooke, "The Allegro Qumran Photograph Collection: Old Photos and New Information," in *The Provo International Conference on the Dead Sea Scrolls: Technological Innovations, New Texts, and Reformulated Issues* (ed. Donald W. Parry and Eugene Ulrich; STDJ 30; Leiden: Brill, 1999), 13–29 (25).

"House of Stumbling Fragment" to the item,[5] but otherwise abstaining from identifying its content or appurtenance.[6]

Two recent brief articles, however, attempt a more precise interpretation of the content of this fragment. David Hamidović suggests renaming the fragment as "Return to the Jerusalem Temple."[7] He conjectures that the text contained a reproach aimed at the Jerusalem priesthood, whose temple the text describes in l. 2 as a בית מכשול, a "maison de scandale," the same line from which Horgan took the name "House of Stumbling" for the text. When the text talks in l. 4 of the gate of God where the righteous enter, according to Hamidović this is an expression of the expectation of the Essenes that they would soon be reentering a newly purified temple. Émile Puech takes issue with a number of the readings of Hamidović, as well as of previous editions,[8] and rejects the idea that a return to the temple is envisioned, but agrees with Hamidović in seeing in the text a series of reproaches against the Levitical priesthood concerning the duties associated with the temple service.

Our attempt at interpretation has focused less on reading a coherent content out of the few remaining words on the fragment, and more on trying to specify the wider literary context within which those few preserved words might fit. Without a doubt, the fragment is aptly described by Strugnell as "unique" in the sense that it is almost certainly the only preserved fragment of the manuscript it once belonged to, and thus there is no question of physically matching it up with other fragments. Nor is there any overlap with other existing texts to identify it as stemming from another copy of a known text. But still, "unique" is a big word, and while there has been universal agreement, since the publication of Strugnell's work, on the fragment's non-association with the manuscript made up by 4QpPs[b] frags. 1–4, it makes sense to consider whether anything can be said of the relative plausibility of linking such an orphaned fragment with one of the known Qumran compositions. In order to determine a literary "matrix," so to

---

[5] Maurya P. Horgan, "House of Stumbling Fragment (4Q173a = 4Q173 frg. 5 olim)," in PTSDSSP 6B. 363–5.

[6] Horgan, *Pesharim*, 266 + appendix, 61; Florentino García Martínez and Eibert J. C. Tigchelaar, *DSSSE* 1. 350–1.

[7] David Hamidović, "Le retour au temple de Jérusalem (*4Q173a olim 4Q173 5*)?," *RevQ* 24/94 (2009): 283–6.

[8] Émile Puech, "*4Q173a*: Note épigraphique," *RevQ* 24/94 (2009): 287–90.

speak, within which it can be plausibly placed due to its inter-textual relations, we have primarily investigated the references or allusions to biblical passages and concepts that it shares with other texts.

We propose the following reading and translation of the preserved writing on the fragment. We have gone less far than Hamidović and Puech in trying to reconstruct what is no longer there, but touch upon the matter below in relation to l. 5, where the interpretation of the one preserved word is heavily dependent on the understanding of the half-preserved ones preceding and following it.

4Q173a (previously 4Q173 frag. 5)

1 [ם מ בּרו[∘∘
2 [בּית מכשול]
3 [∘ת המזבח י∘]
4 זה] השער לאל צדי[קים יבאו בו
5 נ] קִיבי שמות וחרותֹ[
6 [ל ליעקֹוֹבֹ]

1.] [
2.]house of stumbling[
3.]of the altar [
4.]the gate of *El*. The righ[teous shall enter through it
5. app]ointed by name, and engra[ved
6.]to Jacob[

Considered on its own, the only thing that might relate the fragment to the *pesher* genre, is the probable quotation in l. 4 from Ps 118:20, זה] השער לאל צדי[קים יבאו בו, "this is] the gate of *El*. The righ[teous shall enter through it." Strictly speaking, we are not dealing with a literal quotation, as לאל, written in a cryptic script of sorts,[9] has been

---

[9] The writing of the divine name "El" is unusual. According to Emanuel Tov, the letters "look like Greek and Latin letters with Hebrew values (α = א and L = ל), and therefore resemble the Cryptic A script of 4QHoroscope, which includes a few Greek letters", cf. Emanuel Tov, "Letters of the Cryptic A script and paleo-Hebrew letters used as scribal marks in some Qumran scrolls," *DSD* 2 (1995): 330–9, (334). The Cryptic A alphabet, as evidenced in 4Q249, 4Q298, 4Q317, and the other texts cited by Stephen Pfann in "The Writings in Esoteric Scripts from Qumran," in *The Dead Sea Scrolls: Fifty Years after Their Discovery 1947–1997. Proceedings of the Jerusalem Congress, July 20–25, 1997* (ed. Lawrence H. Schiffman, Emanuel Tov and James C. VanderKam; Jerusalem: Israel Exploration Society, 2000, 177–89), does not include Greek letters. The occurrence of Greek *alpha* and *beta* are a special feature of 4Q186. The *aleph* of 4Q173a 4 does,

substituted for the tetragrammaton with a prefixed ל, which is found in the biblical text.[10]

Assuming this identification of the line to be certain, however, Allegro took this as the basis for proposing that the word מזבח in l. 3 is yet another quotation from Ps 118, coming from verse 27, אִסְרוּ־חַג בַּעֲבֹתִים עַד־קַרְנוֹת הַמִּזְבֵּחַ, but even if the preceding word is correctly reconstructed as קרנות, this, in any case, is the most frequent noun to occur in a construct relation to מִזְבֵּחַ in the Hebrew Bible and does not necessarily indicate any connection with Ps 118; in addition, the extant remains of the following word in l. 3 bear no resemblance to the context in Ps 118, so the assumption can hardly be upheld. Furthermore, the root פשר, or other technical terms characteristic of the *pesher* literature, are not found in the fragment, and taken apart from 4QpPs[b], the fragment does not seem to provide any evidence that it was once part of a continuous *pesher* text.

To consider the fragment as part of some sort of thematic *pesher*, or even as a patchwork of scriptural passages without explicit *pesher* content, may do better justice to what remains of this text. Apart from the relatively certain near-quotation of Ps 118:20, the unusual expression "house of stumbling", בית מכשול, in l. 2 seems the most obvious key. It is reminiscent of the "stumbling block", צוּר מִכְשׁוֹל, in Isa 8:14.[11] This passage seems to loom large as the interpretative context of two other occurrences of מכשול in the DSS, although unfortunately

---

however, have a remarkable resemblance to the *aleph* of Cryptic A. The *lamed* is unusually shaped and may be interpreted as an idiosyncratic version of either the paleo-Hebrew or the standard square letter.

[10] Writing the tetragrammaton in Paleo-Hebrew characters (e.g. 4QpPs[a] III 14 and passim) or replacing it by four dots (e.g. 4QTanh 1–2 I, 6–7 and passim) is a well-known phenomenon; cf. Emanuel Tov, *Scribal Practices and Approaches Reflected in the Texts Found in the Judean Desert* (STDJ 54; Leiden: Brill, 2004), 218–21. But it its not entirely undisputed whether the broken line is in fact a quotation at all; cf. Ulrich Dahmen, *Psalmen- und Psalter-Rezeption im Frühjudentum: Rekonstruktion, Textbestand, Struktur und Pragmatik der Psalmenrolle 11QPs[a] aus Qumran* (STDJ 49; Leiden: Brill, 2003), 109.

[11] In the Hebrew Bible, no other construction has מִכְשׁוֹל as the absolute part of a construct relation (and the exact collocation בית מכשול is found neither in the Hebrew Bible, Qumran corpus, Rabbinic writings nor anywhere else). In the DSS, we do find נגע מכשול, "affliction (that causes) stumbling" in 1QH[a] VIII, 33 [XVI, 15] and בזקי מכשול, "with shackles that make one stumble" in 1QH[a] XVI 36 [VIII 35]; translation and line numbering according to Hartmut Stegemann, Eileen M. Schuller and Carol A. Newsom, *Qumrân Cave 1.III: 1QHodayot[a]* (DJD XL; Oxford: Clarendon Press, 2009).

they too are quite fragmentary: 4QBéat (4Q525) 23 9 talks about צדק
וכצור מכ]שול, "justice, and as a rock of st[umbling", and 4QInstruc-
tion^d (4Q418) 168 2 has ל נגף מכשול], reminiscent of the context in
Isa 8:14, וּלְאֶבֶן נֶגֶף וּלְצוּר מִכְשׁוֹל.

Isaiah 8:14 and Ps 118:20 are found in combination in no other
Qumran text, nor is Psalm 118 quoted on its own in any other non-
biblical Qumran text. But one text from antiquity does quote the passage from Isa 8:14 about the stumbling block in connection with a
passage from Psalm 118 (v. 22), namely 1 Pet 2:4–10. Assuming that
the combination of certain passages or motifs might be to some degree
conventional rather than completely arbitrary, and that the usage in
1 Peter might be inherited from other contemporary Jewish schools of
interpretation, could the similarity between our fragment and 1 Peter
conceivably cast light on the relation to other texts within the Qumran
corpus?

One Qumran text that does quote Isaiah 8 (v. 11) is 4QFlorilegium
or *Eschatological Commentary A* (4Q174) which combines its reference to Isaiah 8 with 2 Samuel 7, Deuteronomy 33 and other passages.
The reason for directing attention to 4Q174 is that 4QFlorilegium and
1 Peter share the thematic motif of the temple as a metaphor for the
group or congregation. In 4Q174 frags. 1–3 I, 6–7 we have "and he
commanded to build for himself a temple of man, to offer him in it,
before him, the works of thanksgiving,"[12] and 1 Pet 2:5 exhorts its
readers thus, "like living stones, let yourselves be built into a spiritual
house." The temple metaphor brings to mind 2 Samuel 7, which is
quoted explicitly in 4Q174 and implied by 1 Pet 2:5 talking about the
believers being "built" (οἰκοδομεῖσθε) into a "spiritual house" (οἶκος
πνευματικὸς). Reading 4Q173a in light of these two texts, we seem to
find a shared thematic and terminological (cultic) pattern.

Taking the legible words of 4Q173a in sequence: בית (or οἶκος) is
shared by 4Q174 frags. 1–3 I, 2 and 1 Pet 2:5; and, notably, מכשול too
plays a role in 4Q174 frags. 1–3 I, 8 as well as being shared by 1 Pet 2:8

---

[12] General agreement seems finally to have been reached, on the grounds of physical examination of the actual manuscript, that the passage in question reads מעשי
תודה and not מעשי תורה, cf. Steudel, *Der Midrasch zur Eschatologie*, 94, Brooke,
"Allegro Collection," 21, and Torleif Elgvin, "An Incense Altar from Qumran," *DSD*
9 (2002): 20–33 (28). But divergent voices may still be heard, cf. Jacob Milgrom, "Florilegium: A Midrash on 2 Samuel and Psalms 1–2 (4Q174 = 4QFlor)," in PTSDSSP
6B. 248–63 (248).

(the Greek πέτρα σκανδάλου is a direct rendition of the Hebrew צור
מכשול rather than a quotation from the Septuagint); מזבח is shared
by 4Q174 frags. 6–7 5 (quoting Deut 33:8–11), which links up with
the cultic terminology, used in a metaphorical fashion, in 4Q174 frags.
1–3 I, 6–7 and 1 Pet 2:5. צדיקים is found, in connection with the verb
זבח, in 4Q174 frags. 9–10 1 (quoting Deut 33:19–21); and יעקוב may
be safely reconstructed in 4Q174 frags. 6–7 5 in a quotation from Deut
33:8–11. In schematic fashion, this may be represented thus:

	4Q173a	4Q174	1 Pet
בית	2	frags. 1–3 I, 2	2:5
מכשול	2	frags. 1–3 I, 8	2:8
מזבח	3	frags. 6–7 5	
צדיקים	4	frags. 9–10 1	
יעקוב	6	(frags. 6–7 5)	

If, rather than list shared Hebrew words, we look at shared biblical
references, we notice that beyond the quotation from Psalm 118 and
the seeming allusion to Isaiah 8, we seem to find 4Q173a placing itself
within an inter-textual pattern comprising also 2 Samuel 7 and Deuteronomy 33, a pattern shared by our text with 4Q174 and 1 Peter 2.
4Q173a has elements of all four, while Florilegium and 1 Peter each
leave out one (Florilegium quotes Deuteronomy 33, 2 Samuel 7 and
Isaiah 8, leaving out Psalm 118, while 1 Peter quotes Isaiah 8 and Psalm
118 and alludes to 2 Samuel 7, leaving out only Deuteronomy):

text	Deut 33	2 Sam 7	Isa 8	Ps 118
quoted or alluded to in				
4Q173a	x	x	x	x
4Q174	x	x	x	
1 Pet 2		x	x	x

The combination of motifs from 2 Samuel 7 and Isaiah 8, which recurs
in all three texts, may help us throw light on that peculiar expression of 4Q173a 2, בית מכשול, "house of stumbling." It seems to be
decidedly negative, describing an aspect of the counter-group or

community,[13] and it is reminiscent of the use made of word play on the root כשל to define the position of one group against others, which we find in a number of "sectarian" Qumran texts.[14] As its antithesis, the expression בית נאמן, "an established house," suggests itself, and this is in fact found in 2 Sam 7:16. It seems natural for texts expressing the Qumranic world view by means of exegesis of 2 Samuel 7 to designate the insider community a בית נאמן and its opponents a בית מכשול (the passage of the "tested cornerstone and sure foundation" in Isa 28:16, which is explicitly quoted in our verse from 1 Pet 2:6, would fit in excellently as part of the positive self-portrayal here). In the Qumran-related literature, we do in fact find בית נאמן used for the repentant community in CD III, 19. In that context the opponents are the מואסים, "those who reject" the Torah; in 4Q174 it is the sons of Belial, and in 1 Peter the ἀπιστοῦσιν, "non-believers," but the shared pattern of the faithful securely founded on the rock as opposed to the wayward ones that stumble, is easily discernable.

According to Allegro's reading, one further connection could be posited between 4Q173a and 4Q174 in the form of a shared use of the root שמם. In 4Q173a 5, Allegro—followed by most subsequent work on this fragment—read שמות as the plural of BH שַׁמָּה, and translated the word as "waste places." This was based on the parallel with the following word, which Allegro read as וחריב]ות, "ruins," making the interpretation of שמות as "waste places" an obvious choice.[15] In 4Q174

---

[13] In Isa 8:14 it is God who becomes for Israel a sanctuary, a stone for stumbling, etc.; cf. Hans Kosmala, "The Three Nets of Belial (A Study in the Terminology of Qumran and the New Testament)," *ASTI* 4 (1965): 91–113. In the first of the two Hodayot passages mentioned in note 11, the stumbling-inducing affliction is something *against* which the hymnist prays for divine protection, and even more so in the second of these passages where the shackles which cause stumbling originate with the enemies of the hymnist. While God may thus be the prime mover behind the fact of stumbling, the stumbling itself definitely is negatively defined, and the allusion to Isa 8:14 would make good sense as an implicit identification of the group's opponents with the lapsed "Israel" which is chastised by God in the Isaianic verse.

[14] James E. Harding, "The Wordplay between the Roots כשל and שכל in the Literature of the Yaḥad," *RevQ* 19/73 (1999): 69–82.

[15] That the word חָרְבָּה and the root שמם were used together, is in evidence in Ezek 36:33–35 (I am grateful to Prof. Moshe Bernstein for supplying this connection on the spur of the moment); Ezekiel, incidentally, is responsible for more than half the occurrences of מִכְשׁוֹל in the Hebrew Bible. The biblical passage in question is not interpreted or quoted in any of the Qumran texts, but a passage in 4QPseudo-Ezekielᵃ (4Q386 1 II, 2), in which the prophet sees the land of Israel lying waste, is at least thematically related.

frags. 1–3 I, 5 the word שמה is used in an exegesis of 2 Samuel 7 by means of allusions to passages dealing with the marginalisation of those who are not allowed into the house of the Lord. This metaphorical matrix of juxtaposing those belonging in the בית נאמן to those excluded from it and associated with waste places, would make excellent sense as a context for 4Q173a. The bottom stroke of the proposed ב in the reading וחריב]ות is nowhere to be seen in even the earliest photograph (PAM 41.515), however, and the reading וחרות]ים, or just וחרות], "engraved," proposed by Hamidović and Puech, must be the correct one.[16] The two authors consequently construe the word in 4Q173a 5 as the far more frequent שֵמות, "names," which means that a parallel to the use of שמם in 4Q174 is no longer in evidence.[17]

As 4Q174 is now widely recognised to be part of a collection of eschatological commentaries comprising at least also 4Q177 (formerly "Catena A") and possibly more manuscripts,[18] an association of 4Q173a to one member of this group of manuscripts necessarily involves the rest of the related manuscripts, notably 4Q177. And 4Q177 does in fact share two features of the vocabulary of 4Q173a namely the root כשל (frags. 10–11 7) and the name of Jacob (frags. 1–4 15); so the table above should be expanded to look like this:

	4Q173a	4Q174	1 Pet	4Q177
בית	2	frags. 1–3 I, 2	2:5	
מכשול	2	frags. 1–3 I, 8	2:8	frags. 10–11 7
מזבח	3	frags. 6–7 5		
צדיקים	4	frags. 9–10 1		
יעקוב	6	(frags. 6–7 5)		frags. 1–4 15

---

[16] Hamidović, "Le retour," 285. Puech, "Note épigraphique," 289–90. Cf. the evaluation by Strugnell, "Notes en marge," 220, that the readings of ב here and in l. 3 are "vraiment peu plausibles."

[17] The reading and translation of Hamidović indicate that it is the ones bearing the names that are "engraved," whereas Puech suggests that a new sentence begins with the word וחרות. In favour of the latter it may be mentioned that among the one Biblical (Ex 32:16) and more than a dozen Qumran occurrences of the verb חרת, it is almost exclusively God who does the engraving, and what is engraved is most often his חוק or ברית or the like. Only in 4Q266 11 16 (and the partially reconstructed parallel in 4Q269 16 14) does the root חרת describe the registration of human actions at the hand of the מבקר.

[18] Steudel, *Der Midrasch zur Eschatologie*, 152–7.

Obviously there is no such thing as "proving" that just because texts share frames of reference, they also have a shared origin (and certainly as for 1 Peter, we would ourselves prefer not to entertain any such idea in any serious way), and suggesting that 4Q173a be renamed e.g. *Eschatological Commentary F?* would probably not be a good idea. But the connections or quasi-connections noted above might give a very broad and somewhat fuzzy indication of the sort of literature that the fragment originally belonged to. The question of how to determine at least the very approximate affiliation of "homeless" fragments, however, still awaits a more comprehensive answer.

FROM FLORILEGIUM OR MIDRASH TO COMMENTARY: THE PROBLEM OF RE-NAMING AN ADOPTED MANUSCRIPT

GEORGE J. BROOKE
University of Manchester

INTRODUCTION

On the one hand my mother was very certain on the matter: if one was to acquire a dog as a pet from a dog rescue home, the dog should never be renamed—there should be no disrespect for the integrity of the dog's identity and no deliberate inflicting of psychological harm. On the other hand, although there are many exceptions, especially since the Second World War, often upon marriage women in Anglo-Saxon contexts have adopted the family names of their husbands and stopped using their maiden names. To some extent the subject of this paper concerns whether 4Q174 and its counterparts should be treated like a newly acquired rescue dog or an Anglo-Saxon wife in traditional mode. The possible need to rename compositions has to be considered by all who are responsible for revising principal editions of manuscripts, by all who have in a sense adopted manuscripts from their principal editors; this essay tries to articulate some of the criteria that should be considered when renaming is proposed. What title should be given to 4Q174 and the manuscripts related to it in the revised Discoveries in the Judaean Desert (of Jordan) V? This study gives priority to 4Q174 in the discussion, attempts to set out some of the issues in deciding upon a title, and makes a proposal for a way forward.

When I became the editor of the principal edition of 4Q252, I spent many hours thinking about what the composition should be called. The first fragment of the manuscript to be discussed extensively was published by John M. Allegro with the title *Patriarchal Blessings*.[1] Józef T. Milik soon came to realize that that fragment belonged with several others that contained exegetical passages on various parts of Genesis and he wrote to Allegro arranging a swap: Allegro returned the

---

[1] John M. Allegro, "Further Messianic References in Qumran Literature," *JBL* 75 (1956): 174–87.

Patriarchal Blessings to Milik and in return received 4Q341 and as a result the principal edition of Allegro's allocated manuscripts did not contain an edition of *Patriarchal Blessings*.[2] For Milik the form and content of *Patriarchal Blessings* was that of a *pesher* and the technical term did indeed occur in one of the extant portions of the text in a formula introducing the interpretation of Gen 49:3–4. Milik designated 4Q252 as 4QpGen A, using just part of the contents of the composition to designate the whole. In the *Preliminary Concordance* it was referred to as 4QpGen[a].[3] Milik retained 4QpGen A in his subsequent writings.[4] But when what remained of the whole scroll was released in 1991, it soon became apparent that most of what survived was something other than *pesher* in the strict sense.[5] And so it seemed to me that a new name was required. Because there had been much, generally negative, debate about the use of the term midrash for any of the sectarian exegetical literature from the Qumran caves, in effect that it was an inappropriate emic category, I decided upon the use of what in modern English is a relatively neutral and thus transferable descriptor, an etic category: Commentary.[6] And so 4Q252 and its counterparts were labelled as *Commentary on Genesis A, B, C,* and *D*,

---

[2] Allegro published 4Q341 in John M. Allegro, *The Dead Sea Scrolls and the Christian Myth* (Newton Abbot: Westbridge Books, 1979), 235–40. For other studies of this fragment and further remarks see George J. Brooke, "4Q341: An Exercise for Spelling and for Spells?" in *Writing and Ancient Near Eastern Society: Papers in Honour of Alan R. Millard* (ed. Piotr Bienowski, Christopher B. Mee and Elizabeth A. Slater; JSOTSup 426; London: T & T Clark International, 2005), 271–82; Phillip R. Callaway, "Some Thoughts on Writing Exercise (4Q341)," *Qumran Chronicle* 13/2–4 (2006): 147–51.

[3] Raymond E. Brown, Joseph A. Fitzmyer, William G. Oxtoby and J. Teixidor (arranged by Hans-Peter Richter), *A Preliminary Concordance to the Hebrew and Aramaic Fragments from Qumrân Caves II–X* (Göttingen: Printed Privately, 1988).

[4] Józef T. Milik, "*Milkî-ṣedeq* et *Milkî-reša'* dans les anciens écrits juifs et chrétiens," *JJS* 23 (1972): 95–144 (p. 138).

[5] The text was first offered in transliteration by Ben-Zion Wacholder and Martin G. Abegg, *A Preliminary Edition of the Unpublished Dead Sea Scrolls: Hebrew and Aramaic Texts from Cave Four. Fascicle 2* (Washington: Biblical Archaeology Society, 1992), 212, labelled as "4Q252 Pesher Genesis[a]," a title also used by Florentino García Martínez, *The Dead Sea Scrolls Translated: The Qumran Texts in English* (Leiden: Brill; Grand Rapids: Eerdmans, 1994), 213; also in the list in PTSDSSP 2. 225.

[6] In using the terms "emic" and "etic" I am not implying anything profoundly anthropological, but refer to matters that are "insider" and "culturally specific" or "outsider" and (supposedly) "culturally neutral." The categories have been used to good effect to clarify what is at stake in the debates about labelling texts as "Rewritten Bible" by Anders Klostergaard Petersen, "Rewritten Bible as a Borderline Phenomenon—Genre, Textual Strategy, or Canonical Anachronism?" in *Flores Florentino: Dead Sea Scrolls and Other Early Jewish Studies in Honour of Florentino García Martínez* (ed.

the upper case letters indicating that the manuscripts did not contain copies of the same composition, but something generically similar.[7] To anticipate where this paper is heading, let me say now that I will return to the term "Commentary" below but try to argue that it has both emic and etic qualities.

THE HISTORY OF THE NAMING OF 4Q174

In his first publication to mention the composition John M. Allegro wrote of a text that was "un florilège de passages bibliques avec commentaires tirés de l'Exode, II Samuel, Isaïe, Amos, les Psaumes et Daniel."[8] In another study written shortly afterwards he stated that the extract that he was discussing "comes from a work which I have provisionally entitled 4Q Florilegium."[9] He offered no explanation for his choice of title, but confirmed it in his subsequent publications.[10] J. T. Milik was aware that 4Q174 was named Florilegium not because it contained an anthology of extracts from various compositions, but because it was "un commentaire de caractère messianique dont le text biblique est un florilège,"[11] a "commentary of messianic character on a florilegium of biblical texts."[12] These designations are remarkably similar to Allegro's description in the communication in *Revue Biblique* of 1956: it is the biblical texts that are anthologised, not that the composition contains a bunch of flowers picked from various commentaries. When the principal edition of 4Q174 was published, it was this matter that exercised its main reviewer, John Strugnell: "ce titre [Florilegium], et celui de «Catena», me semble inexacts, un florilège devant être une

---

Anthony Hilhorst, Émile Puech and Eibert J.C. Tigchelaar; JSJSup 122; Leiden: Brill, 2007), 285–306, esp. pp. 297–9.

[7] See George J. Brooke, "Commentaries on Genesis and Malachi," in *Qumran Cave 4.XVII: Parabiblical Texts, Part 3* (ed. G. J. Brooke et al.; DJD XXII; Oxford: Clarendon Press, 1996), 185–236.

[8] John M. Allegro, "Communication," in "Le travail d'édition des fragments manuscrits de Qumrân," *RB* 63 (1956): 63.

[9] John M. Allegro, "Further Messianic References in Qumran Literature," 176.

[10] Especially the principal edition: John M. Allegro with the collaboration of Arnold A. Anderson, "174. Florilegium," in *Qumrân Cave 4.I: (4Q158-4Q186)* (DJDJ V; Oxford: Clarendon Press, 1968), 53.

[11] Józef T. Milik, *Dix ans de découvertes dans le desert de Juda* (Paris: Éditions du Cerf, 1957), 37.

[12] Józef T. Milik, *Ten Years of Discovery in the Wilderness of Judaea* (SBT 26; London: SCM Press, 1959), 41.

sélection de beaux texts, tandis qu'une chaîne est une suite de commentaires; il semble qu'on devrait plutôt interchanger les deux titres."[13] Theodor H. Gaster proposed "A 'Messianic' Florilegium."[14] In all this preliminary searching for a title, it is worth noting how readily the term "commentary" was used; there was little doubt that 4Q174 was a commentary of some sort.

André Dupont-Sommer used Allegro's "Florilegium" and noted that Allegro had suggested the composition was devoted to a "collection of midrashim on certain biblical texts." Dupont-Sommer commented sharply that "the word midrash, which appears once in the document itself (I, 14), must not be accepted here in the exact and limited sense it usually has in Rabbinic literature, where it describes stories depending on 'haggadic' tradition, but as I have indicated earlier (p. 306), in the broad and general sense of 'research, exegesis'. It would be preferable, therefore, to avoid the word midrashim, which is equivocal, and to call them instead pesharim, a term pointing direct to the genre of the Qumran Commentaries."[15] It is notable that Dupont-Sommer is aware of the problematic character of the word "midrash," though we might question nowadays his precise reasons for challenging the suitability of the term on the basis of its association with rabbinic haggadah.[16] Johann Maier used Allegro's "Florilegium", but put in brackets underneath the title "Sammlung eschatologischer Midrašim,"[17] echoing Allegro's own preliminary study on the text. Other early translators of scrolls who followed the principal title of Florilegium included Millar

[13] John Strugnell, "Notes en marge," 220.

[14] Theodor H. Gaster, *The Dead Sea Scriptures in English Translation* (Garden City, NY: Doubleday, 1956), 337.

[15] André Dupont-Sommer, *The Essene Writings from Qumran* (Oxford: Blackwell, 1961; Cleveland: World Publishing, 1962), 310. The French original uses the word "Florilège": André Dupont-Sommer, *Les Écrits esséniens découverts près de la Mer Morte* (Paris: Payot, 2nd edn, 1960), 324.

[16] One can sense in Dupont-Sommer's reservations, the influence of the thinking on "midrash" in terms of both form and content that was emerging in Paris in the early 1950s through the influence in particular of the work of Renée Bloch.

[17] Johann Maier, *Die Texte vom Toten Meer: Erste deutsche Gesamtübertragung* (München: Ernst Reinhardt Verlag, 1960), 1.185. Maier noted: "Nicht wie man an Hand von 10–14 meinte, ein Florilegium messianischer Stellen, sondern eine Sammlung »eschatologischer Midrašim«" (2.165).

Burrows,[18] Frank M. Cross,[19] Hans Bardtke,[20] and Franco Michelini Tocci.[21]

On the other hand, various scholars have pushed the label "midrash" to the fore. A. M. Habermann entitled 4Q174 *mdrš 'l 'hryt hymym*.[22] Until 1997 Geza Vermes provided a more or less straightforward English version of that: "A Midrash on the Last Days."[23] Yigael Yadin was more precise: "A Midrash on 2 Sam. vii and Ps. i-ii."[24] His title was echoed simultaneously by David Flusser.[25] William H. Brownlee noted that in keeping with the general preference for finding an appropriate Semitic name for each composition the title of Allegro's 1958 article might most suitably suggest 4Q Midrashim.[26] Not surprisingly several of these commentators operated in a Hebrew-speaking environment.

In essence, over the years two habitual practices have emerged; it would be too grand to call them schools of thought, since there is something basically pragmatic about each of them. On the one hand there are those who have been inclined to keep to the labels given in Allegro's preliminary studies and kept in the principal edition: Florilegium and Catena. Though there seems to be nothing deliberately

---

[18] Millar Burrows, *More Light on the Dead Sea Scrolls: New Scrolls and New Interpretations with Translations of Important Recent Discoveries* (New York: Viking, 1958), 401: "The Florilegium."

[19] Frank M. Cross, *The Ancient Library of Qumran and Modern Biblical Studies* (Garden City, NY: Doubleday, 1958), 165 n. 44: "Florilegium."

[20] Hans Bardtke, *Die Handschriftenfunde am Toten Meer: Die Sekte von Qumrān* (Berlin: Evangelische Haupt-Bibelgesellschaft, 1958), 298. He labels the extract he cites as follows: "Aus einem Florilegium messianischer Stellen mit Kommentar."

[21] Franco Michelini Tocci, *I manoscritti del Mar Morto* (Biblioteca di cultura moderna 631; Bari: Editori Laterza, 1967), 317–20.

[22] Abraham M. Habermann, *Mgylwt mdbr yhwdh* (Jerusalem: Machbaroth Lesifrut Publishing, 1959), 173.

[23] Geza Vermes, *The Dead Sea Scrolls in English* (Harmondsworth: Penguin Books, 1962), 243; he altered this title to "Midrash on the Last Days (4Q174)" in the 1987 third edition; he changed that to "Florilegium or Midrash on the Last Days" in *The Complete Dead Sea Scrolls in English* (London: Penguin Books, 1997), 493.

[24] Yigael Yadin, "A Midrash on 2 Sam. vii and Ps. i–ii (4Q Florilegium)," *IEJ* 9 (1959): 95–98. Yadin was supported by Menahem Ben-Yashar, "Noch zum *miqdaš ādām* in 4QFlorilegium," *RevQ* 10/40 (1979–1981): 587–8 (p. 587 n. 2).

[25] David Flusser, "Two Notes on the Midrash on II Sam. vii (4QFlorilegium)," *IEJ* 9 (1959): 99–109; reprinted in idem, *Judaism and the Origins of Christianity* (Jerusalem: Magnes Press, 1988), 88–98.

[26] William H. Brownlee, *The Meaning of the Qumrân Scrolls for the Bible with Special Attention to the Book of Isaiah* (New York: Oxford University Press, 1964), 88 n. 52.

anti-Jewish in such titles, they are of course designations that are from outside the literature itself; they are titles derived from genres that are found in their most developed form in early Christian tradition where such literature abounds under such Latin titles.[27] Amongst the group of scholars who have taken this particular pragmatic route have been George Brooke,[28] André Dupont-Sommer,[29] Florentino García Martínez,[30] Johann Maier,[31] Tryggve Kronholm,[32] Ida Fröhlich,[33] and Bodil Ejrnæs.[34]

On the other hand there have been those scholars who have preferred Allegro's other name for 4Q174, "Eschatological Midrash(im)." Some of these scholars have also used this label for 4Q177, and for the compositions on other fragmentary manuscripts which seem to be similar. This might well seem to resonate as a more Jewish label, and echoes the use of one of the terms that occurs in the manuscript itself. Preeminent amongst those taking this approach has been Annette Steudel.[35]

---

[27] Coming from outside the Qumran sectarian literature itself they are principally etic categories, but because they are from literature that does indeed have some affinities with the compositions they are attached to and are only somewhat distant in time and place from what they describe, they have a certain emic feel to them.

[28] George J. Brooke, *Exegesis at Qumran: 4QFlorilegium in its Jewish Context* (JSOTSup 29; Sheffield: JSOT Press, 1985).

[29] André Dupont-Sommer, "Florilège," in *La Bible: Écrits intertestamentaires* (ed. André Dupont-Sommer et al.; Bibliothèque de la Pléiade; Paris: Gallimard, 1987), 405–12.

[30] Florentino García Martínez, *Textos de Qumrán: Introducción y edición* (Madrid: Editorial Trotta, 1992), 183 ("4QFlorilegio"); idem, *The Dead Sea Scrolls Translated: The Qumran Texts in English* (Leiden: Brill; Grand Rapids: Eerdmans, 1994), 136.

[31] Johann Maier, *Die Qumran-Essener: Die Texte vom Toten Meer. Band II: Die Texte der Höhle 4* (UTB 1863; München: Ernst Reinhardt Verlag, 1995), 102.

[32] Tryggve Kronholm, "Qumranlitteraturen och den antika judendomen," in *Qumranlitteraturen: Fynden och forskningsresultaten* (ed. Tryggve Kronholm and Birger Olsson; Konferenser 35; Stockholm: Kungl. Vitterhets Historie och Antikvitets Akadamien, 1996), 80: "florilegiesamling." Kronholm speaks about 4Q174 in more detail as follows: "Florilegiesamlingen sammanställer på motsvarande sätt en rad texter (2 Sam 7:10–14; Ps 1:1; Ps 2:10 [sic]): det rör sig om en liten kommentar (*midrash*) med andragande av bibliskt parallellmaterial och med uppenbar syftning på ändens tid."

[33] Ida Fröhlich, *A Qumráni Szövegek Magyarul* (Studia Orientalia 1; Piliscsaba–Budapest: Pázmány Péter Katolikus Egyetem, Bölcsészettudományi Kar, Szent István Társulat, 2000), 358: "Florilegium (4Q174)."

[34] Bodil Ejrnæs, "Eksegetisk Litteratur," in *Dødehavsskrifterne og de antikke kilder om essæerne. 2. udvidede og reviderede udgave* (København: Forlaget ANIS, 2003), 244–5. Ejrnæs explains the title "(latin 'blomstersamling', dvs. antologi)."

[35] Annette Steudel, *Der Midrasch zur Eschatologie aus der Qumrangemeinde (4QMidr-Eschat[a.b]): Materielle Rekonstruktion, Textbestand, Gattung und traditionsgeschichtliche*

Other scholars have followed her lead, such as Émile Puech,[36] Jacob Milgrom,[37] Armin Lange,[38] and Ludwig Monti.[39]

Some few editions and translations carry both names, as is the case, for example with the Dead Sea Scrolls Reader.[40] This follows the practice of the official catalogue of the Dead Sea Scrolls in DJD XXXIX, which lists 4Q174 as "4Q174 Flor (= MidrEschat[a]?)."[41] Most Dead Sea Scrolls scholars are fully aware that compositions can carry more than one name or have their name changed. The issue now needs to be addressed squarely: should the name of 4Q174, 4Q177, and related fragmentary manuscripts be changed, perhaps for a final time, for the revised edition of DJD V?

Einordnung des durch 4Q174 ("Florilegium") und 4Q177 ("Catena A") repräsentieren Werkes aus den Qumranfunden (Leiden: Brill, 1994).

[36] Émile Puech, *La Croyance des esséniens en la vie future: immortalité, resurrection, vie éternelle? Histoire d'une croyance dans le Judaïsme ancien. II. Les données qumraniennes et classiques* (EB 22; Paris Gabalda, 1993), 572–91: "4QMidEsch = 4Q174 (Florilège) + 4Q177 (Catena)." Puech talks of "4QMidEsch" throughout his edition and commentary on the text.

[37] Jacob Milgrom, "Florilegium: A Midrash on 2 Samuel and Psalms 1–2 (4Q174 = 4QFlor)," in PTSDSSP 6B. 248–63 (248): "*Florilegium* (4Q174) is more appropriately entitled '*A Midrash on 2 Samuel and Psalms 1–2*';" the fragments "preserve a midrash."

[38] Armin Lange with Ulrike Mittmann-Richert, "Annotated List of the Texts from the Judaean Desert Classified by Content and Genre," in *The Texts from the Judaean Desert: Indices and An Introduction to the* Discoveries in the Judaean Desert *Series* (ed. Emanuel Tov; DJD XXXIX; Oxford: Clarendon Press, 2002), 115–64 (130). Lange and Mittmann-Richert prefer to call 174 and 177 "MidrEschat," but list them together with other compositions such as 11QMelch as "*Pesharim*: Thematic *Pesharim*."

[39] Ludwig Monti, *Una comunità alla fine della storia: Messia e messianismo a Qumran* (Studi biblici 149; Brescia: Paideia Editrice, 2006), 65, 145: "4Q174 + 177 (4QMidr, *Midrash escatologico*)." On p. 66 he also calls the composition "*pesher tematico*."

[40] Donald W. Parry and Emanuel Tov (eds), *Exegetical Texts* (DSSR 2; Leiden: Brill, 2004), 2–21: "4Q174 (Flor = MidrEschat[a]?), 177 (Catena A = MidrEschat[b]?), 178 (Unclass. Frags. = MidrEschat[c]?), 182 (Catena B = MidrEschat[d]?)."

[41] Emanuel Tov with the collaboration of Stephen J. Pfann, "List of the Texts from the Judaean Desert," in *The Texts from the Judaean Desert: Indices and An Introduction to the* Discoveries in the Judaean Desert *Series* (ed. Emanuel Tov; DJD XXXIX; Oxford: Clarendon Press, 2002), 27–114 (p. 50).

Two Key Issues

1. *Relevant Proximity*

It would seem to be self-evident that preference in naming a literary composition should be given to its author, compiler, or even copier.[42] No title survives in the fragmentary remains of 4Q174 other than the leading terminology of 4Q174 I, 14: *mdrš mn*. Neither are there any titles in the other manuscripts that have been closely associated with 4Q174. The term *pesher* has sometimes been used in general of this category of manuscripts; they are considered to contain "thematic pesharim,"[43] but it can be readily acknowledged that not every section of these compositions contains *pesher* in the strict sense, and so the term can result in a false view of some aspects of the composition. As a result the only strong candidate for consideration in terms of relevant proximity to what the author, compiler, or copyist might have preferred remains *mdrš*.[44]

Some attention should be given to whether and how the label midrash might be used in Jewish literature in the late Second Temple period.[45] The debate concerning midrash has only really taken off in the last two decades, spurred in part by a rediscovery of the possible significance of the scrolls within the broader fields of the study of rabbinic literature and hermeneutics.[46] Much of the debate in the last twenty years can be considered as focussed on diachronic issues, that is, debate about whether the term *mdrš* should be understood in the light of earlier scriptural tradition read forward to the late Second Temple period, in relation to rather limited contemporary evidence, or in terms of later rabbinic materials read back into the period before the fall of the Temple.[47]

---

[42] Here I am in search of an emic category.

[43] So Shani L. Berrin (Tzoref), "Pesharim," *EDSS* 2.644–47 (p. 646).

[44] This is the descriptive candidate that is clearly emic, i.e., meaningful to the author from within the culture concerned.

[45] Some of what follows on "midrash" is discussed in more detail in George J. Brooke, "*Pesher* and *Midrash* in Qumran Literature: Issues for Lexicography," *RevQ* 24/93 (2009–2010): 79–95.

[46] See the helpful summary of this recent orientation around the concept of midrash by Philip S. Alexander, "The Bible in Qumran and Early Judaism," in *Text in Context: Essays by Members of the Society for Old Testament Study* (ed. Andrew D. H. Mayes; Oxford: Clarendon Press, 2000), 35–62, esp. pp. 35–40, 44–6.

[47] For this approach to debates about interpretation in the Qumran scrolls see George J. Brooke, "From Bible to Midrash: Approaches to Biblical Interpretation in

The sectarian community responsible for this commentary literature was heavily scriptural, as indeed the commentary literature itself attests. So, might the label "midrash" show some continuity with scriptural antecedents? The substantive *mdrš* only occurs twice in the Hebrew scriptures, in 2 Chr 13:22, "the midrash of the prophet Iddo," and in 2 Chr 24:27, "written in the midrash of the book of the kings." In the former the term seems to designate the literary source from which the Chronicler took his account, whereas in the latter the NRSV renders the term not unsuitably as "Commentary." The extent of the influence of the books of Chronicles in the sectarian literature can be debated,[48] but the use of scriptural terminology to help produce a title with resonances of a literary genre has been challenged especially by those who have argued that it is the developing use of the verb *drš* that should be used to follow the changes in the semantic field of the root. In that respect in particular Johann Maier has argued that "scarcely sufficient evidence exists for a connotation of the verb *drš* like 'to interpret' or 'to expound' in early Jewish literature."[49] Maier has argued that as with its scriptural antecedents so the verb *drš* in the Qumran sectarian literature does not mean "to study,"[50] not least because the Greek translators did not use terms of interpretation to render the Hebrew and in the targumim the consistent rendering of *drš* is with forms of

the Dead Sea Scrolls by Modern Interpreters," in *Northern Lights on the Dead Sea Scrolls: Proceedings of the Nordic Qumran Network 2003–2006* (ed. Anders Klostergaard Petersen et al.; STDJ 80; Leiden: Brill, 2009), 1–19.

[48] See George J. Brooke, "The Books of Chronicles and the Scrolls from Qumran," in *Reflection and Refraction: Studies in Biblical Historiography in Honour of A. Graeme Auld* (ed. Robert Rezetko, Timothy H. Lim, W. Brian Aucker; VTSup 113; Leiden: Brill, 2007), 35–48; I argue for some initial influence that waned as the Hasmoneans probably adopted Chronicles for their own ideological project.

[49] Johann Maier, "Early Jewish Biblical Interpretation in the Qumran Literature," in *Hebrew Bible/Old Testament: The History of Its Interpretation. Volume 1: From the Beginnings to the Middle Ages (Until 1300)* (ed. Magne Sæbø; Göttingen: Vandenhoeck & Ruprecht, 1996), 108–29 (p. 113).

[50] Maier, "Early Jewish Biblical Interpretation in the Qumran Literature," 114–5, argues that a key text and context, 1QS VI, 6–8, should be translated as: "In the place where these ten (members) are (living) must not be missing a man advising/instructing/enacting the law, day and night, concerning good relations each one with his companion." Maier's German translation of the passage is: "Und nicht weiche von einem Ort, wo sich die Zehn befinden, ein Mann, der in bezug auf Torah Anweisung(en) erteilt, (und zwar) tagsüber und nachts, ständig, bezüglich des guten (verhaltens) eines jeden zu seinem Nächsten" (*Die Qumran Essener. Die Texte vom Toten Meer* I [UTB 224; München: Reinhardt, 1995], 182).

the verb *ṭbʿ*, "to demand," "to summon."[51] He has concluded forcefully
that "there is no reason to assume for Qumran *dršᵢ/mdrš* a connotation
like 'to expound' or 'to derive from scripture'."[52] But the question has
to be posed to Maier: at what point and on what grounds might he be
willing to permit a widening of the semantic field so that Qumran *drš/*
mdrš could be conceived as sometimes having a connotation like "to
expound" or "to derive from scripture,"[53] and by extension the nominal form *mdrš* might be usable as a description of a particular kind of
sectarian exegetical practice, perhaps even as a label that could be used
as some kind of title for a commentary that reflected such practice.

Perhaps, rather than worrying overmuch about scriptural possibilities and problems, it is more appropriate to consider the sectarian literature itself, especially those compositions that might well predate
the commentary literature such as 4Q174 that is the subject of this
essay. The nominal form *mdrš* occurs eleven times in the extant non-
scriptural scrolls; all its uses are in what most scholars would acknowledge to be sectarian compositions. There are two (three, if parallels are
counted) occurrences in the *Damascus Document*. CD XX, 6 occurs
as part of a description of the judgement of the community against
one who is slow in fulfilling the demands of the righteous: "But when
his deeds are evident, according to the *explanation* of the law (*mdrš*
htwrh) in which the men of perfect holiness walked, no-one should
associate with him in wealth or work."[54] In 4Q266 11 18–20 (// 4Q270
7 II, 12–15) J. Baumgarten has restored and read "Behold, it is all
in accordance with the final *interpretation* of the Law (*mdrš htwrh*
h'hrwn)."[55] Three uses of the term occur in 1QS. 1QS VI, 24 reads:
"And these are the regulations (*hmšptym*) by which they shall judge

---

[51] Paul Heger, "The Development of Qumran Law: *Nistarot, Niglot* and the Issue
of 'Contemporization'," *RevQ* 23/90 (2007–2008): 167–206 (p. 174), argues that the
targum is not quite so monolithic in its renderings as Maier supposes.

[52] Maier, "Early Jewish Biblical Interpretation in the Qumran Literature," 119–20.
Through a presentation of Deut 17:8–12 and its parallel in the *Temple Scroll* (11Q19
LVI, 1–11), Maier has argued that *drš* is priestly activity in legal declaration.

[53] On some aspects of the rabbinic use of *mdrš* see, inter alia, Mayer I. Gruber,
"Biblical Interpretation in Rabbinic Literature: Historical and Philological Aspects," in
The Encyclopedia of Judaism Second Edition (ed. Jacob Neusner, Alan J. Avery-Peck,
W. S. Green; Leiden: Brill, 2005), vol. I (A–E), 217–34.

[54] Trans. Florentino García Martínez and Eibert J. C. Tigchelaar, *DSSSE* 1.579.

[55] Joseph M. Baumgarten, *Qumran Cave 4.XII: The Damascus Document (4Q266–
273)* (DJD XVIII; Oxford: Clarendon Press, 1996), 76–7.

in an examination of the Community (*bmdrš yḥd*) depending on the case."[56] This might be especially important for our purposes because the sentence is in effect the title of a subsection of the *Rule of the Community*; however, it is clear that *mdrš* is not being used here as a label to describe or define a literary genre. In 1QS VIII, 15, the term *mdrš* is used in the identificatory interpretative comment after the citation of Isa 40:3: "This is the study of the law (*mdrš htwrh*) which he commanded through the hand of Moses, in order to act in compliance with all that has been revealed from age to age, and according to what the prophets have revealed through his holy spirit."[57] The preparation of the way of the Lord is the *mdrš htwrh*, both in that particular text and in the parallel passage in 4Q259 III, 6: "This is the study of the law ([*md*]r[*š htwrh*]) which he commanded through the hand of Moses. These are the regulations for the Instructor..."[58] 1QS VIII, 26 is part of a passage that lays out the rules for the men of perfect holiness: "If his conduct is perfect in the session, in the investigation (*bmdrš*), and in the council according to the Many, if he has not sinned again through oversight until two full years have passed." Here the term *mdrš* refers to the examination of other members of the community. This last text has a partial parallel in 4Q258 VII, 1–3: "he should be excluded from pure food and from the council and the judgment for two full years. And he may return to the interpretation (*bmdrš*) and to the council if he does not go sinning through oversight until two years have passed."[59] Apart from 1QS VIII, 15 and its parallel in 4Q259, the majority of the occurrences of *mdrš* in the *Rule of the Community* seem to refer primarily to the examination of fellow members of the community. It is the interpretation of people as much as it is the study of texts, but it is indeed some kind of interpretation and explanation.

The other occurrence of the term *mdrš* in the *Rule of the Community* is in 4Q256 IX, 1 which has a verbatim parallel in 4Q258 I, 1: "Midrash for the Instructor concerning the men of the law who freely volunteer..."[60] This titular usage of the term is also reflected in two

---

[56] García Martínez and Tigchelaar, *DSSSE*, 1.85.
[57] García Martínez and Tigchelaar, *DSSSE*, 1.89–91.
[58] García Martínez and Tigchelaar, *DSSSE*, 1.531
[59] García Martínez and Tigchelaar, *DSSSE*, 1.523
[60] García Martínez and Tigchelaar, *DSSSE*, 1.513. Philip S. Alexander and Geza Vermes, *Qumran Cave 4.XIX: Serekh Ha-Yaḥad and Two Related Texts* (DJD XXVI; Oxford: Clarendon Press, 1998), 54, translate *mdrš lmśkyl* here as "Instruction for the Maskil." In relation to the parallel in *4Q258* they state baldly (p. 96): "*mdrš* has the

other texts. On the verso of 4Q249 a title or incipit is preserved: "Interpretation of the Book of Moses (*mdrš spr mwšh*)."[61] And, of course, in the principal fragment of 4Q174, the principal subject of this essay, the term is used to introduce a new section of interpretation. The commentary on the oracle of Nathan is given through the use of demonstrative pronouns rather than with the formulaic use of *pšr*; after that unit of interpretation has been completed, the new section begins with the term *mdrš* followed by the preposition *mn* and the first verse of Psalm 1: "Midrash of Ps 1:1 «Blessed [the] man who does not walk in the counsel of the wicked». The interpretation of this word (*pšr hdbr*):"[62] When this use on 4Q174 is set alongside all the other uses in the sectarian literature, is there enough evidence to suggest that the term *mdrš* might function as a title with some measure of technicality? Some might be tempted to read such a title as denoting a literary genre, others might be more aware that the term is principally concerned with a process, being on a semantic trajectory that at this stage describes an interpretative approach or set of techniques which only in later rabbinic literature were understood as belonging archetypally to particular genres of scriptural interpretation.[63]

What is one to make of these dozen uses of the term *mdrš* in the Qumran sectarian manuscripts? It certainly has to be acknowledged that it is very difficult to find any single term that will cover all the occurrences in the Qumran literature. Timothy Lim has proposed that for the term *mdrš* there are four broad categories of referents.[64] First there are references to "communal study" as in 1QS VIII, 14–16, 26. Second, some uses are best rendered as "inquiry," that is "a judicial inquiry"; such is the case for 1QS VI, 24. Third, Lim understands *mdrš* in CD XX, 6 as "communal regulation."[65] Fourth, the term is used in a titular manner in 4Q258 1 I, 1, 4Q256 5 I, 1, and 4Q249, but Lim

---

meaning of teaching, instruction, or interpretation, as in *1QS* VI, 24; VII [sic] 15, 26; *CD* XX 6; *4QFl* 1 i 14."

[61] García Martínez and Tigchelaar, *DSSSE*, 1.497
[62] García Martínez and Tigchelaar, *DSSSE*, 1.353
[63] Note, e.g., how *4Q174* is the starting point in the significant article on midrash by Philip S. Alexander, "Midrash," in *A Dictionary of Biblical Interpretation* (ed. R. J. Coggins and J. L. Houlden; London: SCM Press, 1990), 452–9.
[64] Timothy H. Lim, "Midrash Pesher in the Pauline Letters," in *The Scrolls and the Scriptures: Qumran Fifty Years After* (ed. Stanley E. Porter and Craig A. Evans; JSP-Sup 26; Roehampton Institute London Papers 3; Sheffield: Sheffield Academic Press, 1997), 280–92.
[65] Lim, "Midrash Pesher in the Pauline Letters," 287.

insists that this titular usage is not a reference to a literary genre of biblical exegesis but something more practical, "'instruction' or 'rule' which the Wise Teacher will impart to the sectarians,"[66] since in the longer corresponding passage in 1QS V, 1 the term *serek* is used synonymously for *mdrš*. In the joint use of *mdrš* with *pšr* in 4Q174, Lim concludes, *mdrš* should be translated as "a study of" or "an instruction deriving from," Ps 1:1 rather than as a reference to a genre of biblical exegesis that is the direct precursor of the rabbinic midrashim and all the assumptions about scripture that those midrashim make and project.[67] So, the term can indeed be used as a title, but there is a risk that it will be misconstrued as a genre label.[68] Is this a matter of splitting hairs or is there a genuine issue here? Put another way, does the use of the term "midrash" cause anachronistic distortion more than it satisfies the need for relevant proximity?[69]

In my revised dissertation, *Exegesis at Qumran*, I was more than content to use the term "midrash" of 4Q174. Being aware of the differences in assumptions and approaches between such a Second Temple sectarian composition and what later emerged variously in rabbinic texts, I drew attention to the differences as well as to the similarities by describing the composition generically in a qualified way as "Qumran Midrash."[70] In the generally mixed reaction to this proposal and

---

[66] Lim, "Midrash Pesher in the Pauline Letters," 288.

[67] Paul Mandel, "The Origins of *Midrash* in the Second Temple Period," in *Current Trends in the Study of Midrash* (ed. Carol Bakhos; JSJSup 106; Leiden: Brill, 2006), 9–34 (pp. 13–4 [italics his]), is similarly cautious: in assessing the origins of midrash in the Second Temple period he concludes that "the word *darash* retained a decidedly non-textual connotation throughout the Second Temple period, and it is this connotation that is also evident in texts from the early rabbinic period. An analysis of the relevant evidence shows that the Jewish scholar, who was indeed named *sofer*, was involved not so much in the *interpretation of a text* (the Bible) but in the *instruction in law*."

[68] The problematic saga of the term "midrash pesher" as a category alongside "midrash haggadah" and "midrash halakhah" illustrates why caution is needed here. This seems to have started with the work of Edward Earl Ellis, "Midrash Pesher in Pauline Hermeneutics," *NTS* 2 (1955–56): 127–33; republished in *Prophecy and Hermeneutics in Early Christianity: New Testament Essays* (Tübingen: Mohr [Paul Siebeck], 1978), 173–81. Amongst those who are similarly happy to see the term "midrash" as often referring to some kind of formal interpretation are Paul Heger, "The Development of Qumran Law: *Nistarot, Niglot* and the Issue of 'Contemporization'," *RevQ* 23/90 (2007–2008): 167–206.

[69] Jacob Neusner, *What is Midrash?* (Guides to Biblical Scholarship; Philadelphia: Fortress Press, 1987), 31–6, distances the concern with contemporary events in what he terms "midrash as prophecy" in the Qumran sectarian works from the later sustained exegetical concerns of rabbinic compositions.

[70] Brooke, *Exegesis at Qumran*, 166–7.

for many other reasons, some of which are difficult to articulate, the situation has now turned itself around. In general it is commentators not working in a Hebrew or Jewish environment who are willing to entitle 4Q174 a "midrash," whereas scholars who have had some specialist training in rabbinic literature proper tend towards a desire to differentiate what is taking place in thematic commentaries like 4Q174 from what is present in such later literature. In light of the impasse, is there a case for retaining Florilegium (and Catena)?

The term "florilegium" is the Latinised equivalent of the Greek word "anthology," meaning literally "a collection or selection of flowers." Florilegia are collections of selected passages from the writings of other authors. The term is widely used as a genre label, especially for some items of Christian literature from the late fourth century CE with a technical confessional sense of collections of passages, either scriptural or by Christian authors.[71] The genre has antecedents in pagan literature traceable to the third century BCE or earlier. Most especially poetic selections were used for didactic purposes, for entertainment and also for philosophical argument. The poetic saying of Aratus in Acts 17:28 is vaguely attributed to "some of your poets" and may derive from such a florilegium. Prose passages were also collected, most commonly, so it seems, for moral edification. These are often lists of pithy maxims and are known especially amongst Epicureans. Clement of Alexandria's late second century CE *Stromateis* might well be the earliest substantial Christian attempt at imitating the genre; it includes extracts from classical sources. As for Catena, "chain," the term is applied to Christian biblical commentaries from the fifth century CE onwards; these works commonly consist of successive biblical verses elucidated by selections from previous commentators linked together in various ways. Neither Florilegium nor Catena fully satisfies the criterion of relevant proximity to the composition(s) we are considering.

In relation to 4Q174 it is also likely that Allegro's original intention was to highlight the selection of scriptural passages in the

---

[71] See especially Henry Chadwick, "Florilegium," *RAC* 7 (1969): 1131–59; George J. Brooke "Florilegia," in *A Dictionary of Biblical Interpretation* (ed. Richard J. Coggins and J. Leslie Houlden; London: SCM Press; Philadelphia: Trinity Press International, 1990), 235–7.

composition,[72] rather than the selection of individual items of exegesis (text + interpretation) in the composition as a whole. It thus seems that as with the label *pesher* a part of the composition has come to be used to describe the whole. Is there a better term? For 4Q252 and its related texts, I opted for the term "commentary," largely for etic reasons on the basis of its modern and somewhat neutral usage. Not least in relation to modern biblical commentaries the term is recognized as embracing both the scriptural passages, usually in sequence, and the interpretative comments upon them. Like Florilegium and Catena, the term "commentary" has a Latin pedigree (*commentarius*), but in the context of pagan literature. As a literary phenomenon the Latin *commentarius* is the heir to much Hellenistic practice, evident in various *hypomnēmata*, that might go back to as early as the fifth century BCE, but which flourished from the second century BCE onwards, not least in Alexandria.[73] In the Latin tradition Aulus Gellius, the late second century CE grammarian, uses the term *commentarius* in association with *liber*, "book," and Suetonius, his contemporary, uses the term of a written journal. The early use of the term implies a wide range of written records such as a sketch, note-book or memorandum, but it has acquired a more technical sense by the second century of "commentary, brief explanation, annotation,"[74] even though first century commentaries exist such as that by Asconius on Cicero's speeches.

The modern discussion of Latin commentaries and the literary traditions to which they belong has been developing apace in recent years.[75]

---

[72] As in Allegro, "Communication," in "Le travail d'édition des fragments manuscripts de Qumrân," *RB* 63 (1956): 63.

[73] On the similarities between the commentary techniques and forms of commentary in the Hellenistic and Qumran continuous pesharim see Markus Bockmuehl, "The Dead Sea Scrolls and the Origins of Biblical Commentary," in *Text, Thought and Practice in Qumran and Early Christianity: Proceedings of the Ninth International Symposium of the Orion Center for the Study of the Dead Sea Scrolls and Associated Literature, Jointly Sponsored by the Hebrew University Center for the Study of Christianity, 11–13 January, 2004* (ed. Ruth A. Clements and Daniel R. Schwartz; STDJ 84; Leiden: Brill, 2009), 3–29. Bockmuehl's study has extensive notes on relevant secondary literature. He permits himself some "genetic" speculation, wondering about the suitability of setting the Qumran continuous pesharim in the context of its contemporary Hellenistic commentary tradition in terms of (1) its attention to citing the source in sequence, (2) lemmatisation, (3) the implied claims to authority in the comments, and (4) the move beyond the plain sense through something akin to allegorisation.

[74] Charlton T. Lewis and Charles Short, *A Latin Dictionary* (Oxford: Clarendon Press, 1962), 377.

[75] See, e.g., Roy K. Gibson and Christina Shuttleworth Kraus (ed.), *The Classical Commentary: Histories, Practices, Theory* (MnemosyneSup 232; Leiden: Brill, 2002).

Most scholars are agreed that this tradition begins to take shape in the first centuries BCE and CE, which is also the time of the Jewish traditions that we see in the sectarian literature found at Qumran.[76] Of a recent conference volume dedicated to the discussion of commentaries, including Latin ones, James O'Donnell has commented: "there is little attention to the material form of the thing called 'commentary', and this is unfortunate. The term is used, in my experience, for a range of things including but not limited to: transcription (with or without editing) of oral presentation of exposition of a text read aloud to a broad public...; marginal notes and interlineations in an authoritative text... compilations of marginalia... and deliberate writing of a 'commentary' as a vehicle for the exposition of the commentator's own views. To continue to lump those practices together as often as this volume does is to leave the task of distinction to a future conference."[77] O'Donnell has called for classical scholars to clarify what particular uses of "commentary" they are referring to. In whatever way such scholars might proceed with their specification, these items are all very much the kind of things that are to be observed in the Qumran manuscripts too, not least those that display some kind of exegetical process. In fact, Qumran scholars are similarly engaged in adequate description and classification. In its classical use, then, the label "commentary" is near in time, if not quite in place, and covers a wide range of relevant literary phenomena. Its use for the so-called "Thematic Pesharim" would enable scholars to avoid the problem of presenting an oversimplified trajectory from Qumran phenomena to rabbinic literature, whilst also using a term that has an umbrella catch-all competence. Perhaps it is no surprise that in their translation of the Dead Sea Scrolls, a translation which has paid particular attention to the naming of texts (sometimes problematically so), Wise, Abegg and Cook opt to call both the continuous and the thematic pesharim,

---

[76] On the history of literary development in the sectarian commentary literature see the preliminary and stimulating analytical work of Annette Steudel, "Dating Exegetical Texts from Qumran," in *The Dynamics of Language and Exegesis at Qumran* (ed. Divorah Dimant and Reinhard G. Kratz; FAT 2/35; Tübingen: Mohr Siebeck, 2009), 39–53.

[77] James J. O'Donnell, "Review of: Glenn W. Most (ed.), *Commentaries—Kommentare* (Aporemata: Kritische Studien zur Philologiegeschichte 4; Göttingen: Vandenhoeck & Ruprecht, 1999)," *Bryn Mawr Classical Review* (19 May 2000).

"commentaries," though for 4Q174 the content is given priority: "The Last Days: A Commentary on Selected Verses."[78]

2. *Generic Suitability and Content Qualification*

Several of the compositions among the more fragmentary Dead Sea Scrolls are simply given titles according to a few words of their surviving content; sometimes even when considerably more text survives a key item of content is used for the title: 11QMelchizedek is a case in common, though some have sought to entitle this more precisely and informatively as "Midrash on Melchizedek."[79] More commonly the editors of Dead Sea Scrolls have attempted to provide some kind of title with a genre label in it, even if it is the very common and very vague word "Apocryphon." Often such generic labels will also be accompanied by something more specific related to the content of the text. Thus, commonly the titles of scrolls have two words in them, one that refers in some way to genre and another that specifies the composition by reference to its content.

Generic labels can be extremely helpful: "an interpreter's preliminary generic conception of a text is constitutive of everything that he subsequently understands;"[80] or again, "without helpful orientations like titles and attributions, readers are likely to gain widely different generic conceptions of a text, and these conceptions will be constitutive of their subsequent understanding."[81] But all genre labels carry with them ideological baggage. Thomas O. Beebee has crisply identified the four stages of generic criticism: "genre as rules, genre as species, genre as patterns of textual features, and genre as reader conventions" which for him correspond more or less with "the four positions in the great debate about the location of textual meaning: in authorial intention, in the work's historical or literary context, in the text itself, or in

---

[78] Michael O. Wise, Martin G. Abegg, Edward M. Cook, *The Dead Sea Scrolls: A New Translation* (San Francisco: HarperSanFrancisco, 1996), viii. To distinguish 4Q174 from 4Q177, the latter is called: "The Last Days: An Interpretation of Selected Verses."
[79] E.g., Steudel, "Dating Exegetical Texts from Qumran," 46–7.
[80] Eric D. Hirsch, *Validity in Interpretation* (New Haven: Yale University Press, 1967), 74.
[81] Hirsch, *Validity in Interpretation*, 74. Cited in relation to the definition of pesher by George J. Brooke, "Qumran Pesher: Towards the Redefinition of a Genre," *RevQ* 10/40 (1979–1981): 492.

the reader."[82] For Beebee genres are principally of use to readers; for him generic differences "are grounded in the 'use-value' of a discourse rather than in its content, formal features, or its rules of production."[83] His work is principally in the area of reader-response and the instability of genres, but most generic definition of early Jewish literature is carried out not on the basis of what ancient readers would find "useful," but on the basis of the following of ever-developing conventions in the production of texts. In Jewish commentary such conventions are also tangled up with the developing authority of the texts being interpreted. It is issues to do with a set of conventions that make the term "midrash" problematic as a genre label for exegetical texts from the Qumran caves: those problematic issues concern how the formal structure of the whole text and the application of hermeneutical techniques are discernible.

For commentaries many issues arise out of Beebee's four perspectives, issues that it is not possible to address in any detail here. Christina Shuttleworth Kraus has identified three particular features of the genre commentary, whether ancient or modern: segmentation ("atomization," "morselization," or "lemmatisation"), tralaticiousness, and parallels.[84] How a text is divided for reading and commentary is obviously important, both for commentator and for the reader or hearer. The division breaks the whole that is commented upon, and when the commentary is selective rather than continuous such fragmentation is all the more apparent. This first characteristic has to do principally with form, with structure, with textual organisation. For 4Q174 it is all too easy to point out how various scriptural texts have been taken as units for interpretation, and then broken up yet again into short sequences to be interspersed with independent comments, some of which include further scriptural lemmata that seem to bolster

[82] Thomas O. Beebee, *The Ideology of Genre: A Comparative Study of Generic Instability* (University Park, PA: Pennsylvania State University Press, 1994), 3.
[83] Beebee, *The Ideology of Genre*, 7.
[84] Christina S. Kraus, "Introduction: Reading Commentaries/Commentaries as Reading," in *The Classical Commentary: Histories, Practices, Theory* (ed. R. K. Gibson amd C. S. Kraus MnemosyneSup 232; Leiden: Brill, 2002), 10–20. Notice how Kraus tries to tie textual production with textual reception in her title. I prefer Kraus' broader definition to that of Bockmuehl, "The Dead Sea Scrolls and the Origins of Biblical Commentary," 4, who has insisted that commentary consists "primarily of sequential, expository annotation of identified texts that are themselves distinguished from the comments and reproduced intact, whether partially or continuously," with the emphasis on sequential.

the authority of the interpretative remarks. In some instances too, the scriptural lemma is placed on the manuscript in a distinct way, such as starting at the margin, or after a space. There is an ongoing and stimulating debate to be had about how much unquoted text an author intended his reader or hearer to be aware of; the presentation of a lemma of scripture does not automatically exclude the reader from perceiving a textual resonance with unquoted material. In 4Q174 this issue is acute in the way in which Ps 1:1 and 2:1 are probably intended to be taken as incipits rather than as excerpts or extracts.

Tralaticiousness in commentary is the tendency of both lemmata and illustrative material to reproduce themselves from generation to generation; as an observable process it challenges the idea that any commentator can engage in an autonomous act of commentary; for Kraus the commentary tends to complicate rather than simplify the voices of a text. When there is not a very wide range of texts to consider, it is difficult to see the real significance of this definitional point. But two items can be mentioned briefly. First, with regard to the ongoing representation of the same or similar lemmata, there seems to be value indeed in recognizing that the combination of commentary on Psalm 2 and 2 Samuel 7 in 4Q174 is largely, if not totally, independent of the same combination in the Letter to the Hebrews. On the topic of messianism, these two texts readily suggest each other through their shared vocabulary of sonship.[85] Second, as far as the interpretation in 4Q174 goes, its overall concern with the latter days is most certainly also echoed in 4Q177 and in other thematic interpretative texts too, such as 4Q178, 4Q182, and 4Q252, not to mention the so-called continuous pesharim. This element of commentary definition is strongly suggestive that any one commentary is unlikely to have been copied out in multiple copies without addition and adaptation. The scribal transmission of commentaries was an ever-developing operation with the possibility for new additions to the interpretative comments at each copying.

---

[85] This was one of the points I tried to make in George J. Brooke, "Shared Intertextual Interpretations in the Dead Sea Scrolls and the New Testament," in *Biblical Perspectives: Early Use and Interpretation of the Bible in Light of the Dead Sea Scrolls: Proceedings of the First International Symposium of the Orion Center for the Study of the Dead Sea Scrolls and Associated Literature, 12–14 May, 1996* (ed. Michael E. Stone and Esther G. Chazon; STDJ 28; Leiden: Brill, 1998), 35–57.

Kraus's third element concerns the use in commentary of parallels. She is particularly exercised by the modern commentators use of cf. and e.g.; she suggests that the use of parallels in commentaries ancient and modern offers the reader both a single line of thought and the possibility of polyphony. In a thematic commentary like 4Q174 the use of subordinate texts superficially proposes a single trajectory of interpretation, such as the interpretation of the texts in terms of the community of readers in the latter days, but at the same time it invites the reader or hearer to wonder how the combination of textual elements has been done, to consider how such parallels enhance the authority of the interpretative comments, and so to reflect on whether the parallel is suitable and appropriate.

Scholars of the Dead Sea Scrolls have become increasingly aware of the variety of genres in which and through which scriptural interpretation can take place. For the kind of lemmatised handling of scripture that builds on earlier traditions implicitly and uses parallels to enhance the comment being made, the term "commentary" seems not only convenient but also right. Its generality enables modern readers not to be distracted by debates about midrash as method and genre, as rabbinic preserve or not; its specificity, informed through the contemporary Latin commentary tradition, turns out after all to be useful.[86]

But part of the point of this section of the paper is to acknowledge that the label "commentary" by itself is perhaps too general, just as for some scholars the category of "rewritten Bible" has needed closer definition.[87] In this respect I think that it is indeed important that there should be some kind of reference to the content of the compositions that are under generic scrutiny here, as many scholars have ascertained. One of the two options that lie before us is the term "thematic," already widely used to distinguish compositions like that in 4Q174 from "continuous" commentaries such as are present in *Pesher Habakkuk*. To my mind there are problems with this label. First, it does not say very much about the content, other than that there is some theme that lies behind the choice of lemmata. In fact, it seems to me that

---

[86] There may also be elements in the earlier and contemporary Greek commentary tradition that make the generic comparison suitable too: see Bockmuehl, "The Dead Sea Scrolls and the Origins of the Biblical Commentary," 6–13.

[87] See, e.g., Moshe J. Bernstein, "'Rewritten Bible': A Generic Category which has Outlived its Usefulness?" *Text* 22 (2005): 169–96; Michael Segal, "Between Bible and Rewritten Bible," in *Biblical Interpretation at Qumran* (ed. Matthias Henze; Studies in the Dead Sea Scrolls and Related Literature; Grand Rapids: Eerdmans, 2005), 10–28.

similar themes can also be found in the continuous commentaries as well. This then implies that the term "thematic" is also concerned with the structure of the commentary: rather than the structure being one of a continuous running text of a scriptural book with comment, the commentary is made up of a selection of different scriptural texts, sometimes themselves broken into lemmata, chosen because of the way they illuminate a theme. A further problem arises when the difference between these kinds of commentary is investigated more closely. It soon becomes apparent that there can be no rigid classification that distinguishes the two groups.[88] There is rather a continuum with some examples closer to being purely on a single running text, others very much based on a selection of primary and secondary texts.

A better description of the content of these commentaries might well be "eschatological," the second of the two options that is widely used of 4Q174 and its counterparts.[89] To my mind this is more informative for four reasons at least. First, it assists in the differentiation of these sectarian commentaries from other Jewish commentary literature by highlighting one particular item that seems to have been significant for the sectarian movement in various ways. Second, it is suggestive of these compositions as concerned with an appropriate understanding of prophetic texts, broadly conceived,[90] perhaps especially those that were considered to be unfulfilled in some sense. Third, usually by implication but sometimes the texts are quite explicit about this, it hints at what is at stake in the making known of all the divine mysteries, inspired exegesis ratified by the use of hermeneutical techniques. In other words, the content of these eschatological commentaries concerns the identification of the end times or latter days. Fourth, because it was a term being used by the first scholarly readers of these compositions, the use of the term enables the modern reader to see continuities between the new understandings of these texts and

---

[88] A point made clear by Moshe J. Bernstein, "Introductory Formulas for Citation and Recitation of Biblical Verses in the Qumran Pesharim: Observations on a Pesher Technique," *DSD* 1 (1994): 30–70.

[89] Bockmuehl, "The Dead Sea Scrolls and the Origins of the Biblical Commentary," 29, has noted that within the range of similarities between the continuous *pesharim* and the Hellenistic running commentaries of Philo of Alexandria one of the key differences concerns the character of the content in each: the former are eschatological and the latter philosophical.

[90] That is, including some passages of the Torah, such as the blessings of Jacob, the oracles of Baalam or the Song of Moses, as well as passages within narrative frameworks, such as the oracle of Nathan, together with the literary prophets proper.

the way in which they were perceived from the very outset over fifty years ago.[91] Overall "eschatological" seems to be the most suitable term that, by highlighting a key aspect of the content, assists in the closer definition of 4Q174 and its affiliated compositions as commentary.

Conclusion

And so the proposal of this essay is that 4Q174 (and 4Q177 and related fragmentary manuscripts) should be treated not like a dog from the rescue home. This is so not least because the dog seems, Janus-like, to have two names (*Florilegium* and/or *Eschatological Midrash*). Rather the proposal is to treat 4Q174 and its friends, somewhat traditionally, like Anglo-Saxon wives. As they are adopted and come under the influence of new editors, so they take on new names. 4Q174 can become *Eschatological Commentary A*, 4Q177 can become *Eschatological Commentary B*, and so on, with capital letters to indicate affinity, rather than that they are necessarily copies of a single exemplar.[92]

---

[91] Note the use of the word "commentaire" by Allegro, "Communication," in "Le travail d'édition des fragments manuscripts de Qumrân," 63; and by Milik, *Dix ans de découvertes dans le desert de Juda*, 37: "un commentaire de caractère messianique dont le text biblique est un florilège."

[92] It might be that these manuscripts should be put in some other order in relation to each other, their current order being based, somewhat arbitrarily, largely on the size of their extant fragments—but that might be a step too far.

4QTANḤUMIM (4Q176): BETWEEN EXEGESIS AND TREATISE?

Jesper Høgenhaven
University of Copenhagen

Within the context of Qumran literature, to describe any particular text (such as 4Q176) as "strange" or unusual or indeed as a unique document may seem either a commonplace or an exaggeration. Yet the fact remains that this manuscript does exhibit a number of features which make it stand out among the many manuscripts from Cave 4. This has to do with the scribal character of the manuscript—4Q176 bears the marks of two different scribal hands—and, above all, with its contents. 4Q176 is composed in part from an extensive series of scriptural quotations, most of which—if indeed all—are derived from the Book of Isaiah, and in part from non-scriptural passages. The literary nature of the latter and the relation to the scriptural quotations raise a number of intriguing and to a large extent unanswered questions. This study attempts to examine some of these questions and to suggest some tentative answers. A brief presentation of the manuscript precedes the analysis.

THE MANUSCRIPT

4Q176 (as published in DJD V by Allegro) comprises 57 fragments. Fragments 1 and 2 can be joined with material certainty to from one large composite, preserving substantial remains of two consecutive columns of text. This composite shows two different and clearly distinguishable scribal hands. The first is found only in the extant parts of the first column. The second hand is found in frags. 1–2 col. II as well as in the rest of the manuscript.

From the remaining fragments, it is possible with a high degree of plausibility to reconstruct five columns of the original scroll. Of these five columns, some of col. I, all of column II and the greater part of col. III are made up of text known to us from the Book of Isaiah. In other words, a very considerable portion of the extant text is made up by a long apparently uninterrupted series of quotations which we can without much difficulty identify as passages from Isaiah 40; 41; 43; 44; 49; 51; 52; and 54.

Whether all the fragments Allegro assigned to 4Q176 do in fact belong to the same manuscript, has been a matter of some dispute. Menahem Kister has identified fragments 19–21 as belonging to a Hebrew copy of the Book of Jubilees.[1] Kister's identification, which is based on the material quality, the handwriting, and the palaeography of the fragments mentioned, has gained widespread acceptance among Qumran scholars.[2]

4QTanhumim exhibits two different scribal hands. The first of these (hand A) is confined to the preserved parts of frags. 1–2 col. I, while the second hand (hand B) is found in frags. 1–2 col. II and in the rest of the scroll. The combination of fragments 1–2 into one large composite with two consecutive columns is materially certain, so the occurrence of both types of handwriting within the same manuscript is not to be doubted. Both scribal hands may be characterized as belonging to a Hasmonean "semiformal" tradition with a number of "semicursive" elements. The number of "semicursive" elements is greater in hand B than in hand A, and in hand B they occur with increasing frequency in the later parts of the scroll.[3] The palaeographical findings point to a tentative dating of the scroll in the first half or possibly the middle of the first century BCE.

---

[1] Menahem Kister, "Newly-Identified Fragments of the Book of Jubilees. Jub. 23:21–23, 30–31," *RevQ* 12 (1985–1987): 529–36.

[2] Cf. G.-Wilhelm Nebe, "Ergänzende Bemerkung zu 4Q 176, Jubiläen 23,21," *RevQ* 14/53 (1989–91): 129–30; James C. VanderKam, "The Jubilees Fragments from Qumran Cave 4," in *The Madrid Qumran Congress. Proceedings of the International Congress on the Dead Sea Scrolls Madrid 18–21 March, 1991* (ed. Julio Trebolle Barrera and Luis Vegas Montaner; STDJ 11.2; Leiden: Brill 1992), 635–48. For further references see Hermann Lichtenberger, "Consolations (4Q176 = 4QTanh)" in PTSDSSP 6B.330, note 17.

[3] In hand A we note the simplified, "semicursive" forms of the letters *alef*, *ṣade* and *qof*. In hand B we find cursive forms of *gimel* (which is curved, the left leg connecting near the middle of the right), *ṭet* (with a sharp angle at the bottom, and the right down-stroke curling into the base-stroke), and *tav* (which occasionally has the left down-stroke and the upper part of the right leg crossing). Strugnell described hand A as an "imitation" of the formal script carried out by a scribe used to the "semicursive" style. Hand B, according to Strugnell, is another "semiformal" script with "semicursive" elements, which becomes, in the later part of the scroll when the citations from Isaiah have ended, a standard "semicursive" (Strugnell, "Notes en marge," 229). A more objective description of both hands would be to speak of "semiformal" styles with elements of "semicursive." On the Hasmonean cursives and semicursives, see Frank M. Cross, "The Development of the Jewish Scripts," in *The Bible and the Ancient Near East* (ed. G. E. Wright; Garden City: Doubleday, 1961), 133–202; Cross, "Palaeography and the Dead Sea Scrolls," in *The Dead Sea Scrolls After Fifty Years. A Comprehensive Assessment. Volume 1* (ed. Peter W. Flint and James C. VanderKam; Leiden: Brill, 1998), 379–402, esp. 390–401.

Allegro published the 4Q176 fragments in DJD V without attempting to reconstruct further columns of the original scroll apart from
the materially certain combination of frags. 1–2 into two consecutive
columns. John Strugnell laid the foundations for a more comprehensive reconstruction, and his results were confirmed and further refined
by Christopher D. Stanley.[4] The re-editions of 4Q176 by Florentíno
García Martínez and Eibert J. C. Tigchelaar and by Hermann Lichtenberger reflect in part these reconstructions but fail to take full advantage of their results.[5] In fact, it is possible, based on the sequence of
biblical passages, to reconstruct frags. 3–5 (Isa 43:1–6) as the beginning of and frags. 6–7 (Isa 51:22–23) as the end of the second column
partly preserved on frags. 1–2 (Isa 49:7.13–17). This column may be
regarded as col. II, although we cannot know whether col. I (the first
column preserved on frags. 1–2) was actually the first column of the
original scroll. The column preserved in frags. 8–11 (containing passages from Isa 51:23; 52:1–3; 54:4–10 and non-scriptural text) would
then have been the following column (col. III). This reconstruction,
obviously, rests on the assumption that the scriptural passages followed the order known to us from the Book of Isaiah. Less certain
is the reconstruction of frags. 12–15 and 42, into a fourth column
(col. IV). The non-scriptural text in frag. 14 seems to connect well
with the non-scriptural passage at the end of col. II, and could be
interpreted as its continuation, meaning that this fragment should
be placed near the top of col. IV. Frags. 12–13, with which frag. 42
may be combined,[6] preserve a bottom margin and must be placed at
the end of the column. Frag. 15, which contains a quotation from or
an allusion to Zech 13:9, could tentatively be located to col. IV. Like
frag. 15, it exhibits the more "formal," less "cursive" version of hand
B, and should therefore be placed before the transition to the more
"cursive" style found in the subsequent part of the scroll. Frags. 16–18,
22–23, 33, 51, and 53 were combined by Strugnell into one column,
with the top margin preserved on frags. 17–18, and 53, and the right

---

[4] Christopher D. Stanley, "The Importance of 4QTanhumim (4Q176)," *RevQ* 15/60
(1991–1992): 569–82.
[5] Florentino García Martínez and Eibert J. C. Tigchelaar, *DSSSE* 1.358–61;
PTSDSSP 6B.329–49.
[6] The combination was proposed by Strugnell, "Notes en marge," 233.

margin on frags. 33 and 51.[7] This column, in which a considerable number of "cursive" elements occur in the handwriting, and which contains non-scriptural text, may have followed col. IV in the original scroll, and could conveniently be designed as col. V, but the sequence here is not certain.[8]

THE GENRE OF 4Q176

The genre, structure and literary character of 4Q176 remain elusive. This is clear from the attempts at generic descriptions found in recent studies. In 1992 Stanley maintained that in terms of genre 4QTanḥumim holds a unique position within the Qumran library.[9] Hermann Lichtenberger notes in his 2002 edition that "further research" into the literary character of the document is desired.[10] According to Johann Maier the scroll consists of "literary texts of various genre."[11] In fact, various parts of the text seem to contain generic features pointing in very different directions. If all we had of 4Q176 were fragments from col. II and the first part of col. III, we would conclude without the slightest hesitation that we were dealing with an Isaiah manuscript. On the other hand, if all that was preserved of the manuscript comprised some or most the fragments that have here been combined to form col. V we would be inclined to assume that we were dealing with some sort of treatise-like text, possibly a composition akin to Qumran wisdom texts such as *Instruction* or *Ways of Righteousness*.

4QTanḥumim is not one of those DJD V texts that have received massive scholarly attention. However, in what has been written about the text, terms such as "exegesis" and "exegetical" have been rather prominent in peoples' attempts to describe its genre and character. In fact, many scholars have tended to classify 4Q176 as an exegetical composition of some sort. This can be clearly perceived from the way 4Q176 has been treated in various editions and translations of

---

[7] Strugnell, "Notes en marge," 235. The combination of fragments is shown on PAM 44.192.

[8] The suggested reconstruction of columns is presented with greater detail in Jesper Høgenhaven, "The Literary Character of 4QTanḥumim," *DSD* 14 (2007): 99–123.

[9] Stanley, "The Importance of 4QTanḥumim," 569–82.

[10] PTSDSSP 6B.329–49.

[11] Johann Maier, "Tanhumin and Apocryphal Lamentations," *EDSS* 2.915.

Qumran texts.[12] Jonathan Campbell describes 4Q176 as an "interpretative anthology of scripture."[13]

The obvious and indisputable closeness to biblical literature is undoubtedly the reason 4Q176 has so often been viewed as in some sense an "exegetical" composition. However, the preserved non-scriptural passages of 4Q176 contain nothing which is explicitly exegetical or interpretative. The scriptural passages from Isaiah are not interspersed with interpretative additions, comments, or explanations of any kind. And in the non-scriptural parts of 4Q176 we encounter no interpretative expressions; nothing like the interpretation formulae of the *pesharim* occurs. We find no employment of pronouns to equate particular entities in a scriptural source with entities outside scripture. In fact, the only feature of 4Q176 that could be described as interpretative is the very application of the term *tanhumim* to designate the chain of quotations (4Q176 I, 15). This way of designating the scriptural passages quoted, clearly marking them as something different from the surrounding (non-scriptural) text, shows that the author of the document distinguished between scriptural quotations and his own text: when quoting the Book of Isaiah, he is obviously conscious of importing text from a particular source into his own work. At the same time, we encounter in 4Q176 a long passage (the reconstructed col. V) which is not directly related to the scriptural quotations, but speaks of God's creation of the world and of his ordering of human destiny in a style seemingly akin to theological treatises or wisdom texts. This raises the question of how we are meant to view the relationships between the large blocks of scriptural text extant in 4QTanhumim on the one hand and the extensive non-scriptural sections on the other. We shall first examine the non-scriptural passages of 4Q176, to gain an impression of their character, and the literary traits they have in common. In particular, we shall try to assess the nature of the implied speaker and reader of the text.

---

[12] Geza Vermes, *The Dead Sea Scrolls in English* (4th ed.; London: Penguin Books, 1995), 363, places 4Q176 in the section "Biblical Interpretation." Florentino García Martínez, *The Dead Sea Scrolls Translated. The Qumran Texts in English* (2nd ed.; Leiden: Brill, 1996), 208–09, places 4Q176 under the heading "Exegetical Literature ("Other Texts")." In PTSDSSP 6B, 329–49, 4Q176 is also placed among texts of "exegetical" nature. Jonathan G. Campbell, *The Exegetical Texts* (Companion to the Qumran Scrolls 4; London: T. & T. Clark, 2004), 78–87, treats 4Q176 among "exegetical" texts.

[13] Campbell, *The Exegetical Texts*, 82.

The non-scriptural passages in 4QTanḥumim

If we look at the way the chain of quotations from Isaiah are introduced in the first extant non-scriptural section (4Q176 I 12–15) we
note that these passages are explicitly introduced as quotations.

4Q176 frags. 1–2, col. I

‫ועשה פלאכה והצדק בעמכה והיו֯ן֯]‬ 12
‫מקדשכה וריבה עם ממלכות על דם֯]‬ 13
‫ירושלים וראה נבלת כוהניכה]‬ 14
‫ואין קובר ומן ספר ישיה תנח֯ומים֯]‬ vacat ‫נחמו נחמו עמי]‬ 15
‫יומר אלוהיכם דברו אל לב ירושלים וק֯ר֯]או אליה]כ֯]יא מלא[֯ה]‬ 16
‫צבא[֯ה כיא‬

12 and perform your marvel, and do justice to your people and...
13 your sanctuary, and strive against kingdoms over the blood of...
14 Jerusalem, and see the corpses of your priests...
15 and there is no one to bury them. And from the Book of Isaiah
    consolations: [Comfort, comfort my people]
16 says your God. Speak tenderly to Jerusalem, and cr[y to her] that her
    [warfare is end]ed, that...

Johann Maier characterizes this section as belonging to a "lament-like
poetic genre."[14] Interestingly, he has chosen to present 4QTanḥumim in
a combined article in *EDDS* together with *Apocryphal Lamentations A*
(4Q179) and *Apocryphal Lamentations B* (4Q501).

An analysis of the non-scriptural part of col. I as liturgy or prayer
is supported by the use of the second person singular as direct address
to God. The verbs, accordingly, should be read as imperatives. In the
language of the collective lament God is called upon to perform his
marvel, and to do justice to his people, and "strive" or "fight" against
the kingdoms which apparently represent an enemy force. In accordance with the lament style, the present desolation of the lamenting
people is described. Jerusalem is mentioned, and we find references to
the corpses of God's priests with the explicit addition that there is no
one to bury them. There is no explicit first person (singular or plural)
speaker in these lines, but the implied speaker would most naturally
be understood as a lamenting "psalmist," representing the "voice" of
the congregation or liturgical body.

---

[14] Maier, "Tanhumin and Apocryphal Lamentations," *EDSS* 2.915.

Allegro points to the obvious points of contact between these lines in 4Q176 and the initial verses of Psalm 79.[15] The phrase ואתן קובר also occurs as the closing words of Ps 79:3. The expression נבלת כוהנתך closely resembles נבלת עבדתך in Ps 79:2. The "blood" (דם) mentioned in line 13 may recall the reference to "their blood" (דמם) in Ps 79:3, and the reference to "your sanctuary" (מקדשך) in line 13 corresponds to התכל קדשך in Ps 79:1. Allegro's characterization of these lines (14–15) as a "pesher" on Psalm 79 does not seem justified, since none of the terms of interpretation peculiar to the *pesharim* are found here. The text speaks directly to God in the style of a lament or prayer, using vocabulary from a scriptural source. The situation envisaged would seem to be basically the same as the situation reflected in Psalm 79. Disaster has hit God's people, his sanctuary, and his priests. His city and temple have been defeated by enemies. Such a situation is the sinister background for the appeal to God to perform his marvel and do justice to his people. The expression "your marvel" (פלאכה) in line 14 is often found in biblical poetic passages,[16] and the term seems to imply a definiteness associated with the idea that God has performed well-known marvels in the past. The appeal to God is made, in other words, within a context of covenantal theology or "salvation history". The passage shares the perspective and to a large extent the language not only of Psalm 79 but also of the Qumranic compositions *Apocryphal Lamentations A* (4Q179) and *Apocryphal Lamentations B* (4Q501), both of which also describe a devastated Jerusalem.[17]

Against this background the use of an introductory quotation formula seems to stand out. Such a formula does not read very naturally as part of a prayer addressed to God.

The chain of quotations is introduced by a brief nominal sentence: "and from the Book of Isaiah consolations" (ומן ספר תשתה תנחומים). The conjunction would seem to imply some sort of semantic connection (even in the form of contrast) with the preceding lament, which is a description of the disastrous situation where there is "no one to bury" (ואין קובר). The "voice" speaking through the introductory formula seems to be different from the voice heard in the lament. It belongs,

---

[15] DJD V, 61.

[16] The word פלא is the object of the verb עשה (with God as the subject) in Ps 78:12; 88:11. Cf. Exod 15:11; Ps 77:12: 88:13; 89:6.

[17] The appeal to God to "see" the misery of his people (ראה, imperative) is also found in 4Q501 5.

as it were, to a second layer within the literary structure of the document, representing an organizing force having the function of giving
structure and meaning to the text as a whole. What this ordering voice
does is to set apart the following passages as quotations with a specific
function—consolations—and to assign to these passages their proper
place within the literary framework of the document. In this context,
the quotations are expressly introduced as something different from
the lament and prayer preceding them.

In fact, what we have here could very well be interpreted as a liturgical rubric or a prescription for a liturgical reading of scriptural passages
from a named source. The implied speaker might be characterized as
an authoritative figure in charge of organizing and ordering a liturgical celebration, which comprises the reading of scriptural passages.
The implied readers of the text would then be someone responsible
for carrying out the liturgical instructions in practice. This impression
is confirmed when we look at the next non-scriptural section, which
follows after the large block of quotations from Isaiah.

4Q176 frags. 8–11, col. III

בֹּ[	נ]ואש עד דברי תנחומֹיֹם וכבוד רב כתוב	*vacat*	13
	[בֹּאוהֹבֹ]י [אין עוד מעת]		14
]°° ת°[	בלי]עֹל לענות את עבדיו בו[		15
	י ישמחֹ [ ] וֹ[ ] אריֹסֹ[ ] יושבת]		16
	°בֹּתֹ[ ]°[תמֹעֹ]°		17

13   ...de]sperate until the words of consolation, and great glory is written
     in...
14   ...among those who love [me] there is no more since the time of...
15   [Beli]al to oppress his servants...
16   ...shall rejoice...I shall rise up...she that sits...
17   ...she shall be diminished(?)

This section clearly marks the end of the chain of quotations, and
indeed there seems to be a very conscious correspondence between
the words that signal the end of the quotation section and the words
used at its introduction. Unlike 4Q176 I, 12–15 these lines cannot be
described as a prayer text. There is no direct address to God, but there
seems to be at least one instance of God speaking in the first person
(the verb אריֹם in line 16, possibly to be compared with the reconstructed first person suffix in בֹּאוהֹבֹ[י, line 14). At the same time, however, the word עבדיו (line 15) seems to show that God is spoken of
in the third person. The exact relationship between the non-scriptural

sections before and after the quotations thus remains somewhat unclear. The findings, however, would seem to be compatible with what we should expect from a liturgical text, in which the voice of God may be heard, alternating with the voice of his lamenting congregation. The shifts between speaking to God, listening to God's words, and speaking of God in the third person, may be interpreted as a feature well at home within the liturgical genre. The implied speaker in these lines would be the same as in the prayer text in 4Q176 I, 12–15, the voice of the psalmist or congregation.

The first line in 4Q176 III, 13–16 is particularly difficult to interpret. The initial word has been partly restored as נואש on the basis of Isa 57:10, where we find this niphal form of the root יאש. However, very little is preserved of the first letter, and there could be several other possible ways of reading this word.[18] The use of the term "written" (כתוב) in this context is both interesting and intriguing. There are two ways of analysing the syntax of the last four words of this line. We may interpret the words as a nominal sentence with כבוד רב as the subject, and כתוב as the predicate: "and great glory is written." An alternative understanding would be to combine the words כבוד רב with the preceding words דברי תנחומים to form the phrase "words of consolation and great glory." In that case, the following כתוב must be understood as the beginning of a new sentence: "It is written…" The first understanding seems to be the most plausible. If כתוב was the first word in a new sentence, we would expect it to have a copula. In any case, however, the implied speaker of line 13 clearly seems to be the same as the implied speaker of 4Q176 I, 15. Here, we encounter the same ordering, structuring "voice," explicitly setting apart different parts of the document, and regulating the order existing between these parts, as well as their function within an overall framework that would seem to be liturgical in its character and purpose.

The employment of the passive participle כתוב to mark a scriptural quotation would seem to echo a series of well-known quotation formulae used in various Qumran texts.[19] However, the specific formulation used here, "great glory is written in…" followed by a designation of the scriptural source, is to the best of my knowledge not mirrored

---

[18] We may note that באש occurs in one of the smaller fragments of 4Q176 (frag. 26). Other possible readings would be אש or ראש.

[19] Cf. Moshe J. Bernstein, "Scriptures: Quotations and Use," *EDSS* 2.839–42.

anywhere else in the material. Nowhere else in a Qumran text do we find the exact phrase "X is written in..." (From a grammatical point of view, the closest parallels are phrases like הנה הכול כתוב בלחות (4Q177 1–4 12) or הנה הכול כתוב על מדרש התורה (4Q270 7 II, 14)). It is a noteworthy aspect of this text, though, that it contains a reference in absolute terms to something written in terms of a summary of the scriptural contents itself.

In terms of thematic contents, the expression כבוד רב could be understood as an allusion to the revelation of the glory of the Lord described in Isa 40:5. This would seem to be the most plausible background for the expression, given the massive block of quotations from Isaiah 40–55 found in 4Q176. In Isa 40:5 the revelation of glory summarizes the transition from affliction and doom to salvation and blessing. A similar notion of change from doom to salvation would seem to be the theme of line 16. We have the verbs ישמח ("rejoices" or "causes to rejoice") and ארים ("I shall rise up"), both of which could be construed as having God as their subject, even if one verb is in the third person, and the other one in the first person singular. The word יושבת ("she that sits") could very plausibly be understood as referring to Zion/Jerusalem, depicted as a person now "sitting" in agony and distress, but also the object of God's saving acts.[20] He is about to raise her up and cause her to rejoice, making her enter a new state of peace and blessing. This passage, in other words, continues the theme of the affliction of God's people also found in the lament passage 4Q176 I, 12–15, and at the same time it represents a development in the direction of explicitly describing a transition from doom to salvation. The underlying theology of salvation history would seem to be the same in both passages.

If we move to the non-scriptural text in fragment 14, which would seem in the original scroll to have followed some 6 lines after 4Q176 III, 13–17, we may note that here the "prayer style" with its direct address to God reappears:

4Q176 frag. 14, col. IV(?)

[בכשו]ל	1
[ס שנאתה]ο	2
[שונאנו שברנו	3
[א הבטתה אולינו]	4
מ[כה על מכה בו]	5

---

[20] Cf. Lam 1:1 (and the allusion in 4Q179 III, 4).

6 [אין לוא דורש]
7 [°[אׄוׄבֿדׄה °ל]

1 in stumbl[ing]
2 you hate…
3 he has hated us, he has broken us…
4 you look upon us…
5 [wo]und upon wound on him/it…
6 there is no one who seeks him…
7 she/it has perished…

In fact, as far as the scant remains will allow us to draw any conclusions, this section has the characteristics of a liturgical text also found in 4Q176 I, 12–15 and 4Q176 III 13–17. The text has an explicit first person plural ("we"), which is the object of God's punishing acts. The situation described in these lines is clearly similar to that of 4Q176 I, 12–15: The people of God is afflicted and suffering. The phrase אין לוא דורש seems formally parallel to 4Q176 I, 15. We note that here God is both addressed in the second person and spoken of in the third person, in itself not an uncommon feature in a liturgical text. The implied speaker here is clearly the lamenting congregation ("we").

The last extensive non-scriptural passage is the reconstructed column V. This section seems to be of a somewhat different literary character when compared with the other sections, since most of the text apparently consists of a description of God's creating and governing activities:[21]

4Q176 frags. 16, 17, 18, 22, 23, 33, 51, 53, col. V

1 [יׄרׄ] [וגם אף בׄ°קדוש][נׄחלת ידו כי לוא יצדק]
כול איש
2 מׄל[פׄניו [כׄיא הוא ברא את כול] דור]ׄות עולמים וׄ]הכין כמש]פׄטו
דרכי כולם וׄהׄאׄר]ץ
3 ברא°[נו בימׄי]נׄו טרם היותם ובעצׄ°תו פק]ׄד° על כול א[יש וכ]רׄזו הפיל
גורל לאׄיׄשׄ לתׄתׄ]
4 ל] ל] ל] [וׄל אמרׄ] [במלאך פׄ]° [ ] יׄת קודש ולתת פעלתׄ
איש ל]
5 °[ ]°° [ ] שמונה שׄ] ר על אוהבו ועל שומי
מצׄ]וׄתׄיׄו

---

[21] For the reconstruction of 4Q176 V see Høgenhaven, "The Literary Character of 4QTanhumim," 106–7. The reconstruction was first suggested by Strugnell ("Notes en marge," 234), whose proposals are followed by Martínez/Tigchelaar (DSSSE 1. 358–61) and Lichtenberger (PTSDSSP 6B.344–5). Since the column, as reconstructed by Strugnell, would be unusually wide in comparison with the extant columns of the scroll, I have reconstructed col. V assuming a slightly smaller distance between the fragments.

6 ‏[וׄיׄפׄע לנו מפׄרׄן]   [שׁכח את בריתו   ]וׄל[

7 ‏עׄ[שׁׄו התורה ו]   [שׁׄנאתה להיותׄ]   ]ל[

8 ‏[התורה   ]   [כלותם]   ]ל[   ]◦[

1 ...and even also in the sanctuary...the possession of his hand, for no [man] is justified

2 be[fore him], for he created all of the eternal ge[nerations, and according to] his [jus]tice [established] the ways of them all. And the la[nd]

3 he created [with] his [right hand] before they had come into being. And by his co[unsel he look]ed after every m[an. And according to] his secret he made the lot fall...for men to give...

4 ...said...by the angel of...holy...and to give the reward of man to...

5 ...eight...over those who love him and over those who keep [his] command[ments]

6 ...to us .. forgot his covenant. *vacat* And to...

7 ...they [d]o the law and...you hate. To be...

8 ...the law...to destroy them...

The style and terminology of column V, according to Maier, point to a "mixture of sapiential and hymnic elements."[22] The text emphasizes God's determining and governing activities; his acts consist in creating, ordering, and casting the lots of men, and as a result of these acts mankind is divided into two parts. The explicit references to "those who love him" and "those who keep his commandments" (line 5)[23] would seem to imply the existence of a "counter-group" consisting of people who do not love God or keep his commandments. Indeed, this negatively connoted group appears to be mentioned in lines 7–8, where the fragmentary text speaks again of the "law" (התורה) in connection with God "hating" somebody, and with certain people being the object of destruction or destined for destruction (לכלותם). In other words, the text clearly envisages a division between the just and the wicked, eventually resulting in the destruction of the latter group. The image conveyed is that of an ultimate divine judgment putting an end to the activities of evil forces in the world.

The reference to the "sanctuary" (במקדש) in line 1 constitutes a link to the section 4Q176 I, 12–15, where the sanctuary is mentioned within the context of an appeal to God to become aware of the disas-

---

[22] Maier, "Tanhumin and Apocryphal Lamentaions," *EDSS* 2.915.

[23] To these references we may add those who "do the law" in line 7. An alternative reading instead of עׄ[שׁו התורה would be עו]שׁי התורה, "doers of the law," but a *waw* seems materially preferable.

trous state of his people. The text is fragmentary, and the context for the reference here in 4Q176 IV, 1 is lost. However, the emphasis conveyed by the preceding words וגם אף would suit a description (similar to that in 4Q176 I, 12–15) of enemies having destroyed, or defiled, not only the city but "even also" the sanctuary of God and his people.

The context in 4Q176 IV, 1–8 is a theology of "salvation history," and, as in 4Q176 I, 12–15 the focus seems to be on a transition from a state of oppression and affliction suffered by the righteous/the people of God to a state of glory and peace, brought about by divine judgment, which annihilates the wicked.

In 4Q176 IV, 6 we find the first person plural (לנו), a feature reminiscent of the liturgical style found in 4Q176 I, 12–15 and 4Q176 IV. Lines 1–6 speak of God and his acts in the third person, but at the end the text seems to address God directly in the second person (שנאתה). The shift between addressing God and speaking about God is a characteristic that this passage shares with 4Q176 IV. In 4Q176 V, however, the third person discourse seems to play a more prominent role.

4Q176 I, 12–15 uses the second person address exclusively, while 4Q176 III, 13–17 appears to have a combination of God speaking in the first person, and third person references. 4Q176 IV (fragment 14) and 4Q176 V combine second person address with third person discourse. The implied speaker, in all these passages, could be understood as the liturgical "voice" of the congregation or of a "psalmist" representing the congregation.

The language and contents of 4Q176 V show a considerable degree of similarity to Qumran "wisdom" texts such as 4QInstruction and 4QTimes of Righteousness. A particularly impressive number of thematic links exist between 4Q176 V and 4Q418 81 (4QInstruction). Both texts describe God's creation of the universe, his determination of the lots of humans, and the twofold division of mankind explicitly associated with the divinely established order.[24] It is not unusual within poetic, liturgical texts to find passages of a more treatise-like, "doctrinal" nature. It may well be that the similarity in thought and terminology which connects 4Q176 V with specific passages in other Qumran texts reflects their common origin in a traditional body of doctrine.

---

[24] Cf. Høgenhaven, "The Literary Character of 4QTanhumim," 119–21. There are also overlaps in theme and vocabulary with 4Q 215a 1 II, 8–10. The combination of creation motifs and the theme of God's division of mankind is also found in "sectarian" documents such as the *Rule of the Community* (1QS III, 13–IV, 26) and the *Damascus Document* (CD II, 3–13).

We have established that the non-scriptural passages of 4Q176 may all be plausibly read as belonging to a liturgical genre. We find God addressed in the second person, speaking in the first person, and spoken of in the third person. Such shifts are to be expected in a liturgical text. Furthermore, we find that these passages use a first person plural (meaning, in all probability, the "congregation"/God's people, as well as a third person plural (designating the righteous/God's people and their "counter-group," the wicked), and also a feminine singular (referring to Zion/Jerusalem). The passages seem to contain two different layers or "voices," the first voice being that of the congregation addressing God, and being addressed by him, and the second "voice" belonging to an implied speaker organizing and structuring the liturgical event. The words of this implied speaker take the form of rubrics, setting apart the various parts of the liturgy, and marking the beginning and end of the scriptural quotations.

THE SCRIPTURAL QUOTATIONS

We now turn our attention to the chain of quotations from the Book of Isaiah which occupy the greater part of 4Q176 I–III. The first point to be noted is that apparently all of the passages within this large block of quotations are cited in their "canonical" order. Even though large portions of text are not cited, there is no instance of a verse or passage being cited out of order. Incidentally, as far as can be ascertained from the extant fragments, all the quotations comprise entire biblical verses, according to the later system.[25]

Against this background, it is remarkable that outside the chain of quotations—and separated from it by a non-scriptural section—we find what may be a regular quotation from another scriptural source,

---

[25] Interestingly, the Isaiah text found in 4Q176 would seem, as far as its fragmentary nature allow any such conclusions, to belong to a tradition akin to that of 1QIsaᵃ and 1QIsaᶜ. While not representing a textual tradition different from the "proto-Masoretic" type generally found in the Isaiah manuscripts from Qumran, these manuscripts share both a number of features characteristic of the "Qumran" scribal school, and a relatively large number of textual harmonizations and similar secondary variants. See Høgenhaven, "The Literary Character of 4QTanhumim," 108–10. On the textual tradition of the Qumran Isaiah manuscripts, see Emanuel Tov, "The Text of Isaiah at Qumran," in *Writing and Reading the Scroll of Isaiah. Studies in an Interpretive Tradition* (ed. Craig C. Boyles and Craig A. Evans; VTSup 70.2; Leiden: Brill 1997), 2.491–511.

Zech 13:9, as well as a renewed quotation from Isa 51:23–52:2, a text that has already been quoted within the chain of quotations above.

The following passages are quoted in col. I–III: Isa 40:1–5; 41:8–10; 43:1–7; 44:3; 49:7, 13–17; 51:22–52:3; and 54:4–10. It goes without saying that any conjecture as to the criteria which controlled the selection process must remain highly speculative. Nevertheless, it may be possible to point to some noteworthy traits connecting the passages cited.

Most of the selected texts contain words spoken by God. God speaks in the first person in Isa 41:8–10; 43:1–7; 44:3; 49:7; and 51:22–52:3.[26] The first quotation, the famous opening of Isaiah 40, consists of a divine uttering followed by a prophetic message speaking of God in the third person. Isa 49:13–17 starts out with a reference to God, then continues into a dialogue between the Lord and Zion.

If we turn our attention to the addressees of these passages, a revealing picture emerges. Isa 40:1–5 is again the exception, addressing the prophet, who is instructed to bring forth a divine message to "my people." However, the subsequent quotations (41:8–10; 43:1–7; 49:7) are all addressed to God's people, Israel, in the second person masculine singular, while the last three quotations (49:13–17; 51:22–52:3; 54:4–10) are addressed to Zion or Jerusalem in the second person feminine singular. This double form of address to God's people and to Zion could be said to correspond with the occurrence in the non-scriptural passages we have analyzed of a first person plural ("we" clearly representing God's people) and of a third person feminine which may with great plausibility be construed as representing Zion as subject to present affliction and future glory. The form of divine address to the people or to Zion, prevailing in the scriptural passages, is, as we have noticed, also mirrored at least once in the non-scriptural liturgical sections (4Q176 III, 16). In these passages, however, the people's address to God takes up most of the space, and they may be said to function, in relation to the quotations, as the "other" part of a liturgical dialogue.

We may note that the formula אל תירא is found in two of the passages (Isa 41:10; 43:1, 5). However, the same words "fear not" in 44:2 are apparently omitted. The use of this specific formula, in other words, does not seem to have been the criterion governing the selection of the scriptural passages. But if formal considerations were not

---

[26] This feature was observed and commented upon by Stanley, "The Importance," 577, and Campbell, *The Exegetical Texts*, 82.

the determining factor, we may indeed point to a considerable degree
of coherence when it comes to the content of the passages chosen. As
Stanley rightly observed, it is not difficult to identify the criteria behind
the selection. The passages quoted emphasize the love and faithfulness
of God towards his chosen people, and contain divine promises of a
future restoration. Stanley speaks of the passages being held together
by a common interpretative "story," in which the present is viewed
as a crucial moment in God's plan for his people, the time of divine
punishment and oppression by enemies nearing its end, and the new
era of unprecedented glory finally approaching.[27]

Again, we detect an evident degree of correspondence between the
main themes of the scriptural quotations and the non-scriptural passages surrounding these quotations. The idea of a transition from a
period of punishment and affliction to a new glorious state for Israel
is a dominant motif throughout 4Q176. The selection of passages from
Isaiah would appear to be to a large extent governed by the same
notion of a "salvation history" which we found to be prominent in the
non-scriptural sections. If this was indeed the criterion for choosing
these particular passages from Isaiah, it becomes less surprising that
themes of obvious importance within Isa 40–55 are altogether omitted.
Thus, no text referring to the servant of the Lord seems to have been
quoted in 4Q176; and the whole theme of polemics against idolatry
was apparently also left out. When viewed as a whole and held up
against the extant non-scriptural sections of 4Q176, the passages from
the Book of Isaiah exhibit a remarkable thematic and formal similarity
with those parts of the document. The selection of scriptural sources,
in other words, seems to have been carried out not for any "exegetical"
purposes, but rather to serve a particular function within the liturgical
framework apparently governing the composition in its entirety.

Conclusion

As the observations made above have shown, it would seem that the
terms "exegesis" and "treatise" are both inappropriate when it comes
to describing the content and genre of 4QTanḥumim. 4Q176 is not
an exegetical text in the sense of a text which has as its primary aim
to give an exposition of scriptural passages. In a broader sense, obvi-

---

[27] Stanley, "The Importance," 576–7. Cf. Campbell, *The Exegetical Texts*, 84.

ously, interpretation of scripture also takes place in 4Q176, but this interpretation is carried out indirectly, through the selection of certain passages, above all from the Book of Isaiah, and through the installation of these passages within a liturgical framework structured around a number of important themes—explicitly using, and referring to, the scriptural passages quoted as "words of consolation" to be heard in their new context. Our analysis has confirmed that 4Q176 should be regarded as a liturgical composition. The "treatise-like" elements, while showing remarkable similarities to passages from Qumran wisdom literature, may be naturally interpreted as parts of the liturgical whole, the discourse taking on, occasionally, a more "doctrinal" style, drawing, in all probability, on well-established traditional expressions. Interestingly, we encounter, at crucial points of transition from scriptural quotations to other liturgical material, rubrics or ordering and structuring sections with an implied speaker that is clearly different from the voice of the congregation heard in the liturgical passages.

A number of questions, obviously, remain unanswered at this point. We have no means of determining whether 4Q176 was a document actually meant to be used in some kind of liturgical celebration, even though such an assumption would seem natural. The nature of this festival or liturgical event, if indeed it existed, remains unknown.[28] Furthermore, it cannot be determined whether there once was a special relation between 4Q176 and other liturgical compositions from Qumran such as *Apocryphal Lamentations A* and *Apocryphal Lamentations B*. The implied readers of 4Q176 would be a "congregation" or a group of people expected to perform liturgical acts of recitation and listening. In itself, the composition shows no evidence of specifically "Qumranic" or "sectarian" terminology, and there is no direct proof that this text originated within the Qumran community. There are points of contact between 4Q176 and undisputedly "sectarian" documents, but with non-sectarian wisdom and liturgical texts as well.

As it happens, I believe the word "tanḥumim" as used in 4Q176, does not fit the document as a whole. However, I am also convinced that for practical purposes there is here a very strong case for retaining the name also in the future, since this is one of the designations that has become very widely accepted.

---

[28] As pointed out by Campbell, there is no real correspondence between 4Q176 and the later rabbinic work known as *Tanḥuma*, which contains homilies on the weekly Pentateuchal synagogue readings (Campbell, *The Exegetical Texts*, 86).

THEME AND GENRE IN 4Q177 AND ITS SCRIPTURAL SELECTIONS

Mark Laughlin and Shani Tzoref
Jerusalem

4Q177[1] has conventionally been classified as a "thematic pesher,"[2] or, more recently as "thematic commentary,"[3] or "eschatological midrash."[4] It is one of a group of Qumranic compositions in which the author cites and interprets biblical texts, applying them to the contemporary experience of his community, which he understands to be living in the eschatological era. Unlike the continuous pesharim, thematic pesharim are not structured as sequential commentaries on a particular

---

[1] John M. Allegro first pieced together the thirty fragments that he identified as comprising 4Q177, which he labeled 4QCatena A. Cf. John M. Allegro and Arnold A. Anderson. *Qumran Cave 4.I (4Q158–4Q186)* (DJD V; Oxford: Clarendon Press, 1968), 67–74, Pls. XXIV–XXV. John Strugnell subsequently added four additional fragments, and suggested improvements to Allegro's readings and reconstructions ("Notes en marge," 236–48). Annette Steudel re-worked the order of the material in 4Q174 and 4Q177, and argued that the two manuscripts should be regarded as parts of a single composition, which she termed 4QMidrEschat. See George J. Brooke, "From Florilegium or Midrash to Commentary: The Problem of Re/Naming an Adopted Manuscript," in this volume. Cf. Annette Steudel, *Der Midrasch zur Eschatologie aus der Qumrangemeinde (4QMidrEschat^{a,b}): Materielle Rekonstruktion, Textbestand, Gattung und traditionsgeschichtliche Einordnung des durch 4Q174 ("Florilegium") und 4Q177 ("Catena^a") repräsentierten Werkes aus den Qumranfunden* (STDJ 13; Leiden: Brill, 1994). The current discussion will touch upon the relationship between 4Q177 and 4Q174 but is primarily concerned with the composition of 4Q177 itself.

[2] The term was introduced by Jean Carmignac, "Le document de Qumrân sur Melkisedek," *RevQ* 7/27 (1969–1971): 343–78. For this classification of 4Q177, see John G. Campbell, "4QCatenae A–B (4Q177, 182)," in *The Exegetical Texts* (Companion to the Qumran Scrolls 4; London: T & T Clark, 2004), 45–55, esp. 47–49.

[3] See George J. Brooke, "Thematic Commentaries on Prophetic Scriptures," in *Biblical Interpretation at Qumran* (ed. Matthias Henze; Grand Rapids: Eerdmans, 2005), 134–57.

[4] See Steudel, *Der Midrasch zur Eschatologie.* On the general question of taxonomy and nomenclature, see the paper by Brooke in this volume. See also Steudel, "4QMidrEschat—'A Midrash on Eschatology' (4Q174 + 4Q177)," in *The Madrid Qumran Congress; Proceedings of the International Congress on the Dead Sea Scrolls, March 1991* (Vol. 2; ed. Julio Trebolle Barrera and Luis Vegas Montaner; Leiden: Brill, 1992), 531–41; "Eschatological Interpretation of Scripture in 4Q177 (4QCatena^a)," *RevQ* 14/55 (1990): 437–81.

biblical text.[5] Rather, they cite eclectically from a number of texts, purportedly in order to convey a particular theme. In this study, we suggest that the key to identifying the unifying theme of 4Q177 lies in the investigation of the criteria for the selection of biblical verses cited in the text.[6]

In continuous pesharim, the biblical feature that influences, or guides, the pesherist in structuring his composition is the structure of the biblical work being interpreted. In thematic pesher, and similar works, there is no single biblical composition exerting such direct control upon the commentator. But might there be an analogous process in which non-continuous exegetical works are shaped by the structure of their biblical base-texts? Certainly an important step in seeking to discern a unifying theme in such a composition is the attempt to identify shared features among the biblical verses cited in the text, and particularly the framing texts.[7]

Standard descriptions of the base-texts in 4Q177 include the observations that the framing texts are taken from Psalms, with subordinate citations deriving from diverse prophetic works and, in one case, from Deuteronomy.[8] The verses quoted from Psalms in the extant portion of the manuscript can be found listed in the table below. The verses

---

[5] On the continuous pesharim, see *inter alia* Maurya P. Horgan 1979, *Pesharim*; Shani L. Berrin, "Pesharim," *EDSS* (2000), 2.644–47; Timothy H. Lim, *Pesharim* (Companion to the Qumran Scrolls 3; London: Sheffield Academic Press, 2002).

[6] Hanan Eshel observed that analysis of 11QMelch and 4Q252 proceeded along a similar model, of isolating the cited biblical texts and then seeking their commonalities (personal communication, 2 November 2008). George Brooke discussed the necessity for determining the selection criteria in 4Q177 in his review of Steudel's monograph, "Review: Annette Steudel. *Der Midrasch zur Eschatologie aus der Qumrangemeinde (4QMidrEschat^{a,b}): Materielle Rekonstruktion, Textbestand, Gattung und traditionsgeschichtliche Einordnung des durch 4Q174 ("Florilegium") und 4Q177 ("Catena^a") repräsentierten Werkes aus den Qumranfunden,*" *JSJ* 26 (1995): 380–84.

[7] This is an adaptation of the approach to pesher interpretation advocated in Shani L. Berrin, *The Pesher Nahum Scroll from Qumran: An Exegetical Study of 4Q169* (STDJ 53; Leiden: Brill, 2004). We aim to be both "holistic and detail-oriented," (cf. ibid., p. 306) and sensitive to "lemma-pesher correspondence," i.e., to attend to the relationship between pesher and its base-text, both at the level of individual lemma-pesher units and on the larger-scale of compositional structure.

[8] Thus, Brooke, "Thematic Commentaries," 149; idem, "Catena," in *EDSS* 1.121–22; Steudel, *Der Midrasch zur Eschatologie*, 60; Campbell, *Exegetical Texts*, 51.

Table of Primary and Subordinate Citations[9]

4Q177	PSALMS	Non-Psalms
col. a *4Q174 frags. 13–14[10] Col. I frags. 5, 6, 8 (= Steudel's Col. VIII)	Ps 5:3 [Ps 10: ?3] Ps 11:1–2 Ps 12:1	Isa 37:30; Isa 32:7 Micah 2:11 (probable) Isa 27:11 (probable) Isa 22:13
Col. II frags. 7, 9, 10, 11, 20, 26 (= Steudel's Col. IX)	Ps 12:7 Ps 13:2–3 Ps 13:5a	Zech 3:9 Ezek 25:8
Col. III frags. 1, 2, 3, 4, 14, 24, 31 (= Steudel's Col. X)	Ps 16:3 Ps 17:1	Deut 7:15; Joel 2:2; Nah 2:11 Hos 5:8
Col. IV frags. 12–13 col. 1 (= Steudel's Col. XI)	Subordinate citation: Ps 6:2–3 Ps 6:4,5	Jer 18:18; Joel 2:20 (Isa 29:23; 35:10/51:11)

quoted from other works, in the subordinate citations, appear in the right-hand column of the table.

Looking at the cited verses from Psalms, it is clear that we are not dealing with a running verse-by-verse pesher. Thus, as stated by Jonathan Campbell, "4QCatena A is unlikely to be a Continuous Pesher on the Psalms in the way that 4QPsalms[a] appears to be."[11] It is worth noting, however, that even while 4Q177 differs from 4QPsalms[a] (4Q171) in that it does not cite any whole psalm, but only quotes snippets, or even just an initial verse or superscription (similar to the treatment of Psalms 1 and 2 in 4Q174),[12] it is actually more faithfully "consecutive" than 4Q171. In the latter pesher, classified as a continuous pesher, the commentary on Psalm 37 is followed by citation of Psalm 45:1–2, and

---

[9] The column numbers follow those found in the edition of Florentino García Martínez, DSSSE 1.362–68; *Dead Sea Scrolls Translated*, 209–11. Steudel's numbering presumes continuity of 4Q177 with 4Q174; cf. n. 1 above.

[10] We propose that the fragmentary citation and interpretation of Psalm 5, currently designated 4Q174 frags. 13–14 may in fact belong to 4Q177, as discussed below.

[11] Campbell, *Exegetical Texts*, 47, following Brooke, "Catena," 121; Geza Vermes, "Catena A or Midrash on the Psalms (4Q177)" in Emil Schürer, *The History of the Jewish People in the Age of Jesus Christ (175 B.C.–A.D. 135)* (rev. English version, ed. Geza Vermes and Fergus Millar; Edinburgh: T & T Clark, 1986) 3.1:448–49.

[12] 4Q174 III, 14, 18.

the next extant citation is from Psalm 60. In 4Q177, there are successive excerpts from Psalms 11, 12, 13, 16, and 17; it is also likely that a pesher interpretation of Psalm 10 is preserved directly prior to the citation of Psalm 11.[13]

The exploration of the continuity and non-continuity of these and related works is an important enterprise, but one that is beyond our immediate scope. For now, we are interested in the structural unity of 4Q177, through the choice of the above-mentioned psalms, in terms of both sequence and genre. Specifically, we propose that the extant portion of 4Q177 stands together as a commentary on the prayers that are clustered in the initial section of the book of Psalms (according to the arrangements of the Psalms as found in the MT).[14]

It is not necessary to enter into intricate form-critical analysis in order to characterize Psalms 3–17. Taking Limburg's entry on Psalms in the *Anchor Bible Dictionary* as a representative indicator of general scholarly assessment, we may note that he categorizes the following as individual laments: Psalms 3, 4, 5, 6, 7, 9, 10, 13 and 17.[15] Psalms 11

---

[13] In the first line of col. I. See Brooke, "Catena," 121; Campbell, *Exegetical Texts*, 49. The composition also includes citations from Psalm 6. Steudel has demonstrated that these citations must come later in the manuscript than the previous columns (on the basis of the physical damage patterns of the extant leather, using the "Stegemann method"); but she has also shown, on the basis of the use of citation formulas, that the quotations from Psalm 6 are subordinate rather than framing texts. Cf. Steudel, *Der Midrasch zur Eschatologie*, 142. Devorah Dimant accepts Steudel's characterization of these quotations as subordinate, in her review of Steudel's monograph. Cf. D. Dimant, "Review: Annete Steudel, *Der Midrasch zur Eschatologie aus der Qumrangemeinde (4QMidrEschat^a,b): Materielle Rekonstruktion, Textbestand, Gattung und traditionsgeschichtliche Einordnung des durch 4Q174 ("Florilegium") und 4Q177 ("Catena^a") repräsentierten Werkes aus den Qumranfunden*," *DSD* 10 (2003): 305–9. Although this explanation of the significance of the citation formula is persuasive, it is worth noting that the specific formula used in the citation of the excerpts from Psalm 6 (in 4Q177 IV, 7), אשר אמר without a conjunctive *waw*, is not common enough to justify definitive conclusions. It could plausibly be used as an introduction to a new primary text, rather than as a segue to a supporting citation. Steudel further believes that 4Q177 contains a quotation of Ps 5:10, between the citations of Psalm 12 and 13, in col. II, 5 (= Steudel's IX, 5), but the words כי אין do not require this restoration.

[14] There is no evidence from Qumran for any difference in sequence in this section of Psalms. See Eugene Ulrich et al., *Qumran Cave 4: XI; Psalms to Chronicles* (DJD XVI; Oxford: Clarendon, 2000); Peter W. Flint, *The Dead Sea Psalms Scrolls and the Book of Psalms* (STDJ 17; Leiden: Brill, 1997); idem, "Psalms, Book of," *EDSS* 2.702–10. It has been similarly observed of 4Q179, that "the sequence of the quotations seems to be given by the order of the biblical books (Ex., Num., Dt., and Jos.)" (A. Steudel, "Testimonia," *EDSS* 2.936. See also Hanan Eshel, *The Dead Sea Scrolls and the Hasmonean State* (Jerusalem: Yad Ben-Zvi, 2008), 66–67.

[15] James Limburg, "Psalms, Book of," in *ABD* 5.522–36.

and 12 are similar pleas to God for salvation against enemies, and Psalm 16 is considered a "song of confidence," which resembles the lament and plea in form and content. Of this group, psalms [10],[16] 11, 12, 13, 16, and 17 are represented in 4Q177 in the order in which they appear in Scripture. We further propose to add to this list, by relocating the fragments currently labeled frags. 13 and 14 of 4Q174, and placing them in 4Q177.[17] It is most likely that the three columns we have labeled 1 through 3 are consecutive, as reconstructed by Strugnell,[18] and followed by Annette Steudel,[19] so that Psalms 14 and 15 would not have been represented in the composition.[20] This would support the suggestion that the represented psalms are those in which an individual addresses God in the belief that God will hear his prayer and save him from his wicked enemies.

To summarize our evaluation of the use and placement of Psalms in our composition, we have observed that the framing texts of 4Q177 are excerpts from a series of individual prayer psalms, taken from some of Psalms 5 through 17 of the traditional psalter, in the traditional order. The inclusion of Psalm 5 is somewhat speculative. Psalm 6 is cited as well, but out of order, and as a subordinate citation rather than a primary one, as noted above. Our proposal about genre as a selection criterion for the framing texts can stand regardless of the placement of these citations of Psalm 6 in frags. 12–13. It would, however, be smoother for our overall thesis if these fragments could be positioned in accordance with the order of the biblical psalter, or if these subordinate citations could be viewed as secondary re-citations of material that had been cited earlier in the composition. Strugnell had stated that "without doubt" frags. 12–13 belonged earlier in the manuscript, in

---

[16] See above, n. 13.

[17] See the first row of our table above. Cf. Brooke, *Exegesis at Qumran*, 127. The text of these fragments was reconstructed by Strugnell as containing a citation of Ps 5:3 along with eschatological comment. Brooke (241 n. 141), noted that Strugnell ("Notes en marge," 237), may have already had this placement in mind.

[18] "Notes en marge," 236–46.

[19] *Der Midrasch zur Eschatologie*, 57–80 (though she labels these cols. IX to XI).

[20] Psalm 14 is a communal lament and Psalm 15 is a Torah psalm pertaining to Temple liturgy. As such, they would have been out of place, according to our proposed schema. Psalms 7, 9, and 10 could have appeared prior to the extant col. I, which begins with the apparent interpretation of Ps 10:3 and proceeds to a citation from Psalm 11 (Psalm 8, a thanksgiving hymn, is unlikely to have been included.)

keeping with the sequence of Psalms.[21] Steudel, however, has ruled out this possibility on the basis of the methodology of material reconstruction, firmly placing frags. 12–13 in the final column of the preserved sections of the composition.[22] Despite the puzzling placement of the Psalm 6 material, its inclusion in the list of quoted Psalms contributes to the evidence for the use of individual prayers in 4Q177.[23]

Sensitivity to the genre of these framing texts, as prayers for salvation from one's enemies, sharpens our understanding of 4Q177 in three ways. It offers insight into (a) the overall structure of the composition, (b) the selection of subordinate citations, and (c) the comments on the individual lemmas. The primary focus of our investigation below is the structure of columns I–III, but we shall also examine column IV, and conclude with some observations about subordinate citations and individual lemma/pesher sections.

[21] "Avec leur citation de l'*incipit* du Psaume 6, ils venaient sans doute avant les fragments 5–6" (Strugnell, "Notes en marge," 245). Thus, Edward Cook presents the fragments in sequential order according to the numbering of the biblical psalms, beginning with the citations from Psalm 6 (in Michael Wise, Martin Abegg, and Edward Cook, *The Dead Sea Scrolls: A New Translation* [San Francisco: Harper, 1996], 234–7.

[22] James C. VanderKam objects to her conclusion in "Review: Annette Steudel, *Der Midrasch zur Eschatologie aus der Qumrangemeinde (4QMidrEschat^{a,b}): Materielle Rekonstruktion, Textbestand, Gattung und traditionsgeschichtliche Einordnung des durch 4Q174 ("Florilegium") und 4Q177 ("Catena^a") repräsentierten Werkes aus den Qumranfunden," CBQ* 57 (1995): 576–7.
After the publication of Steudel's reconstruction in her monograph, Émile Puech suggested an alternative reconstruction for this column, removing Fragment 19 (which contained the lines labeled 1–6) from 4Q177, and placing this fragment in 4Q525 Beatitudes instead. Cf. Émile Puech, "4QBéatitudes," in *Qumran Grotte 4 XVIII* (DJD XXV; Oxford: Clarendon Press, 1998), 115–78, Pl. IX, XIII.
Even with the removal of frag. 19, the damage patterns of the manuscript do not justify a configuration of frags. 12 and 13 that would permit placing these pieces earlier in the manuscript (Steudel, personal communication, 18 June, 2009). The placement of the Psalm 6 material in the composition remains somewhat of a conundrum.

[23] Note that among the fragments of 4QPsalms^a (4Q83), the only preserved text up until ch. 25 is from Ps 5:9–6:4. In his entry on "Catena" in *EDSS* (p. 121), Brooke notes that these fragments appear after Ps 31; however, the subsequent publication of the official edition of this manuscript does not offer any indication of the placement of Pss 5–6 out of sequence, and the fragment containing this text is labeled "frag. 1." There is other material in this manuscript that differs from the sequence of MT, but this concerns later chapters of the Psalms. Cf. "4QPs^a," in DJD XVI, 7–22; Pl. I–II; esp. p. 8. Of the other Psalms manuscripts from Qumran, Psalm 6 appears only in 4QPs^s. This manuscript contains only Ps 5:8–6:1 (ibid. 153–64; Pl. XIX.)

STRUCTURE

The sectarian exegesis of 4Q177 is conveyed in a form that is modeled on the psalms of David used in its composition.[24] Examination of the texts cited in 4Q177 indicates that the author saw many similarities between the (then) current situation of his community and the situation ascribed to David in several of the psalms explicated in this text. The central theme of the work can thus be identified more precisely than the usual designation of "eschatological salvation."[25] The theme and the unifying structural focus is trust in divine salvation from persecution, in the manner of an Individual Lament or "Psalm of Confidence" in the Masoretic Psalms. More specifically, there is a discernible sequence in the extant portion of 4Q177 that corresponds to the elements of the individual lament isolated by modern form-critics,[26] as follows:

1. ADDRESS (PRAISE) TO GOD / CRY OF DISTRESS
2. COMPLAINT / LAMENT (at times with protestation of innocence)
3. EXPRESSION OF TRUST.
4. REASONS why God should help the one(s) praying (protestation of innocence/acknowledgment of sin accompanied by repentance)
5. [oracle of salvation]
6. VOW to offer PRAISE or SACRIFICE when the petition is heard.
7. [Grateful PRAISE to God.]

---

[24] Compare Flint's proposal that that ascription of Davidic authorship was a primary force in the structure of 11QPsᵃ. See Flint, *The Dead Sea Psalms Scrolls*, 174, 176, and 193–4.

[25] See the characterizations of the content in Brooke, "Catena," 122; Steudel, *Der Midrasch zur Eschatologie, passim*; Campbell, *Exegetical Texts*, 45; 51–4; Cook, *The Dead Sea Scrolls*, 233–4; Vermes, *The Complete Dead Sea Scrolls in English* (5th ed.; New York: Penguin, 1998), 504; Jacob Milgrom with Lydia Novakovic, "Catena A (4Q177 = 4QCatᵃ)," in PTSDSSP 6B.286–303 (the relevant description is on p. 285).

[26] Cf. Limburg, "Psalms, Book of," 531–2; Hermann Gunkel, *Introduction to the Psalms: The Genres of the Religious Lyric of Israel* (Mercer Library of Biblical Studies; Macon, GA: Mercer University Press, 1998), 152–86; Claus Westermann, *Praise and Lament in the Psalms* (Atlanta: John Knox Press, 1981), 176–94; Erhard S. Gerstenberger, *Psalms Part 1, With an Introduction to Cultic Poetry* (FOTL 14; Grand Rapids: Eerdmans, 1988); Sigmund Mowinckel, *The Psalms in Israel's Worship* (Sheffield: JSOT Press, 1992), 229–35.

The extant material in 4Q177 follows a sequence that matches the logical formal succession outlined above. Progression in the text has already been noted in previous studies. Thus, Brooke observed that the composition offers "a description of the sequence of events in the last days."[27] He stated that "the running narrative within the interpretation covers the flight of a persecuted community, description of various participants in the last days, a statement of the sure blessings that will be given to the Sons of Light, and the defeat of Belial and the end of his lot."[28] Cook too traced a progression, from a "sketch... [of] the 'Last Days' in general terms," to particular descriptions of the persecution and flight of the righteous, through the perceptions of the author about the time of testing during the flourishing of the wicked, and the assertion that the faithful will ultimately be vindicated in the Last Days.[29]

The development which these scholars recognized, and which they explained in terms of narrative sequence, is even more effectively understood in formal terms. The author of 4Q177 moves through the conventional elements of the lament, from the Address to God, through descriptive Complaints about the trials of the Community, and their persecution and frustrations, into Expressions of Faith and, probably, Praise.[30] Before turning to the text to illustrate this point, it is necessary to clarify two basic premises in our approach. (1) Although we will point out the significance of the specific cited verses, in each case, the Psalm in its entirety is relevant to the adaptation. Our discussion is thus informed by the principle that the original biblical context must be used to understand the new composition, with regard to both the framing-texts and the citations of texts other than Psalms.[31] (2) The claim

---

[27] "Catena," 122.

[28] Ibid.

[29] Wise, Abegg, and Cook, *The Dead Sea Scrolls*, 233–7.

[30] Once again, recall that Cook placed frags. 12 and 13, with the citation of Psalm 6, at the start of the preserved section of the manuscript (see n. 6 above). As in the case of the selection criteria for the base-texts, our observations about the structure of 4Q177 would be highly effective with Cook's arrangement, but they can also stand securely if this material is understood as reflecting subordinate citation later in the composition.

[31] Esther G. Chazon, "The Use of the Bible as a Key to Meaning in Psalms from Qumran," in *Emanuel: Studies in the Hebrew Bible, Septuagint, and Dead Sea Scrolls in Honor of Emanuel Tov* (ed. Shalom M. Paul et al.; Leiden: Brill, 2003), 85–96; eadem, "Scripture and Prayer in 'The Words of the Luminaries',," in *Prayers That Cite Scripture* (ed. James L. Kugel; Cambridge, Mass.: Harvard University Press [Center for Jewish Studies], 2007, 25–41). On evaluating the significance of the larger context of biblical citations and allusions in Qumran texts, see also Julie A. Hughes, *Scriptural Allusions: Exegesis*

for the adoption of the form of the individual lament pre-supposes a typological adaptation of the biblical base-texts such that the biblical prayers of individual leaders are taken to reflect the experience of the Community.[32]

Turning to the text, we begin our survey with the proposed column "a".[33] The restored citation from Ps 5:3 reflects an **ADDRESS**; a persecuted individual cries out to God.[34]

---

in the Hodayot (STDJ 59; Leiden. Brill, 2006), 41–55; H. Eshel on 4Q175 (4QTestimonia) in *The Dead Sea Scrolls and the Hasmonean State*, 80–3. Devorah Dimant proposed succinctly that an implicit quotation "may be defined as a phrase of at least three words, which stems from a specific recognizable context," ("Use and Interpretation of Mikra in the Apocrypha and Pseudepigrapha," in *Mikra; Text, Translation, Reading and Interpretation of the Hebrew Bible in Ancient Judaism and Early Christianity* [CRINT II/1], ed. Martin J. Mulder [Assen: van Gorcum; Philadelphia: Fortress Press, 1988], 401).

[32] On the identification of messianic biblical references as pertaining to the Community, see, for example, CD VII, 16–17, in which the "king" of Amos 5:26 is interpreted as the "congregation"; and 4Q174 I, 19, in which the "anointed one" of Ps 2:2 is interpreted as the plural "chosen ones." See Joseph Angel, "*The Traditional Roots of Priestly Messianism at Qumran,*" in *The Dead Sea Scrolls at 60: The Scholarly Contributions of NYU Faculty and Alumni* (ed. Lawrence H. Schiffman and Shani Tzoref; Leiden: Brill, forthcoming). See further, John J. Collins, "The Nature of Messianism in the Light of the Dead Sea Scrolls," in *The Dead Sea Scrolls in their Historical Context* (ed. Timothy H. Lim; Edinburgh: T. & T. Clark, 2000), 216–7. In Collins' view, these examples indicate that the biblical verse is taken "non-messianically"; this is technically accurate, but the the appropriations strengthen the Community's self-perception as the eschatological Elect. Compare Gunkel's objection that modern scholars tended to misconstrue individual laments as collective, and "universally related the 'I' of the complaint songs to the 'community'," (*Introduction to the Psalms*, 122).

[33] Our transcription and translation generally follow the versions found in Accordance 8 (roughly corresponding to that of E. Cook, *The Dead Sea Scrolls*, 234–37, with some rough adaptations, primarily on the basis of Steudel's edition and translation (*Der Midrasch zur Eschatologie*, 71–80). The text is provided for utilitarian purposes; no attempt has been made to create an accurate new edition. The official re-edition of the text is under preparation by Annette Steudel and George Brooke.

The Psalms citations are marked by *underlining* in the Hebrew and **bold italics** in the English. Citations from scripture other than psalms are indicated by *italics* in the English.

[34] It is possible that Psalms 3 and/or 4 would have been cited as well. Neither of these two psalms are represented in any of the ancient Psalms manuscripts found in the Dead Sea region. Of Psalms 1–89, Flint counts 19 psalms as not being found in these manuscripts. Another five psalms from 90–150 are not represented. (Cf. Flint, *The Dead Sea Psalms Scrolls*, 48 n. 139 and 142 n. 21.) Flint surmises that "all or most of the twenty-four 'missing' Psalms were most likely included, but these are now lost due to the fragmentary state of most of the scrolls" (idem, 48).

*col. "a" (currently 4Q174 frags. 13–14)
Persecuted individual cries out to God

ADDRESS

יֹחֹרוֹבֹ 1

הקשיֹבֹה לקוֹ]ל שועי מלכי ואלוהי כיא אליכה אתפלל... 2

הדבר לאחרית ה]ימים 3

[...]כיא המה] 4

1 °°*rw*°
2 **He[e]d the sou[nd of my cry, my king and God, for I pray to you** (Ps 5:3)
3 the word for the end of d[ays]
4 for they

In column I, the citations are from the opening verses of Psalm 11 and Psalm 12, as we move to COMPLAINT and expression of TRUST:

Col. I 4Q177 frags. 5, 6, 8 (= Steudel col. VIII) comment to Ps 10:[3];
Ps 11:1–2; Ps 12:1
Arrogant Speakers of Falsehood oppress the humble ones,
but they will be destroyed.
COMPLAINT; Comments: Expression of TRUST

[...ה ההוללים אשר יֹ]... [בֹא על אנשי היֹ]חד 1

הנ]ביא אכול השנה שפֹ]יח ובשנה השנית שחיס vac ואשר אמ]ר השפיח הוֹ]א... 2

[...רֹה עד עת המצֹ]רף ...[אחרי כן יעמוד] 3

[...כֹיא כולם ילדים]...[אמרו ההולליֹ]ם 4

... כתוב] עליהם בספר יֹשעיה ...[יֹא תורת ההוֹ] 5

[...קרא להם כאשר]... הוא זֹ]מות יעץ לחֹ]בל ענוים 6

-- באמרי שקר ...[הלצון את ישרא]ל. למנצח] לדויד ביהוֹה] חסיתי 7

כי הנה הרשעים ידרכון קשת]ויכי]נֹ<ו> חצים עֹ[ל יתר לירות במו 8

אפל לישרי לב פשרו א[שר ינודו אן] 9

... כצֹ]פור ממקומו וגלֹ]ה ... עליהֹ]ם בספר הֹ] 9

[... ץֹ לה איש הלך רֹ]...[רֹ]°°° ∘∘[...]°°° סם היאֹ] 10

[... °]אֹשר כתוב עליהם בספר]...[חֹד ערומי ∘] 11

[... דֹ {{ר}}אוֹ   למנצח על הֹ]שמינית...] כיא לוא עם ∘] 12

[... המה העונה השמינית]... 13

... אֹ]ין שלום אשר המה דוֹ]...]∘ 14

[... הֹרוג בקר ושחוט צואן אֹ]כול בשר ושתות יין 15

[... סֹ∘[... ת התורה עושי היחד ס] 16

1 ...] the *boasters* who [...] against the men of the Com[munity...
2 as it is written in the book of Isaiah the p]rophet, *This year eat what grows [by itself, and next year the aftergrowth* (Isaiah 37:30)... sa]ys "*what grows by itself*" is [...
3 ...] up to the time of refi[ning...] and afterwards shall appear [...
4 ...] for all of them are children [...] said the boaste[rs...]

5   ...that is written] about them in the book of I[saiah the prophet...for]
     the Law of the *hw*[
6   ...]calls them, as [...*He thinks up p*]*lots to [destroy the humble with
     lying words*" (Isa 32:7)
7   ...] of scoffing Israe[l...*For the leader.] Of David. In the Lord [I take
     refuge; how can You say to me, 'Flee to your mountain, bird.' For see
     the wicked bend]*
8   *bow,] they set their arrow on [the string to shoot from the shadows
     at the upright of heart* (Psalm 11:1–2) ...th]at the me[n...] will flee.
9   ...like] a bird from its place and th[ey] will be exil[ed...written
     about] in the book of the[...
10 ...]it belongs to *a man who walks in w[indy, baseless falsehoods.*
     (Micah 2:10?–11)...
11 ...] as is written about them in the book of [... ???
12 ...] ∘∘ *For the leader. On the [eighth. A psalm of David*... (Psalm 12:1)
     for it is not a nation of [discernment... (Isa 27:11)
13 ...]*hmh* the eighth season [...
14 ...*there is n]o peace* (Jer 6:14; 8:11; Ezek 13:10), that they *dw*[...
15 ...] *killing cattle and slaughtering sheep, ea[ting meat and drinking
     wine* ..." (Isaiah 22:13)....]
16 ...]∘t of the Law, the doers of the Community *s*∘[....]

As noted above, we follow Brooke's suggestion that the initial lines of
this column reflect a commentary on Psalm 10, specifically verse 3,
which contains the root הלל, found in the first line of this column in
the word הוללים.[35] In the citations from Psalms 10 and 11, the composition moves to **COMPLAINT**. The citation from Psalm 12 seems
to be comprised of the incipit alone. This affords the commentator the
opportunity to elaborate upon the Expression of **TRUST**.

    At the beginning of this column, we encounter the sort of theological
give-and-take that is characteristic of the classic lament, but with a
noticeably Qumran twist. In the list of formal elements above, we noted
that "protestations of innocence" are often incorporated into the Complaint. Here, in place of that element, which would challenge the justification for his suffering, the author puts forth the theodicy of "the
period of refinement," apparently asserting the belief that the suffering
itself is an expression of God's intervention on behalf of His Elect.[36]

---

[35] Ps 10: 3 כִּי-הִלֵּל רָשָׁע עַל-תַּאֲוַת נַפְשׁוֹ, "The wicked one **boasts** about his unbridled
lust." Cf. n. 13 above; Brooke, "Catena," 121; Campbell, *Exegetical Texts*, 49. The term
הוללים appears in line 4 as well.

[36] Steudel points to the phrase על (ה) המצרף הבא (עת) as unique to 4QFlor and
4Q177 (*Midrasch zur Eschatologie*, 149), but the term מצרף for a period of eschatological testing is found also, e.g., in CD XX, 27 (יומי מצרפותיו) and in 1QS I, 17; VIII, 4.

In the final section of this column, the commentator atomizes the word "eight" from Ps 12:1 to express his own message, which is best understood as an affirmation of trust.[37] The term "eight" has a purely technical sense and function in the biblical text, presumably indicating a musical notation (שמינית). The author of 4Q177 apparently takes this word as signaling the anticipated arrival of the final era of Judgment.[38] The words העונה השמינית are best understood in light of the *Apocalypse of Weeks*:

> After this there will arise an *eighth week* of righteousness, in which a sword will be given to all the righteous to execute righteous judgment on all the wicked, and they will be delivered into their hands. And at its conclusion, they will acquire possessions in righteousness, and the temple of the kingdom of the Great One will be built in the greatness of its glory for all the generations of eternity.[39]

At this juncture, our author has taken up the element of Affirmation of Confidence, which is typically at the center of a psalm of individual lament. Atomization enables the author to use Psalm 12:1 to suit his literary purpose, even though it is the opening verse of the psalm. He uses the word "eight" as a springboard for introducing the idea of an eighth week, in which the Elect will triumph over their enemies.

Column II continues the Affirmation of **TRUST**.

4Q177 col. II frags. 7, 9, 10, 11, 20, 26 (= Steudel col. IX)
Ps 12:7; Ps 13: 2–3, 5
A divinely inspired leader will overcome the sophists; faith despite delay; mockery of the wicked
TRUST; REASONS **for divine intervention**

---

[37] The term "atomization" here denotes interpretation of a word in a manner that is incompatible with its original biblical context. Although atomization ought not be viewed as a fundamental hermeneutic in pesher, it is certainly one of the implements in the exegete's toolbox. See Berrin, *The Pesher Nahum Scroll*, 12–3, 28, 131–3, 140–1, 157.

[38] In her commentary on the words העונה השמינית, Steudel notes with a question mark the possible relevance of the *Apocalypse of Weeks*, as an alternative to Milik's association of the use of this phrase here with priestly courses (*Midrasch zur Eschatologie*, 88 n. 2; cf. Józef T. Milik, "Milki-sedeq et Milki-resha dans les anciens écrits juifs et chrétiens," *JJS* 23 [1972]: 132–3).

[39] *1 Enoch* 93:12–13 (= ch. 91) (transl. George W. E. Nickelsburg, *1 Enoch: a Commentary on the Book of 1 Enoch* [Hermenia: a Critical and Historical Commentary on the Bible; Minneapolis: Fortress Press, 2001], 434). On the significance of the *Apocalypse of Weeks* in works found at Qumran, and for bibliography on the eighth week as the beginning of a "meta-historical cycle" in this schema, see Hanan Eshel, "*Dibre Hame'orot* and the Apocalypse of Weeks," in *Things Revealed: Studies in Early Jewish and Christian Literature in Honor of Michael E. Stone* (ed. Esther G. Chazon, et al.; JSJSup 89; Leiden: Brill, 2004), 149–54, esp. 149–50.

אמרות יהוה אמרות טהרות כסף צרוף בעליל לארץ מזק[ק   1
שבעתים כאשר כתוב

...על אבן אחת שבעת עיניים מפ[תחת פתוחה נואם יהוה אשר   2

...א[שר עליהם כתוב ורפאתי את   3

...כ[.]ל אנשי בליעל וכול האספסוף   4

...]המה דורש התורה כיא אין   5

...]איש על מצורו בעומדם   6

...]ס[...]המכשילים את בני האור   7

...עד אנה יהו[ה תשכח[ני נצח עד אנה תסת[יר פניכה ממני עד   8
אנה אשיתה

עצות[בנפשי]יגון ב[לבב]י י[ומם עד אנה יר]ום אויבי עלי[פשר   9
הדבר [ע]ל נצח לב אנשי

...]ה[.]...[.]..ה באחרית הימים כיא[...]לבוחנם ולצורפם   10

...]יהם ברוח וברורים ומזוקק[ים...א[]מר פן יאמר אויב   11

יכלתיו...]המה עדת דורשי ח[ל]קות המ[...]ד אשר יבקשו לחבל   12

...]בקנאתמה ובמשטמ[ה...] ל פש[...כאש[]ר כתוב בספר יחזקאל   13
הנ[ביא

...] יהודה ככול העמ[י]ם [...] .[...]הימים אשר יקבצו עליה[ם   14

...]עם צדיק ורשע אויל ופתי[...]י האנשים אשר עבדו אל[]הים   15

...הס[]רו ערלות לב[ן]ב[שרם בדור הא[חרון...]..].[ ]וכ[ו]ל אשר   16
להמה טמא ול[

1   *The words of the Lord are pure words, silver refined in an earthen
    crucible, purg]ed sevenfold.* (Ps 12:7), as it is written,
2   *...upon a single stone are seven eyes. I am engr]aving an inscription,
    declares the Lord* (Zech 3:9) that
3   *...wh]ich it is written concerning them, And I shall heal the*
4   *...a]ll the men of Belial and all the rabble*
5   ...]*hmh the Interpreter of the Torah, for there is no*
6   ...] each man on his watch-tower when they stand
7   ...]°*m* [...] who causes the Sons of Light to stumble
8   ... *How long, O Lor]d? Will You forget [me forever? How long will
    You hi]de Your face from me? How long will I set*
9   *cares] on my soul, [grief on my] heart [all day]? How long [shall
    my enemy exult over me?* (Psalm 13:2–3)] The interpretation of the
    statement concerns the eternity of heart(s) of the men of
10 in the last days, for [...] to test them and to refine them
11 ...] their [...] with spirit, and pure and refin[ed...] *Lest the enemy say*
12 *'I have overcome him...'* (Psalm 13:5)] they are the congregation of
    the Seekers After Smooth Things *hm*[...] seek to destroy
13 ...] in their zeal and in th[eir] hatred [...a]s is written in the book
    of Ezekiel the pro[phet...
14 *Because Moab has said, 'Behold, the house of]* Judah *is like all the
    nations"* (Ezek 25:8). [...to the Last] Days, when [the...] will gather
    together against [them ..
15 ...] with the righteous, but the wicked, foolish and simpl[e...] of the
    men who have served Go[d...
16 ...] who have removed the *foreskins of their heart* of flesh in the in the
    la[st] generation [...] and all that is theirs is unclean and n[ot...

In col. II, the lemma comes from the end of the psalm, Ps 12:7, which is well-suited to the affirmation of TRUST. The citations from Psalm 13 return to the complaint, and move forward to offer **REASONS**, both for the current suffering and for the anticipated divine salvation. The rationale for the suffering as a time of testing is repeated, and incorporates a statement about the fidelity of the righteous in lines 9 to 11.[40] In its original context, the reference to the exultation of the enemies in Ps 13:5 ("Lest the enemy say 'I have overcome him…'") probably functions as an elaboration of the individual's plea—the psalmist's fear that his situation will worsen even further in the absence of divine intervention (continuing the thread in the previous verse, "lest I sleep the sleep of death"). 4Q177 does not seem to adopt this tone of near-despair; lines 11–14 may perhaps adapt the phrase as a statement of incentive, suggesting that one reason for God to save His Community is to prevent the wicked from denying the truth regarding God and the Community, as they are wont to do in their arrogance.[41]

Column III appears to offer closure.
4Q177 col. III frags. 1, 2, 3, 4, 14, 24, 31 (= Steudel col. X) [13:6?];
Ps 16:3; Ps 17:1
Vow to offer PRAISE; ADDRESS (inclusio?)

1   ...כו?]ל דבריהם [...]ₒ[...]ת.[שֹׁבחֹת הכבוד אשר יואמֹ]ר...
2   ...והסיר יהוה] מֹמֹכֹה כול חלי לקדֹו[שים אשר]בא[רץ] הֹמה ואדֹירֹי כול חפצֹי [בם ...
3   ...]ₒ נהיה כמוהֹו [...ולב נמס ו]פֹיק[ב]רכים וחלחלה בכול מתֹנ[ים]...

---

[40] In the biblical psalm, vv. 2 and 3 comprise the address and complaint: "How long, O Lord…?" The author of 4Q177 uses these words to reflect upon the rationale for the prolonged time of trial, to perfect the Community and prove its faithfulness. Cf. 1QpHab VII, 5–14.

[41] Cf. Deut 9:28, "else the country from which you freed us will say (פֶּן יֹאמְרוּ), 'It was because the Lord was powerless to bring them into the land that He had promised unto them';" Deut 32:27, "But for fear of the taunts of the foe, their enemies who might misjudge and say (פֶּן יֹאמְרוּ), 'Our own hand has prevailed; none of this was wrought by the Lord'." See also Num 14:15–16. There may even be a sort of *gezera shava* in operation in the use of this expression, since (ו)יאמרו + פן occurs in only one other verse in the HB besides Ps 13:5, Deut 9:28, and Deut 32:27. See Elieser Slomovic, "Toward an Understanding of the Exegesis in the Dead Sea Scrolls," *RevQ* 7/25 (1969–1971): 5–10, and sources cited there, p. 6 n. 16. The subsequent verses in Deuteronomy 32 read "for they are a folk void of sense, lacking in all discernment; were they wise, they would think about this, gain insight into their future (אחריתם)" (vv. 28–29). In CD V, 17, Deut 32:28 is applied to the enemies of the community. Note the similarity of גוי...ואין בהם תבונה in Deut 32:28 to Isa 27:11 כי לא עם בינות הוא, probably cited in 4Q177 I, 2, as a subordinate citation in a comment to Ps 12:1.

[...] ‎[.]‎ר‎[...]‎ ‎[...]‎ל‎[...]‎ל‎°‎תמה שמעה‎] יהוה צדק‎] הקשׁיבה רנתי   4
האזינה ל‎[תפלתי

‎[...]‎וׄ‎[באחרית הימים בעׄת אשר יבקש ‎°[...]‎° את עצת היחד הוׄא   5
ה‎[...

‎[...]‎° פשר הדבר אשר יׄעמוד איש מבי‎°[...]‎°° רי °°°° ‎[.]‎ל‎[

‎[...]‎היו כׄאׄש לכול תבל והמה אשר כתוב עליהם באחרית ‎] הימים   7
‎[...]°°‎ה פוחׄזים

‎[...]‎מׄ‎°°[גׄ]‎ורל אור אשר היׄה מתאבל בממשלת בל‎[יׄ]‎על‎[...]‎אשר   8
היה מתאבל ‎]

‎[...]‎בה ממנו וׄ‎[...]‎ לרׄאשי אבל שוב °°° ‎[-- א]‎לׄוהי הרחמים   9
ואׄל ישרא‎[ל...]‎מׄול כׄ‎[...

‎[...]‎אׄשר הׄ‎[ת]‎גׄוללו ברוחׄ‎[י ב]‎לׄיעל ונסלחׄ להם לעולם וברכׄם ‎[...]   10
עודׄ<מידׄ>לעולם יברכםׄ‎.. פׄ‎[לׄ]‎אׄי קציׄהם

‎[...]‎ת אבותם בׄמספר שמותׄ‎[ם]‎ מפורשים בׄשמות לאיש ואיש   11
‎[...]°‎ שׄ‎[נ]‎ותיהם וקץ מעמדם וׄ ‎[...]‎ יׄ לשונגם‎]

‎[...]‎אׄ את צאצׄ‎[אי יהודה] ו]‎עׄתה הנה הכול כתוב בלוחות   12
אשׄר‎[...]‎ אׄל ויׄ‎[דׄ]‎יׄעהו את מסׄפר ‎°[...]‎ותׄ וינחׄ‎[

‎[...]‎°°[...]‎לׄ ‎[ו] ‎ולזׄרׄעו ‎[עד] עׄולם ויקום משׄנה ללכת מן   13
ארם ‎[...]‎תקעׄו שופר בגבעה השופר הואה ספר‎]

‎[...]‎°°[...]‎היׄ‎[...]‎אׄה ספר התורה שנית אשרׄ מאסו כ‎[ול א]‎נׄשׄיׄ עצתו   14
וידברו עליו סרה וישלחׄ‎]

‎[...]‎או‎[תׄות]‎{{עׄ}} גדולות על ה‎°[...]‎°‎° ויעקוב עומד על הגתות ושמח על   15
רׄדׄתׄ‎]

‎[...]‎תׄ בתׄרׄב אׄ‎[...]‎לׄאנשי עצתו המה החרב ואשר אמר‎]   16

1 ...]*l their words* [...]° [...*pra*]*ises of glory that* [...] *shall utter*

2 ...*The Lord shall remove*] *from you* **every illness** (Deut 7:15) **To the ho[ly ones that are] in the la[nd] and the mighty ones in [whom] is all my delight** [...

3 ...] *has* [n]*ever been like it* [...] (Joel 2:2); [...*and*] *knocking of knees and trembling in everyone's loins* (Nahum 2:11) [...

4 ...]*l°tmh* **Hear, [O Lord, justice.] Listen to my cry, give ear to [my prayer** (Psalm 17:1) [...

5 ...]*w in the Last Days in the time when He shall seek* ° [...] *the council of the Community. That is* [...

6 ...] *The meaning of the verse is that a man shall arise from b*[...

7 ...] *they will be like a fire on the whole earth. They are the ones about whom it is written, in the last* [days...]°°*h pwh*[??? (Zeph 3:4 *reckless* פוחזים)

8 ...*s*]*aid concerning the* [l]*ot of Light who grieved during the rule of* Be[lial], [...] *who grieved* [...

9 ...]*bh from him* [...] *mourning. Return, O Lord,* [...*G*]*od of mercy and to Israe*[l *re*]*compense k*[...

10 ...] *who have defiled themselves with the spirit*[s of Be]*lial, but let it be forgiven them forever, and bless them* [...] *He will bless them forever* [...*won*]*ders of the*[ir] *periods*[...

11 ...] their fathers, according to the number of [their] names, specified
     by names, for each man ○ [...] their [y]ears and the period of their
     position, an[d...]*y* their tongue [...

12 ...] the descendants of Judah. [And] now, behold, all is written on
     the tablets that [...] God, and He told him the number of [...]○*t* and
     he will cause them to i[nherit...

13 ...] and to his offspring forever. And he arose from there to go
     [from Aram]. *Blow the horn in Gibeah* (Hosea 5:8). The *"horn"* is
     the [...] book of [the Law...

14 ...] is the book of the second Law that [...] men of his council
     rejected, and they spoke rebelliously against him and th[ey] sen[t...

15 ...] great [si]gns upon the [...] and Jacob is to stand on the wine-
     presses and he will rejoice over their downfall[...

16 ...] chosen [...] the men of his council. They are "the *sword*." And
     that which said [....

It is not clear why Strugnell reconstructed line 1 of this column as pertaining to songs of praise,[42] but this certainly suits the schema we have been
tracing. The final essential element in the individual lament is the Vow to
offer **PRAISE** or sacrifice when the petition is heard. Strugnell most likely
considered this text to reflect Ps 13:6, the concluding verse of the Psalm:

> I, in Your lovingkindness I have trusted; My heart shall rejoice in Your
> salvation. I will sing to the Lord, for He has dealt bountifully with me

> (וַאֲנִי בְּחַסְדְּךָ בָטַחְתִּי יָגֵל לִבִּי בִּישׁוּעָתֶךָ אָשִׁירָה לַיהוָה כִּי גָמַל עָלָי)

This song of **PRAISE**, especially if dependent upon 13:6 "I will sing,"
as a Vow of Praise, is precisely in place for the conclusion of a lament
or song of confidence. The subsequent citation, Ps 16:3, is somewhat
obscure; it does not seem to be followed by any direct commentary, but
only by two subordinate citations. The function of this text ("To the
ho[ly ones that are] in the la[nd] and the mighty ones in [whom] is all
my delight") seems to be to emphasize the sectarian belief that the exclu-
sive beneficiaries of the anticipated salvation, when God heeds the plea
inherent in the lament form, will be the deserving Elect, i.e. the Community. The subsequent citation, Ps 17:1, is once again an **ADDRESS**
to God, selected from the beginning of the psalm, "Hear, [O Lord, justice.] Listen to my cry, give ear to [my prayer." If our above proposal
is correct, and the cycle of Psalms citation and comments that we
have surveyed here originally began with Psalm 5, then Psalm 17 pro-

---

[42] "Notes en marge," 237–8; 240.

vides effective closure, in that it echoes the opening words of Psalm 5.[43] The cycle does seem to end in this column; after the citation of Ps 17:1, there are no more citations of psalms in this column. The Community has been brought to salvation, and there is a discernible shift in tone from pleas and affirmations to descriptive language.

Although column III completes the cycle we have traced—the creative use of excerpts of individual lament psalms from Psalms 5–17 to construct a commentary with a literary structure based on the form of such a lament—this column is not the end of the manuscript. It is important here to bear in mind observations such as those of Jesper Høgenhaven on 4QTanḥumim and of Moshe Bernstein and Eileen Schuller on 4Q371–373, regarding the need to attenuate our expectations of homogeneity for Qumran compositions.[44] With this in mind, if the lengthy citation from Psalm 6 in "col. IV" is correctly placed after the citation of Psalm 17, and is indeed a subordinate citation, then it is not integral to creating the structure and framework outlined in the previous columns. Its precise relationship to the preceding material is not entirely clear, but it is noteworthy that col. IV incorporates all the essential elements of the lament:

col. IV 4Q177 frags. 12, 13[45]
persecuted individual cries out to God
ADDRESS; COMPLAINT. Comments: Expression of Trust

6	[...]מֹֿנביא [תורה מֿכֿ [והן ועצה מחכם ודבר]
7	... [לאחרית הֿ [י]מים אֿשר אמר דויד יֿהֿ [ו]הֿ אל באפכה
	תוֹ[כיחני ... כי]א אמלל אני
8	... [ונֿפשי נבהלה מאדה ועתה יהוה עד מתי חונני חלצה
	נפֿ[שי...ש]יֿ[...]∘מים על
9	... [ב]ליעל להאבידמה בחרונו אשר לוא יותיר ל[...]ח∘∘לבליעל
10	... [∘הם עד עשרה צדיקים בעיר כיא רוח אמת ה∘[...]א כי]∘א אין
11	... [מֿה ואחיהמה במחשבל בליעל ויחזק עליוֿן[...]∘∘∘ל[...]∘∘∘

---

[43] If Psalms 3 and 4 were part of this commentary on Psalms, it would be less simple to account for the citation of Psalm 17. It would presumably function as a summary of the preceding Plea for Deliverance even without an inclusio.

[44] Jesper Høgenhaven, "The Literary Character of 4QTanhumim," *DSD* 14 (2007): 99–123, and idem, "4QTanḥumim (4Q176): Between Exegesis and Treatise?" in this volume. Eileen Schuller and Moshe J. Bernstein, "4Q371–373. 4QNarrative and Poetic. Composition a–c" in *Qumran Cave 4.XXVIII. Miscellanea, Part 2* (ed. E. Schuller et al. DJD XXVIII; Oxford: Clarendon, 2001), 151–4.

[45] The line numbering begins with line 6, to maintain the conventional numbering found in previous publications, before Puech moved frag. 19 to 4QBéatitudes (see above n. 22).

[... מלאךֹ אמתֹו יעזור לכול בני אור מיד בליעֹל ...]   12

ידיהם[...]◦ ◦◦◦[...]ולפזר[ם] באֹרֶץ ציה וׁשׁממהˣ היא עת ענות   13
המ[...]

כיא ה[...]תמדֹ ידוד ה[..]◦ ויד אל הגדולה עמהמה לעוזׁרם מכול   14
רוחו[ן]

[...]◦◦[◦אׁו אל יֹקדיׁשו שמו ובאו ציון בסמחה וירושלים]   15

...ב[ל]ל[יע]ל כול אנשי גורלו ו[..]◦[..] לעד וֹנֹאֹספו כול בני א[ור...   16

6   ...] Instruction [shall not fail] from the pr[iest, nor counsel from the
sage, nor oracle] from the prophet (Jer 18:18).

7   ...] for the Last Days, as David said, **O Lord, do not pu[nish me]
in Your anger [...fo]r I languish.**

8   **Heal me, O Lord, for my bones shake with terror], my soul is stricken
with terror. And now, O Lord. How long? Have mercy upon me. Rescue
my soul.** (Psalm 6:2–5) [...Latter D]ays about

9   ...Be]lial to destroy them in his wrath, that he will not leave °[...]°
to Belial

10   ...Abra]ham up to ten men in the city (cf. Gen 18:32) for the spirit
of truth °[...fo]r there is no

11   ...] and their brothers by the wiles of Belial, and he will strengthen [...

12   ...] the angel of His truth will help all the children of light from the
hand of Belial [...

13   ...] and to scatter [them] in *a dry and desolate land* (Joel 2:20). This
is the time of (tribulation/response?) *hm*[...

14   ...]*tmd* the °[..]° will flee and the great hand of God is with them
to help them from all spirit[s....

15   ...]°°of God will *sanctify his name* (Isa 29:23), and *they shall enter Zion
with joy* (Isa 35:10/51:11) and Jerusalem [...

16   ...B]el[ia]l and all the men of his lot, [...] forever and all the sons of
li[ght] will be gathered [...

The citation in this column includes an ascription of Davidic authorship
for the biblical psalm, but his words are taken to reflect the emotions
and experience of the Community. The quotation in line 7 again begins
with an **ADDRESS** ("O Lord") from Psalm 6:2, and then moves on to
the **COMPLAINT**, including the words "how long." As in the exegesis
of Ps 13:2 in col. ii, these words offer a **REASON** for the suffering, and
a rationale for why the community is deserving of redemption. In the
text following the citation, the author of 4Q177 moves beyond the complaint to express his **TRUST** in divine salvation and justice.

SUBORDINATE CITATIONS

To this point, we have focused on the Psalms citations as framing-texts for the extant material in 4Q177. Any analysis of the citation of biblical works other than Psalms in this composition must be considered tentative, due to the imperfect state of preservation of the manuscript. The fragmentary state of the document interferes with identification of biblical citations and their functions, and systematic treatment of this material will best be undertaken after the new edition of the text has been produced. Nonetheless, some preliminary remarks are appropriate here, particularly with respect to the function of the non-Psalms citations in light of our proposal that the structure of the work is modeled on individual laments. The use of biblical language is pervasive in this text, as is typical of Qumran compositions, and it is often unclear whether a particular biblical expression should be viewed as simply reflecting the allusive idiom of the commentator, or whether it serves a more formal role as a subordinate citation, or prooftext.[46] There are, moreover, a number of instances where citation formulas introduce words or phrases that simply cannot be identified with any known biblical text (e.g., col. II, line 3, "…. written concerning them, *And I shall heal the*…"). With the above caveats, we have nonetheless produced a preliminary list of cases identified as citations, as found in the table at the beginning of this paper. There is room for some debate, but basically, the criteria for inclusion in this table were either (a) the presence of a quotation formula or identification formula accompanying the biblical expression,[47] or (b) the length of the expression and the distinctiveness of its terminology.[48]

The texts we will focus upon briefly here are Isa 37:30, Jer 18:18, and Joel 2:20. In col. 1, apparently within a comment on Psalm 10, there is an excerpt from Isa 37:30. This verse is a response to Hezekiah's prayer

---

[46] See the sources cited in n. 29, above.

[47] On the formulas used in 4Q177 to introduce biblical quotations and to introduce interpretive identifications, see Steudel, *Der Midrasch zur Eschatologie*, 129–31.

[48] Thus we have included Joel 2:20, בְּאֶרֶץ צִיָּה וּשְׁמָמָה from line 13 of col. IV in the table, even though the verb in 4Q177₂, וּלְפֹזְר]ם, reflects a paraphrase of MT וְהִדַּחְתִּיו rather than a direct quote, since צִיָּה וּשְׁמָמָה בְּאֶרֶץ is a distinctive collocation and it is followed by the identifying formula "הִיא" in הִיא עֵת עֲנוּת.

earlier in the chapter;[49] it describes the sign given by Isaiah to Heze-kiah when Hezekiah receives word from the Rabshakeh that the Assyr-ians will destroy Jerusalem.[50] In spite of Hezekiah's record as a good king, he came under the threat of an enemy army. In this situation, Hezekiah acted righteously and turned to the Lord for help and God gave good news to Hezekiah through Isaiah. The introduction to Isa-iah's words, in verse 21, reads, "Thus said the Lord, the God of Israel to whom you have prayed…" Thus, the original context of the cited text is a positive divine response to the prayer of a leader.

The citations from Jer 18:18 and Joel 2:20 likewise derive from con-texts in which God responds to the prayers of victims of persecution. Jeremiah's prayer begins "Listen to me, O Lord, and take note of what my enemies say" (vs. 19; יריבי...הקשיבה ה' אלי ושמע לקול). This would create an effective inclusio with Psalm 5:3 הקשׁיָבה לקון[ל שועי which we have posited as having been cited at the beginning of this section of 4Q177.[51]

Joel 2:20 is not the lament of a leader, like David or Jeremiah. It is, however, an excerpt from God's response to the prayer of the nation earlier in the chapter, that was intended as part of a penitential program to obtain God's mercy from before the Gentiles. The response is intro-duced in verse 19, "In response to His people, the Lord declared" (ויען ה' ויאמר לעמו). I therefore suggest that the phrase עת ענות in line 13, fol-lowing the phrase from Joel 2:20, may not be related to the time of fast-ing in 4Q171, as proposed by Strugnell (with the root ענה as affliction),[52] but rather may be the time of God's response (ענה as response.).[53]

---

[49] On the prayers of Hezekiah and Isaiah, see Hanan Eshel and Esther Eshel, "4Q448, Psalms 154 (Syriac), Sirach 48:20, and 4QpIsaᵃ," *JBL* 119 (2000): 649–50.

[50] The author of 4Q177 may have attributed particular significance to the "sign" in the biblical context, for this transitional section where the tone shifts to expressions of confidence. Zech 3:9, cited in the comments to Psalm 12 in the following column of 4Q177, also speaks of a sign of the fulfillment of the word of the Lord, in this case about eschatological salvation.

For an analysis of psychological and formal considerations in the transition from lament to hope in biblical psalms, see Yair Hoffman, "The Transition from Despair to Hope in the Individual-Lament Psalms," *Tarbiz* 45:2 (1986): 161–72 (Heb.).

[51] If frags. 12 and 13 were located earlier in the composition, then the connection between the uses of קש"ב in Jeremiah 18 and Psalm 5 would be one of contiguity rather than inclusion.

[52] 4Q171pPsᵃ II, 9; III, 3; Strugnell, "Notes en marge," 246.

[53] Although it is not a citation, line 5 in frags. 12–13 seems to be an allusion to Abraham's prayer on behalf of the inhabitants of Sodom (Genesis 18). Strugnell had proposed that a common thread in 4Q177 might be its concern with "événements de

The above examples offer an indication of how the subordinate citations in 4Q177 contribute to the flow of the composition as a prayer, particularly that of an "individual" as standing in for the Community. A more comprehensive analysis of the individual citation/interpretation components must await the forthcoming publication of this manuscript in the reworked DJD, as we suggested above. The primary aim of this study has been to demonstrate that 4Q177 reflects a systematic use of biblical psalms as generic models, and that the citations function as formal building blocks in a literary structure, as well as lemmas for interpretation. Like 4Q176 *Tanḥumim*, as it has been characterized by Høgenhaven, 4Q177 is not only an exegetical work, but it also has a literary identity of its own. It is more than a catena or commentary, and whether the work as a whole is designated as an eschatological midrash or a thematic pesher (or any mix of the above), cols. I–III ought also be acknowledged as an adaptation of a lament. In these columns, and perhaps in col. IV, the text progresses from Address, through Complaint, and onto affirmation of Trust, and Praise, adapting prayers attributed to historical leaders and applying them to the Community's perceptions of its experience as situated in the End of Days.

---

l'histoire plus ancienne," pointing to references to Abraham (12–13, line 5), Joshua (22), Jacob (frags. 1–4) ("Notes en marge," 236). The reference to Jacob seems to refer to the nation rather than the patriarch, and the relevance of the reference to Joshua in frag. 22 to this portion of the text is unknown. However, Abraham's prayer does seem to be directly relevant, as it is a prayer by a leader intending to avert catastrophic retribution, though the context (and God's response) differ from the other examples here. Adapting Strugnell's observation, Abraham's prayer may be added to the evidence of the other biblical texts addressed in this composition, concerning pleas for deliverance, especially prayers by individuals on behalf of the collective.

4QSAPIENTIAL ADMONITIONS B (4Q185):
UNSOLVED CHALLENGES OF THE HEBREW TEXT

Mika S. Pajunen
University of Helsinki

Manuscript 4Q185 contains the remains of an intriguing wisdom text that has usually been given the title *Sapiential Work*,[1] but will in the future bear the slightly more informative title *Sapiential Admonitions B*. The text was published by John Allegro in 1968 and subsequently John Strugnell and Hermann Lichtenberger have made further contributions to the reading of the Hebrew text.[2] Apart from these textual studies the work has not received much attention, though recently some attention has been paid to the contents.[3] While this development is welcome indeed, the problem is that these interpretations of the contents do not have as their basis an edition of the Hebrew text as accurate as could be hoped for. In places the manuscript is very difficult to read and all the challenges presented by the text have not yet been met in a satisfactory way. In addition, while every editor so far has been able to read a bit more of the text, there are still ink traces and supralinear letters left unaccounted for. While these problems also occur with other texts among the Qumran finds, in this particular case it is important to address this issue, because the text is rather short

---

[1] Cf. Emanuel Tov, *The Texts from the Judaean Desert Indices and an Introduction to the Discoveries in the Judaean Desert Series* (DJD XXXIX; Oxford: Clarendon Press, 2002).

[2] John M. Allegro with the collaboration of Arnold A. Anderson, *Qumrân Cave 4.I (4Q158–4Q186)* (DJDJ V; Oxford: Clarendon Press, 1968), 85–7; John Strugnell, "Notes en marge," 163–276; Hermann Lichtenberger, "Der Weisheitstext 4Q185: Eine neue Edition," in *The Wisdom Texts from Qumran and the Development of Sapiential Thought* (ed. Charlotte Hempel, Armin Lange and Hermann Lichtenberger; BETL 159; Leuven: Peeters and Leuven University Press, 2002), 127–50.

[3] E.g., Thomas H. Tobin, "4Q185 and Jewish Wisdom Literature," in *Of Scribes and Scrolls. Studies on the Hebrew Bible, Intertestamental Judaism and Christian Origins* (ed. H. W. Attridge, J. J. Collins and T. H. Tobin; Lanham: University Press of America, 1990), 145–52; Benjamin G. Wright III, *Praise Israel for Wisdom and Instruction. Essays on Ben Sira and Wisdom, the Letter of Aristeas and the Septuagint* (JSJSup 131; Leiden: Brill, 2008), see esp. pp. 9–11, 20, 34–5.

and hence its interpretation is based on certain key terms that are not always as certain as the present editions would seem to indicate. The re-edition of DJD V will eventually fill the need for a reliable edition of this text, but until that happens it is worthwhile drawing attention to the problematic readings and to offer some possible answers to them. In some instances the solutions are still preliminary and, although a complete Hebrew text is presented for the benefit of the reader, it is not meant as a final edition of this text. First, observations on the manuscript as a whole as well as placement of fragments are given; then the preliminary Hebrew text and a translation are presented; and finally the differences from the previous editions are analyzed.

Manuscript 4Q185

The manuscript 4Q185 is made up of one large piece having remains from three columns as well as five smaller fragments.[4] Taking all of the fragments into account, there is evidence for two sheets with writing on them and altogether four columns. The holes for stitching on the right edge of frag. 1 prove that there was either still another sheet of text or a handle sheet preceding the text of col. I. The remaining columns are 9 and 11 cm wide. The text has only fifteen lines, which, together with the fact that sheets with two columns are quite rare and that the scribe has tried to save space already on col. II, give the impression that this text might have been quite short. In addition, the damage on the fragments suggests that the manuscript might have been folded instead of rolled.[5] Many pieces of damage correspond well with each other, but are mirror images of one another, rather than the usual pattern of corresponding pieces of damage being nearly identical. If the remaining parts are

---

[4] The large fragment is a combination of several smaller fragments. The gradual process of putting these fragments together is well documented in the PAM photos. The joins of these fragments appear convincing and thus they are treated as one large whole, as also in the previous editions.

[5] Practically all of the manuscripts from Qumran appear to have been rolled, but there are some exceptions to this rule in short texts. For these see Annette Steudel, "Assembling and Reconstructing Manuscripts," in *The Dead Sea Scrolls after Fifty Years. A Comprehensive Assessment, Vol. 1* (ed. Peter W. Flint and James C. VanderKam; Leiden: Brill, 1998), 525; Emanuel Tov, *Scribal Practices and Approaches Reflected in the Texts Found in the Judaean Desert* (STDJ 54; Leiden: Brill, 2004), 38–9. Other short texts might also have been folded, but with only small fragments remaining from almost all of them it is in most cases practically impossible to tell if a text was folded or rolled.

folded in roughly 8 cm sections, the places with vertical damage correspond very well with each other as do many holes and cuts, etc.[6] This would also help explain why col. II is so well preserved in comparison with cols. I and III; the remains of col. III would have been on top of col. I and that on top of col. II. The small amount of material remaining of the manuscript and the rarity of folding instead of rolling leave some amount of doubt concerning this interpretation, but it seems to be the best available explanation for the damage patterns.

The text is difficult to read in many places as there is much abrasion on the surface of the leather. The script also varies quite considerably and because of this at times some letters are hard to tell apart, e.g., ב and מ. Still another issue is that the scribe has made many small mistakes and corrected them afterwards with supralinear letters, but these are also in many instances faded or abraded, which makes reading some parts of the text really challenging.

Strugnell has dated the writing of the manuscript by paleographical analysis to the late Hasmonean period.[7] According to Lichtenberger the composition itself is to be regarded as pre-Qumranic.[8] The most comprehensive attempt at dating the composition of the text itself has thus far been that by Thomas Tobin. By analyzing the appearance of the characteristic features of 4QSapiential Admonitions B in other wisdom writings, he suggests that the text was written in the last part of the third century or the first part of the second century BCE.[9] His analysis gives a rough *terminus a quo* for the composition in the period he suggests, but neither his nor Lichtenberger's arguments for dating the text prior to the writings usually associated with the Qumran movement (e.g., 1QS, 1QH, 1QM, etc.) are totally convincing. They have shown that the composition does not share the characteristic features of the texts of the movement, but that only means that the text was most likely not composed by that movement. It does not, however, give an answer as to who wrote it and exactly when. A date in the second

---

[6] The first fold would have been a centimeter or so to the right of the present right edge of frag. 1, i.e., it would have been just to the right of the stitching. The next fold would have been through the ל's on פעמים and לפניה on col. I, 6–7, where there seems to be a line going straight down the manuscript. Then the fold after that would be along a straight line of abrasion going through יבולה and וישועות in II, 12–13. The final preserved fold would have again been along the stitching between the sheets.

[7] Strugnell, "Notes en marge," 269.

[8] Lichtenberger, "Der Weisheitstext," 129.

[9] Tobin, "4Q185 and Jewish," 145.

century BCE is quite plausible, but further work on this matter is still needed. Thus, it is safest at present to put the *terminus ad quem* of the composition to the time when the manuscript was written.

There appears to be no other extant copy of the composition. However, Carol Newsom has shown that there is some kind of textual connection between 4QSapiential Admonitions B and 4QAdmon-Flood (4Q370).[10] The exact nature of this connection and the way the influence goes remains an open question.

Placement of Fragments

Frag. 3 cannot be placed together with 1–2 III, 7–10 where it is placed in some PAM photos (e.g., 43.514).[11] The line divisions seen at the beginning of the lines do not match with the ones on the fragment; the lines would have to slant in a different direction than they otherwise do. But most of all, there is a clear ink trace on III, 10 which has no counterpart on frag. 3. The stroke is right where a trace from a letter going below the baseline should be, if line 10 ran where it is supposed to be.

The shape of frag. 3 corresponds very well with III, 10–14 and also the line divisions match perfectly, meaning that frag. 3 could be from the same sheet and the same lines but further along. It could be two folds away, which would probably put it in col. IV, a distance from the left edge of col. III c. 12.5 cm. The placement is possible but hypothetical and the fragment is edited as a separate piece, not as lines 10–14 of col. IV.

Frag. 4 is from between columns as it has text from two columns, perhaps III and IV. The damage on it would fit a pattern found on col. II very well, i.e., the straight cut on the right edge, but beneath col. II. If so, it could be placed roughly 9 cm from the beginning of the lines on col. III. This would indicate that col. III would be c. 11 cm wide which would fit well with the width of columns I and II. The placement is possible but hypothetical and the fragment is edited as a separate piece.

---

[10] Carol A. Newsom, "4Q370: An Admonition Based on the Flood," *RevQ* 13/49–52 (1988): 23–43.

[11] Strugnell, "Notes en marge," 272, and Lichtenberger, "Der Weisheitstext," 128, 131, accept this placement of the fragment.

Lichtenberger separates two small fragments in his edition that have been attached to frags. 1–2 III, 1–3. Lichtenberger justifies the separation by the difference in the width of the margin.[12] It is clear that the upper piece of these two is not correctly placed at the moment but the lower one seems well welded with frag. 1 and the only apparent reason to deal with it as a separate piece would be to see the first visible letters as the beginning of the line. However, even from the photos it is clear that there is extensive abrasion before the visible letters, so there is no need to suppose that they are the first letters on the line. The upper fragment has the same problem with the margin, but the fragment should actually be placed a bit more to the right as is clear from the imprint of stitching, i.e., the fragment should be under the visible stitching and if placed like that the margin is in line with the other lines. The other problem concerning that fragment is that the traces of the letters on line 3 do not fit with the current placement. If the placement is done as suggested above, the letters could be read as belonging to the abraded beginning of the lower fragment (especially as one of the traces probably belongs to ע which is written high up on the line). If a material join is impossible, it is not a problem to put the upper fragment a bit higher having traces of lines 1–3, and then the lower fragment would be from line 4. Line divisions are not necessarily exactly the same on different sheets, but the first four lines are written pretty tightly also on the first sheet. One more thing supports the upper fragment being at the beginning of col. III and that is the feminine figure that is present at the end of col. II and the first line of the upper fragment. The figure is present only in the latter half of col. II (and possibly once in col. I) which implies that the fragment should probably be placed quite close to the end of col. II. Therefore, the fragments are read, following Allegro and Strugnell, as forming lines 1–3 of frags. 1–2 III.[13]

Strugnell suggests that PAM 44.191 fragment h should be considered part of 4Q185 (as fragment 7) and placed at the beginning of lines 14–15 in col. III.[14] Lichtenberger has correctly argued on the basis of several material indicators that the placement is not possible. Furthermore, he doubts whether the fragment could be part of manuscript 4Q185

---

[12] He numbers them as fragments 7 and 8, see Lichtenberger, "Der Weisheitstext," 129, 132.

[13] Allegro, *Qumrân Cave 4.I*, 86; Strugnell, "Notes en marge," 271–2.

[14] Strugnell, "Notes en marge," 272. The small fragment can be seen for example on PAM 43.514 between fragments 1–2 and 4.

because the handwriting seems different.[15] Although only a few words are preserved on the fragment, it is enough to deduce that the fragment most likely does not come from 4Q185. Lichtenberger drew attention to the differences in writing, especially ב and ק, but an even more obvious case is ע, which is drawn in a distinctly different way than anywhere on 4Q185. Therefore, the fragment is almost certainly not part of 4Q185.

TEXT AND TRANSLATION

Preliminary Hebrew Text of 4Q185[16]

Fragments 1–2, Col. I

מ̇[	] 1
[	] 2
[° כ̇י °]	] 3
[טהור וקדוש]	] 4
[מתו וכח̇מתו̇]	] 5
[ל̇] [ש ועד עשר °פעמים̇]	[ ] 6
[ואין כח לעמוד לפניה וא̇י̇ן מקוה]	7
לזעמ̇] [ומי יכלכל לעמוד לפני מלאכיו כי באש	8
להבה ישפט] [ו̇ רוחתיו ואתם בני אדם א̇] [כי ה̇גה	9
כח̇צ̇יר יצמח מארצו יפרח כציץ חסדו נשב̇[ה בו] רוחו	10
ויבש ש̇ט̇ו וציצו תשא רוח עד א̇נ̇קום לעמ̇ו̇]ד [פ̇ד	11
ולא ימצא כ̇י רוח vacat יבקשוה̇ו̇ ולא ימצאהו ואין מקוה	12
והוא כצל ימ̇י̇ם ע̇ל הא̇ר̇ץ ועתה שמעו נא עמי והשכילו	13
לי פתאים ותצמק מן̇] [ג̇בורת אלהים̇] וזכרו נפלאו̇ת̇ עשה	14
במצרים ומופתיו̇ ב̇]ארץ חם] ו̇יערץ לבבכם מפני פחדו	15

Col. II

נ̇]פ̇שכם כחסדיו̇ הטבים חקרו לכם דרך	ועשו רצ̇]ונו 1
[לשארית לבניכם אחריכם ולמה תתנו	לחיים ומסל̇ה̇] 2
מ[ש̇פט שמעוני בני פ̇ע̇ל תמרו דברי יהוה	[ ] כ̇ם לשד̇] 3
י̇[עקב ו̇נ̇תיבה חקק לישחק הלוא ט̇ו̇ב יום	אל ת̇צ̇עדו [ ] 4
אחרו]ן מי̇]ו̇ם̇ בעשר̇] [בי̇ראתו ולא לעתת מפחד ומפח יקוש	5
]ל̇°[ ] ד̇[ ] א̇יה̇ [ ] ד̇[ ] °°ב̇כ̇°ל̇ו [°]]מן מלא̇כ̇יו כי אין חשך	6
]°°°	°°הו̇א מ̇ד̇] [וה̇°ה ידעתי ואת̇מג̇° 7
מה תת̇] [צ̇ו̇]	]מ̇לפניו תצא רע̇ד̇] ע̇ל כל עם אשרי אדם 8
	נתנהלו

---

[15] Lichtenberger, "Der Weisheitstext," 129.
[16] This is still a work in progress and at this time is based only on the various photos and electronic images.

9]יתׄן אׄ°[   ]בׄכׄם ואל יתׄהׄללׄ[ו]ן רׄשעים לאׄמור לאׄ נׄתׄנה
10 לו ולאׄ[   ]לישראל ומׄ°בׄד[   ]°ב נׄמׄדׄו וׄכׄל עמו גׄאל
11 והרׄג שנׄאׄ עׄמׄמׄ°י [   ]אבׄ[   ]וׄאמר המתׄיׄטׄבׄה בׄהׄ וׄשאׄנה °[   ]שה
12 ומצאה לוׄ[ ]°ׄת בׄהׄ יבולה ועמהׄ[   ]מׄים ורשׄףׄ עׄ°ׄנׄ°ׄם ושמחת לבב
    עשׄ°[ ]ׄדׄ
13 וחסדיו לׄעׄמיה וישׄוׄעׄוׄתׄ על °°[   ]°° אשרי אדם יעשנה ולא יגׄ°ׄמׄ°ׄל
    על° °[
14 מרמה לא יבקשנה ובׄחׄלקות לאׄ יׄחׄזׄׄיׄקנה כן תתן לאבתיו כן
    ירשׄנׄהׄ°[
15 בכל עוז כחו ובכל[   ]דׄו לאין חסׄרׄ° ויורישנה לצאצאיו וד[ ]עׄתׄׄי°
    לעם[ ]וׄב°

Col. III

1 אליה כי פׄנׄיׄ°[
2 וממאׄׄורות יתהׄ°[
3 °°[ ]°[ ]°ׄעׄ°[ ]ומׄ°
4-6 [...]
7 הׄנׄוׄ°[
8 תׄבׄ°[
9 והׄואׄ[
10 ולׄאׄ עׄ°[   ]אׄ[לׄ]הׄׄיׄׄם °[   ]°[
11 הׄ°לׄוׄ° °[   ]°ׄם עשה לביתו ויׄפׄ°[
12 אלׄ כׄל חרׄׄמׄׄי בטן ויחפש כליתוׄ[
13 לשון וידע דברה אלהים עשה ידים[
14]טוב ואם רעׄ[   ]
15]°מחשׄ[   ]

Fragment 3

1]°ׄם כוׄׄ[   ]°[
2]הׄים יבחן כל וׄעׄ°ׄ[
3]°עׄשה דברי ברׄׄׄיׄ[
4]פׄט במסורׄתׄ[

Fragment 4
Col. I

1]° לעולׄ[
2]עׄוטהׄ אׄוׄרׄ וׄישׄבׄׄוׄ[
3]קׄודש

Col. II

3 ולׄעׄׄמׄׄׄיׄ[
4 ונׄׄׄׄׄריבה וׄ°[

Fragment 5

1 וׄ°[
2 מיׄפׄ[
3 הדׄׄרׄׄ[

Fragment 6

]מָ֥ע֥וֹ[1
[וֹהריאתי א°]   2
[בנ°]   3

4Q185 English Translation

Col. I

1 [...]...
2 [...]
3 [...]...[...]...
4 [...]pure and holy[...]...
5 [...]...and according to his rage [...]...
6 [...]...[...]...and up to ten times[...]
7 [...] and no strength to stand before her/it and there is no hope
8 for the fury[...] and who can endure to stand before his angels for with a burning
9 fire he judges [...]...his spirits. But you sons of man...[...]because (it is) a sigh.
10 Like grass it (man) springs forth. From its earth it sprouts. Like a flower is its loveliness. His (God's) wind blows [upon it]
11 and its reed withers and its blossoms are carried away by the wind until nothing rises up to stan[d...]...
12 and nothing but the wind is found. *vacat* They shall search for him (man) but he will not be found and there is no hope;
13 and he, like a shadow are (his) days upon the earth and now hear, I pray, my people and pay attention
14 to me simple ones! Shrivel up at the [mi]ghty deeds of God and remember the wonders he did
15 in Egypt and his portents in[the land of Ham] and your hearts will tremble before his dread

Col. II

1 and will do [his] wi[ll...]your [s]ouls according to his good mercies. Search for a road
2 to life and a highway[...] for a remnant to your sons after you. And why do you give
3 your [...] to ruin[...ju]dgment. Hear me, sons of the Maker/deed! You rebel against the words of Yahweh!
4 Do not step[...J]acob and the path he decreed to Isaac. Is not welfare in the time
5 to come [better than a d]ay in riches[...] in his fear and not for ages from dread and the net of the fowler.
6 [...]...[...]^{no}[...]...[...]...from his angels for there is no darkness

7   …[….]…[…]… I know and you…

8   What …[…]…[…]from before him goes trembling upon all people. Blessed is the man to whom she/it has been given.

9   He gives …[…] and let not the wicked boast by saying that it has not been given

10 to him and not[…] to Israel and besides […]… they have been measured and all his people he has redeemed

11 and kills the one who hates people[of …]…[…]and he will say: shall man have welfare in her and be secure in her …[…]…

12 and finds her…[…]… in her and carries her and with her[…]… and sparkle of eyes and joy of heart …[…]…

13 and his mercies to her people and salvation upon[…] Blessed is the man who does her/it and does not repay […]…

14 in treachery does not seek her and in flatteries does not grasp her. As she was given to his fathers so he will inherit her[…]…

15 in all the power of his strength and in all […]… without lack. And he will give her as inheritance to his descendants and my knowledge to…[…]…

Col. III

1   to her for the face of […]

2   and from the luminaries…[…]

3   […]…[…]…[…]…[…]

4–6 […]

7–8 …[…]

9   and he[…]

10 and no…[…G]od…[…]

11 …[…]…he has done to his/its house and…[…]

12 to all bans/devotion of the innermost body and he tested his inmost parts[…]

13 tongue and he knows its advice. God made the hands[…]

14 […]good and if evil[…]

15 […]…[…]

Fragment 3

1   […]…[…]…[…]

2   […]…he tests everyone and…[…]

3   […] does words of…[…]

4   […]…in bonds[…]

Fragment 4
Col. I

1   […]…[…]

2   […]…light and they dwell[…]

3   […]holy

Col. II

3   and to people of [...]
4   and we shall strive and...[...]

Fragment 5

1   and [...]
2   ...[...]
3   ...[...]

Fragment 6

1   [...]...[...]
2   [...] and I will show...[...]
3   [...]...[...]

Notes on Readings

Fragment 1–2, Col. I

Line 1: Lichtenberger suggests in his textual comments that the last letter of the line could be ה.[17] Although the traces are only faintly visible the letter is reasonably well recognizable as a final ם.

Line 6: Lichtenberger reconstructs ש[ו]ל[ש,[18] at the beginning of the line but there is too much space for just ו between ל and ש which makes the reconstruction impossible. Strugnell suggests that there might be a ל preceding פעמים, but Lichtenberger doubts it.[19] Practically the entire ל is visible in the images, but it starts at the upper right hand corner of פ, not at its right side as usual (where there would be no space for it). Thus, it is likely to be a supralinear correction made after the text was written.

Line 8: The first letter in באש is a clear ב as read by Strugnell and Lichtenberger, not a כ as Allegro has it.[20]

---

[17] Lichtenberger, "Der Weisheitstext," 132.
[18] Lichtenberger, "Der Weisheitstext," 130.
[19] Strugnell, "Notes en marge," 269; Lichtenberger, "Der Weisheitstext," 132.
[20] Allegro, Qumrân Cave 4.I, 85; Strugnell, "Notes en marge," 269; Lichtenberger, "Der Weisheitstext," 130.

Line 9: Reading the first two letters of the last word on the line is made difficult by a tear going through the middle of the letters. Allegro, Lichtenberger (and presumably also Strugnell) read the word as הנה.[21] The first letter is most likely ה although it is not the only option, but the second letter is not נ. There is no horizontal stroke at the bottom and, more importantly, the vertical stroke branches in two directions from a little from the top of the letter. The right hand branch is clearly observable on both sides of the tear and the left branch connects with the right vertical stroke of ה. The only letter fitting these traces is ג. The word הגה "sigh" might at first seem strange in the context, but it is connected with the shortness of human existence before the wrath of God in Ps 90:9. The same Psalm also draws upon other images to express the same idea including the image of a growing, blossoming and finally withering grass that is used also in the next lines of 4Q185 (although those lines seem to draw their language specifically from Isa 40:6–7, 23–24). The reconstruction should probably express the idea that in comparison with the power of God and his angels man is nothing but a sigh and the duration of his existence is comparable to grass. One possibility might be to reconstruct א[כח ין] following Lichtenberger.[22] The reconstruction would fit the lacuna nicely and the same word pair has already been used before (I, 7), but it is by no means the only available option.

Line 10: Lichtenberger reads ופארתו instead of following Allegro and Strugnell in reading מארצו.[23] Allegro's and Strugnell's reading is to be prefered, as there is no uncertainty about the letters in this particular word. A spot of ink obstructs the מ at the beginning, but it is still visible and recognizable. The penultimate letter cannot be read as ת because it would be too wide, as the observable tip of ר demonstrates; furthermore, there is no indication that the letter would have a right vertical stroke.

[21] Allegro, *Qumrân Cave 4.I*, 85; Strugnell, "Notes en marge," 272; Lichtenberger, "Der Weisheitstext," 130, 133.

[22] Lichtenberger, "Der Weisheitstext," 130, 133.

[23] Allegro, *Qumrân Cave 4.I*, 85; Strugnell, "Notes en marge," 272; Lichtenberger, "Der Weisheitstext," 130, 133.

Allegro and Strugnell read the first letter of יפרח as ו which remains
a possibility, but the shape of the head and the size of the letter make
the י that Lichtenberger reads the more likely of the two alternatives.[24]

Line 11: Strugnell reads the second word of the line as עגזו and
suggests a meaning for it from Arabic or that the ע is a mistake.[25]
However, the traces are far from clear. The first letter(s) is either ע
with ו/י written after it or most likely ש as the angles of the strokes
match perfectly only with that letter. The second letter is not ג, because
the legs would start too high up and the trace that should be the left leg
is not a straight stroke, as it should be, but curves strongly downward
near its bottom. However, there is an abraded baseline stroke that can
still faintly be seen, which makes the letter, when combined with the
letter Strugnell read as ז, a ט. The scribe apparently wrote the ש and
then miscalculated the space needed for ט and ended up drawing it
slightly too large and as such partly over the lower portion of ש. This
seems to be the preferable reading of the traces as it accounts for all
of them, but this is a difficult case and if one prefers to read the traces
as Strugnell does then the most likely solution is the one offered by
Skehan (according to Strugnell) that there is a metathesis and the text
should read as גזעו as in Isa 40:21.[26] The passage is close to Isa 40:24
that the author of 4Q185 most closely follows in this line which makes
the suggestion appealing, but, as noted, the traces do not favour it and
the question would also arise why the scribe did not later correct the
mistake as he has done with so many others.

Allegro and Lichtenberger read אי׳קום and interpret the word as
meaning "non-existence" which is what would be expected in the context.[27] But as Strugnell has noted the form seems a bit unusual.[28] When
one looks at the second letter it is clear that it does not have a "head",
i.e., it is not ו/י and an ink trace belonging to a horizontal stroke at the
bottom makes the letter a medial נ. Strugnell reads it the same way,
but the resulting word אנ׳קום does not mean anything.[29] However,

---

[24] Allegro, *Qumrân Cave 4.I*, 85; Strugnell, "Notes en marge," 272; Lichtenberger, "Der Weisheitstext," 130, 133.

[25] Strugnell, "Notes en marge," 269–70. So also Lichtenberger, "Der Weisheitstext," 130, 134.

[26] Strugnell, "Notes en marge," 270.

[27] Allegro, *Qumrân Cave 4.I*, 85, 87; Lichtenberger, "Der Weisheitstext," 130, 134.

[28] Strugnell, "Notes en marge," 270.

[29] Strugnell, "Notes en marge," 270, 272.

there is a faint shape resembling a י on top of א. If it is indeed ink, there would seem to be two words written together by the scribe אֹוֹ and קֹום'. An additional argument for this is that in the previous line the author was using Isa 40:6–8, but on this line he has switched to Isa 40:24. In Isa 40:23 אין is used with the meaning "nothing", which fits well into this sentence.

The next word is read as לעמוד[30] because it fits the traces, has been used already previously in the same section (I, 7, 8), and continues the line of thought begun with the previous words. Strictly on paleographical grounds Strugnell's reading of לעבור remains a possibility, but its meaning does not fit the sentence. Lichtenberger reconstructs the lacuna near the end of the line as לעמ]דו מל[בד.[31] The reconstruction is not possible as the upper vertical stroke of ל should be visible and the reconstruction is much too short to fill the lacuna. Strugnell and Lichtenberger read the penultimate letter of the line as ב,[32] but it is most likely פ or possibly כ, because ב is written a little above the baseline in this manuscript and this letter is on a level with the line and the upper horizontal stroke does not go as far left as it should in ב.

Line 12[33]: There seems to be no basis for Lichtenberger's reconstruction of ו[34] at the beginning of יבקשוהו as there is no lacuna nor any abrasion visible on the photos and no traces of ink before the י.

Line 13: Strugnell and Lichtenberger read ימיו על האר]ץ [.[35] The ink traces belonging to the first word are difficult to read after the first two letters because of abrasion, but reading them as יו leaves ink traces unaccounted for and would leave a very large lacuna between words, so it is unlikely to be correct. The last letter is best seen as a final ם because the traces cover a large area and go below the baseline. The letter(s) before the ם is either י with a thick head (as on the first י of

---

[30] Allegro has only seen the first letter of the word and Lichtenberger the first two, but there is a minimal trace remaining of the fourth letter at the edge of the lacuna. So also Strugnell, "Notes en marge," 270.

[31] Lichtenberger, "Der Weisheitstext," 130, 134.

[32] Strugnell, "Notes en marge," 270; Lichtenberger, "Der Weisheitstext," 130, 134.

[33] The Hebrew text in Lichtenberger's edition, "Der Weisheitstext," 130, has changed position so that the text before the vacat on the manuscript is after it in the edition and vice versa: a technical mistake as the translation is correct.

[34] Lichtenberger, "Der Weisheitstext," 130, 134.

[35] Strugnell, "Notes en marge," 270; Lichtenberger, "Der Weisheitstext," 130, 135.

the word) or perhaps ה, or the traces might belong to two letters that do not take much space like י and ו. There is a small trace of ink on the left side of the lacuna that is the bottom end of a vertical stroke. This makes Allegro's reading of האו[ר] impossible.[36] The stroke does not go below the baseline so there is some doubt whether reading final ץ, as Strugnell and Lichtenberger do,[37] is correct, but it is by no means impossible and because of the sense of the overall sentence, it is the best available option.

Line 14: The size of the penultimate letter in פתאים makes י more likely than the ו read by Allegro.[38] The next word on the line: ותצמק, is very difficult to read leaving open different possibilities. Allegro only reads the last three letters as תמו, Strugnell reads והכמו, acknowledging that the ה would be mutilated and the כ is doubtful, and Lichtenberger reads יתומו.[39] The first letter has a minimal head, making ו much more likely than י. The second letter seems to be a clear ת with part of the left leg abraded. The third letter is definitely not ו as there is a horizontal baseline stroke that makes a large bend before continuing upward. כ could be a possibility if all of the ink is not part of the letter, but the best option is צ because in addition to the curving vertical stroke and the connected baseline horizontal stroke there are traces on top of ת that would fit as the right arm of צ as well as spots of ink continuing upward just where the left arm of צ should be. The penultimate letter is a clear מ, but the last letter is again difficult. It could be ו, but then one should read י between מ and ו to account for all the visible traces. A more likely reading of the final letter is ק because it fits the ink traces best.

Strugnell and Lichtenberger read [ג]בורת.[40] There is a stroke under the right part of ב that conforms well with the angle of the left leg of ג. Allegro's reading of [ח]בורת[41] is not possible as the left leg of ח would not go under ב but remain beside it.

---

[36] Allegro, *Qumrân Cave 4.I*, 85.

[37] Strugnell, "Notes en marge," 270; Lichtenberger, "Der Weisheitstext," 130, 135.

[38] Allegro, *Qumrân Cave 4.I*, 85. Strugnell, "Notes en marge," 270; and Lichtenberger, "Der Weisheitstext," 130, 135; read the letter as י.

[39] Allegro, *Qumrân Cave 4.I*, 85; Strugnell, "Notes en marge," 270; Lichtenberger, "Der Weisheitstext," 130, 135.

[40] Strugnell, "Notes en marge," 270; Lichtenberger, "Der Weisheitstext," 130, 135.

[41] Allegro, *Qumrân Cave 4.I*, 85.

Allegro reads אלהים but Strugnell and Lichtenberger אלהינו.[42] It is next to impossible to decide which option is the correct one as neither fits perfectly with what remains of the letter(s) on the manuscript. However, as אלהים is used also elsewhere in this composition (at least III, 13) and אלהינו is not, that tips the scales slightly in favour of reading אלהים.

The size of the first letter in וזכרו and its small head indicate that it is more likely to be the ו read by Strugnell and Lichtenberger than the י read by Allegro.

Allegro and Lichtenberger read נפלאים, but as Strugnell observes ו and ת at the end of the word are clear and נפלאות should thus be read.[43] The horizontal stroke of the last letter is completely visible and it has the characteristic protrusion of ת. Final ם has two protrusions on top of the upper horizontal stroke of which one would be completely missing; there is no sign of a lower horizontal stroke and the letter does not go below the baseline as final ם does.

Line 15: Lichtenberger reads ויעדץ instead of ויערץ as Allegro and Strugnell do.[44] The penultimate letter is completely visible and does not have the characteristic protrusions at both ends of the horizontal stroke as ד has, but only the left one as a typical ר does. However, Lichtenberger does not comment on this reading and as there seems to be no such verb root in Hebrew, it is possible that this is a typing error and he meant to write ויערץ. This is also what his translation suggests.[45]

Col. II

Line 2: There is a ו at the beginning of ומסלה that Allegro does not note, but Strugnell and Lichtenberger correctly read.[46]

---

[42] Allegro, *Qumrân Cave 4.I*, 85; Strugnell, "Notes en marge," 270; Lichtenberger, "Der Weisheitstext," 130, 135.

[43] Allegro, *Qumrân Cave 4.I*, 85; Strugnell, "Notes en marge," 270; Lichtenberger, "Der Weisheitstext," 130, 135.

[44] Allegro, *Qumrân Cave 4.I*, 85; Strugnell, "Notes en marge," 270; Lichtenberger, "Der Weisheitstext," 130.

[45] Lichtenberger, "Der Weisheitstext," 144.

[46] Allegro, *Qumrân Cave 4.I*, 85; Strugnell, "Notes en marge," 270; Lichtenberger, "Der Weisheitstext," 130, 136.

Lichtenberger reads an unidentifiable ink trace after the lacuna which would belong to a word other than שארית.[47] However, there is no space between the ink trace and שׁ and as the trace is high up it fits the ל suggested by Allegro best,[48] but ו remains an option.

Line 3: The letter(s) after לשׁ belonging to the second word of the line have been seen differently by the three editors. Allegro reads לשׁא ○[, Strugnell לשׁוא and Lichtenberger לשׁח]ת.[49] The third letter is not א as Allegro reads it, because there is a horizontal stroke with two protrusions on top of it visible as well as a faded, but readable, straight vertical stroke next to ל that does not fit א. The horizontal stroke also makes Strugnell's reading doubtful and although Lichtenberger's reading of ח fits the traces better, the horizontal line goes further than the left protrusion and there is no sign of the left vertical stroke of ח below the horizontal line. Thus the letter seems to be ד.

Allegro reads שמעתי,[50] but as Strugnell has correctly observed the letter(s) before the last one are certainly נו instead of ת.[51]

An ambigious case is how to read the word after בני. Allegro read יצל which might be paleographically possible, but does not fit the sentence (and is somewhat tied in with his reading of שמעתי discussed above).[52] Strugnell (followed by Lichtenberger) reads ואל because the context demands it, but the reading is paleographically very difficult which Strugnell himself concedes.[53] The first letter is more likely י than ו, but more importantly there are two separate ends of horizontal strokes below ל and neither of the traces are possible for א unless the א was written completely sideways. The letter before ל might be ע because the other horizontal stroke could then belong to a letter preceding it that continues below it and the angle of the stroke connecting to the head of the first letter fits well with ע as well. The first letter looks like י at the moment but it seems to start a protrusion to the left at the lower end just before the abrasion and the head of י is similar to

---

[47] Lichtenberger, "Der Weisheitstext," 130.

[48] Allegro, Qumrân Cave 4.I, 85.

[49] Allegro, Qumrân Cave 4.I, 85; Strugnell, "Notes en marge," 270; Lichtenberger, "Der Weisheitstext," 130, 136.

[50] Allegro, Qumrân Cave 4.I, 85.

[51] Strugnell, "Notes en marge," 270. Thus also Lichtenberger, "Der Weisheitstext," 130, 136.

[52] Allegro, Qumrân Cave 4.I, 85.

[53] Strugnell, "Notes en marge," 270; Lichtenberger, "Der Weisheitstext," 130, 136.

that of פ. Therefore, the letter might perhaps be a פ with a long lower stroke as on col. I, 7, 15. Reading פעל is perhaps the better option paleographically, but Strugnell's reading of ואל is further supported by 4Q370 that has some kind of textual connection with this text. According to Newsom it reads אל תמרו דבר]י יהוה (4Q370 II, 9).[54] Thus, one interpretation is supported by the context and the other by the ink traces and no definite answer can be given on the basis of the photographs. Study of the original can hopefully shed more light on this reading but before that פעל is taken as the preferable reading, albeit with hesitation.

Line 4: It is possible to read the beginning of the line following Allegro as אל or like Strugnell and Lichtenberger as א[ו]ל.[55] The choice depends on how one understands the previous sentence.

Strugnell's and Lichtenberger's reading of ונתיבה instead of Allegro's התימה is practically certain.[56]

Line 5: Allegro reads the beginning of the line: אחד[   ] ₒₒₒ [מעשר]ה.[57] Strugnell supplements Allegro's reading by reconstructing בבי]תו.[58] Lichtenberger rightly points out the difficulties with Strugnell's reading of the letters after the lacuna and the first letter of the last word and instead reads: תער]וך בעשר. The difficulties with these readings stem from reading the third letter of the first word as ד which it is not. The right protrusion on top of the horizontal stroke typical of ד is not there and thus the letter is a clear ר followed before the lacuna by the head of a ו with an abraded, but still faintly visible, vertical stroke. Reconstructing the expression as יום אחרו]ן "future days" (cf. Isa 30:8, Prov 31:25) fits the context well. Lichtenberger is correct in reading the first letter of the last word as ב as the letter is quite clear, but the final letter of the previous word is not a final ך, as there is a clear horizontal stroke connecting with the lower end of the left vertical stroke. The

---

[54] Newsom, "4Q370: An Admonition," 24.

[55] Allegro, *Qumrân Cave 4.I*, 85; Strugnell, "Notes en marge," 271; Lichtenberger, "Der Weisheitstext," 130, 137.

[56] Allegro, *Qumrân Cave 4.I*, 85; Strugnell, "Notes en marge," 271; Lichtenberger, "Der Weisheitstext," 130, 137.

[57] Allegro, *Qumrân Cave 4.I*, 85.

[58] Strugnell, "Notes en marge," 271.

letter is quite obviously a final ם. Reconstructing מי[ום בעשר brings out the contrasting alternatives present in the expressions.

The first readable traces after the lacuna are part of the first complete word, as read by Allegro, as there is no word space between them.[59] Lichtenberger reads the traces as belonging to a previous word, but in his notes he suggests the possibility of reading ביראתו[60] which indicates that there might be an error in his edition. The letter in question is either ב or מ because two horizontal strokes are visible. The lower of the two is quite high on the line. This makes ב the more likely alternative.

Line 6: The beginning of the line is especially heavily abraded and no letters have been identified by others before the lacuna. A few of the traces can be reasonably well identified as a ר and a ד, but there are also three supralinear letters that are quite clear and best read as אין.

The first partly readable word after the lacuna is seen by Allegro as ולה∘∘, Strugnell suggests that either ולהבדיל or ולהשמר should be read and Lichtenberger supplies ולהא[מן].[61] The third letter is not ה as there is both an upper and lower horizontal stroke connecting with the left vertical stroke, meaning that a possible reading of that letter would be ו followed by כ and unclear traces.

Lichtenberger suggests that there might be a supralinear ו on top of חשך.[62] There seems to be an ink trace above שׁ, but it does not resemble ו and it is unclear whether it is meant as a letter.

Line 7: Because of abrasion the beginning of the line is next to impossible to decipher. Strugnell and Lichtenberger read it as ואפלה.[63] All of the letters remain doubtful and the third(?) letter of the word seems to be ר. Thus, although the reading cannot be totally dismissed, it is quite unlikely to be correct.

The first clearly visible letters after the lacuna are הוא as read by Allegro and Lichtenberger,[64] but that is apparently not the whole word.

---

[59] Allegro, *Qumrân Cave 4.I*, 85.

[60] Lichtenberger, "Der Weisheitstext," 130, 137.

[61] Allegro, *Qumrân Cave 4.I*, 85; Strugnell, "Notes en marge," 271; Lichtenberger, "Der Weisheitstext," 130, 137.

[62] Lichtenberger, "Der Weisheitstext," 138.

[63] Strugnell, "Notes en marge," 271; Lichtenberger, "Der Weisheitstext," 130, 138.

[64] Allegro, *Qumrân Cave 4.I*, 85; Lichtenberger, "Der Weisheitstext," 130.

There is a trace of a baseline stroke below the right leg of ה and a trace connecting also with the upper part of ה, so there is at least one more letter in this word. The letters visible after א belong to the next word and look like מ followed by ד, but the traces are far from clear.

The abrasion continues and the next few words are all but gone. The ending of the third last word on the line is partly preserved and has led to different interpretations. Allegro reads it as ‏[יע, Strugnell as ר‏[צונו and Lichtenberger as ב.‏[י‏[נ‏[תו.[65] The last letter is not ו or י because the letter continues to the right of the vertical stroke. It is the left vertical stroke of ה and its crossbar. The right vertical stroke is also visible. Below the right vertical stroke there seems to be a slanted horizontal stroke that could belong to ע; at least it is not typical for נ or ת. The letter next to the totally abraded portion could be י as Allegro and Lichtenberger have it, but the leg is long and the head is not very thick which makes ו more likely.

The penultimate word of the line is clear and should be read with Allegro as ידעתי.[66] However, Strugnell and Lichtenberger read both the first and last letter as ו instead of י.[67] Although sometimes hard to tell apart, the two letters are generally distinguishable from each other in this script. י is shorter and has a thicker head than ו. Both of the letters in this word have very short vertical strokes and thick heads which makes them almost certainly י's and interpreting both of them as ו's is questionable.

The penultimate letter on the line is a final ם that seems to be followed by ה (so Allegro and Lichtenberger).[68] However, the same word was in col. I, 9 written without ה. When looked at closely the last letter is not ה at all. The left vertical stroke is slanted and connects with the right vertical stroke before the top. Above the left vertical stroke is a trace of still another vertical stroke which most likely belongs to another letter as there is a short space separating the traces. The best reading of the ink traces is ג followed probably by י or ל. If there were more letters, they are now abraded. Additional support for this reading is given on the next line where the penultimate and ultimate words are also written without a word space between them.

[65] Allegro, *Qumrân Cave 4.I*, 85; Strugnell, "Notes en marge," 271; Lichtenberger, "Der Weisheitstext," 130, 138.

[66] Allegro, *Qumrân Cave 4.I*, 85.

[67] Strugnell, "Notes en marge," 271; Lichtenberger, "Der Weisheitstext," 130, 138.

[68] Allegro, *Qumrân Cave 4.I*, 85; Lichtenberger, "Der Weisheitstext," 130.

Line 8: The last visible letters before the lacuna near the beginning of
the line have been identified as two נ's by Strugnell and Lichtenberger,
allowing the reconstruction of תת[בו]נ[נ]ו.[69] The first of these letters is
most likely צ as the vertical stroke slants heavily to the left, but נ or
ת cannot be completely ruled out as possibilites. The second letter is
nearly certainly a final ז as it goes below the line without turning into
a horizontal stroke.

There is a small ink trace before לפניו that fits well with מ that Lichtenberger has previously offered as a reconstruction.[70]

The third word after the lacuna is read by Allegro as רעה.[71] Strugnell
notes that this is the preferable reading, but suggests a textual correction to דעה which Lichtenberger accepts.[72] However, the first letter is
indeed a ר as there is no protrusion on the right side above the horizontal stroke. If it was a scribal mistake it should have been corrected
later as so many others have been. However, the unclear letter in this
word is not the first, but the final one which does not look like ה.
There is no left vertical stroke and the horizontal stroke has two protrusions on top of it. The letter seems to be ד although at an odd angle,
but other solutions might also be possible.

The next clear letter after רעד is ל. It is usually read as the first letter
of the next word because there is just a short space between ל and the
כ in כל.[73] But there is a small space between them and more importantly there is a small trace of a stroke connecting with the right side
of the ל which means there was a letter preceding it and the trace fits
with ע. In addition, the word space would be somewhat large without
the ע, but with it a more typical length is achieved.

Line 9: All three previous editors read the first word of the line differently. Allegro reads מן, Strugnell כן and Lichtenberger בן.[74] The last
letter is a clear final ז, but the penultimate letter is just as certainly ת.
Both vertical strokes, the crossbar, the hook of the leg and the protru-

[69] Strugnell, "Notes en marge," 271; Lichtenberger, "Der Weisheitstext," 130, 138.
[70] Lichtenberger, "Der Weisheitstext," 130, 138.
[71] Allegro, *Qumrân Cave 4.I*, 85.
[72] Strugnell, "Notes en marge," 271; Lichtenberger, "Der Weisheitstext," 130, 138.
[73] Allegro, *Qumrân Cave 4.I*, 85; Strugnell, "Notes en marge," 273; Lichtenberger, "Der Weisheitstext," 130.
[74] Allegro, *Qumrân Cave 4.I*, 86; Strugnell, "Notes en marge," 271; Lichtenberger, "Der Weisheitstext," 130, 138.

sion above the crossbar are visible. However, that is not the first letter of the word. A faint י can be seen on the edge of the crack.

The letters after the lacuna have been interpreted as ‎[‎○דם by Allegro and as ‎[‎עים by Strugnell and Lichtenberger.[75] The last letter is certain, the penultimate could be ד, but the vertical stroke curves to the left at the bottom which means it might also be כ with abrasion. The reading ‎[‎עים is unlikely because the head of the penultimate letter is different from a י and the ink on the right side of the vertical stroke at the top would be left without explanation. Depending on whether one reads ד or כ as the penultimate letter the first visible traces are best read as א or ב.

Strugnell's reading of the last word of the line as נתנה seems correct and preferable to Allegro's reading of ימנה.[76]

Line 10: The first word of the line has been read as לי,[77] but the second letter has a long leg and a narrow head making ו more probable than י.

The sentence after לישראל is difficult because each of the three words can be interpreted in a number of ways. Allegro (followed by Strugnell in his translation) has read the sentence as וממד]ת ט[ב ימדה and Lichtenberger וכזבד [ט] וב זבדה.[78] The second letter of the first word is most likely מ but ב might be a possibility. However, כ offered by Lichtenberger is not suitable because the upper horizontal stroke is too long and there is a protrusion near the end of it. There is a letter written above this one that Allegro has not noted. Lichtenberger reads it as ז, but the stroke begins high and curves strongly and so ל, if not the only possibility, is the best reading and ז is not a convincing option. The fourth letter is probably ב, but מ might also be a possibility. Therefore, the two best readings for the word would be ומלבד or ומלמד.

The second word has only one clear letter, i.e., ב at its end, and seems to have two or three preceding letters. The reading of these min-ute specks depends on how one reads the surrounding words, but טוב is a good option.

---

[75] Allegro, *Qumrân Cave 4.I*, 86; Strugnell, "Notes en marge," 271; Lichtenberger, "Der Weisheitstext," 130, 138.

[76] Allegro, *Qumrân Cave 4.I*, 86; Strugnell, "Notes en marge," 271;. Lichtenberger, "Der Weisheitstext," 130, 138; follows Strugnell's reading of the word.

[77] Allegro, *Qumrân Cave 4.I*, 86; Strugnell, "Notes en marge," 273; Lichtenberger, "Der Weisheitstext," 131.

[78] Allegro, *Qumrân Cave 4.I*, 86; Strugnell, "Notes en marge," 273; Lichtenberger, "Der Weisheitstext," 131, 138–39.

The third word does not start with a ו/י, as suggested by Allegro, because the letter has no head. Lichtenberger's reading of ז is an option, but below the next letter is an ink trace that seems to belong to a baseline horizontal stroke and makes ג the best choice. The second letter is מ because the upper part curves too much for כ and the protrusion is in the middle not at the tip as it is usually in ב. The third letter is ד by all accounts but the final letter is not ה as suggested by Allegro and Lichtenberger. There is a trace of at least a short baseline stroke in this letter which implies that it could be ב or כ. However, the letter looks like it was corrected by the scribe and not abraded (but it is impossible to be certain of this without seeing the original). If so, then the final letter is ו.

Line 11: At the beginning of the line after והרג Allegro and Lichtenberger have only read the first letter of the next word but Strugnell supplies: שנאי[ן ח]כמ[תו.[79] The traces after ש leave open many possibilities, but conform well to ג and א. There is no sign of י and reading both י and ח between the words would in practice mean that the words would have been written together. The visible letters of the second word could be כ and מ, but then ח at the beginning is not possible because there is a horizontal stroke connecting with the middle of the curve of כ. That stroke is either part of the letter in which case the letter would be צ or it could belong to the previous letter. If so, the letter fitting the stroke is ע. Only the lower parts of the two following letters (if the first is ע) remain. Therefore, there are several possible readings for them, i.e., פ, כ, ב and מ.

The letter beginning the word ואמר has been read as י,[80] but the shape of the head and the length of the leg make ו more likely.

The second word after the lacuna defies any easy interpretations and Strugnell aptly describes the attempt as "désespérée".[81] Allegro reads המתמooo, Strugnell suggests reading המתשבח and Lichtenberger offers המתכבד.[82] The first three letters are clear, but the fourth is neither ש, מ nor כ. ש would account for all the traces, but the letter would be

[79] Allegro, *Qumrân Cave 4.I*, 86; Strugnell, "Notes en marge," 271; Lichtenberger, "Der Weisheitstext," 131, 139.

[80] Allegro, *Qumrân Cave 4.I*, 86; Strugnell, "Notes en marge," 273; Lichtenberger, "Der Weisheitstext," 131.

[81] Strugnell, "Notes en marge," 271.

[82] Allegro, *Qumrân Cave 4.I*, 86; Strugnell, "Notes en marge," 271; Lichtenberger, "Der Weisheitstext," 131, 139.

very strangely drawn with thick branches and an almost straight, long baseline stroke. כ is not possible because the upper horizontal stroke is long and curves and moreover in Lichtenberger's reading the clear vertical stroke Strugnell takes as part of שׁ is left completely unexplained. מ fits with most of the strokes, but again the vertical stroke is left without explanation and the protrusion on the curving horizontal stroke would be missing. Between ת and this letter there seems to be a trace beside and going slightly higher than ת that fits the shape of a head of י. Then comes the difficult letter that is most likely ט because that accounts for all the traces. The only problem with this reading is that it means that the scribe wrote two words together. However, the scribe apparently miscalculated the space needed for ט once before (I, 11); thus it could have happened again. Above ט is a faded supralinear letter that seems to be ו and the next letter is most likely ב. The final letter is probably ה as the left vertical stroke and both ends of the crossbar can be seen.

There seems to be a supralinear ת between this word and the next, but it is not clear enough in the images to be sure that it is indeed ink.

Whether one reads ו or י at the beginning of ושׁאנה is dependent on how one interprets the preceding words.[83] Both options can be argued for as the head is more in line with י, but the leg is long as in ו.

Line 12: The three words after the first word of the line have been interpreted in different ways. Allegro read וˑ[ ]°[בה יכילה, Strugnell וחזק בה ונחלה and Lichtenberger לו[[כי] רבה יבולה.[84] The first letter is ל because all but the upper vertical stroke are visible. The second letter could be ו, but ר and ד are possible alternatives. There is no word space after the second letter as Lichtenberger has read. Instead, heavy abrasion has deleted the ink traces. The traces following the abrasion are part of the final letter of a word and cannot be read with בה because there is a clear word space between the traces and ב. If the thick spot of ink is just a smudge, then the letter is probably ת because a vertical stroke with a hook at the lower end is visible.

Allegro's reading of the final word remains a possibility, but Lichtenberger's reading is to be preferred because the second letter looks

[83] Allegro, *Qumrân Cave 4.I*, 86; and Lichtenberger, "Der Weisheitstext," 131, read it as י.

[84] Allegro, *Qumrân Cave 4.I*, 86; Strugnell, "Notes en marge," 271; Lichtenberger, "Der Weisheitstext," 131, 139.

much more like a ב than כ. Strugnell's reading is not an option, as
the uneven line he takes as the right leg of ח is not ink but a crack in
the leather that goes all the way through the middle of ב.

The second and third words after the lacuna have been seen in two
different ways. Allegro read ורשף עינים but Strugnell suggested that
ודשן עצם should be read instead.[85] The second letter of the first word is
clearly ר and there is nothing hampering the reading. Strugnell admits
that ד is a very difficult read, but in this case it would mean that the
scribe made a mistake. The final letter of the first word is not preserved
in its entirety, but the stroke curves strongly to the left which is not
typical of final ן. Thus Allegro's reading of final ף is preferable. The first
letter of the second word is either ע or possibly ש. The next letter is
unclear as there is only a single spot of ink remaining, but reading י
is one possibility. Then there is a clear נ before the final ם. If it were צ
the vertical stroke should curve to the left but it is straight, and there
should be something remaining of the right hand of צ which there
is not. There is no י between נ and ם as Allegro has read, but the י is
there as a supralinear addition written above the נ. The letter is faint,
but still clearly recognizable.

Line 13: Allegro reads the second word of the line as עלמיה but
Lichtenberger suggests לעמיה instead.[86] The stroke remaining of the
first letter is a curving horizontal stroke that might belong to ל, ש
or ס. It is unlikely to be ע because of the angle of the stroke and the
absence of any sign of the left branch. The second letter is either ע or ל.
The crucial factor in this is whether there is a horizontal stroke connecting to the top of the vertical. If there is, the letter must be ל and if
not then it is ע. There seems to be a faint trace on the left side of the
vertical stroke but whether it is indeed ink from a horizontal stroke
cannot be judged from the images. Hopefully the original fragment
can yield the answer to this question but before that Lichtenberger's
reading is prefered.

Lichtenberger reconstructs י and ו at the end of וישועות. The reconstruction would bring the word very close to the next visible traces
that probably belong to ע and ל. Moreover, not all of the skin between

---

[85] Allegro, *Qumrân Cave 4.I*, 86; Strugnell, "Notes en marge," 271. Lichtenberger,
"Der Weisheitstext," 131, 139, has in his edition ודשן עעם but in his notes he claims
to follow Strugnell; thus the second ע should be read as צ.
[86] Allegro, *Qumrân Cave 4.I*, 86; Lichtenberger, "Der Weisheitstext," 131, 140.

the words seems abraded so some spots of ink should be visible if Lichtenberger's reconstruction were correct.

The last completely visible word has proven difficult to read. Allegro reads it as יאל, Strugnell hesitantly proposes דגל and Lichtenberger suggests יג[ע]ל.[87] The first letter is either ו or י that seems to have been written on top of an erased מ. The second letter is messy, but א and ג are the possibilities of which ג fits the traces better. Above that letter is a clear supralinear מ that has gone unnoticed until now and the final letter is ל. There is no possibility to read anything between the second letter and ל as Lichtenberger has done and certainly not in a lacuna.

Line 15: There is a clear ו, as recognized also by Allegro between ע and ז of the second word of the line, but Lichtenberger takes no note of it in his edition.[88]

Allegro and Strugnell read חקר and Lichtenberger חסר.[89] Both options are paleographically possible but Lichtenberger's seems better suited to the context.

Allegro and Strugnell read the last completely visible word of the line as ידעתי and Lichtenberger differs slightly from them by reading ודעתו.[90] There is a slice of leather missing between ד and ע which means that if it were still present at the time of writing, then a letter is missing, but the ד ends just before the damage and ע starts straight after it, so it is likely the damage was present when the text was written. The first letter looks like a typical ו, but the final letter is more ambiguous. The short leg and size of the head favour י, but the shape of the head is more like a ו. This means that the choice depends on how one interprets the context. At this point י is prefered because of the parallel idea of knowledge coming from the speaker found at II, 7.

Col. III

Line 1: The first word is read by Allegro and Strugnell as אליה.[91] For some reason Lichtenberger reads only the first and last letter and

---

[87] Allegro, *Qumrân Cave 4.I*, 86; Strugnell, "Notes en marge," 271; Lichtenberger, "Der Weisheitstext," 131, 140.

[88] Allegro, *Qumrân Cave 4.I*, 86; Lichtenberger, "Der Weisheitstext," 131.

[89] Allegro, *Qumrân Cave 4.I*, 86; Strugnell, "Notes en marge," 271; Lichtenberger, "Der Weisheitstext," 131, 140.

[90] Allegro, *Qumrân Cave 4.I*, 86; Strugnell, "Notes en marge," 271; Lichtenberger, "Der Weisheitstext," 131, 140.

[91] Allegro, *Qumrân Cave 4.I*, 86; Strugnell, "Notes en marge," 272.

marks a lacuna in the middle.[92] There is no lacuna and the traces are
best read the way Allegro and Strugnell have done.

Allegro suggests the last visible letters on the line should be read as
פני but Strugnell (followed by Lichtenberger) reads טו instead.[93] On
the basis of the images the preferable reading is difficult to decide. The
first letter looks like פ as the upper stroke does not curve long enough
for ט. But it might of course be a slightly incomplete ט. The deciding
factor is whether there is a horizontal stroke going from the vertical
stroke, that is either part of נ or the left side of ט, under י/ו. There is
a faded line there that looks like ink in the images and on that basis
Allegro's suggestion seems preferable at this point.

Line 2: The first word is best read with Allegro and Lichtenberger as
וממאורות, but Strugnell's reading וממגרות cannot be entirely dismissed.[94]

There are some visible traces of the first three letters of the second
word that Allegro has read as יתºº and Lichtenberger וººº.[95] The first
letter is most likely י because of the size of the head and the length of
the leg. The second letter is probably ת as the horizontal stroke with
the characteristic protrusion at the left end is visible. The third letter is
perhaps ת as the visible horizontal stroke matches the crossbar of ת.

Line 8: There are traces belonging to three letters at the beginning of
the line. The first letter seems to have a horizontal stroke typical of
ת as well as parts of two vertical strokes. The second one could be ב as
it starts slightly higher than the previous letter and has two horizontal
strokes starting from a vertical one. The remains of the third letter are
too unclear for even a tentative identification.

Line 11: The first word suffers from heavy abrasion starting after the
first letter. Allegro reads הלºººº and Lichtenberger הלא.[96] There is some
space between ה and the vertical stroke of ל and it is possible that a
letter that does not require too much space horizontally (e.g., ו, י, ל)

[92] Lichtenberger, "Der Weisheitstext," 132. In his edition the text is on fragment
7 line 1.
[93] Allegro, *Qumrân Cave 4.I*, 86; Strugnell, "Notes en marge," 272; Lichtenberger,
"Der Weisheitstext," 132, 143.
[94] Allegro, *Qumrân Cave 4.I*, 86; Strugnell, "Notes en marge," 272; Lichtenberger,
"Der Weisheitstext," 132, 143.
[95] Allegro, *Qumrân Cave 4.I*, 86; Lichtenberger, "Der Weisheitstext," 132.
[96] Allegro, *Qumrân Cave 4.I*, 86; Lichtenberger, "Der Weisheitstext," 131, 142.

was between them. The ל is almost certain, but the last letter is unlikely to be א as there is only one stroke partly visible and that does not easily fit as part of א. It looks like ו, but the head is partly abraded which makes other alternatives possible. After the third letter there seems to be a word space.

The last complete word on the line should be read following Allegro and Strugnell as לביתו.[97] Lichtenberger reads לבות,[98] but the size of the third letter favors י and there is a ו written above the hook of ת.

The last visible letter seems to be פ as the vertical stroke curves slightly and the short downward stroke at the top is visible. A faded baseline stroke seems also to be present.

Line 12: All previous editors read the third word as חדרי.[99] The second letter might be ד, but it is missing the protrusion on the right side of the horizontal stroke and thus ר is more likely. The third letter cannot be ר as the letter clearly curves into a baseline horizontal stroke that is still partly preserved. This means that the letter is either מ or ב of which מ seems to fit slightly better; reading either חרמי or חרבי is possible.

The last word on the line has thus far been read variously by the editors. Allegro has כלותו, Strugnell כליתי and Lichtenberger כליתו.[100] Looking at the letters Lichtenberger's reading is preferable, but the others are also possibilities. The choice depends partly on how one understands this and the preceding colon which is not an easy task because the context is largely missing. The cola have been understood in the translation as expressing parallel ideas, but translating the latter sentence with Allegro as "and he sought his destruction"[101] is certainly a possibility.

Line 13: The reading וידע suggested by Strugnell and Lichtenberger for the second word of the line is preferable to Allegro's יודע which nevertheless remains an alternative.[102]

[97] Allegro, *Qumrân Cave 4.I*, 86; Strugnell, "Notes en marge," 273.
[98] Lichtenberger, "Der Weisheitstext," 131, 142.
[99] Allegro, *Qumrân Cave 4.I*, 86; Strugnell, "Notes en marge," 273; Lichtenberger, "Der Weisheitstext," 131.
[100] Allegro, *Qumrân Cave 4.I*, 86; Strugnell, "Notes en marge," 272; Lichtenberger, "Der Weisheitstext," 131, 142.
[101] Allegro, *Qumrân Cave 4.I*, 87.
[102] Allegro, *Qumrân Cave 4.I*, 86; Strugnell, "Notes en marge," 272; Lichtenberger, "Der Weisheitstext," 131, 142.

Line 14: Allegro reads the final letters on the line as °ד but Strugnell's reading רע (followed by Lichtenberger)[103] is more accurate because ר is certain and although ע is partly in a lacuna the remaining upper ends make it the most probable reading.

Fragment 3

Line 2: Strugnell and Lichtenberger read the last word as מזמ]ות. However, if the first letter is מ it is shaped like a sharp angled triangle, i.e., the descending stroke's angle is very steep in comparison with other מ's. Additionally, the descending stroke not only touches the next vertical stroke but seemingly makes a curve with it and there is no sign of the baseline stroke. An alternative is to see the first letter as ו followed by ע with its right end touching the head of ו. The remains of the third letter leave open many alternatives with no real means to choose between them.

Line 3: Lichtenberger reconstructs and reads the beginning of the line אלהים] עשה.[104] There is an end of a horizontal stroke visible below and to the right of ע at the edge of the leather. It is unclear whether it is part of the first visible word or a previous one. If it is part of the last letter of the previous word, it is noteworthy that it does not fit as part of a final ם.

Fragment 4

Col. I, line 2: Allegro reads the first two words of the line as וטי °°°.[105] Lichtenberger leaves the second word unread but suggests שפטי for the first word.[106] However, most of the letters are identifiable. The first letter is ע as its slanting downward stroke and separate upward stroke are visible. The second is a certain ו. Lichtenberger apparently read these letters together without paying note to the head of ו nor to the absence of any strokes starting from the vertical stroke to the right as in ש. The third letter is ט. The fourth is unclear. It is not י as the head would continue too straight and long to the left. There is a stretch of

---

[103] Allegro, *Qumrân Cave 4.I*, 86; Strugnell, "Notes en marge," 272; Lichtenberger, "Der Weisheitstext," 131, 142.

[104] Lichtenberger, "Der Weisheitstext," 131, 141.

[105] Allegro, *Qumrân Cave 4.I*, 87.

[106] Lichtenberger, "Der Weisheitstext," 131.

the surface of the skin missing that is visible even in photos, so part of the letter was probably lost because of that. The remains best fit the right leg and crossbar of ה but there might be other options. The word possibly comes from the root עטה "to enwrap, envelope."

The last two letters of the second word are most likely ו and ר with ר being practically certain. The first letter can be identified only tentatively and other options will remain open, but א fits the traces and available space well.

Col. II, line 3: Lichtenberger argues that Allegro's reading ולעמי is uncertain and reads only the ו at the beginning.[107] When one connects the cracks on the fragment at the appropriate places Allegro's reading seems, if not certain, then at least highly likely and should be accepted.

Col. II, line 4: Allegro's reading of the line as ונריבה ו○ should be preferred to Lichtenberger's ונדריבה[108] as there is no letter nor any space for one between נ and ר. The ו at the beginning of the next word is also nearly certain.

Fragment 5

Line 2: Allegro reads מיפ and Lichtenberger מופ[ט.[109] The second letter is more probably י than ו because of the shape and size of the head and the short leg.

Fragment 6

Line 1: The only one to read any of the traces on this line is Allegro who correctly saw מ in the middle of it.[110] Following the מ is a nearly certain ע as one can see the slanting stroke and the upward stroke branching out of it. After ע is a letter starting on top of the slanting stroke which points to it possibly being ו or י.

---

[107] Allegro, *Qumrân Cave 4.I*, 87; Lichtenberger, "Der Weisheitstext," 131, 142.
[108] Allegro, *Qumrân Cave 4.I*, 87; Lichtenberger, "Der Weisheitstext," 131.
[109] Allegro, *Qumrân Cave 4.I*, 87; Lichtenberger, "Der Weisheitstext," 131, 143.
[110] Allegro, *Qumrân Cave 4.I*, 87.

CONCLUSIONS

This study of the Hebrew text of 4Q185 is meant as a contribution to the ongoing process of making a thorough and reliable edition of this challenging text. It has highlighted the areas where the difficulties lie in this text and provided some suggestions as to how they might be solved. The "new" readings offered do not change the meaning of the text in a drastic way; rather, it is a question of fine tuning. However, they do give further insights into the nuances of the text and into its structure. This study has once again pointed out the need to continue the careful reading of texts even when multiple editions are already available. One of the lessons to be learned here concerns the many supralinear letters that have previously gone unnoticed. Because these letters were not noticed before now, the words these supralinear corrections were found in have been subject to many different interpretations as scholars have tried to find the reasons behind the odd word forms. Scholars have resorted to e.g., reading almost certain letters as mutilated forms of other letters, textual corrections, and sometimes even leaving letters unread. While these measures are sometimes necessary, it has been shown here that solutions to some seemingly difficult problems can still be found by carefully reading the manuscripts. This is not the only text where these kinds of supralinear letters have gone unnoticed (Cf. 1Q27 2 between lines 2 and 3). The examples discussed here will hopefully encourage further investigation of other texts as well.

4Q186. 4QZODIACAL PHYSIOGNOMY. A FULL EDITION

Mladen Popović
Qumran Institute, University of Groningen

Bibliography

M. Albani, 'Horoscopes in the Qumran Scrolls', *The Dead Sea Scrolls After Fifty Years: A Comprehensive Assessment* (ed. P. W. Flint and J. C. VanderKam; 2 vol.; Leiden: E.J. Brill, 1999) 2:279–330; P. S. Alexander, 'Physiognomy, Initiation, and Rank in the Qumran Community', *Geschichte—Tradition—Reflexion: Festschrift für Martin Hengel zum 70. Geburtstag, Band I Judentum* (ed. H. Cancik, H. Lichtenberger and P. Schäfer; Tübingen: J. C. B. Mohr [Paul Siebeck], 1996) 385–94; J. M. Allegro, 'An Astrological Cryptic Document from Qumran', *JSS* 9 (1964) 291–4; R. Bergmeier, *Glaube als Gabe nach Johannes: Religions- und theologiegeschichtliche Studien zum prädestinatianischen Dualismus im vierten Evangelium* (BWANT 112; Stuttgart: W. Kohlhammer, 1980) 78–81; J. Carmignac, 'Les Horoscopes de Qumrân', *RevQ* 5/18 (1965) 199–217; M. Delcor, 'Recherches sur un horoscope en langue hébraïque provenant de Qumrân', *Religion d'Israël et Proche Orient Ancien: Des Phéniciens aux Esséniens* (M. Delcor; Leiden: E. J. Brill, 1976) 298–319 (originally published in *RevQ* 5/20 [1966] 521–42); A. Dupont-Sommer, 'Deux documents horoscopiques esséniens découverts à Qoumrân, près de la Mer Morte', *CRAI* (1965) 239–53; R. Gordis, 'A Document in Code from Qumran—Some Observations', *JSS* 11 (1966) 37–9; J. Licht, 'Legs as Signs of Election', *Tarbiz* 35 (1965–1966) 18–26 (Hebrew); H. Lichtenberger, *Studien zum Menschenbild in Texten aus der Qumrangemeinde* (SUNT 15; Göttingen: Vandenhoeck & Ruprecht, 1980) 142–8; G.-W. Nebe, 'אבר in 4Q186', *RevQ* 8/30 (1973) 265–6; M. Philonenko, 'Deux horoscopes Qoumrâniens: Identification des personnages', *RHPR* 65 (1985) 61–6; M. Popović, 'A Note on the Reading of שמונה and עמוד השני in *4Q186 2 i 7*', *RevQ* 21/84 (2004) 635–41; idem, *Reading the Human Body: Physiognomics and Astrology in the Dead Sea Scrolls and Hellenistic-Early Roman Period Judaism* (STDJ 67: Leiden: Brill, 2007); F. Schmidt, 'Astrologie juive ancienne: Essai d'interprétation de *4QCryptique (4Q186)*', *RevQ* 18/69 (1997) 125–41 ('Ancient Jewish Astrology: An Attempt to Interpret 4QCryptic (4Q186)', *Biblical Perspectives: Early Use and Interpretation of the Bible in Light of the Dead Sea Scrolls* (ed. M. E. Stone and E. G. Chazon; STDJ 28; Leiden: E.J. Brill, 1998) 189–205); J. Strugnell, 'Notes en marge du volume V des "Discoveries in the Judaean Desert of Jordan"', *RevQ* 7/26 (1970) 274–6.

Introduction

The genre designation 'horoscope' was quickly applied to 4Q186 as the text was preliminary published, and the text came to be officially known as *4QHoroscope*. This name, however, creates the wrong impression that the text represents a horoscope or a collection of horoscopes, which it does not.[1] Notwithstanding the presence of certain astrological notions, 4Q186 as such cannot be characterized as a horoscope text. It does not contain the actual horoscopes of particular individuals. The text lacks many elements that would qualify it as belonging to the genre of horoscopes as known from Babylonian, Greek or later Jewish examples. Most significantly, 4Q186 does not have any explicit reference to the zodiacal position of the sun, moon or any of the other five planets known in antiquity.[2] Alexander suggests renaming it '4QAstrological Physiognomy'. Schmidt aptly refers to 4Q186 as 'un texte de physiognomonie zodiacale'. Schmidt's more limited characterization fits the content better. I have suggested renaming 4Q186 *4QZodiacal Physiognomy*.

4Q186 is a list of physiognomic and astrological content. The text contains different physical descriptions of individual types of people. The astrological information concerning the horoscope under which a type of person was born is listed subsequently to the physiognomic description of the person's body. The text of 4Q186 is structured according to these physiognomic descriptions. The idea behind this order is that the human body may signify certain astrological data concerning the individual. From a person's physiognomy an observer may gather astrological knowledge. According to 4Q186 the human body reveals the zodiacal sign that ascended at the moment of birth.[3] Although the division between the 'house of light' and the 'house of darkness' is astrologically the result of the ascendant zodiacal sign's position vis-à-vis the eastern horizon, I suggest that this was understood in terms of the zodiacal spirit being divided between light and darkness.

Various interpretations have been suggested for the meaning of enigmatic terms and elements in 4Q186 against an astrological background.[4] It will be clear that the significant elusiveness inherent in the terminology and the fragmentary nature of the manuscript preclude any final interpretation. Astrology was not a fixed and unified system

---

[1] It is regrettable that the recent name given to the Aramaic physiognomic text 4Q561 creates a similar mistaken impression; see É. Puech, *Qumrân Grotte 4.XXVII: Textes araméens, deuxième partie (4Q550–4Q575a, 4Q580–4Q587)* (DJD 37; Oxford: Clarendon, 2009) 303–5.

[2] Popović, *Reading the Human Body*, 18–9.

[3] Popović, *Reading the Human Body*, 34–8, 112–8.

[4] For the physiognomic background see Popović, *Reading the Human Body*, 68–112.

of concepts and terminology during the Hellenistic and Early Roman period. There was much terminological inconsistency and conceptual confusion, reflecting the still unsettled state of astrology. One has to bear in mind the possibility of multiple developments and trajectories, not all of which are recognizable anymore. Against this background, and taking into account the late first-century BCE date for the manuscript, 4Q186 can perhaps be seen as a text representative of the incipient stages of horoscopic astrology in Second Temple period Judaism, attempting to render concepts foreign to Jewish culture into Hebrew. The text may represent a translation effort of astrological terminology and concepts into Hebrew.

PHYSICAL DESCRIPTION AND MATERIAL RECONSTRUCTION

The leather is a rather dark brown. Of the fragments, only 4Q186 4 has something like a whitish layer of 'dust-like' substance on its surface. Allegro did not comment on this in his short description of the leather of 4Q186,[5] perhaps because this is not very unusual. Other manuscripts have a 'dust-like' white substance also. It is possibly a clue that 4Q186 4 does not belong together with 4Q186 1 or 2 on the same sheet or on the same part of the sheet, because no such whitish layer is found on the leather of those fragments.

On inspecting the museum plate, it is evident that the fragments are now more damaged than in the photograph in *DJD* 5 (Plate XXXI).[6] Gaps have appeared in places where before there were none, and gaps that were there already have become larger.

4Q186 consists of ten fragments. Inspection of the original fragments confirmed my arguments against Allegro's material reconstruction of the second fragment.[7] The two parts of 4Q186 2 cut in half by Allegro have been put together again, clearly after the photograph for *DJD* 5 was taken.[8] Due to the fact that the two halves have been

---

[5] Allegro, 'An Astrological Cryptic Document', 291. He described the leather as 'a soft reddish-brown skin'.

[6] September 22, 2005 at the Dead Sea Scrolls Laboratory of the Israel Antiquities Authority, Jerusalem. I wish to thank the curators Tamar Rabbi-Salhov and Lena Liebman for their kind assistance during my visit.

[7] See Popović, 'A Note'.

[8] It seems unlikely that Allegro is responsible for this because it contradicts his reconstruction. The current curators at the IAA have informed me that the scrolls

rejoined, 4Q186 4 1 is no longer in line with 4Q186 2 i 7.[9] 4Q186 4 1 has shifted down slightly, and thus does not continue in 4Q186 2 i 7 nor provide evidence for the numerical sequence reconstructed by Allegro ('eight and o[ne'). But the placement by the IAA is also highly improbable because it does not take into account the spacing between the lines in either this fragment or 4Q186 2 i 7–9.[10] 4Q186 4 cannot, therefore, be placed directly below 4Q186 2 i as it has been by Allegro and, more recently, by the IAA. Finally, the current placement on IAA #109 seems to show a clear join between 4Q186 4 and 4Q186 5. However, the whitish layer may argue against such a join because 4Q186 5 does not have this. It is difficult to assess whether the two fragments really fit. After inspection with the microscope it seems that someone at the IAA has put them together in such a way that part of fragment 5 lies under fragment 4, especially in the upper part, whereas in the lower part the edges of both fragments curl up and stand back to back to each other. The current material reconstruction has resulted in an extant text of 4Q186 consisting of two main fragments, 4Q186 1 and 2, and four smaller, separate fragments.

Bearing in mind the inverted writing and the reversed order for reading the lines, there is no clear indication as to the order in which the columns have to be read, from right to left or vice versa. 4Q186 1 contains the remains of four columns. Of these four columns three have a bottom margin measuring 1.5 cm, but the top margin of all four columns is lacking. This makes it difficult to establish the direction in which a bottom line continued in the next column: whether the sentence resumed at the top of the column to its left or to its right. 4Q186 2 preserves the top margin of one column (measuring 2.0 cm),

---

laboratory recently placed the fragments thus on IAA #109, but the reason why is not clear.

[9] Below יושבות in 4Q186 2 i 6 the leather of the manuscript extends slightly further, revealing the blank between the lines. There is clearly not enough space to place 4Q186 4 and 4Q186 5 between this piece of leather and the leather of 4Q186 2 i 7–9, nor join the latter to 4Q186 2 i 7–9. It is obvious that precisely because of this the IAA curators must have placed 4Q186 4 *below* the leather extension and not next to it to the right as Allegro did in *DJD* 5.

[10] The placement of 4Q186 4 below 4Q186 2 i 6 in the way it is now on IAA #109 results in too much space between line 6 and line 1 of 4Q186 4 (עֲמוֹד השני ש[ן]ה). Moreover, 4Q186 4 1 has been joined to 4Q186 2 i 8. This leaves 4Q186 2 i 7 isolated. The discontinuation of the lines is also clear in the case of 4Q186 4 2 (מולדו) and 4Q186 2 i 9, where the traces of the upper parts of two letters stand significantly lower than 4Q186 4 2.

and also contains the meagre remnants of a second column at the lower left part of the fragment. Furthermore, 4Q186 2 preserves the edge of a sheet. Not only is part of the margin on the right preserved, the stitches by means of which another sheet was attached are unmistakably visible also. Unfortunately, this does not enable the order in which the columns were organised to be reconstructed. I have, therefore, retained Allegro's ordering of the columns so as not to cause unnecessary confusion with previous scholarship on 4Q186.

An estimation of the entire amount of text cannot be determined on material grounds alone, but depends on one's understanding of the text. A crucial element is the number of typological entries one assumes the original text to have had. As no complete account has been preserved, it is impossible to establish a set number of lines for an entire account. But it seems reasonable to assume that an average entry had no less than seven or eight lines. Three examples are indicative, if not for the complete text, at least for the remaining fragments. Assuming 4Q186 1 ii 9 to be the end of the account, it at least began in 4Q186 1 ii 4, but probably before that. 4Q186 2 i 1 is most probably not the beginning of an account that continues at least until 4Q186 2 i 7. Finally, the account in 4Q186 1 iii at least includes line 5 and probably continued in another column following the end of line 9.

We do not know how many typological entries appeared in one column. If one assumes three entries to a column, such a column would consist of 21–24 lines. An average leather height can be suggested on the basis of the vertical space covered by a certain number of lines in combination with the measurements of the top and bottom margins of the manuscript. The height of five lines in 4Q186 1 ii and 4Q186 2 i measures ca. 3.5 cm (including the space between the lines at ca. 0.5 cm). To this one should add a top margin of 2.0 cm and a bottom margin of 1.5 cm. The column height would then be between 15–17 cm and the leather height ca. 18.5–20.5 cm.[11] An estimation of the entire amount of text depends on the number of typological entries it had. Assuming that the typological entries in 4Q186 are intrinsically related to the average number of nine subdivisions of each zodiacal sign, the result is an elaborate catalogue that may have listed almost

---

[11] According to Tov's classification a scroll with a medium-sized writing block. Cf. E. Tov, *Scribal Practices and Approaches Reflected in the Texts Found in the Judean Desert* (STDJ 54; Leiden: Brill, 2004) 86–8.

a hundred physiognomic and astrological typologies. For example, if one assumes three entries to a column 32 columns would be needed for 96 physiognomic accounts. Bearing in mind a column width of ca. 8–9 cm together with a margin of ca. 0.5–1 cm, 4Q186 could have been a scroll of ca. 2.7–3.2 meters. But a column may have had an average of between two and three entries, which would result in a shorter scroll. We simply do not know.

Contents

4Q186 represents a sort of list or compendium of physiognomic and astrological content. The text lists different entries that, as far as can be observed from the extant fragments, consist of three set elements at least.

First, the entries contain the physiognomic descriptions of 'ideal types' of individuals. These descriptions of the human body are structured according to the *a capite ad calcem* principle, i.e. they run from head to toe.

Second, they register a division of numbers with regard to the person's רוח ('spirit') in the 'house of light' and the 'house of darkness'.[12] It is possible that this division is made on a nine-point scale, but this is neither certain nor necessary.

Third, the different entries provide certain zodiacal information with regard to the moment of birth of the aforementioned person: his horoscope (מולד).

In addition, the text lists predictions concerning the described type's future state or gives an indication of people's characters. But, due to the fragmentary state of the manuscript, this can only be verified for one type of description (4Q186 1 ii 9: עני יהיה: 'he will be poor', or ענו יהיה: 'he will be humble').

Although one should allow for the possibility that the words העמוד השני ('the second column') in the phrase והואה מן העמוד השני ('and he is from the second column')[13] are a set element, it is questionable

---

[12] 4Q186 1 iii 8–9 actually mentions first the 'house of darkness' and secondly the 'house of light'. It is unclear whether this reversal is significant, and, if so, in what way.

[13] 4Q186 4 1 only has ה[עֳמוד השני, but it is likely that the same phrase is implied as in 4Q186 1 ii 6. See also 4Q186 6 2: העמוד ה[שֹני.

whether the phrase represents a fixed part of the text. Only in 4Q186 1 ii 6 is its position clearly set between the physiognomic description and the part concerning the 'house of light' and the 'house of darkness'. This is certainly not the case in 4Q186 1 iii and 4Q186 2 i where the words ורוח לו ('and there is a spirit for him'), introducing the part concerning the 'house of light' and the 'house of darkness', follow immediately upon the physiognomic sections. Also, 4Q186 4 1 shows that when a reference to עמוד occurs it is not necessarily followed by רוח לו. Here the phrase ה[ע̊מוד השני is certainly not followed by רוח לו as in 4Q186 1 ii 6–7, but by a word beginning with *šin* (see also 4Q186 6 2). This means that the phrase העמוד השני, whatever its exact sense may be, is perhaps optional in the entries listed in 4Q186.

Finally, it is possible that the different accounts in 4Q186 listed certain stones in relation to a person's physiognomic traits and zodiacal sign. Both Babylonian and Graeco-Roman astrology were familiar with various connections between the zodiacal signs and stones. Perhaps the stones mentioned in 4Q186 were deemed to have some sort of magical powers. It is clear that a stone (אבן צונם) is listed in 4Q186 1 ii 2, but its exact sense is uncertain due to the fragmentary context.

Palaeography and Orthography

The copying of the manuscript has been executed in a fine hand. The writing gives the impression that trouble was taken with it, not strange considering the reversed direction of writing.

The way that 4Q186 is written is unique among the Dead Sea Scrolls. The lines as well as the words have to be read in reverse order from left to right. Another scribal peculiarity is that the scribe wrote the medial instead of the final form of the letters *kap*, *mem* and *nun* at the end of a word. The reason for this is not entirely clear. One might suppose that although the text is basically read from left to right, the scribe actually wrote in the usual way from right to left. But this seems unlikely since, first of all, the flush left is straight which suggests that the scribe started writing there. Secondly, there are no ligatures in the manuscript where this may have been expected had the direction of writing been right to left.[14] Finally, had the direction of writing been

---

[14] Except for יפי in 4Q186 3 3.

right to left, the scribe could still have written final forms at the beginning of words read from left to right, which is not the case.

Only two words have to be read in the regular order from right to left. In 4Q186 1 ii 2 the scribe wrote the words אבן צונם ('a granite stone') from right to left.[15] In this case the copyist did use the final forms of the characters.

In addition to the inverted writing, the manuscript exhibits another distinct scribal feature, namely the use of mixed scripts.[16] Characters from other scripts were used alongside the usual square script: palaeo-Hebrew, Greek and cryptic letters. The palaeo-Hebrew letters are *gimel, he, waw, ḥet, yod, lamed, mem, nun, samek, ṣade, reš, šin* and *taw*.[17] Two Greek letters were used, *alpha* and *beta*.[18] Only one Cryptic A letter seems to appear in the remaining fragments, namely *yod*,[19] but it is also possible that it represents a simplified palaeo-Hebrew *yod*. Finally, there is one letter that cannot be identified. In 4Q186 1 iii 4 a letter occurs, the third one from left, which many scholars have read as a Greek *beta*, but this is extremely unlikely. Its exact identification remains unknown.[20] Although difficult to detect a 'cryptographic' system, it is interesting to note that when non-square characters are used the entire word is written in non-square characters.[21]

The square script of 4Q186 can be characterized, according to the typology of Frank Moore Cross, as a Herodian 'Round' semiformal hand, showing both earlier and more developed forms.[22] 'Alep has a right arm thickened at the top, which develops into a *serif*,[23] and the

---

[15] יפי in 4Q186 3 3 was perhaps also written from right to left, because of the ligature.

[16] There is only one other manuscript from Qumran that perhaps has mixed scripts in the running text, namely *4QcryptC Unidentified Religious Text* (4Q363a). The text uses the palaeo-Hebrew script (note also the dots that function as word dividers) and characters unknown to us that have been called Cryptic C script. Only a photograph has been published of 4Q363a, see M. Bernstein et al., *Qumran Cave 4.XXVIII: Miscellanea, Part 2* (DJD 28; Oxford: Clarendon, 2001), Plate XLIII.

[17] 4Q186 1 i 8: רחבים and סגלגלים; 1 i 9: רֹושׁ[ו]; 1 ii 4: נצֹר[ו]ת; 1 ii 7: האור; 1 ii 8: החושך; 1 iii 4: וא.ה; 1 iii 8: בבית; 2 i 2: ממֹע[ט.

[18] 4Q186 1 i 8: רחבים; 1 ii 7: בבית (twice); 1 ii 7: האור; 1 iii 4: וא.ה; 1 iii 8: בבית.

[19] 4Q186 1 ii 7: בבית.

[20] See NOTES ON READINGS.

[21] Exceptions are 4Q186 1 iii 7: בבית; 1 iii 8: החושך; 2 i 2: ממֹע[ט; 4 2: מולדו.

[22] F. M. Cross, Jr., 'The Development of the Jewish Script', *The Bible and the Ancient Near East: Essays in Honor of William Foxwell Albright* (ed. G. E. Wright; Garden City, New York: Doubleday, 1961) 133–202, at 173–81.

[23] 4Q186 1 iii 6: לאבר.

left leg is bent to the right. *Bet* still has its tick at the right, upper shoulder in some cases,[24] but is losing it in others.[25] *Gimel* has a right down stroke that is gently curved and bent to the right at the top, without *serif*, and to the left at the bottom. The left leg is connected low on the right down stroke. *Dalet* has an 's'-shaped right leg characteristic of the semiformal style.[26] *He* has a crossbar or roof that is thick and heavily shaded. Also, at the top of the right down stroke above the roof a small projection to the right appears. *Waw* and *yod* are not always easily distinguished. Sometimes *yod* is longer than *waw*. *Zayin* has both forms that appear in the early Herodian style: a simple stroke thickened or slightly bent to the right at the top,[27] and a doubly curved down stroke.[28] *Ḥet* has a right leg curved inward, and a crossbar set rather low in some cases. *Ṭet* is broad and squat, tending more to the developed Herodian formal script. *Kap* has a down stroke that curves outward to the right, and the base is sometimes rather broad.[29] *Lamed* has a large, sometimes rounded hook. *Mem* conforms to the late Hasmonaean style according to which the left oblique is penned last. *Nun* appears with a down stroke bent to the right and thickened at the top, but without *serif*.[30] *Samek* is fully closed. *ʿAyin* has a right down stroke that is sometime thickened.[31] *Pe* has a sharp head. *Sade* appears with a left arm that characteristically curves inward to the right at the top,[32] and the right arm is bent up and thickened at the tip.[33] *Qop* has two forms of the down stroke: straight,[34] and 's'-shaped, resembling that of *dalet*.[35] *Reš* has some variation in the width of the head. *Šin* has a left down stroke that continues below the right arm, and the middle arm is gently curved. *Taw* was not drawn in a continuous stroke, and is not yet squat and broad.

---

[24] 4Q186 1 i 9: מעורבים; 1 ii 9: ברגל; 1 iii 6: לאבר; 2 i 6: יושבות.

[25] 4Q186 1 iii 7: עבות; 3 2: בכתפ[י.

[26] 4Q186 1 ii 5: ודקות; 1 ii 8: המולד.

[27] 4Q186 2 i 1: וזקנו; 6 2: זות.

[28] 4Q186 1 ii 8: וזה.

[29] Perhaps implying a final form? Cf. 4Q186 1 ii 8: החושכ; 1 iv 7: תוכ; 2 i 3: ארוכ. The base is broad when the letter is in final position. This shows that the scribe did have the tendency to give some letters different forms when they are in word-final or line-final position.

[30] 4Q186 1 ii 2: צונם; 2 i 2: ענוה.

[31] 4Q186 1 i 9: מעורבים; 1 iii 8: עבות; 2 i 3: על.

[32] 4Q186 2 i 4: קצר.

[33] 4Q186 1 iii 8: ואצבעות.

[34] 4Q186 2 i 5: חלקות.

[35] 4Q186 1 ii 6: דקות; 2 i 2: קולו.

On palaeographic grounds a date for the manuscript between ca. 30 BCE–20 CE, according to the Cross-dating, seems probable.[36]

Regarding orthography, 4Q186 consistently writes *plene* using *waw* for long and short /o/ and /u/, e.g.: לוא, שחורות, וראושו, החושך, ושלוש, ארוכות, מעורבים.[37] 'Alep is dropped in רֹוֹשׁ[ו] (but not in וראושו)[38] and זות.[39] Regarding morphology, 4Q186 shows the long form of the singular personal pronoun הואה (once הוא)[40] and היאה, and the lengthened pronominal suffix of the third persons plural in סרכמה. These features concur with Emanuel Tov's criteria for a Qumran Scribal Practice.[41]

INVENTORY AND PLATE NUMBERS

Mus. Inv. 109
PAM 40.615, 41.314, 41.804, 41.892, 42.616, 43.344, 43.438

Frg. 1 i

הֹ]	4
ה]	5
] *vacat*	6
ואיש אשר יהיה קֹ]	7
רחבים <ו>סגלגלים]	8
מעורבים ולוא שאר רֹוֹשׁ[ו]	9

bottom margin

Notes on Readings[42]

L. 7]קֹ. The long down stroke curves to the left ('s'-shaped). This feature makes it probable that *qop* should be read here.

---

[36] Matthias Delcor mentions in passing that Józef T. Milik and Jean Starcky suggested to him a date in the second half of the first century BCE for the manuscript. See Delcor, 'Recherches sur un horoscope', 319 n. 36.

[37] Cf. E. Qimron, *The Hebrew of the Dead Sea Scrolls* (HSS 29; Atlanta, Georgia: Scholars Press, 1986) 17–8.

[38] Cf. also n. 46 below.

[39] Qimron, *Hebrew of the Dead Sea Scrolls*, 20, 22.

[40] Popović, *Reading the Human Body*, 259.

[41] But the table in Tov, *Scribal Practices*, 341 wrongly lists that the verbal form *qtlth* occurs in 4Q186.

[42] For a full discussion of notes and comments on readings in 4Q186, see Popović, *Reading the Human Body*, 240–62.

L. 8 סגלגלים<ו>. Allegro reads וְגָלֹגֹלִים, 'rounded',[43] but palaeo-Hebrew samek is clearly visible. Strugnell proposes reading סגלגלים<ו>, assuming a leap by the copyist from waw to samek in palaeo-Hebrew.[44]

L. 9 רֹוֹשׁ[ו]. A tear beneath this line that runs upward right through the strokes of ink after שאר hampers any reading of the final letters of this line. The manuscript also seems to have suffered a crinkle at this point. To the left of the tear the tip of a head is clearly visible, either from palaeo-Hebrew reš or square script waw or yod. Beneath this head a trace of ink that must be the end of a stroke is still observable. In PAM 41.804 the two elements are clearly not connected, which would seem to rule out the possibility of waw or yod, but PAM 42.616 is less clear and it even seems as if the head has part of the leg attached to it. Two elements are clearly discernable to the right side of the tear. First, one sees a small trace of ink, and, second, below the trace a down stroke with a stroke to the left on top is patently visible. Again, neither element is clearly connected in PAM 41.804, but this is not so clear in PAM 42.616.

Adopting Strugnell's reconstruction, the first letter is palaeo-Hebrew reš. It consists of three elements. The first part is the head at the left side of the tear that must have been connected with the second element, which is the trace of ink to the right side of the tear. This was the connection between the upper stroke of the head and the down stroke of the leg.[45] The third element is the small trace of ink to the left side of the tear and below the head. The manuscript has crinkled causing the displacement of the leg of palaeo-Hebrew reš diagonally underneath the head. This also resulted in the fourth element, the second letter waw, moving slightly lower. The last stroke of ink could be the left edge of palaeo-Hebrew šin.

Reading רֹוֹשׁ[ו], differs from the full spelling וראושו in 4Q186 1 iii 5, but does not speak against this reconstruction.[46]

---

[43] Allegro, DJD 5:88–89 (the italics are Allegro's).

[44] Strugnell, 'Notes en marge du volume V', 274.

[45] Cf. 4Q186 1 ii 7: האור, where the head is elongated and pointed (completely different from the palaeo-Hebrew reš in 1 i 8: רחבים.

[46] Cf. also 4Q186 2 ii 5: הוא, whereas otherwise הואה is written. Admittedly, there are only a few cases where one and the same manuscript has alternative spellings of ראש. See 4Q403 1 ii 24 (לראשי, רוש); 1 ii 34 (ראוש); 4Q418 9+ 5 (ברושכה); 43–45 i 1 (ראש); 126 ii 7 (ראוש). In biblical manuscripts only in the Isaiahª scroll from Cave 1; see for the form without ʾalep (רוש) Isa 40:21; 41:26; 48:16.

Translation

4. ...[
5. ...[
6. *blank*   [
7. And someone (whose)...will be[
8. broad <and> rounded [
9. mixed, but the rest of [his] head is not [

Comments

L. 7 ‏וְאִישׁ אשׁר יהיה קֹ]‏. This line begins a new entry for a physiognomic description. As the physiognomic descriptions in 4Q186
seem to be structured *a capite ad calcem*, the account in 4Q186 1 i
7 might have begun with the head or crown of the head (‏וְאִישׁ אשׁר‏
‏יהיה קֹ]דקדו‏), with a qualification of the described person as being bald
(‏קֹ]רח‏), or with a description of the tone of his voice (‏קֹ]ולו‏). But it
is also possible that the description began with a general bodily characterization about the individual's height (‏קֹ]ומתו‏), or a more direct
qualification, such as that the person is small (‏קֹ]טן‏), short (‏קֹ]צר‏), or
has a dark complexion (‏קֹ]דר‏).

It is possible to understand ‏וְאִישׁ אשׁר יהיה קֹ]‏ as a *protasis* in the sense
of 'and if someone (whose)...will be, then...', expressing the conditional
clause similar to that used in Babylonian omen lists. Support for such an
understanding of the beginning of an entry in 4Q186 comes from material in the Qumran penal codes, where the construction ‏(ו)אִישׁ אשׁר‏ or
‏(ו)האִישׁ אשׁר‏ is used to introduce the protasis.[47] In 4Q186 it is likely that
this phrase introduced a string of physiognomic descriptions such as one
finds in 4Q186 1 ii, iii, and 2 i, not just of one body part.[48]

L. 8–9 ‏רחבים‏, ‏סגלגלים‏ and ‏מעורבים‏. These expressions are used
in later physiognomic texts to describe various parts of the human
body, making it probable that 4Q186 1 i 7 indeed concerns an opening description of the human body that continued in lines 8–9.[49] Given

---

[47] See 1QS 6:12.24; 7:4.13.15.17.18.22; 4Q270 i 12. Cf. also CD 9:9; 1QM 7:5–6.

[48] Interesting comparative material comes from a later medieval Jewish text, *The Book of the Reading of the Hands by an Indian Sage*. See G. Scholem, 'Physiognomy and Chiromancy', *Sefer ʾAssaf: Qoveṣ maʾamre meḥqar* (ed. M. D. Cassuto, J. Klausner and J. Gutmann; Jerusalem: Mossad Harav Kook, 1953) 459–95, at 488–92.

[49] *b. Ned.* 66b; *b. Šabb.* 30b–31a; *The Physiognomy of R. Ishmael*; *The Book of the Reading of the Hands by an Indian Sage*; T.-S. K 21.88 1/‏ב‏ 22. See the discussion in Popović, *Reading the Human Body*, 36–7.

the other occurrences of רחב ('broad') and סגלגל ('round'), it is likely that 4Q186 1 i 8 describes an individual's face, or perhaps even more specifically his eyes, as broad and round.[50]

In addition, part of the head is described with the word מעורבים. There are two possible interpretations. מעורבים is a *puʿal* participle derived from the root ערב, 'to be sweet, pleasing', or it is a *puʿal* participle from ערב, 'to mix, confuse'. The second interpretation is to be preferred. In 4Q561 the passive participle מערבין occurs too, and it is also followed by the negative adverb ולא. In this Aramaic text the sense 'mixed, confused' is clearly intended. The word is followed by the qualification that it is 'not too much' (ולא שגיא), hardly said of something if the sense were 'pleasing'.[51] In *The Book of the Reading of the Hands by an Indian Sage* the use of ערב in the sense of 'to be sweet, pleasing' is also attested. A person's voice can be sweet and pleasant (ואותו שקול ערב ומתוק).[52] 4Q186 1 i 9 probably continues the description of a certain feature or part of the head as being of mixed character, but at the same time stresses the limited extent of this; the rest of the person's head should not show this characteristic.

Frg. 1 ii

ג טמא[	1
אבן צונם[	2
איש עוֹ֯ו[ר	3
(ו)אר]וֹכֹות ו֯/יֹה֯[]ֹ·· נ֯צר]וֹ[ו]ת	4
ושוקיו ארוכות ודקות ואצבעות רגליו	5
דקות וארוכות והואה מן העמוד השני	6
רוח לו בבית האור שש ושלוש בבית	7
החושך וזה הואה המולד אש‍‍ר הואה ילוד עליו	8
ברגל השור ענו יהיה וזה בהמתו שור	9

bottom margin

---

[50] Cf. also Delcor, 'Recherches sur un horoscope', 299. Unfortunately, no body part is mentioned in the extant text in 4Q561 7 3 where סגלגל also occurs, but it is possible that it refers to the eye. See also Puech, *DJD* 37:320.

[51] See 4Q561 1 i 1.

[52] Scholem, 'Physiognomy', 491.9. But the first interpretation is confirmed also by this same text, and, even more, in exactly the same form as in 4Q186 1 i 9 (in another manuscript of this text Scholem notes the reading מעורבים). It is said that the lines on the palm of the hand are mixed, that they are intertwined with each other (וכל אשר יהיה כפו מעורבבים אלו עם אלו); Scholem, 'Physiognomy', 489.12.

Notes on Readings

L. 1 טמא. In PAM 42.616 it is clear that the scribe drew part of the down stroke that is attached to the horn of *mem* and descends to the left.

L. 2 אבן צונם. The only two words in 4Q186 that have to be read in the regular order from right to left.

L. 3 עו[ר. Allegro reads עי[,[53] but the second letter might also be *waw*. There seems to be a small crinkle in the leather below the second character, or it may be that a small part of the surface has fallen off. This makes it difficult to determine whether the down stroke continued further down.

L. 4 (ו)אר[וכות. The final letter is palaeo-Hebrew *taw*, and the third letter is square script *waw*, with part of the head still visible in PAM 42.616. Of the second letter, a down stroke and a base are extant. The first letter is only present in a small trace of ink (PAM 41.804; 42.616) and is in itself not indicative.

 וה[/··[]. The manuscript is damaged and the surface layer of the leather is partly missing. Only a few dots are visible in this damaged section. When the top layer of the leather is present again one can discern a small horizontal stroke that seems to have a curve upwards at the left, like the upper stroke (the sting) of *bet, dalet, kap, mem* or *reš*, but it is very vague (PAM 41.314, 41.804, 42.616). There are two problems with Allegro's reconstruction וה[נ]ה.[54] First, the gap seems too large for one letter (even if it were palaeo-Hebrew *nun*), and, second, final *he* is difficult to read, since the curve seems to go upward.

נצר[ו]ת. The final word is entirely written in palaeo-Hebrew characters. The fourth letter, filling the gap, is palaeo-Hebrew *waw*. In PAM 41.804 one can observe a small stroke to the left of the gap and to the right of the palaeo-Hebrew *taw*. This perhaps represents the horizontal stroke of palaeo-Hebrew *waw*.

L. 7 בבית. The third letter can be either *waw* or *yod*, and the fourth letter is read either as *reš* or *taw*. It is not possible to give a clear identification of the last letter on palaeographic grounds. Given the other occurrences of בית in 4Q186, the reading בבית instead of בבור is to be preferred.

---

[53] Allegro, *DJD* 5:88–89.
[54] Allegro, *DJD* 5:88–89.

L. 8 הֹחושך. Part of the upper horizontal stroke and left down stroke of palaeo-Hebrew *het* is still visible (PAM 41.804, 42.616).

L. 9 ענו. The reading עני ('he will be poor') is also possible.

Translation

1. [   ]…unclean
2. [   ] a granite stone
3. [   ] a bli[nd (?)] man
4.   (and) lo]ng,…[…]…sec[re]t parts (?)
5. and his thighs are long and slender, and his toes are
6. slender and long. And he is from the second column.
7. There is a spirit for him in the house of light (of) six (parts), and three (parts) in the house of
8. darkness. And this is the horoscope under which he was born:
9. in the foot of *Taurus*. He will be humble, and this is his zodiacal sign: *Taurus*.

Comments

L. 2 אבן צונם.[55] Contrary to the otherwise inverted written character of the text the words אבן צונם, a kind of granite, are written in the normal order from right to left. In various ancient magical texts inverted writing or the use of different scripts was used to enhance its magical power or effect. In 4Q186, however, the entire text is written in an inverted manner and words that are written with mixed scripts also appear in normal, square characters. These considerations make it unlikely that these two scribal features were intended for magical effect. Yet, it may suggest that the regular order of writing represented some form of magical power. Perhaps the granite stone represents a magical stone, and maybe it was thought that the normal direction of writing enhanced its magical power in this otherwise inverted written text. Josephus ascribed to the Essenes an interest in the medicinal function of stones and plants. Both Babylonian and Graeco-Roman astrology were familiar with various connections between the zodiacal signs and particular stones, as well as other elements. It is thus possible that the original text of 4Q186 associated certain stones with different physiognomic types and zodiacal signs. Similar to its Babylonian and

---

[55] Cf. Popović, *Reading the Human Body*, 51–4, 213–5, 235–7.

Graeco-Roman counterparts, 4Q186 is an example of a tendency to bring together various branches of knowledge in one type of text, such as compendia or catalogues.

L. 3 ר[ו]ע איש. If one reads עו[ן instead of עי[a reconstruction such as איש עו[ר is possible. Another possibility could be that line 3 introduced a certain type of character. One might reconstruct איש עו[ל ('an unjust man'),[56] or איש עו[רמה ('a shrewd man').[57] If the text is arranged according to physiognomic criteria, it seems more likely that a bodily feature is being described rather than a character trait. If, in addition, אבן צונם in line 2 represents the end of a previous account, it follows that line 3 would be the beginning of another account in 4Q186 1 ii. Perhaps line 3 mentioned first the head and then commented on the eyes by stating the person was blind. Two lines further on the thighs are described as long and slender.[58]

L. 4 נצר[ו]ת. The exact sense here of נצרות is hard to determine. It is a *qal* feminine passive participle plural from the root נצר, 'to watch, keep, guard'.[59] Following the sequence of the description of the human body, it could refer to the genital area of the body, which is kept secret.[60] In Babylonian as well as in medieval Jewish physiognomic tradition the penis is the object of physiognomic inquiry.[61] And in Greek *zodiologia*

---

[56] 4Q417 2 i 7: ואיש עול.

[57] 4Q525 23 5: באנשי ערמה.

[58] In 4Q186 1 iii 5 the head is mentioned and two lines down the thighs are described as thick and hairy.

[59] Cf. Carmignac, 'Les Horoscopes', 202, who refers to Isa 48:6: נְצֻרוֹת, ('hidden things').

[60] Carmignac, 'Les Horoscopes', 202–3. Carmignac quotes part of a *zodiologion* that speaks of moles on the secret parts of a person born in the zodiacal sign *Aries*: 'he has moles on the eyes, on the breast and on the secret parts' (ἐλαίας ἔχει ἐπὶ τῆς ὄψεως, ἐπὶ τοῦ στήθους καὶ ἐν τῷ κρυπτῷ, see CCAG 12.174.14–15). Cf. also Delcor, 'Recherches sur un horoscope', 299–300.

[61] In the Babylonian physiognomic omen series *Šumma alamdimmû* the tenth tablet is devoted to descriptions of the penis and testicles (X:64–125), see B. Böck, *Die babylonisch-assyrische Morphoskopie* (AfO.B 27; Vienna: Institut für Orientalistik der Universität Wien, 2000) 122–27. There is an astrological-physiognomic text in the Cairo Genizah (T.-S. NS 252:2) that gives descriptions of the male genitals, see I. Gruenwald, 'Further Jewish Physiognomic and Chiromantic Fragments', *Tarbiz* 40 (1970–1971) 301–19, at 317–9. For a comparison between some Babylonian omens and this Cairo Genizah text, see Böck, *Die babylonisch-assyrische Morphoskopie*, 67. The Babylonian series *Šumma alamdimmû* also pays attention to the vagina in the subseries devoted to the woman, see Böck, *Die babylonisch-assyrische Morphoskopie*, 165. It seems that Graeco-Roman physiognomic tradition did not regard the sex organs as objects of physiognomic inquiry, but see the occurrence in the Anonymous Latin author, *De physiognomonia liber* §85: *qui virilia habent magna laneaque, stolidi*

as well as the Mandaean *Book of the Zodiac* the secret or private parts are also referred to.[62] Ptolemy, *Tetrabiblos* 3.13.15, mentions injuries and diseases of the secret parts (κρυπτῶν τόπων) caused by the planet Mars. Firmicus Maternus, *Mathesis* 5.3.38, says that if Saturn is positioned in *Scorpio* he causes tireless pains in the concealed and private parts (*absconsorum et latentium locorum assiduos dolores*). However, if a part of the body were referred to one would expect a suffix attached to נצרות. As far as one can tell, in 4Q186 the individual's body parts are always followed by a personal suffix.[63]

L. 6 והואה מן העמוד השני.[64] The exact sense of the phrase והואה מן העמוד השני ('And he is from the second column') is difficult to ascertain. The subject of הואה is the described person in the preceding physiognomic account, referred to by the suffixes attached to the different parts of the body.[65] No new subject has been introduced. It is, therefore, probable that it is the described individual who is 'from the second column'. Furthermore, it is evident that a new element is introduced following the physiognomic description. The conjunctive-*waw* in והואה makes this clear.[66]

In the Hebrew Bible the word עמוד can have an architectural sense, it can function as a reference to the divine presence, or it can have a metaphorical sense. Occurrences of עמוד in the Dead Sea Scrolls fall primarily within the category of architectural usage,[67] while the rest are mainly analogous to the second sense describing the divine presence.[68] The sense of העמוד השני ('the second column') cannot be reconciled with any of the various meanings of עמוד in the Hebrew Bible, the

---

sunt ('those who have large and hairy testicles are stupid'), and also the Greek *zodiologia* in n. 62.

[62] CCAG 4.159.12; 160.1–2, 18–19, 31–32; 162.1; 163.3–4; 166.15; 167.1, 23–24; 168.23; 169.10; 10.102.8–9; 103.26–27; 105.11–12; 108.15–16; 109.28–29; 114.25; 117.3; 118.19; 119.29; 183.21–184.1; 12.176.6–7; 178.8–9; 181.28; 184.25–26. E. S. Drower, *The Book of the Zodiac* (OTF 36; London: Royal Asiatic Society, 1949) 9, 13, 30, 33, 35.

[63] See 1 ii 5: ושוקיו and ואצבעות רגליו, 1 iii 5: וראושו, 1 iii 6: ושני, 1 iii 6–7: ובת, 2 i 2: וזקניו and וע]יניו, 2 i 1: ואצבעות רגליו, 1 iii 8: ושוקיו, 1 iii 7: ואצבעות ידיו, 2 i 5: ושוקיו and וכפות רגליו, 2 i 4: ואצבעות ידיו, 2 i 5: ושני and קולו.

[64] For a detailed discussion see Popović, *Reading the Human Body*, 38–48, 248–9.

[65] 4Q186 1 ii 5: ושוקיו and ואצבעות רגליו.

[66] In 4Q186 1 iii 8 and 4Q186 2 i 6 another element subsequent to the physiognomic parts is introduced in the same manner by the use of conjunctive-*waw* in ורוח לו.

[67] See 1QM 5:10; 3Q15 4:1; 6:1; 11:3; 4Q403 1 i 41; 11Q13 3:10; 11Q19 10:11; 30:9; 31:9; 34:2–3.15; 35:10; 42:11. See also the Aramaic *New Jerusalem* texts 1Q32 1 1–2; 4Q554 1 iii 22; 5Q15 1 ii 4; 2 4–5; 11Q18 9 2; 11 6.

[68] See 4Q365 6a i 9; 4Q470 3 5; 4Q504 6 10; 4Q505 128 2 (?); 4Q506 126 2.

Dead Sea Scrolls, or rabbinic literature for that matter. It seems to be unique and particular to 4Q186.

The word עמוד is best translated by 'pillar' or 'column', but scholars have given various interpretations for the specific sense of the phrase העמוד השני in 4Q186. There are basically three astrological explanations and one non-astrological understanding. The most widely held interpretation is to connect העמוד השני with the zodiacal sign *Taurus* and to take the term עמוד as a reference to the zodiacal sign or more specifically a position within the zodiac; in the case of *Taurus* the second position. Secondly, Schmidt suggests that עמוד refers to a zodiacal quadrant, which contains three zodiacal signs. Consequently, 'the second column' denotes the second quadrant containing the zodiacal signs of *Aries, Taurus* and *Gemini*. Thirdly, Wise suggests in passing that עמוד is a reference to one of the phases of the moon,[69] but this seems unlikely. Fourthly, Alexander argues עמוד refers to a 'column' or a 'list' in a heavenly scroll. But there is no other evidence in 4Q186 that the concept of heavenly books plays a role in the text. Also, the term עמוד is not attested this early in such a sense and other terms were available. It is evident that all the proposals for the specific sense of העמוד השני in 4Q186 can be no more than hypothetical. The simplest, but unsatisfactory, solution seems to be to take it as a reference to the second position in the zodiacal circle. Only in 4Q186 1 ii does it occur in context, and then in relation to the zodiacal sign *Taurus*, which is the second sign of the zodiacal circle according to the most common view.[70] This is unsatisfactory, however, because it is superfluous (the explicit reference to *Taurus*, שור, in 1 ii 9 makes clear that the second signs of the zodiac is meant) and does not add any significant information to a text that is otherwise succinct and meaningful.

L. 7 רוח לו.[71] Most scholars read רוּחַ ('spirit') and assume that רוח לו ('his spirit') refers to the human spirit, i.e. the spirit of the described person. Contrary to the general understanding, Gordis proposes to read רֶוַח לוֹ ('it has a space...'). Bergmeier and Albani accept this read-

[69] M. O. Wise, 'A Horoscope Written in Code (4Q186)', *The Dead Sea Scrolls: A New Translation* (M. O. Wise, M. G. Abegg, Jr. and E. M. Cook; New York: HarperCollins, 2005) 275–8, at 277.

[70] For details about the not yet satisfactorily resolved matter of the selenodromion in 4Q318, beginning with *Taurus* as the first sign in the month of Nisan, see Popović, *Reading the Human Body*, 39–40 n. 88; J. Ben-Dov, *Head of All Years: Astronomy and Calendars at Qumran in their Ancient Context* (STDJ 78; Leiden: Brill, 2008) 256–57.

[71] For a detailed discussion see Popović, *Reading the Human Body*, 172–208.

ing and understand the zodiacal sign as the object of reference. However, when Albani takes רֶוַח as a reference to the space occupied by the different parts of the zodiacal sign in the areas above and below the earth he ignores the identity of the subject of לֹו: it is unlikely that this is the zodiacal sign. In the physiognomic descriptions, the suffixes refer to the types of people whose bodies are described. A new subject has not been introduced in the text. The subject, therefore, of רוח לו is the individual type of human being with which the entries of the list are concerned, not the zodiacal sign.[72] The most plausible reading remains רוּחַ.

The general understanding is that 4Q186 visualizes the human spirit as divided between light and darkness. This division of the human spirit between light and darkness is taken as a dualistic feature of the text and 4Q186 is therefore related to the *Two Spirits Treatise* in the *Rule of the Community* (1QS 3:13–4:26). The assumption is that the partition of the human spirit in the *Two Spirits Treatise* is expressed arithmetically on a nine-point scale in 4Q186.

But it is questionable whether רוּחַ denotes the human spirit. First of all, it is important to realize the context in which רוח appears in 4Q186. The text explicitly connects the numbers in the 'house of light' and the 'house of darkness' with the word רוח: 'There is a spirit for him in the house of light (of) six (parts), and three (parts) in the house of darkness' (1 ii 7–8).[73] Any explanation for the meaning of רוח in 4Q186 should also be able to account for the realization of the numbers divided between the 'house of light' and the 'house of darkness' in relation to the concept behind that terminology. Second, the use of the nominal construct רוח לו ('there is a spirit for him') instead of רוחו ('his spirit') suggests the possibility that another, external spirit is meant. The regular way of referring to people's innate spirits in Second Temple period texts is רוחו.[74] It is thus possible that the distinct construction רוח לו was chosen precisely for the purpose of drawing attention to the fact that the human spirit is not meant as the object

---

[72] A change of subject occurs in 4Q186 1 ii 8 (וזה הואה), but its object of reference is immediately explicated by the word מולד ('horoscope'). This is not the case with רוח לו. There is, therefore, no reason to assume a change of subject.

[73] Cf. also 1 iii 8–9.

[74] Cf. CD 3:3; 20:24; 1QS 2:14; 4:26; 6:17; 7:18.23; 9:15.18; 4Q279 5 5; 4Q416 7 3 (=4Q418 77 4); 4Q417 1 i 18 (=4Q418 43–45 i 14); 2 i 1.3; 4Q426 11 3; 11Q29 1. Cf. A. E. Sekki, *The Meaning of* Ruaḥ *at Qumran* (SBLDS 110; Atlanta, Georgia: Scholars Press, 1989) 118–21, 123, who does not comment on the construction רוח לו.

of reference, but another, external spirit in this case. In the physiognomic descriptions the suffix is immediately attached to the nouns, as already noted above,[75] and that is also the case with the reference to the person's zodiacal sign in 4Q186 1 ii 9 (בהמתו, 'his animal'). The construction רוח לו seems thus to stand out in the text.

Instead of the human spirit, רוח refers to the zodiacal spirit. Since 4Q186 relates the numbers to a 'spirit', רוח should also be considered within the astrological framework of the text. If the allocation of numbers between the 'house of light' and the 'house of darkness' is astrologically the result of the ascendant zodiacal sign that is divided between the areas above and below the horizon (see below), then the 'spirit' should probably also be related to the zodiac. In other words, the spirits mentioned in the text are zodiacal spirits: one for each of the twelve zodiacal signs. Although there are no other attestations for this specific type of spirit in texts from this period (unlike from late antiquity, see e.g. the *Testament of Solomon*), various Second Temple texts imagine angels and spirits performing a variety of cosmological functions and understand stars as animated beings (see e.g. Dan 12:3; *1 En.* 21:1–5; 39:4–5; 43:1–4; 60:14–22; 72:1; 74:2; 75:3; 79:6; 80:1; 82:10; *Jub.* 2:2; 1QHᵃ 9:9–13; *2 En.* 4–6; 11; 19). Against this background 4Q186 understands spirits to accompany the zodiacal signs so that these were believed to be animated beings, possessing a spirit.

L. 7–8 בבית האור שש ושלוש בבית החושך. The mention of numbers in relation to 'house of light' and 'house of darkness' terminology occurs twice, while a third occurrence can be assumed.[76] Many scholars relate this to the light/darkness dualism of sectarian texts, especially the *Two Spirits Treatise* of the *Rule of the Community*. But the use of בית in combination with אור and חושך occurs in no other text from Qumran and cannot, therefore, just be taken as another example of Qumran dualism.

Scholars have proposed various interpretations for the term בית and the conceptual framework behind the 'house of light' and the 'house of darkness'. Delcor and Lichtenberger take בית as an astrological *termi-*

---

[75] See n. 63 above.

[76] Also in 4Q186 1 iii 8–9. In both cases the words (ו)רוח לו begin the sentence. Whatever the exact sense of (ו)רוח לו, from its basic connection with the 'house of light' and the 'house of darkness', one can assume that a third occurrence of these words originally stood in 4Q186 2 i 7, following the words ורוח לו] in line 6. But the exact division of numbers in the 'house of light' and the 'house of darkness' is lost there.

nus technicus for a planetary house, equivalent to Greek οἶκος, Latin *domus* and Syriac *bēṭ*.[77] But one of the problems with these interpretations is that a planet, even if 4Q186 would make mention of planets at all, cannot be in both of its houses at the same time, being divided between them.[78] The double use of בית must therefore indicate something else than a planetary house. Gordis and Bergmeier suggest that the phrases 'house of light' and 'house of darkness' represent day and night as times of light and darkness. Bergmeier further suggests that the moon's position in a specific part of the zodiacal sign explains the division of numbers between the 'house of light' and the 'house of darkness'.[79] However, it is not clear how day and night are conceptually related to the position of the moon 'in the foot of *Taurus*' (4Q186 1 ii 9) in a proportion of six to three. Schmidt argues that the 'house of light' and the 'house of darkness' represent diurnal and nocturnal zodiacal signs.[80] The division in 4Q186 between diurnal and nocturnal signs is based on the date of conception and an arithmetic that involves counting the duration of pregnancy in relation to the zodiacal signs. Schmidt uses the subdivision of the zodiac into thirty-six decans (three for each zodiacal sign), assumes half of them are diurnal (in the 'house of light'), half nocturnal (in the 'house of darkness'), and presupposes a nine-month duration of pregnancy. The number of eighteen invariable decans is common to every mean period of pregnancy of nine months. This means that nine variable decans remain to be designated as diurnal or nocturnal, which explains the division between light and darkness in 4Q186. Schmidt's explanation for the number nine is based on the combined assumptions that the horoscope is determined by the moment of conception and that twenty-seven decans equal a mean period of pregnancy. If, however, these assumptions do not hold water, the reference to a typology of diurnal and nocturnal zodiacal signs as a third assumption loses its explanatory function with regard to the words 'house of light' and 'house of darkness'. Finally, Albani suggests that the 'house of light' and the 'house of darkness' are related to cosmological rooms above and below the horizon.[81] 4Q186 envisages the partition of the zodiacal sign (see further below on ברגל

---

[77] For the notion of planetary houses see Popović, *Reading the Human Body*, 126–7.
[78] See Popović, *Reading the Human Body*, 132–5.
[79] See Popović, *Reading the Human Body*, 137–41.
[80] See Popović, *Reading the Human Body*, 142–55.
[81] See Popović, *Reading the Human Body*, 155, 157–9.

השור in line 9). The horizon functions as the dividing line between the different parts of the sign. The 'house of light' contains the parts of the zodiacal sign that have risen above the horizon, while the 'house of darkness' refers to those parts that are still below the horizon. This background explains the division of numbers between the 'house of light' and the 'house of darkness'. Greek astrological texts provide evidence for the association of the area above the horizon with light and the area below the horizon with darkness. Babylonian sources show that the word *bītu* ('house') had a spatial sense as a reference to an area in the sky or a part of the ecliptic, so that a similar semantic field can be assumed for בית in 4Q186.

L. 8 מולד.[82] The noun מולד ('horoscope') does not occur in the Hebrew Bible.[83] In rabbinic Hebrew מוֹלָד refers to 'descendant', while מוֹלָד refers to the 'birth-time', especially of the new moon.[84] In the Dead Sea Scrolls מולד is used in a general and, in some of the wisdom texts, more specific, astrological, sense, especially in the case of the phrase בית מולדים.[85] In 4Q186, מולד is a technical term that refers to the astrological sign under which people were born. In 4Q186 1 ii 9 the statement concerning the מולד under which the person was born is followed by a specific reference to a part of the zodiacal sign *Taurus* (ברגל השור, 'in the foot of *Taurus*'). Such a context makes general understandings of the noun מולד, such as the time of birth,[86] the occasion of birth itself,[87] or to the one born,[88] improbable here. The astrological context in 4Q186 warrants understanding מולד more specifically as a technical astrological term for the nativity of an individual,

---

[82] For more details Popović, *Reading the Human Body*, 48–51.

[83] Biblical Hebrew has the abstract noun מולדת in the sense of 'relatives' or 'offspring', and the *hiʿpil* participle מוליד (Isa 66:9), מולדים (Jer 16:3) 'to beget, deliver', but these occurrences do not shed light on the use of מולד in 4Q186.

[84] Cf. M. Jastrow, *A Dictionary of the Targumim, the Talmud Babli and Yerushalmi, and the Midrashic Literature* (1903; repr. New York: Judaica, 1996) 742; S. Gandz, 'The Problem of the Molad', *Studies in Hebrew Astronomy and Mathematics* (S. Gandz; New York: Ktav, 1970) 120–49.

[85] For מולד see 4Q415 11 11; 4Q416 2 iii 9 // 4Q418 9+ 8; 4Q416 2 iii 20 // 4Q418 10a, b 3; 4Q417 2 i 11 // 4Q416 2 i 6; 4Q418 202 1. For בית מולדים see 4Q299 1 4; 3a ii–b 13; 5 5; 4Q415 2 ii 9. Cf. e.g. M. Morgenstern, 'The Meaning of בית מולדים in the Qumran Wisdom Texts', *JJS* 51 (2000) 141–4; E. J. C. Tigchelaar, *To Increase Learning for the Understanding Ones: Reading and Reconstructing the Fragmentary Early Jewish Sapiential Text 4QInstruction* (STDJ 44; Leiden: Brill, 2001) 238.

[86] Allegro, *DJD* 5:89.

[87] Carmignac, 'Les horoscopes', 203.

[88] Dupont-Sommer, 'Deux documents horoscopiques', 242.

analogous to γένεσις and *genitura* in Graeco-Roman astrology.[89] The
nativity is the constellation of planets in relation to the zodiac at the
moment of birth, but in 4Q186 this is restricted to the zodiacal sign, or
rather part of it, under which people were born. The term 'horoscope'
is used in modern parlance for the configuration of planets in relation
to the zodiacal signs, but in antiquity ὡροσκόπος was used only for the
zodiacal sign rising in the east at the moment of birth, the ascendant.[90]
But because 4Q186 is primarily interested in the ascendant (see below
on ברגל השור in line 9), the translation 'horoscope' is appropriate
for מולד.[91]

L. 9 ברגל השור. Allegro's translation 'on the Festival of Taurus' has
met with little approval.[92] Several scholars understand these words as a
reference to a part of the constellation *Taurus* in which the sun or the
moon was positioned at the moment of birth. But it is impossible for
the sun, the moon, or any of the other five planets to reach this section
of the constellation *Taurus* so far below the ecliptic. The phrase רגל
השור cannot, therefore, refer to the constellation, but rather refers to a
specific part of the zodiacal sign.[93] Schmidt suggests it refers to the first
decan of the constellation *Taurus*. But the decans are a subdivision of
the zodiacal signs into three parts of 10° and as such have nothing to
do with the actual constellations. Also, there is no evidence that the
first decan of *Taurus* is referred to as 'the foot of *Taurus*'. Finally,

---

[89] On γένεσις in an astrological sense, see the references in J. N. Bremmer, 'Foolish
Egyptians: Apion and Anoubion in the *Pseudo-Clementines*', *The Wisdom of Egypt:
Jewish, Early Christian, and Gnostic Essays in Honour of Gerard P. Luttikhuizen* (ed. A.
Hilhorst and G. H. van Kooten; AJEC 59; Leiden: Brill, 2005) 311–29, at 313 n. 10.

[90] For the meaning of the term ὡροσκόπος, see e.g. A. Bouché-Leclercq, *L'astrologie
grecque* (Paris: Ernest Leroux, 1899) 257–75; H. G. Gundel and A. Kehl, 'Horoskop',
RAC 16 (1994), 597–662, at 599–600; W. Hübner, 'Zur Verwendung und Umschreibung
des Terminus ὡροσκόπος in der astrologischen Lehrdichtung der Antike', *Mene* 1
(2001) 219–38, at 221.

[91] Cf. also the occurrence of מולדה, "his horoscope," in 4Q534 1 i 10; 1 ii+2 1–2,
6; 4Q535 2 1. For the astrological sense here, see already J. Starcky, 'Un texte messianique araméen de la grotte 4 de Qumrân', *Mémorial du cinquantenaire 1914–1964,
École des Langues Orientales Anciennes de l'Institut Catholique de Paris* (TICP 10;
Paris: Bloud & Gay, 1964) 51–66, at 61–2.

[92] Allegro, *DJD* 5:89.

[93] Cf. Popović, *Reading the Human Body*, 122, 136–7, 156. There is a difference
between zodiacal *constellations* in the zodiacal belt, which comprise actual stars, and
zodiacal *signs* on the ecliptic, which are derived from the constellations but are nonetheless symbolic entities of 30° longitude. The constellations are of varying size and
some extend well beyond the zodiacal belt, which is given a width of ±12°, i.e. 6°
latitude on either side of the ecliptic.

even if רגל השור were a reference to the forefeet of the zodiacal constellation *Taurus* rising above the eastern horizon, it is impossible to
understand it as the first part of the constellation to appear, because
the constellation *Taurus* rises backwards and not head first (the rear
hooves are impossible too, because the constellation is imagined as a
halved animal, cut from the middle).[94] Bergmeier rightly emphasizes
that the words ברגל השור presuppose a division of the zodiacal sign
Taurus. He refers to an astrological list by Rhetorius-Teucer[95] in which
the sign of *Taurus* is divided into nine parts. In this text the enumera-
tion of the nine parts of the zodiacal sign *Taurus* indicates the successive rising of the ecliptical parts of that sign, imagined as the limbs
of the sign. Bergmeier argues that 4Q186 concerns the position of the
moon in the foot of *Taurus* and that with recourse to the Rhetorius-
Teucer text this means that this part together with two more parts of
the sign are in the house of darkness and the six other parts are in
the house of light. Bergmeier's lunar interpretation is problematic, but
his inference that ברגל השור indicates a division of the zodiacal sign
Taurus is the key to understand the astrological framework of 4Q186.
Instead of the moon, Albani proposes that ברגל השור refers to the
ascendant, i.e. that ecliptical part of the zodiacal sign *Taurus* rising
above the eastern horizon at the time of birth. It takes approximately
two hours before the entire 30° section of the sign has entirely risen
above the horizon. This means that during the time of ascension an
ever-greater part appears above the horizon, leaving an ever-smaller
part below the horizon. Assuming that the 'foot of *Taurus*' in 4Q186
1 ii 9 is equivalent to the 'feet' of *Taurus* in the Rhetorius-Teucer text,
which are listed as the seventh part of the body (22°–24°), Albani suggests that this part is in the ascendancy from below the horizon. It
being the seventh part means that six parts or limbs of the sign *Taurus*
have risen above the horizon (in the 'house of light') while three parts
are still below the horizon (in the 'house of darkness'). Thus the division of numbers in 4Q186 1 ii is coherently explained in relation to the
astrological data provided in that entry. However, from an astrological
perspective it does not make sense to count the ascendant part (רגל
השור) as belonging to the 'house of darkness' as it is by definition the

---

[94] Cf. Popović, *Reading the Human Body*, 153.
[95] See *Catalogus codicum astrologorum Graecorum* 7 (Brussels: Henri Lamertin, 1908) 192–213.

point rising above the eastern horizon.[96] An exact match between the data in 4Q186 and the Rhetorius-Teucer text is not necessary in this case. Ancient astrological texts demonstrate that there was not one fixed set of divisions for the signs according to their imagined bodies. Neugebauer has shown that the divisions in these lists are the result of mixing the concept of *dodecatemoria* with another astrological notion, that of *melothesia*,[97] and of misunderstanding both notions.[98] Thus these texts rounded off the dodecatemorial division and altered the meaning of the described body parts; instead of referring to the human body they now referred to parts of the signs. The lists were understood to enumerate the consecutively rising limbs of the signs, which were purely imaginative.[99] 4Q186 may belong to a similar astrological tradition in which the concepts of *dodecatemoria* and *melothesia* were merged together. In 4Q186 'the foot of *Taurus*' was the sixth section of nine that ascended above the horizon, into the 'house of light', while three parts still remained below the horizon. The words 'foot of *Taurus*' seemingly refer to one of the limbs of the zodiacal sign. Whereas the dodecatemorial part behind it originally controlled both or one of the feet of the human body, it is now understood as that body part of the zodiacal sign that influences the appearance of the entire human body, since 4Q186 lists physiognomic descriptions of the entire human body.

בהמתו שור.[100] Most scholars render בהמה simply with 'beast, animal', but it possibly reflects an attempt to translate a foreign word to convey the astrological concept referred to by the Greek ζῴδιον or the Latin *animal*. The word בהמה is not known from other Hebrew texts to be a *terminus technicus* for zodiacal sign. In later texts a zodiacal sign is referred to with the word מזל. But at times more terms were used to refer to this concept. Thus far, only one occurrence of the word מלוש, widely used in Syriac and Mandaean sources, is known

---

[96] For more details and references see Popović, *Reading the Human Body*, 164–70.

[97] *Dodecatemoria* is the division of the signs into twelve parts of 2;30° each. *Melothesia* is the idea that astrological entities (planets, zodiacal signs, or their parts) control a specific part of the human body.

[98] O. Neugebauer, 'Melothesia and Dodecatemoria', AnBib 12 (Studia Biblica et Orientalia 3, *OrAnt*; Rome: Pontificio Istituto Biblico, 1959) 270–75.

[99] This also explains why *Taurus* is imagined as a whole animal, rising head first, whereas in ancient astrology it is normally presented as a halved animal, rising backwards.

[100] For references see Popović, *Reading the Human Body*, 105.

from a Hebrew text from the Cairo Geniza in the sense of 'sign of the zodiac'.[101] And recently, it has been argued that the term is also used in this sense in Qumran Hebrew.[102] Since different terms were used over time, it is perfectly possible that בהמה has the meaning 'zodiacal sign' in 4Q186.

Frg. 1 iii

[	וא°ה] 4
[ ]°°[	] וראושו 5
ושניו רומות לאבר ואצבעות [	] מיראות 6
ידיו >ע<בות ושוקיו עבות ומלאות שער לאחת	7
ואצבעות רגליו עבות וקצרות ורוח לו בבית	8
[החושך ש[מ]ונה ואחת מבית האור ו°°ש	9

bottom margin

Notes on Readings

L. 4 וא°ה. The third character is problematic. Allegro reads וא°ה and does not give a translation. The third letter is legible, but Allegro places a question mark over this character in his table of the scripts used in 4Q186. Carmignac, however, reads the third character as a damaged Greek letter *beta*, ואבה, and translates 'et il consentira (?)'. But Allegro's unwillingness to read the third character as a Greek *beta* is understandable. First, this character evidently differs from the other occurrences of Greek B in 4Q186.[103] It is more rounded and, more importantly, it lacks an upper 'belly',[104] resembling Greek minuscule *beta*. However, and secondly, the minuscule writing system does not predate, in its definitive form, the eighth century.[105] It seems unlikely that within the same script variant characters were also used to express the same letter. The third letter remains, therefore, unidentified.

---

[101] T.-S. K 21.95.L.

[102] M. Kister, 'Three Unknown Hebrew Words in Newly-Published Texts from Qumran', *Lešonénu* 63 (2000–2001) 35–40, at 35–6 (Hebrew).

[103] Cf. 4Q186 1 i 8: רחבים; ii 7: בבית (twice); iii 8: בבית.

[104] It is clear from PAM 42.616 that the leather is sufficiently intact to determine that this character is not damaged in the sense that it might originally have had an upper 'belly'. This observation was confirmed by use of the microscope at the Dead Sea Scrolls laboratory of the IAA, September 22, 2005.

[105] Cf. E. M. Thompson, *An Introduction to Greek and Latin Palaeography* (Oxford: Oxford University Press, 1912; repr., New York: Burt Franklin, 1964) 103, 218; B. A. van Groningen, *Short Manual of Greek Palaeography* (Leiden: A. W. Sijthoff, 1940) 33.

L. 6 מיראות. Allegro's reading מיראות is to be preferred over Licht's
מוראות as *yod* is clearly distinguishable from *waw* in this case.[106]

L. 7 <ע>בות. '*Ayin* is not written; one has to correct the scribe and
read <ע>בות.

שער. Allegro reconstructs [ש]ער, but part of the left down stroke
of *šin* is distinguishable.

L. 9 וא̊י̊ש°°. Allegro's reading וא̊י̊ש ('And a man...') is problematic. If
the second letter is '*alep*, the left down stroke is strangely tilted to the
right. Also, if the third letter is *yod*, the down stroke seems to stand
at too sharp a diagonal. It is different from ואיש in 4Q186 1 i 7. From
the photographs it is impossible to determine the reading of the letters
between *waw* and *šin* with certainty.

Translation

4. and... [   ]
5. and his head [   ]...[   ]
6. terrifying [   ] and his teeth are protruding. And the fingers of
7. his hands are <th>ick, and his thighs are thick and each one is
   hairy.
8. His toes are thick and short. And there is a spirit for him in the
   house of
9. [darkness (of) ei]ght (parts), and one (part) from the house of light.
   And...

Comments

Allegro suggests that the small fragment 4Q186 3 possibly belongs
above the left part of 4Q186 1 iii. In *DJD* 5 Plate XXXI, the fragment is
presented separately, but on PAM 43.438 it appears joined with 4Q186
1 iii as the left part of lines 2–4. This join, however, seems unlikely.
First, the left margin of lines 2–3 is out of line with that of lines 4–8,
because it stands ca. 1.0 cm to the right of the left margin of lines 4–8.
Second, it is improbable that the designation 'beautiful' (יפי) in 4Q186
3 3 is part of a description in which other qualifications such as 'terrifying' and 'protruding teeth' (4Q186 1 iii 6) appear. Of course, it is
possible that 4Q186 1 iii 4 is the end of a previous account, thereby

---

[106] Cf. ושני in the same line.

resolving the problem of opposing qualifications, but because it is
impossible to determine this, the fragment is best treated separately.

L. 6 מיראות. Carmignac derives מיראות from מרא ('to be fat') as
a possible qualification of the cheeks. Gordis, however, understands
מיראות to be *pi'el* participle of ירא ('causing fear, frightening, awe-
some'), possibly used to describe the subject's eyes.

ושניו רומות לאבר. Allegro comments that רומות לאבר is a phrase
'presumably indicating a meaning opposite to על סרכמה of the teeth of
the more favored individual of f.2, i 3; so perhaps here = "lying askew"
or the like'. Carmignac suggests to understand רומות in an active sense
and a confusion in hearing occurred between *'alep* and *'ayin* (לעבר, 'à
côté, de travers'): 'ses dents (sont) poussées de travers'. Other scholars
do not emend לאבר and try to make sense of 'the wing'. Dupont-
Sommer and Delcor read דומות instead of רומות and propose that the
teeth resemble a wing. Delcor takes the phrase to mean that the teeth
of the person are raised like the tip of a wing. Nebe rightly remarks
that *reš* and *dalet* are clearly distinguishable in 4Q186. Also, if מבר had
been meant figuratively one would expect כאבר. The passive participle
רומות of the verb רום should be understood as describing 'a more or
less permanent state as the result of a verbal action'.[107] According to
Nebe, the same is true for the active participle ויושבות in 4Q186 2 i 3.
Secondly, אבר is אֲבַר, 'Aussenseite'. It is derived from the noun בר
(*barr*) with *'alep-prostheticum*, according to Nebe. He finds support
for this interpretation in Aramaic אבר(א)י and אבריתא. Nebe, therefore, suggests the translation 'und seine Zähne stehen nach aussen'.

L. 8–9 בבית [החושך ש]מונה ואחת מבית בית האור. There seems to
be a semiotic relationship between, on the one hand, the division of
numbers in the 'house of light' and the 'house of darkness' and, on
the other hand, the shape and appearance of the body as portrayed
in the physiognomic descriptions. The text seems to imply that the
more parts there are in the 'house of light', the better someone looked.
Those born at the moment when there are more parts of light have a
more attractive appearance (4Q186 1 ii), than those born when there
are more parts of darkness. These latter people look less attractive
(4Q186 1 iii).[108] This suggests that the human body is related to the

---

[107] M.H. Segal, *A Grammar of Mishnaic Hebrew* (Oxford: Clarendon, 1927; repr.
1978) 159–60.
[108] Due to the impossibility of Allegro's reconstruction of 4Q186 2 i, there are no
references to the division of numbers for the type of person described in that column.
See Popović, 'A Note', 638.

division of numbers; it signifies that division. The *Genesis Apocryphon* from Cave 1 provides information on the positive appreciation of certain physical characteristics of Sarai.[109] She is said to have a beautiful face and lovely eyes (1QapGen ar 20:2–3); the latter possibly contrasts with 4Q186 1 iii 6, if מיראות ('terrifying') refers to the eyes. Sarai's hands also have an attractive appearance; she has long (אריכן) and slender (וקטינן) fingers (1QapGen ar 20:5). This suggests that the long (ארוכות) and slender (דקות) thighs and toes of the type described in 4Q186 1 ii 5–6 may have been regarded as positive, attractive features, while, in contrast, the thick fingers of the type in 4Q186 1 iii 6–7 may have been seen as unattractive. Thus, the praising description of Sarai in the *Genesis Apocryphon* provides some evidence for a connection between the descriptions of the human body and the apportionment of numbers between the 'house of light' and the 'house of darkness'.

L. 9 מבית. Notice that מבית instead of בבית is written here. Whether it is significant that מן instead of ב is used is not clear.[110] Contrary to the other reference to the 'house of light' or the 'house of darkness', the word is written in square script, except for a palaeo-Hebrew *taw*.[111]

ו··ש. The fact that the last word in this line begins with *waw*-conjunctive is significant because it indicates that a new element is introduced subsequent to the numbers allotted to the 'house of darkness' and the 'house of light'.[112]

Frg. 1 iv

[שמה אלה	] 6
[יהיה תוך	] 7
[ל	] 8

Translation

6. [   ]there. These
7. [   ](he/it) is inside
8. [   ] ...

---

[109] See Popović, *Reading the Human Body*, 286–7.

[110] See also 4Q186 3 1.

[111] Cf. J. Allegro, *The Dead Sea Scrolls: A Reappraisal* (2d ed.; Harmondsworth, Middlesex: Penguin, 1964) 57: 'Having deciphered one column including a particularly puzzling phrase, it was encouraging to find another piece in a further purchase which contained the same phrase written, rather carelessly for the coder, in "clear" Hebrew, confirming the decipherment'.

[112] Cf. 4Q186 1 ii 8: וזה.

Comments

L. 6 שמה. Most scholars do not give a translation, but a few interpret it as 'there'.

L. 7 תוֹן. Perhaps something inside a specific body part was indicated.[113]

> Frg. 2 i

upper margin

1	סרכמֹ[ה וע]ֹיניו בין שחורות ובֹ[ין]מֹנֹמֹריות וזקנו [על]
2	ממעֹ[ט]והיאה תרגל ובת קולו ענוה ושניו
3	דקות ויושבות על סרכמה והואה לוא ארוך
4	ולוא קצר והואהֹ[]ממולדֹוֹ[]אצבעות ידיו דקות
5	ואֹרֹו[כ]ות ושוקיו חלקות וכפות רגליו
6	[ואצבעות רג[ל]יו] יושבות על סרכמה ורוח ל[ו]
7	[ ]סֹ/עֹ/שֹה וא] [
8	[ ]ד הוֹ]אה] [
9	[ ]ᵒᵒ[ ]

Notes on Readings

[על. The beginning of line 1 is a continuation of a previous column that must have ended with על.[114]

L. 1 סרכמֹ[ה וע]ֹיניו. A small dot of ink is visible following *kap* and preceding the gap.[115] This might be part of the down stroke of *mem*.[116]

מֹנֹמֹריות. Allegro reads הֹגֹמֹיות, but Strugnell notes that *gimel* is not very probable, *he* is impossible, and suggests reading מנמריות. *Nun* instead of *gimel* is more probable. This is because the vertical stroke of the letter directly following the lacuna is too close for it to be *gimel*. There seems to be no space for the left down stroke of *gimel*.[117] Furthermore, there are other examples of *nun* in this manuscript where the upper part of the vertical stroke curves to the right.[118] For *he* one

---

[113] Cf. for the use of תוך in relation to body parts, for example, *b. Neg.* 6:8: הפה ובתוך פדחתו :8 א/2 T.-S. K 21.88; תוך העין תוך האון תוך החוטם תוך (Gruenwald, 'Jewish Physiognomic', 310).

[114] Cf. 4Q186 2 i 3.6: על סרכמה.

[115] Cf. PAM 41.804; 42.616.

[116] Cf. 4Q186 2 i 6: סרכמה. See Strugnell, 'Notes en marge du volume V', 275.

[117] Cf. 4Q186 1 ii 5: רגליו; 1 ii 9: ברגל; 1 iii 8: רגליו; 2 i 2: תרגל; 2 i 5: רגליו.

[118] See 4Q186 2 i 1: בין and וזקנו.

would expect a horizontal stroke to extend to the right, but such is evidently not the case. It could be the upper right corner of *mem*.

L. 2 מֹמֹעֹ[ט. A trace of ink preceding the lacuna may be the upper part of the left down stroke of *ʿayin*, making the reconstruction מֹמֹעֹ[ט possible.

L. 4 מֹמֹולֹדֹו. Following *lamed* the manuscript is too mutilated to discern with certainty whether the traces of ink belong to one or two letters. It is possible to discern the down stroke of *dalet*, but the trace of ink Strugnell understands as the tip of *waw* might also be part of *dalet*.[119] Nevertheless, Strugnell's reading is plausible, either with damaged or reconstructed *yod*.

L. 6 רג]לֹ[יו. A small stroke of *lamed* is visible and there is enough space to reconstruct the beginning of this line as [ואצבעות רג]לֹ[יו].

L. 7]סֹ/עֹ/שֹה ואֹ[.[120] Allegro's reconstruction שמונה ('eight') is to be rejected. The join of 4Q186 4 and 5 with fragment 2 is materially incorrect. Furthermore, the stroke of ink near the left edge of the leather of fragment 2 could be part of *samek*, *ʿayin* or *šin*, but *nun* is excluded. Because, first, a vertical stroke should have been visible on the extant leather of 4Q186 2 i 7, and, second, if Allegro's join of 4Q186 5 to the left of 4Q186 2 i 7–9 is accepted, a stroke of the base of *nun* should appear following *waw* in 4Q186 5 1.[121] Strugnell's reconstruction based on Allegro's join of fragments is therefore also rejected.

Translation

[…]

1. [are] well ordered. [And] his [ey]es are between black and speckled (?). And his beard
2. is sp[arse]and it is wavy (?). And the sound of his voice is kind. And his teeth
3. are fine and well ordered. And he is neither tall
4. nor short, and that[]because of his horoscope.[]His fingers are slender
5. and lo[n]g, and his thighs are smooth. And the soles of his feet
6. [and the toes of his]f[eet] are well ordered. And there is a spirit for [him]

---

[119] See PAM 41.804 and 42.616.
[120] For more details see Popović, *Reading the Human Body*, 257–8.
[121] Cf. 4Q186 1 iii 9: שׁ[מֹונה.

7. [   ]...and...[   ]
8. [   ]...h[e]
9. [   ]...[   ]

Comments

L. 1 מֹנֹמריות. The reading and understanding of the word following the second lacuna are difficult, and most translations add a question mark or leave a blank space. Allegro reads הֹגֹמיות, compares it with Aramaic גומרא ('glowing coals') but adds that 'the "gentilic" form is strange unless it presupposes an adjective *גומרי "glowing"', which is 'possibly here an error for גומרות'.[122] Strugnell suggests that מנמריות ('speckled') from נמר ('to give a checkered/striped appearance') should probably be read. But he has no better explanation for the ending יות-. The text attempts to specify the colour of the eyes as being between black and a somewhat lighter shade of black. In the mediaeval physiognomic text *The Secret of Physiognomy*, a person's yellow eyes are specified as being between light yellow and reddish: צהובה בין ירקות לאדמות מי שעינו (perhaps orange is described?).[123] The construction בין...ל is equivalent to ובין...בין used in 4Q186, and also occurs in the Aramaic physiognomic text 4Q561. The translation 'between' is to be preferred either to 'both', or 'neither/nor', which is expressed by the use of לוא...ולוא in 4Q186 2 i 3–4. Perhaps מנמריות ('speckled') is used in 4Q186 as a reference to the stripes that are visible in the iris and that are better observed in a somewhat light-coloured iris. If so, it is reasonable to assume that in 4Q186 2 i 1 it is used to differentiate between pitch black and a lighter colour of black. In ancient physiognomics the eye received a lot of attention, and many specifications as to colour were made.[124]

L. 2 ממעֹ[ט. Maier and Wise presumably read the *pu'al* participle ממועט.[125] But the lacuna hardly provides enough space for three letters and a blank space preceding the next word והיאה. One should then assume a reading ממעט for the *pu'al* participle of מעט.

---

[122] Allegro, *DJD* 5:91.
[123] See Scholem, 'Physiognomy', 493.4.
[124] See Polemo, *Physiognomonikon* 1.106.19–170.22F; Anonymous Latin, *De physiognomonia liber* §§ 20–43.
[125] Johann Maier, *Die Qumran-Essener: Die Texte vom Toten Meer* (3 vol.; Munich: Ernst Reinhardt, 1995) 2:136; Wise, 'Horoscope Written in Code', 278.

תרגל. This word presents a difficulty because this form is unknown in Hebrew or Aramaic.[126] Allegro makes sense of it by recourse to 'Arab *rajila* "of a quality between lankness and crispness or curliness"'.[127] According to the classical Arabic-Arabic dictionary *Lisān al-ʿarab*, the phrase *šaʿr rajal* (or *rajil* or *rajl*) is explained as 'hair between lankness and curliness'.[128] The translation 'wavy' seems therefore apt.

L. 4 מִמּוֹלדֹו. I understand the preposition מן to have causative meaning ('because').[129] The person's physiognomic appearance, in this case being neither tall nor short, is said to be so because of his horoscope. This means that the physiognomic description is interrupted by a reference to the person's horoscope. But, more significantly, it signals awareness of the notion that the configuration of heavenly bodies at the moment of birth influences human appearance.

Frg. 2 ii

°[	] 4
הוא[	] 5
מ[עׄורב	] 6
שלוג/גולש[	] 7

Notes on Readings

L. 6 מ[עׄורב. Strugnell states that *dalet* instead of *reš* should be read, but this is incorrect. In PAM 41.804 and 42.616 a small diagonal stroke of ink is discernable that could be the right down stroke of ʿ*ayin*. Allegro's reading is, therefore, plausible.

L. 7 שלוג/גולש. This small fragment appears separately in PAM 42.616. The amount of space to the right of *gimel* suggests גולש/שלונ to be the final word of a column. In PAM 43.438 this fragment is joined as another line under 4Q186 2 ii 6. In addition to understanding the word as written in reverse order in accordance with the rest of the manuscript, Allegro suggests that it might not be 'coded', similar to אבן צונם in 4Q186 1 ii 2.

[126] It also occurs in 4Q561 4 2. Cf. Puech, *DJD* 37:315, 317.
[127] Allegro, *DJD* 5:91.
[128] *Lisān al-ʿArab* (Beirut: Dār Iḥyāʾ al-Turāṯ al-ʿArabī, 1988), s.v. *rjl*.
[129] Cf. B.K. Waltke and M.P. O'Connor, *An Introduction to Biblical Hebrew Syntax* (Winona Lake, Indiana: Eisenbrauns, 1990) 213.

Translation

4. [   ]...
5. [   ]he/it
6. [m]ixed
7. [   ]fair/flowing

Comments

L. 7 שלוג/גולש. From the context it is impossible to decide which bodily feature is described in this line, and also whether the word should be read 'non-coded' or reversed. If read as גולש it might refer to a quality of the hair, either in the sense of 'flowing hair' as poetically expressed in Song 4:1 and 6:5, or in the sense of 'baldness'.[130] On the other hand, one should allow for the possibility that the word is written in reverse manner in accordance with the rest of 4Q186 as שלוג, and that it is related to the word שלג ('snow'). In this sense it may describe a physical characteristic, for example the skin, as being white or fair. In the medieaval physiognomic text *The Book of the Reading of the Hands by an Indian Sage* the sole of someone's foot is described as having the appearance of either red wine or snow, i.e. being a burgundy red or white (כתואר יין אדום או כתואר שלג).[131] The problem with this reading is that 4Q186 2 ii 7 has שלוג, not שלג. The reading שלוג remains possible, but its sense is not clear.

Frg. 3

1 מבית] האור/החושך וזה (הואה) המולד אשר הואה ילוד עליו[
2 בכתפ]י
3 [°[] יפי]

Notes on Readings

Upon inspection of the plate with the fragments, I found that 4Q186 3 is not on this plate. One of the curators told me it should be on another plate, but it has not been located yet. The readings, therefore, could not be checked.[132]

---

[130] Cf. N. Gordon, '4Q186 (4QHoroscope)', *Additional Genres and Unclassified Texts* (ed. D.W. Parry and E. Tov; DSSR 6; Leiden: Brill, 2005) 220–3, at 223.

[131] Scholem, 'Physiognomy', 491.21–22.

[132] Checked at the scroll laboratory of the IAA on September 22, 2005.

L. 1 מבית. A small trace of ink appears to the left of *yod*, which might be the bottom stroke of *taw* (PAM 43.344, 43.438).

L. 2 בכתפ֯י]. Another letter is attached to the right leg of *taw* (PAM 43.344, 43.438), which might be *pe*.

L. 3 יפי. Read יפי instead of ופי.

Translation

1. from the house[of light/darkness. And this is the horoscope under which he was born:]
2. in the shoulder[s of...
3. []...[] beautiful[

Comments

L. 1 מבית. As in 4Q186 1 iii 9, this probably refers to the 'house of light' or the 'house of darkness', again using מן instead of ב. If the space to the left of both מבית and בכתפ֯י] represents the column margin, the entire first line could originally have had something like that in 4Q186 1 ii 8. It would probably be too long if 1 ii 8 were exactly copied, but this can easily be solved by leaving וזה הואה המולד הואה in 1 ii 8 out.

L. 2 בכתפ֯י]. A plausible reconstruction is בכתפ֯י)ו] ('with his shoulder(s)'). It could be a reference to the shoulder(s) of a described individual. Another possibility is to understand it as analogous to ברגל השור in 4Q186 1 ii 9. In this case it refers to the shoulders of a zodiacal sign. If this were so, בכתפ֯י] refers to a position in a sign of the zodiac in which an individual is said to have been born.

L. 3 יפי. It is possible to translate יפי as 'beautiful', but due to the fragmentary state it is impossible to determine what was referred to as such.

Frg. 4

```
והואה מן ה[עׄמוד השני ש]            1
     [ מולדו ]                      2
וזה ה[ואה בה<ב>(מ)(ת֯]ו            3
```

Notes on Readings

Although this fragment is very small, it is interesting for two reasons. First, it shows that the phrase העמוד השני is not followed directly by רוח לו as in 4Q186 1 ii 6–7, but a word beginning with *šin*. One may read והואה מן ה[עׄמוד השני ש]. Unfortunately, it is not possible to determine which word might follow the reference to 'the second column'. But it is evident that the reference to 'the second column' in 4Q186 does not occupy a set position in the text. Second, this fragments shows several elements known from 4Q186 1 ii to appear near each other but also some differently from 1 ii. In line 2 מולדו occurs, which can be understood equivalent to המולד in 1 ii 8 as a reference to a person's horoscope. But it is also clear that, different from 1 ii 6–8, there are fewer lines between the reference to העמוד השני and that to מולדו in 4 1–2. On the other hand, the number of lines between מולדו and וזה ה[in 4 2–3 is equal to that between המולד and וזה בהמת[ו in 1 ii 8–9. Due to the amount of space available (assuming a regular column width of ca. 8–9 cm), it can almost certainly be ruled out that a reference to the 'house of light' and the 'house of darkness' stood between both words in 4 1–2. But the fragmentary state does not allow a clear reconstruction.

L. 4 בה>ב<(מ)תֹ[ו. בהבת is possibly a scribal error for בהמת[ו.[133]

Translation

1. and he is from the] second column…[
2.   ] his horoscope [
3.   and th]at is [his] zodiacal sign[

Comments

L. 4 בה>ב<(מ)תֹ[ו. Bergmeier suggests a reconstruction, following Allegro's arrangement, in which 4Q186 2 i is part of the section concerning the zodiacal sign *Taurus*. He therefore reads 4Q186 2 i 9 as בפרסות השור וזה ה[ואה בהמתו ש[ו]ֹ[ר] ('in the hoofs of *Taurus*. And this is his zodiacal sign: *Taurus*'). This reconstruction is entirely based on Allegro's arrangement of the fragments. It is impossible to determine its plausibility for the isolated fragment 4Q186 4. In this case only the reading בהמתֹ[ו remains. It is not possible to identify the zodiacal sign referred to, assuming that this is what בהמה refers to. Maier, however, does not suppose a scribal error and translates 'e]s ist in der Jungf[rau (?)]', probably reading ה.[ואה בהבתו]לה.[134] But

---

[133] The reading of *taw* is based on the emendation, so we should be cautious about accepting בהמתו as a certain reading.

[134] Maier, *Texte vom Toten Meer*, 2:136.

Maier's reading is without basis in the text and does not clarify its interpretation.

Frg. 5

]מו[1
]ילו[2
] ו[3

Notes on Readings

This fragment appears only in PAM 43.438 where it facilitates Allegro's arrangement of fragments for 4Q186 2 i. It cannot be joined to another extant fragment of 4Q186. The fragment is too small to provide any meaningful information. Perhaps line 1 originally had ד[העמ]ד, and line 2 ד[ו]ילו.

Frg. 6

]°°[1
]והואה מן העמוד ה[שֹני זות   2
]ל[]נֹהֹ/גֹ°[3

Notes on Readings

Allegro joins this small fragment to 4Q186 4, but this join seems incorrect. The two small strokes of ink in 6 1 cannot belong to 4 3 (PAM 41.804, 42.616). The legs of *he* in ה[ואה (4 3) are too far apart to be the continuation of these strokes. Fragment 6 is, therefore, best regarded as a separate fragment.

L. 2 ה[שֹני. The remaining stroke of ink to the left is possibly the upper part of a right down stroke of ʿayin or šin (PAM 41.804, 42.616), reading עני or שני, in which case it is possible to reconstruct והואה מן העמוד ה[שֹני.

L. 3 ל[]נֹהֹ/גֹ. Subsequent to a small trace of ink to the left, there is a stroke of ink that might be the down stroke of *gimel* or *nun*, although the latter seems more likely because the trace of ink seems to stand too close for it to be a *gimel*. This letter (probably *nun*) is most likely followed by *he*. It is not possible to determine if *lamed* is part of one word with]נֹהֹ/גֹ[, or if it begins a new word.

Translation

1.]...[
2. and he is from the] second [column]. This[
3.]...[

Comments

L. 2 ה[שֿני. This would be a third occurrence of the phrase העמוד
השני. If this reconstruction is accepted, it also demonstrates, like 4 1,
that the words העמור השני are not necessarily directly followed by
רוח לו as in 1 ii 6–7.

ALLUSIONS TO THE END OF THE HASMONEAN DYNASTY IN *PESHER NAHUM* (4Q169)

GREGORY L. DOUDNA
Bellingham, Washington

Through the accident of the early editorial selections Allegro was assigned most of the pesharim, which have produced much speculation. Historical scenario proposals have a notorious track record of being wrong. Nevertheless I would like to suggest a new framework for an historical context for these texts that I hope will advance discussion, with a revisiting of several elements of *Pesher Nahum*.

COLUMN I

(1) As can be seen in fragments 3–4, column I, line 1, Jerusalem is a dwelling for the nations. The theme of conquest by gentiles runs throughout these columns and is the most basic theme in this text. In lines 1–2 in the quotation there are two lions. The second lion may be a lion whelp or cub as commonly translated, a גור ארי, but this does not mean he is the cub of the first lion or subordinate to the first lion. גור ארי is used in Biblical Hebrew for a young lion fearsome and active in its own right. The tribe of Judah is called a גּוּר אַרְיֵה at Gen 49:9 and Dan is called a גּוּר אַרְיֵה at Deut 33:22. The גור ארי, the lion whelp, simply names a second active independent lion.

As I read it, the ancient authors interpreted the first lion as Demetrius and the second lion as the Lion of Wrath. The authors seem to have interpreted the two lions in terms of a contrast between two foreign powers. Demetrius represents the kings of Yavan of the past and the Lion of Wrath represents the Kittim of the present. The first lion, Demetrius, of the past, failed to conquer Jerusalem. The second lion, the Lion of Wrath, of the present, does conquer Jerusalem.

(2) In col. I, line 5, "his great men and his men of counsel" refers to the regime of a doomed Israelite ruler. These pronouns, "*his* great men" and "*his* men of counsel," refer to the same figure as do the pronouns at lines 10–11 and II, 1, "*his* army detachments," "*his* great men," "*his* envoys." All of these pronouns, in line 5 and again at lines

10 and 11 and II, 1, refer to the same figure in the world of the text, a doomed ruler of Israel who is different from the Lion of Wrath and who is the Lion of Wrath's victim.

Later in cols. III and IV the identical pronouns and language appear as in col. I. It is the same doomed ruler of Israel, the same warriors and great men and armies. In cols. III and IV this figure is named "Manasseh." The real uncertainty is not whether there was a doomed Israelite ruler in col. I who is the same figure as in the later columns, but how the wording worked exactly in the lacunae.

(3) In line 8 the reference to something that happened in Israel in the past, בישראל מלפנים, is likely to be an allusion to the crucifixions by Alexander Jannaeus, since the Demetrius episode in which those crucifixions occurred has been named in the immediate context as the past event of interest to the text, in lines 2–3. (We know that the Demetrius episode is in the text's past because it is expressed with a perfect verb and is situated by the text temporally prior to the Kittim. By contrast, the text never situates the Lion of Wrath or other of its conquest images in its past.)

(4) The final words of the pesher in line 8, כי לתלוי חי על העץ הֹעֹץ [יק]רא, are ungrammatical as they stand. Either there was a missing expression, "accursed of God," finishing the sentence or else the text is not mistaken in which case it is a continuous reading and the following lemma or quotation provides the expected imprecation or curse from God. This is not a choice between two ways of reading the existing text. The existing text as it stands can only be read grammatically as the continuous reading. The question is whether to emend the text on the assumption that a scribal mistake or intentional omission has made the text ungrammatical. But there are three good reasons that support reading the text at line 8 as it stands. First, the continuous reading is grammatical. Second, it fulfills the exact expected words of a curse from God. And third, it introduces the ruler of Israel of the next pesher as hung up alive to die, and this makes very good sense in the larger context of the pesharim.

This last point might sound surprising in light of all the speculation in earlier times concerning a mysterious crucified Teacher of Righteousness. But that is not what is being said here. First of all, as Shani Tzoref has pointed out, if the closing words of the pesher in line 8 are read with only the first phrase of the following quotation and then one stops there, the phrase reads as an indefinite and generic comment concerning the accursedness of all of the ones hung alive of line 7, without referring to any one of them specifically.[1] But if the line 8 words are read as continuous with the full following quotation and pesher, the text makes the same point while at the same time alluding to a specific case illustrating the point, namely the wicked ruler of lines 10 to II, 1, who is hung up alive and accursed. And that reading— of line 8 as continuous with the next pesher of lines 10 to II, 1— makes the best sense for this reason: it provides a fate for the wicked ruler himself of lines 10 to II, 1, which otherwise is missing from that unit.

The important point is that *textually* there is nothing surprising or unusual in an image of the ruler of Israel himself being hung up alive, because that is parallel to the depictions in *Pesher Habakkuk* and *Pesher Psalms A* of the fate of the wicked rulers of Israel in those texts. *Pesher Habakkuk* and *Pesher Psalms A* are very graphic in their depictions of torture and death at the hands of gentiles for their wicked ruler of Israel. This would simply be *Pesher Nahum*'s allusion to the same theme.

The major objection raised in secondary literature to this reading of *Pesher Nahum*, as alluding to a doomed ruler of Israel hung up alive, has actually been a non-textual reason: a perception that nothing corresponds with such an image in known history. Was there ever a Jewish ruler, a Hasmonean king or high priest, in the era of these texts who was hung up alive? Actually, there was. But first it is necessary to consider some other matters.

READING PESHER NAHUM AS ALLUDING TO CONTEMPORARY EVENTS

Usually the sobriquet-bearing figures of the pesharim are assumed to be situated in or drawn from the dim past with respect to the time of the authors. But is that a sound reading of these texts? Early voices such as André Dupont-Sommer, J. P. M. van der Ploeg, Jean Carmignac, Karl Elliger, and others, read the contexts and sobriquet-bearing figures in these texts as contemporary with these texts' authors. That insight of those early voices came to be ignored for non-textual reasons but was never really refuted. The key point is this: if the pesharim

---

[1] Shani Berrin (Tzoref), *The Pesher Nahum Scroll from Qumran* (STDJ 53; Leiden: Brill, 2004), 185–8.

are read without extraneous assumptions, on their own terms, their sobriquet-bearing figures read as if they are contemporary with the world of the texts.

And this raises the question: why insist on reading the temporal settings of the sobriquet-bearing figures of these texts differently than the texts present them? What happens if the figures and settings in these texts *are* read as contemporary with the world of the authors, in keeping with the apparent intentions of these texts? Perhaps some things might make better sense. For example, an historical Wicked Priest of *Pesher Habakkuk*, if there was one, would be active before Herod, because this figure is portrayed as ruling over Israel, but not much before Herod, because the Wicked Priest's regime is portrayed as falling in the context of a Kittim or Roman invasion, and the Romans are not in Judea until the middle of the first century BCE. The texts read as if they allude to first century BCE contexts, with the Kittim as part of a larger landscape or setting which includes the sobriquet-bearing figures, and that landscape as contemporary with the authors of the texts. In this light the Wicked Priest would be situated within a fairly narrow window of time in the world of the texts—between the time of Roman arrival and Herod, which is to say, somewhere between about the 60s and 30s BCE.

And it is important to interject here that in the world of these texts there seems to be only one Wicked Priest. There is no alternative Wicked Priest dying from disease in *Pesher Habakkuk* as is sometimes claimed; that is a misunderstanding. It is all death by torture for this figure in the texts, divine justice carried out at the hands of gentiles.[2] Nor do the "last priests of Jerusalem" of 1QpHab IX, 4 carry an implication of multiple high priest regimes in succession. They are the same as "the priests of Jerusalem" in the parallel pesher at 4QpNah 3–4 I, 11, a collective term for a regime of priests, and the expression reads well as alternative language for the wicked ruler's regime.

In the world of the texts the Wicked Priest is killed by gentiles. In *Pesher Psalms A* this is explicit: God gives the Wicked Priest "into the hand of the ruthless ones of the nations to execute [vengeance] upon him" (4QpPs[a] 1–10 IV, 8–10). *Pesher Habakkuk*'s columns VIII and IX refer to "vengeful acts on his fleshly body" and being "delivered into

---

[2] Gregory L. Doudna, *4Q Pesher Nahum: A Critical Edition* (JSPSup 35; Copenhagen International Series 8; London: Sheffield Academic Press, 2001), 621–2.

the hands of his enemies" in the context of foreign invasion and in parallel with *Pesher Psalms A*. And *Pesher Habakkuk* col. X may allude to this figure's death happening outside Judea among the nations.

There is only one context in the first century BCE with which this portrayal of violent death at the hands of gentiles for a ruler of Israel corresponds, and that is the Roman invasion which ended the Hasmonean dynasty in 37 BCE. That Roman invasion was an army sent by Mark Antony to install Herod as king, and it brought a violent and horrific end to the regime of the last Hasmonean king and high priest, Antigonus Mattathias. There was a siege and a massacre in Jerusalem and the temple was looted by Roman soldiers. Antigonus Mattathias was captured in Jerusalem and killed by gentiles in a foreign country. And of particular interest in light of the allusion in *Pesher Nahum* is the fact that Cassius Dio, the Roman historian, says that Antigonus Mattathias was hung up alive on a cross and tortured in the process of being executed by Mark Antony.[3] In his death at the hands of gentiles Antigonus Mattathias corresponds with the portrayal of the death of the Wicked Priest, and Antigonus Mattathias is the only Hasmonean ruler of the first century BCE who does.

And so it seems to me that the wicked ruler of these texts reflects Antigonus Mattathias, and that the Lion of Wrath alludes to Mark Antony who hung up alive Antigonus and perhaps other members of Antigonus's regime similarly unremarked in Josephus, and that key Qumran pesharim such as *Pesher Habakkuk, Pesher Psalms A, Pesher Nahum, Pesher Hosea B* and others all allude in their various ways to the downfall of this last Hasmonean ruler, Antigonus Mattathias. And it is surprising to me that this suggestion seems to be new. Despite the striking correspondences between Antigonus Mattathias and the Wicked Priest just named and no obvious counter-indication, so far as I have been able to discover there has never previously been a scholarly suggestion that the Wicked Priest might allude to Antigonus Mattathias. And in asking how Antigonus Mattathias was missed I am including myself, for I too missed this in my study of *Pesher Nahum* of 2001. Now let us return to *Pesher Nahum* again.

---

[3] Cassius Dio, *Roman History* 5.49, 22.

COLUMNS II–IV

(5) In column II, line 8, Shani Tzoref is correct that grammatically the expression מתעי אפרים, "leaders-astray of Ephraim," which is another term for the Seekers-after-Smooth-Things, is a partitive genitive.[4] That is, the text is calling the Seekers-after-Smooth-Things Ephraimites. In the world of the biblical and Qumran texts Israel consists of Judah and Ephraim, and Ephraim is more or less everyone of Israel from north of Judah. The image in *Pesher Nahum* is that these Seekers-after-Smooth-Things are non-Judeans. In col. II, line 2, the "city of Ephraim" is Jerusalem controlled by the Seekers-after-Smooth-Things, and reads as an image of Jerusalem as a city of non-Judeans, that is, a city dominated or ruled over by Ephraimites. At the same time the Seekers-after-Smooth-Things in *Pesher Nahum* seem to correspond with Josephus's Pharisees who may have been more widespread and diverse than just in Judea.

It can indirectly be argued that Antigonus Mattathias had the support of Pharisees and the Sanhedrin. Josephus says Herod killed the entire Sanhedrin when he came to power.[5] This Sanhedrin functioned under Antigonus after Antigonus deposed Hyrcanus II. Meanwhile, Shani Tzoref has argued that there was hostility from the Pharisees towards Hyrcanus II in the later years of Hyrcanus's high priesthood over the issue of his protection of Herod from their prosecution, which could reinforce a motive for their support of Antigonus Mattathias in accomplishing the removal of Hyrcanus II and Herod.[6]

Antigonus Mattathias lived most of his life away from Judea and raised his army from outside Judea. When Antigonus entered and took control of Jerusalem the upheaval in power may have involved non-Judeans arriving in significant numbers with Antigonus to Jerusalem. The non-Judean components of Antigonus's regime could be alluded to in *Pesher Nahum* as "Ephraim."

(6) Starting in col. III, line 9, the wicked ruler of Israel of the pronouns of col. I appears again, named "Manasseh." Manasseh's name is taken from the name of the famous wicked king Manasseh of Jerusalem of the Bible, who is credited with having brought about the ancient

---

[4] Berrin, *Pesher Nahum Scroll*, 198–9.
[5] *Ant.* 14.9.4 (175).
[6] Berrin, *Pesher Nahum Scroll*, 233 n. 132.

destruction of Judah through his wickedness. The text is comparing the current ruler of Israel with king Manasseh of old.

The most common geographical description of Israel in both biblical and Qumran texts is two-part, Judah and Ephraim. In fact there is no use of Manasseh as a third geographical or ethnic term in any Qumran sectarian text with the sole exception of *Pesher Psalms A* where there are wicked ones of Manasseh named along with wicked ones of Ephraim, Judah, and Israel, that is, wicked ones from all Israel (4QpPs[a] 1–10 II, 14–16; 18–20; III, 12). But Israel in the world of *Pesher Nahum* should be understood in terms of the more basic two-part scheme in which Israel consists of Judah and Ephraim. *Pesher Nahum* adds the name "Manasseh" not as a third ethnic component but as its name for the wicked ruler of Israel.

THE TEACHER OF RIGHTEOUSNESS

An accurate identification of the wicked ruler of these texts could also potentially help identify the wicked ruler's contemporary in the world of the texts, the elusive Teacher of Righteousness, the מורה הצדק or True Lawgiver. For a lot of reasons, including his titles and functions, the Teacher of Righteousness reads as a high priest figure in the world of the texts, even though the texts portray him as in exile. The high priest was the "lawgiver" or one who decided halakhic matters, and as John Reeves and others have shown, that is what מורה הצדק means: law-interpreter or halakhic interpreter.[7] All of the Teacher's titles, the Unique Teacher, the Interpreter of the Law, the Priest, and so on, evoke a high priest. George Wesley Buchanan noted that the Teacher of CD XX, 27–34 leads the people in confessing sins and receiving atonement from God, which is what the high priest did. Buchanan concluded that the Teacher of CD was regarded as a high priest, and that the expression מורה הצדק which in later centuries uncontroversially is used as a term for high priest was another way of saying "high priest" in these earlier texts as well.[8] The high priest may have gone to heaven mystically in certain rites, and in some Qumran texts the

---

[7] John C. Reeves, "The Meaning of Moreh Sedeq in the Light of 11QTorah," *RevQ* 13/49–52 (1988): 287–98.
[8] George Wesley Buchanan, "The Priestly Teacher of Righteousness," *RevQ* 6/24 (1969): 553–6.

Teacher seems to have gone to heaven mystically. There is much more that supports this high priestly identification.

In short, when all the text allusions are put together, the characterization of the Teacher is as a high priest figure. The texts talk about this figure as if he is a high priest, but he is not in the temple in Jerusalem functioning as a high priest in the world of the texts. What is to be made of this? Why is this figure portrayed in this way? Some scholars long ago including the late Hartmut Stegemann gave a solution which has been accepted by many: the reason this figure is so much like a high priest is because he *was* a high priest, *had been* high priest before he became the exiled figure whose followers regard him still as the legitimate high priest. As noted, this solution is not new. It already has a wide circulation in Qumran scholarship. What *is* new is combining that valid insight with the first century BCE dating, which has rarely been done before. And if this is correct—that the Teacher was both a former high priest *and* contemporary with the authors—then the Teacher, instead of being an *unknown* high priest of the second century BCE, might become one of the *known* high priests of the first century BCE. Is it possible that the mysterious Teacher of the Qumran texts, so ethereal and reified in his anonymity in scholarly portrayals, has been visible and unnoticed all this time in plain view, so to speak?

Was there a contemporary ex-high priest in exile whose supporters would have reason to portray Antigonus Mattathias in the worst possible light?

There was. By 40 BCE Hyrcanus II, the oldest son of Alexander Jannaeus, had been high priest in Jerusalem for over thirty years. But in that year Antigonus Mattathias, who from Hyrcanus's point of view was his evil nephew, overthrew Hyrcanus with the help of a Parthian army, took over as king and high priest and, as told by Josephus, unkindly cut off Hyrcanus's ears, thereby disqualifying Hyrcanus from being high priest and no doubt further straining the family relationship. Hyrcanus was then exiled to Babylon, where Josephus says he was regarded with honor and acclaimed as the legitimate high priest by the Jews of Babylon.[9] That is, Hyrcanus II in exile was regarded as

---

[9] "When Hyrcanus was brought there, the Parthian king Phraates treated him very leniently because he had learned of his distinguished and noble lineage. For this reason he released him from his bonds and permitted him to settle in Babylon, where there was a great number of Jews. These men honoured Hyrcanus as their high priest

the legitimate lawgiver at the same time that he was opposed to the Hasmonean high priest ruling in Jerusalem.

If this sounds familiar, perhaps it is because this is the picture evoked by the traditional portrayal of the Teacher of Righteousness as so often described. After his overthrow by Antigonus Mattathias, Hyrcanus II echoes the basic features of the Teacher of Righteousness in being an ex-high priest, expelled from the temple, cast into exile and opposed to a regime in Jerusalem which fell in a brutal Roman conquest.

But just as was the case with Antigonus Mattathias as the wicked figure, there is no sign in the history of scholarship that Hyrcanus II ever was considered an even hypothetically possible candidate for identification as the Teacher. Why was this?

There was of course a chronological presupposition which is part of the explanation: many scholars have held a notion over these past decades that the buildings at Qumran were built on the orders of the Teacher of Righteousness around 150 BCE. It is doubtful that many today still adhere to this particular reason, since the rebuilding at Qumran is now generally believed to have started in the first century BCE, and since even more fundamentally there never has been any evidence that the dating of the Teacher had anything to do with constructing buildings at Qumran. But even as an historical explanation this is not a full explanation, since there were a number of scholars in earlier years who did read the pesharim as alluding to contemporary contexts, who were looking at figures and settings in the 1st century BCE, and without exception *they too* never considered Hyrcanus II as a possible identity for the Teacher. Why was that?

One reason may have been that it has sometimes been thought that Hyrcanus II was pro-Pharisee whereas the Qumran texts are anti-Pharisee. But a close reading of Josephus shows no evidence that Hyrcanus II favored the Pharisees, as distinguished from relating to the Pharisees as rivals to the Hasmonean family fortunes.[10]

---

and king, as did all of the Jewish nation occupying the region as far as the Euphrates" (Josephus, *Ant.* 15.2.2 (14–15); trans. Marcus).

[10] Jean Le Moyne's 1972 *Les Sadducées* saw no Hyrcanus II/Pharisee alignment. Nor did Anthony Saldarini in his 1997 *Pharisees, Scribes, and Sadducees in Palestinian Society*. James VanderKam notes that "the sources say nothing" about Pharisees exercising influence on Hyrcanus II (*From Joshua to Caiaphas. High Priests after the Exile* [Minneapolis: Fortress Press, 2004], 338). And so on. Hyrcanus II's sectarian orientation is now generally understood to have been Sadducee: e.g., Rachel Bar-Nathan: "it is known that the Hasmonean rulers, with the exception of Queen Alexandra,

There also used to be an idea that the Hasmonean priests were non-Zadokites who had replaced the Zadokite Oniads in the 160s BCE, whereas the Zadokite priests of the Qumran texts were from the earlier Oniad line and opposed to the non-Zadokite Hasmoneans. But there never was any evidence for that construction either—either that the Hasmoneans did not claim to be Zadokites or that the Oniads did. No ancient text or inscription attests to either of those notions, and a number of studies in recent years, from Liver 1967 (the Hasmonean course of Joiarib was Zadokite), DeQueker 1986 (the Hasmoneans understood themselves to be Zadokites), Hjelm 2000 (the Hasmoneans identified themselves as Zadokites), Grabbe 2004 (no evidence the Oniads were Zadokites), Schofield and VanderKam 2005 (considerable reason to believe the Hasmoneans were Zadokites, no evidence to the contrary), Hunt 2006 (the Oniads were not Zadokites), and others have put an end to this idea as well. This means that when the Qumran *Rule of the Community* texts refer to its priests as sons of Zadok, there is no indication in that expression of a difference between those priests and priests of the temple in the era of the Hasmoneans. And any assumptions that the people of the Qumran texts used a different calendar than that of Hyrcanus II are no more well-founded than these other notions, since there is no independent knowledge of the calendar practices of any of the Hasmonean high priests, and therefore no basis for assuming Hyrcanus II would have been on the opposite side of the calendar disputes in the Qumran texts, as opposed to on the same side.[11]

---

who leaned toward the Pharisees, belonged to the Sadducee sect" (*Hasmonean and Herodian Palaces at Jericho. Final Reports of the 1972–1987 Excavations. Volume III. The Pottery* [Jerusalem: Israel Exploration Society, 2002], 186). Bar-Nathan noted similarities in material remains associated with the Hasmonean high priests and Qumran but deflected the question of whether this reflected similar sectarian practices and identity: "[T]he great resemblance of the pottery in Hasmonean Jericho to that of Qumran Period Ib is notable...we shall not discuss whether this similarity indicates a similar sect in both sites, or common Jewish laws and habits, which were practiced throughout Judea" (*Hasmonean and Herodian Palaces at Jericho*, III, 197–8). David Stacey, who excavated with Bar-Nathan, argues that Qumran was "an integral, though outlying" part of the Hasmonean estate at Jericho (David Stacey, "Archaeological Observations on the Aqueducts of Qumran," *DSD* 14 [2007]: 237). That is, for much of Qumran's 1st century BCE history, the site and its workers may have been directly or indirectly answerable to Hyrcanus II.

[11] At 1QpHab XI, 4–8, I believe the two sentences in this pesher allude to two distinct events in the world of the text, not one as commonly read. The first is a murder-

1QS and the Essenes

However, the biggest factor in the background of everything, shaping thinking and consciousness whether expressed or not, is surely the Essene identification itself. The correspondences between details in the *Rule of the Community* texts and the classical descriptions of the Essenes are striking to most people including me. And so in the back of some people's minds may be this question: how could Hyrcanus II as Teacher of Righteousness be compatible with the identification of the sect of the Qumran texts as Essenes?

To put this question into a larger context: a number of studies of Qumran legal texts have shown "Sadducee" affinities, whereas another substantial set of arguments situates the Qumran texts in the context of an "Essene" identification. While everyone agrees both Sadducees and Essenes are sects, they evoke significantly different phenomena—the one sect associated with ruling Hasmonean high priests in power; the other sect removed from power and separated from the rest of society. The dilemma is that these two lines of textual argument each appear compelling if viewed in isolation, yet if considered together they appear contradictory. The resolution of these two lines of argument is one of the fundamental unresolved scholarly puzzles in understanding the Qumran texts. Here is my attempt at making better sense of this picture.

There is nothing in 1QS concerning any of the sobriquet-bearing figures of the pesharim. Nor is there anything in 1QS which is opposed to the temple. 1QS reads as rules of a religious order, a Hellenistic association, a communally structured association of lay people, ruled over by priests. I suggest considering that 1QS might reflect in its origins something like a ruling regime in Jerusalem sponsoring local party organizations in the countryside. The *yahad* groups of 1QS are subject to the control of priests at every turn. The priests get to eat first, decide things, they have the highest status, and so on. There is

---

ous pursuit by the Wicked Priest of the Teacher driving the Teacher to a place of exile. The second takes place in Jerusalem, in the temple, where the Wicked Priest appears in glory on the Day of Atonement and casts the righteous into disarray. The issue, from the point of view of the text, is a usurpation of the high priesthood by the Wicked Priest. The Wicked Priest drives the Teacher into exile, and then the Wicked Priest assumes the office of high priest vacated by the Teacher. If this reading is correct, the issue at 1QpHab XI, 4–8 is not a calendar dispute but rather a legitimate high priest and usurpation dispute.

no known reason to assume the priests of Zadok of 1QS to be other than priests of the temple in Jerusalem in the world of the text. The *yahad* groups of 1QS are not portrayed as a grassroots lay movement. Lay people are forbidden in 1QS from having meetings of over ten people unless a priest or party officer or commissar is present. That sounds like a rule that priests wrote, not lay people. The formation of the 1QS *yahad* groups may correspond with what the *Damascus Document* calls the revival of Israel, likened to a plant coming back to life (CD I, 5–8). If that is the sense of that allusion, then according to that text's chronological scheme the 1QS *yahad* groups started a couple of decades before the Teacher of Righteousness arose.

So let us imagine that the 1QS rule and *yahad* groups began before the Teacher of Righteousness and were sponsored by priests in power in Jerusalem—perhaps beginning in the time of Alexander Jannaeus, perhaps associated with Alexander Jannaeus's conquests and expansion of the Jerusalem state to areas which he turned into "Israel" again, reviving Israel to its former status of old, as at least a possible context for this. The *yahad* groups might represent a means by which a ruling elite in Jerusalem, a priestly sect in power, extended its influence and control, and projected its practices and ideology, into the countryside and outlying areas.

Hyrcanus II, then, in this picture would have come to the high priesthood with the 1QS *yahad* groups already in existence. According to the *Damascus Document* these groups recognized the leadership of the Teacher when he arose twenty years after Israel revived back to life again. But according to the picture in Josephus, for the first nine years of Hyrcanus II's high priesthood, even though he controlled the temple, Hyrcanus and the priests with him were a minority party and did not control the state or the larger society outside the temple. That is, the picture during this early period is that although Hyrcanus II controlled the temple he was actually not in power. In fact Hyrcanus II never in his life held unchallenged civil power directly, although during the later years of his high priesthood he became revered and influential throughout the eastern Mediterranean world as the nation's most highly respected religious leader or lawgiver. But throughout Hyrcanus II's ups and downs as high priest during these turbulent decades he would have been the leading priest of Zadok, and regarded as the moral authority and lawgiver within the *yahad* groups scattered throughout the countryside.

And so by this reconstruction 1QS *does* describe a sect, but it was an extension of the ruling sect in Jerusalem.[12]

But when Hyrcanus II lost power to Antigonus Mattathias and then Antigonus was killed and Hasmonean rule was no more, what would have happened to these *yahad* groups? Many of these groups might be more or less orphaned, rudderless, without leadership. And that is exactly the way the *Damascus Document* Manuscript B closes, with a picture of the Teacher dead, no replacement Teacher or leader, everyone on their own. The B text of the *Damascus Document* alludes to the recent death of the Teacher and the new situation of the righteous ones being without their Teacher and lawgiver, like the scattered sheep of Zechariah that the B text quotes. In 30 BCE the aged, deposed Hyrcanus II, the longest-serving high priest of the first century BCE, having suffered exile and betrayal, was executed by Herod. Josephus says Herod then attempted to exterminate the remaining members of the Hasmonean dynasty. Some of the orphaned S-groups may have come to terms at this time with living under Herod who agreed to let them practice their ways. These surviving *yahad* groups, now existing independently, might then turn up as the idealized, glorified Essenes of the classical sources.

And so in this way there would be a direct S-Essene connection or continuity, but without any notion that S reflects opposition to the priests of the temple, for nothing in the S texts calls for that notion. In the *Damascus Document* there *is* separation from the priests of the temple, an adversarial relationship, but that text postdates the Teacher and the Teacher's expulsion from the temple. But none of those developments are alluded to or assumed in the world of 1QS, which is explained very simply if 1QS is in fact from earlier, before those events. The key insight here is that when 1QS refers to a separation from the "way of the people," that can be read as a sectarian orientation *held by priests of the temple.* 1QS *extends* the ideology of priestly separateness to selected lay initiates, but nothing in

---

[12] Compare Jutta Jokiranta's discussion of the terms "sect" and "sectarian": "the use of the term 'sect'—if insisted—of a group behind the Scrolls should be free of presuppositions such as that this group had a very marginal position…or that it protested against the Temple establishment" (Jutta Jokiranta, "'Sectarianism' of the Qumran 'Sect': Sociological Notes," *RevQ* 20/78 [2001]: 239 n. 48).

1QS requires reading that as meaning *rejection of* the priests or the temple.

CHRONOLOGY OF THE DAMASCUS DOCUMENT

It is often suggested that there is a 490-year chronological scheme, so basic to other Qumran texts, underlying the *Damascus Document* as well: 390 plus 20 to the rise of the Teacher (CD I, 3–11), 40 for the Teacher, and then a final 40 after the death of the Teacher until the new age (CD XIX, 35–XX, 1/XX, 13–15): 490 in total.[13]

The first number, the 390 years, is widely acknowledged to be of no historical usefulness since there is no reason to suppose the authors knew the true date of Nebuchadnezzar or the length of the Persian period.[14] But the other numbers of the scheme from the authors' own time or recent memory could be approximately correct. The revival of Israel like a dead plant coming back to life of CD I, 5–8 might allude to the conquests and expansions of Alexander Jannaeus viewed favorably by the authors of the Qumran texts.[15] The rise of the Teacher twenty

---

[13] For example Geza Vermes, *The Complete Dead Sea Scrolls in English* (5th ed.; New York: Penguin, 1998), 58.

[14] Well summarized by Michael Wise: "The year 587 [for Nebuchadnezzar] is a date modern scholars have deduced only because they have cuneiform writings to combine with the biblical clues. Ancient Jewish chronographers were less fortunate. Indeed, no one in the time of the scrolls was quite sure how long the Persian period had been...Second Temple Jews calculated the length of the Persian period using the 490 years of Dan 9:24–27. Standard practice was first to decide when those 490 years had ended or shortly would end (i.e. when Daniel's prophecies would be fulfilled). Then one reckoned backwards from that very debatable standpoint.... Since, therefore, the author of the *Damascus Document* cannot be presumed to have posited the year 587 BCE for Nebuchadnezzar's siege of Jerusalem, the only proper methodology for understanding CD 1:3–11 is to turn the usual approach on its head. One must first determine when the Teacher lived, then work backwards from that point to calculate when the author believed Nebuchadnezzar was on the scene" (Michael Wise, "Dating the Teacher of Righteousness and the *Floruit* of his Movement," *JBL* 122 [2003]: 63–4).

[15] Seth Schwartz: "By the death of Alexander Jannaeus...all of Palestine except for the territory of Ascalon and much of Transjordan were under Hasmonean control...Jerusalem changed from a small hill-country town far from the main trade routes, whose chief distinction was a not very distinguished temple, to the capital city of one of the largest of the kingdoms which succeeded the Seleucid Empire. Alexander's grandfather had been a village priest, low-level rebel leader and brigand; Alexander was an important king. Palestine had been a mosaic of Greek cities and little Hellenized semitic tribal and ethnic units, of which the Judaeans were only one, and possibly not the largest; now it was almost entirely 'Jewish'..." (Seth Schwartz, "Israel

years later (CD I, 8–11) might allude to the start of Hyrcanus II as high priest. Josephus gives a figure for Hyrcanus II as in office for "forty years" after Pompey at *Antiquities* 15.6.4 (180). Either that is some sort of round number—Hyrcanus II was high priest for about thirty-two years in total, only twenty-three of which were after Pompey, according to Josephus's account otherwise—or it is a garbled tradition of a calculation of some actual year-span of Hyrcanus II.[16] In any case that is what Josephus says: forty years for Hyrcanus II. The death of the Teacher would be the death of Hyrcanus II in 30 BCE. The authors' "present" in the *Damascus Document* B text, meanwhile, is probably about year 450 or 460 or so into the 490, not too long after the death of the Teacher, somewhere in the final forty, which would be not long after 30 BCE.

Not long after the death of Hyrcanus II the lights go out completely in the texts found in the caves at Qumran. It has long been noted that there is not a single name, event, ruler, battle, or allusion to anything later than the first century BCE in any of the texts found in the Qumran caves, or indeed any text known to have been composed later than the 1st century BCE among the finds. The deposits of the texts in the caves around Qumran may also have ended at this time instead of at the First Revolt as commonly supposed. The reason for the end of the texts at this time is unknown but could be related to what Josephus says was Herod's attempt to exterminate the remaining family and partisans of Hyrcanus II. As Josephus puts it, "None was left alive of the family of Hyrcanus, and the kingdom was wholly in Herod's power" (*Ant.* 15.8.10 (266)).

In conclusion, the Qumran texts being revised for the new DJD V may echo the final and tragic collapse of the Hasmonean dynasty in ways that have not yet been adequately recognized.

---

and the Nations Roundabout: 1 Maccabees and the Hasmonean Expansion," *JJS* 42 [1991]: 16–7).

[16] If the c. 4 years Hyrcanus II was in Babylon and regarded as legitimate high priest during Antigonus's usurpation before Hyrcanus's return to Jerusalem, and the earlier 4 years of Aristobulus II's usurpation, are included, the total number of years for Hyrcanus II as high priest as his supporters might interpret it could come out to about 40 years.

Revised Pesher Nahum in English with Some Possible Reconstructions

4QpNah Frags. 3–4

[... WHERE IS THE LIONS' PLACE? THE PASTURE FREQUENTED BY YOUNG LIONS?

<*vacat*> Its interpretation ...]

Col. I   1

[_____] a dwelling for the wicked of the nations. WHERE THE OLD LION WOULD GO, THERE WAS A LION WHELP

2

[FRIGHTENED OF NOTHING. <*vacat*> Its interpretation: the 'old lion'—this is Deme]trius, king of Yavan, who sought to come to Jerusalem in the conspiracy of the Seekers-after-Smooth-Things

3

[before. But God did not choose to give the city into] the hand of the kings of Yavan from the time of Antiochus until the standing of the rulers of the Kittim. And after that it is trampled

4

[by the Lion of Divine Wrath, for he is the 'lion whelp'. <*long vaca*]*t*> THE LION PROVIDING A MEAT SUPPLY FOR HIS CUBS, [AND] STRANGLING PREY FOR HIS LIONESSES.

5

[Its interpretation concerns the Lion of Divine Wrath who tears Manasseh in pieces. And its interpretation] concerns the Lion of Divine Wrath who smites his great men and his men of counsel

6

[_____ AND FILLING] HIDEOUT (*sic*) [WITH PREY] AND HIS PLACE WITH TORN FLESH. <*vacat*> Its interpretation concerns the Lion of Divine Wrath

7

[the one coming upon Israel in the last days to execute ven]geance upon the Seekers-after-Smooth-Things, whom he hangs up as living men

8

[to be a horror and a curse, as it was with the traitors] against Israel before. For to the one hanged up alive on [a stake is procl]aimed: "BEHOLD I AM AGAINST [YOU!"]

9

SA[YS YAHWEH OF HOSTS. "I WILL BURN UP IN SMOKE YOUR HORDE!] THE SWORD WILL DEVOUR YOUR YOUNG LIONS! [I] WILL CUT [FROM THE LAND] THE (*sic*) PREY! <*vacat*>

10   [AND THE VOICE OF YOUR MESSENGERS]
WILL NO [LONGER BE HEARD ^{IN IT}." <vacat>] Its
[interpretation:] 'your horde'—these are his army
detachments [^{which are overthrown}]. And his 'young lions'—these
are

11   his great men [^{and his warriors who are destroyed.} And] his 'prey'—this
is [the weal]th which [the prie]sts of Jerusalem have
a[mass]ed which

12   they give in[^{to the hand of the army of the Kittim, for because of their plundering the simple}
^{ones of} E]phraim Israel is given [to be a spoil. <l]ong vacat>.

Col. II   1   And his 'messengers'—these are his envoys whose call is
no longer heeded by the nations. <vacat> ALAS, CITY
OF BLOODSHED! FILLED [WITH DECEIT!] FIL[L]ED
[WITH VIOLENCE!]

2   Its interpretation: this is the city of Ephraim, the Seekers-
after-Smooth-Things in the last days who in deceit and
fal[sehoods] conduct themselves. <vacat>

3   VIOLENCE DOES NOT CEASE—THE CRACK OF
THE WHIP, THE TREMBLING SOUND OF EARTH
SHAKING FROM WHEELS, THE DASHING HORSE,
THE JOLTING CHARIOT, THE H[ORSE]MAN
CHARGING, THE BLADE,

4   THE GLITTERING POINT OF THE SPEAR. MANY
ARE SLAIN AND THERE ARE MASSES OF CORPSES,
NO END TO DEAD BODIES—THEY STUMBLE OVER
THEIR OWN DEAD BODIES. <vacat> Its interpretation
concerns the dominion of the Seekers-after-Smooth-
Things.

5   The sword of the nations, captivity, and plunder do not
cease from the midst of their congregation. Violence is in
their midst, and exile from terror of the enemy. Many

6   guilty corpses fall in th[eir] days. There is no end to
counting their slain. They trip over their own dead
carcasses as a result of their wicked conspiracies.

7 BECAUSE OF THE MA[NY] FORNICATIONS OF THE HARLOT, BEAUTIFUL IN CHARM [AND] MISTRESS OF SORCERIES, WHO DELIVERS NATIONS TO DESTRUCTION BY HER FORNI[CAT]ION, AND CLANS THROUGH HER [SORCER]IES. <vacat>

8 [Its] interpretation con[cerns] the leaders-astray of Ephraim <vacat> who by their false teaching, their lying tongue, and treacherous lip they lead many astray—

9 kings, officers, priests and people, along with the joined stranger. Cities and clans are destroyed because of their counsel. No[bl]es and rul[ers]

10 fall [because of] their insol[ent] tongue. <extra long vacat> "BEHOLD, I AM AGAINST YOU!", SAYS YAHWEH OF H[OSTS]. "YOU WILL RAISE

11 [YOUR] SKIRTS OVER YOUR FACE. [YOU] WILL DISPLAY TO [THE NAT]IONS [YOUR] PRI[VATE PARTS, AND YOUR] SHA[ME] TO KINGDOMS." <vacat> Its interpretation: [this is their assembly] wh[ich]

12 [is become a byword in all] the cities of the east, for the 'sk[irts'—this is the glory of their rulers which is taken away. And they become an object of scorn in the eyes of]

Col. III 1 the nations because of their im[p]urity [and because of] their [fil]thy abominations. "AND I SHALL FLING EXCREMENT UPON YOU [AND] I [SHALL TREAT] YOU [WITH CONT]EMPT. I WILL MAKE YOU

2 LOATHSOME. AND IT WILL COME TO PASS THAT EVERY ONE WHO LOOKS AT YOU WILL RUN AWAY FROM YOU." <long vacat>

3 Its interpretation concerns the Seekers-after-Smooth-Things whose wicked deeds are revealed to all Israel at the last time.

4 Many discern their sin, hate them, and loathe them on account of their guilty insolence. When the glory of Judah is [t]aken away

5   the simple ones of Ephraim flee from the midst of their
     assembly. They abandon the ones leading them astray
     and become joined to [the God of Is]rael. AND THEY
     WILL SAY:

6   "NINEVEH IS DEVASTATED. WHO WILL
     MOURN FOR HER? FROM WHERE SHALL I SEEK
     COMFORTERS FOR YOU?" *<vacat>* Its interpretation
     [concerns the S]eekers-after-

7   Smooth Things whose counsel is destroyed, and whose
     government is disbanded. They no longer lead astray
     [the] assembly. The sim[ple ones]

8   no longer strengthen their counsel. [*<lo]ng vacat>* WILL
     YOU [DO B]ETTER THAN A[MON, SITUATED ON]
     RIVERS? [*<vacat>*]

9   Its interpretation: 'Amon'—these (*sic*) are Manasseh. And
     the 'rivers'—these are the gr[ea]t [men of] Manasseh, the
     nobles of [the city, the ones strengthen]ing Ma[nasseh.]

10   WATER SURROUNDING HER, WHOSE RAMPART
     WAS THE SEA, AND THE WATER, HER WALLS.
     <l[ong vacat>]

11   Its [interpretation:] these are her (*sic*) men of [ar]ms, her
     (*sic*) m[en of w]ar. [CU]SH WAS [HER] STRENGTH,
     [AND SO WAS EGYPT, WITHOUT LIMIT. *<vacat>* Its
     interpretation: this is the assembly of]

12   [wi]ck[ed ones aiding Manasseh,] the [ones joi]n[ed together to ex]alt [Manasseh.
     P]UT AND [THE LIBYANS WERE HER ALLIES.
     <vacat>]

Col. IV   1   Its interpretation: these are the wick[ed ones united,] the
               house of Peleg, the ones joined to Manass[eh]. EVEN
               SHE W[ENT] INTO EXILE, [INTO CAPTIVITY. AND]

          2   HER INFANTS WERE DASHED TO PIECES AT THE
               HEAD OF EVERY WALL. THEY CAST LOTS FOR
               HER NOBLES. ALL OF [HER] G[REA]T [MEN WERE
               BOUND]

3   IN CHAINS. Its interpretation concerns Manasseh at
    the last time. His reign over I[srael] is brought low
    [_____]

4   His women, his infants, and his children go into captivity.
    His warriors and his nobles [are destroyed] by the sw[ord.
    YOU TOO WILL BE DRUNK]

5   AND YOU WILL BE DAZED. *<long vacat>* Its
    interpretation concerns the wicked ones of
    E[phraim _____]

6   whose cup comes af[ter] Manass[eh and his grea]t [men. *<long vacat>*
    YOU TOO WILL SEEK]

7   A STRONGHOLD IN THE CITY FROM THE ENEMY.
    <vacat> [Its] interpreta[tion con]cerns [the wicked ones of Ephraim
    who seek a stronghold against]

8   their enemies in the ci[ty,
    but _____. ALL
    YOUR FORTRESSES]

9   ARE AS F[IG TREES WITH RIPE FRUIT. *<vacat>* Its
    interpretation concerns _____]

4QpHos B Frag. 2

[... _____
EPHRAIM WENT TO ASSYRIA, AND HE SENT TO]

1   [KING JAREB. BUT HE WAS NOT ABLE TO HEAL
    YOU, NOR CURE YOUR] WOUND. *<vacat>* [Its interpretation
    _____]

2   [_____]
    the Lion of Divine Wrath. FOR I AM [LIKE A YOUNG
    LION TO EPHRAIM AND LIKE A LION TO THE
    HOUSE]

3   [OF JUDAH. *<vacat>* Its interpretation concerns the Lion of Divine Wrath, the
    one coming to destroy the assemb]ly of the Last [P]riest, which he
    stretches forth his hand to smite in Ephraim

4   [and in the house of Judah. For because of the violence they did against his chosen ones God
    delivers them into] his [ha]nd. *<long vacat>*

PESHER COMMENTARY AND ITS AFTERLIFE IN THE NEW TESTAMENT[1]

MOGENS MÜLLER
University of Copenhagen

Most of the New Testament writings testify to the importance of the interpretation of the scriptures of Judaism as a major means of establishing the theological worlds of thought characteristic of early Christianity. As a matter of course the earliest Christ-believers—being themselves Jews—continued using the methods of interpretation already being employed in contemporary Judaism. Thus New Testament scholarship has been aware of examples in Early Judaism of both the allegorical interpretation (with Philo as the most excellent representative) and the midrashic interpretation of biblical texts in new contexts, making use of what were to become known as the seven *middot* of Hillel. To this should be added as well the importance of the phenomenon of "rewritten Bible," which has more recently come to the fore in biblical scholarship.

THE "PROOF FROM SCRIPTURE" MODEL OF INTERPRETATION

With regard to the New Testament, however, modern scholars' interpretations of the evidence have often been biased by the concept of "proof from Scripture" which saw to it that nearly every reference to Old Testament sayings received that label. Although it was often impossible to see exactly what was proven by relating the Old Testament saying to the New Testament events, the designation of all this usage as "proof from Scripture" stuck.

The term "proof from Scripture" should indeed be used sometimes for some phenomena in the New Testament. Perhaps the phenomenon turns up for the first time in the Lucan writings.[2] Here we find,

---

[1] For kind help in improving my English I want warmly to thank the Revd Jim West, Th.D.
[2] In Mogens Müller, "The Reception of the Old Testament in Matthew and Luke-Acts. From Interpretation to Proof from Scripture," *NT* 43 (2001): 315–30, I have tried

most clearly in Acts, an understanding that Scripture contains a clear description of what was going to happen that is fulfilled in the life and fate of Jesus. Perhaps the best example is found in Acts 17:2–3 where we read that in the synagogue of Thessalonica Paul, over three Sabbaths, argued with the Jews "from the scriptures, explaining and proving that it was necessary for the Anointed to suffer and to rise from the dead, and saying: 'This Jesus, whom I proclaim to you, is the Anointed'." Here I have chosen to render the Greek ὁ χριστός as "the Anointed," because the widespread rendering with "the Christ" to my mind undermines the whole argument by cutting short the identification of "the Anointed" one as described in Scripture with the person of Jesus.

Analyzing the various methods of interpreting Scripture in the Lucan writings, forty years ago the Münster New Testament scholar Martin Rese declared that in the Jewish use of Scripture we hardly find any model for the sophisticated "proof from Scripture" methodology.[3] In the meantime, however, the Rostock New Testament professor, Eckart Reinmuth, has shown that there is a conspicuous affinity between the use of Scripture in the Lucan writings and in Pseudo-Philo's *Liber Antiquitatum Biblicarum*.[4] But even if the "proof from Scripture" has its roots in Jewish interpretation, it was in Christian exegesis that it was developed and refined as a means to maintain the holy writings of Judaism as—when "rightly" understood—a Christian book.

Be that as it may, the blanket application of the "proof from Scripture" label to interpretation, which was first done by Justin Martyr, often hindered an adequate understanding of the use of Scripture in the letters of Paul and the earlier Gospels. The so-called fulfilment quotations in the Gospel of Matthew suffered especially from being laid in the Procrustean bed of the "proof from Scripture" approach—the prophetic utterances in these ten quotations really prove nothing.

---

to work out the difference between the Gospel of Matthew and the Gospel of Luke with regard to their use of Scripture.

[3] Martin Rese, *Alttestamentliche Motive in der Christologie des Lukas* (SNT 1; Gütersloh: Gütersloher Verlagshaus, 1969), 42.

[4] Eckart Reinmuth, *Pseudo-Philo und Lukas: Studien zum Liber Antiquitatum Biblicarum und seiner Bedeutung für die Interpretation des lukanischen Doppelwerks* (WUNT 74; Tübingen: Mohr Siebeck, 1993).

The "Pesher" Model

Exactly in this context the continuous pesher commentaries discovered among the Dead Sea Scrolls, as well as examples of the similar manner of interpreting Scripture in other writings belonging to this discovery, have been most helpful in aiding our understanding of what was going on in the employment of Scripture in the letters of Paul and foremost in the Gospel of Matthew. It is understandable that the pesher commentaries have attracted a great deal of attention in Dead Sea Scrolls scholarship, because they are widely held to be the most distinctive and typical mode of biblical interpretation by the community behind this library.[5]

What is often found in the pesher commentaries is a running interpretation of a continuous text, not just a commentary on a specific biblical saying. But the hermeneutical presupposition in both the sectarian and in some New Testament cases seems to have been the same: a charismatic interpreter detects the actual meaning of the text by relating its content to events in the present. Thus it is no accident that it is prophetic texts which are the main subject in the pesharim; and since they are produced by prophets, or at least by poets who are similarly inspired and insightful, the Psalms also can be treated this way.

If we take, for example, the two pesher commentaries that were published first, *Pesher Nahum* is characterised not only by some actualizing interpretation but also by offering names of historical persons belonging to the beginning of the first century BCE, while *Pesher Habakkuk* is the one that seems to be most useful for our reconstruction of the sect's hermeneutical presuppositions. For the sake of convenience I assume that the useful description of the characteristics of the pesher literature by my former colleague, Bodil Ejrnæs, is correct.[6] Thus pesher commentary presupposes that the prophetic text, although it may have had something to say to its original audience,

---

[5] For an overview see Devorah Dimant, "Pesharim, Qumran," *ABD* 5 (1992), 244–51. A newer monograph is that by Timothy H. Lim, *Pesharim* (Companion to the Qumran Scrolls 3; London: Sheffield Academic Press, 2002). Lim ascribes the many acknowledged similarities between the Qumran community and the Early Church to "a common sectarian matrix" (p. 85).

[6] "Pesher-litteraturen fra Qumran," in *Dødehavsteksterne og Bibelen* (ed. Niels Hyldahl and Thomas L. Thompson; Forum for Bibelsk Eksegese 8; Copenhagen: Museum Tusculanum, 1996), 27–39.

more importantly speaks about events in connection with the history
of the interpreter's community which is convinced that it is living at
the end of time. In this situation the prophetic utterance, being inspired
by God, contains an important message, but the prophetic utterances
include miraculous secrets which are not in themselves understandable. To be rightly understood, the prophetic utterances thus demand
an interpretation which in reality consists of a new message from God
in the shape of a new revelation, offering special enlightenment which
makes the interpreter fit to decipher it. This special enlightenment is of
course not a gift given to everyone. In the literature produced by the
community behind the Qumran library it is foremost, but seemingly
not exclusively, connected with the enigmatic figure of the Teacher of
Righteousness.

This means that the pesher commentary—and this is the very special feature about it—considers the prophetic utterances to be secrets
which are only fully and rightly understood when a new revelation
reveals their eschatological meaning. Looked at from the outside, what
is going on here is that events in the history of the interpreting community are made the key for understanding the prophetic word. Thus
it can be described as a complementary process where the inspired
prophetic utterance offers the divine authority, and actual contemporary events contribute the exact meaning. Interpreting the scriptural text, in other words, is an enterprise that involves both reading
meaning into the text from the outside (based on the experience of
the community), and reading meaning out of the text by means of
hermeneutical methods linking the pesher with the scriptural text in
ways well known and recognizable to the community.

THE PESHER MODEL AND EARLY CHRISTIAN INTERPRETATION OF SCRIPTURE

The first to recognize the importance of the pesher commentary for
understanding the use of the Old Testament in New Testament, in
this case the Gospel of Matthew, was the Swedish scholar Krister Stendahl (1921–2008), in his seminal doctoral dissertation from 1954, *The
School of Matthew.*[7] However, Stendahl was primarily interested in

---

[7] Krister Stendahl, *The School of Matthew and Its Use of the Old Testament* (ASNU
20; Lund & Copenhagen, 1954; reprint Philadelphia, 1969). See esp. pp. 183–202.

pesher commentary to explain differences in the textual forms of the scriptural texts. And a similar one-sided interest in the text-form of quotations is also dominant in the newer contribution by Marten J. J. Menken, *Matthew's Bible* from 2004.[8]

The question of the text-form is certainly important. However, the question of the hermeneutical characteristic of the pesher commentary also deserves close attention. Thus it could be an eye-opener to see how the hermeneutic of the pesher commentary served as an expedient means for the earliest generations of Christ-believers to proclaim how the events in the life of Jesus unfolded the (until then) hidden meaning of a series of prophetical utterances. In fact what we observe as systematically developed in the fulfilment quotations in Matthew is already present in the genuine letters of Paul and in the Gospels of Mark and John.

The basic assumption in Paul's exegesis of Scripture is that Christ by the institution of the new covenant has initiated the beginning of the end and Christ-believers can therefore regard themselves as living in the last days.[9] And, according to Paul, the story about what happened to the desert generation was "written down for our instruction, upon whom the end of the ages has come" (1 Cor 10:11; cf. 9:8–10). And in Rom 4:23–24 it is said about the saying in Gen 15:6, that Abraham believed God and it was reckoned to him as righteousness, that "it was written not for his sake alone, but for ours also, us to whom it should be reckoned, us who believe in him that raised from the dead Jesus our Lord." And later on in the same epistle, in Rom 15:3–4, a quotation from Ps 69:9 is followed by the statement, "For what was written in former days was written for our instruction, that by steadfastness and by the encouragement of the scriptures we might have hope." Both in the more allegorical interpretation of the story about the fathers in the desert in 1 Cor 10:13 and in the midrashic elucidation of Deut 30:11–14 in Rom 10:5–13, we can observe the complementary relation between Scripture and Christ-belief. The Christ event—to use this very modern designation—is to Paul the very key to his understanding of

---

[8] Marten J. J. Menken, *Matthew's Bible: The Old Testament Text of the Evangelist* (BETL 173; Leuven: Peeters, 2004).

[9] For a fuller documentation see Mogens Müller, "Christus als Schlüssel der biblischen Hermeneutik des Paulus," in *Paulinische Christologie: Exegetische Beiträge. FS Hans Hübner* (ed. Udo Schnelle und Thomas Söding mit Michael Labahn; Göttingen: Vandenhoeck & Ruprecht, 2000), 121–39.

Scripture and for this reason his interpretation may rightly be labelled methodologically as "Christological" exegesis.

An investigation of the use of Scripture in the Gospel of Mark shows no principal difference from that in the Gospel of Matthew of about fifteen years later. In Matthew 1:23, the quotation probably most discussed, Isa 7:14 about the virgin giving birth to a child, can be taken as representative of the method of all the fulfilment quotations. The "virgin" appears properly in the Greek version of the quotation, but the introduction of the Holy Spirit in this connection is new in relation to the Isaianic saying. But it is this very Spirit which explains what is meant in the prophetic utterance. Thus the Scripture quotation does not figure in a proportion of one-to-one with the "fulfilment." Rather, the essential meaning of the scriptural passage is contributed by traditions and events belonging to the Christian experience.

In the Gospel of John, in spite of all the obvious differences between it and the Synoptics, we find a similar pattern in the use of Scripture. The salvation history which is so pronounced in the Gospel of Matthew is nearly invisible, but, even if Scripture has its own voice and independent meaning in the Gospel of John, it is also the case that this meaning is becoming clear only in its methodical Christ-proclamation.[10]

The earliest Christ-believers gained this confidence of possessing the methodological key to the right understanding of Scripture from their conviction that the new covenant spoken of by prophets, especially Jeremiah (31:31–34) and Ezekiel (36:26–27; cf. 11:19–20) was being realized in their experience. It was thus the very Spirit belonging to the new covenant which offered this competence.[11] This covenant theology is obviously the presupposition for Paul's and the older evangelists'

---

[10] See Mogens Müller, "Schriftbeweis oder Vollendung? Das Johannesevangelium und das Alte Testament," in Klaus-Michael Bull and Eckart Reinmuth (eds.), *Bekenntnis und Erinnerung. FS Hans-Friedrich Weiss* (Rostocker Theologische Studien 16; Münster: Lit Verlag, 2004), 151–71.

[11] Although the Qumran community and the Early Church both use the concept of the new covenant, they surely do so in different ways. In the *Damascus Document* and *Pesher Habakkuk* the new covenant refers to the renewal of the old covenant, whereas in the New Testament it really is about a new dispensation, replacing the old. Thus also Lim, *Pesharim*, 83. A more elaborate argument in Mogens Müller, "Forstod essæerne deres pagt som den nye pagt? Pagtsforestillingen i Damaskusskriftet og Sekthånd-bogen," in *Dødehavsteksterne og Bibelen* (ed. Niels Hyldahl and Thomas L. Thompson; Forum for Bibelsk Ekegese 8; Copenhagen: Museum Tusculanum, 1996), 79–99.

interpretation of Scripture.[12] I think that when Paul designates himself as "minister of a new covenant (διάκονος καινῆς διαθήκης)" we stand at the very heart of his self-understanding. In 2 Corinthians 3[13] Paul does not quote Jer 31:31 explicitly because the Spirit is fundamental to his employment of the concept and that is only mentioned in Ezekiel.

Continuous Running Commentaries on Scripture

Interestingly, continuous running commentaries on entire scriptural books seem to be a feature of developed interpretative communities. Within the Qumran library the continuous pesher commentaries belong to the most recent layers. Writing commentaries is apparently an enterprise which is only taken up after some time, perhaps because one felt the obligation of showing that the whole of Scripture was on one's side, not only selected sayings. It took ca. 150 years before the Church fathers began to write commentaries on whole Old Testament books.[14] Such commentaries seem to be the culmination, not the beginning, of an exegetical tradition.

In the second century the "proof from Scripture" model, together with allegorical interpretation as practised by Philo, was soon to dominate interpretation. The methods characteristic of the pesher commentary disappeared, because Scripture was now understood according to the logic of the "proof from Scripture" method. This probably has to be seen in connection with the change that took place in the basic

---

[12] While the concept of the new covenant did not play any substantial role in the understanding of New Testament theology earlier, the picture has changed in recent decades. A pioneering study was Lars Hartman, "Bundesideologie in und hinter einigen paulinischen Texten," in *Die paulinische Literatur und Theologie. The Pauline Literature and Theology* (ed. Sigfried Pedersen; Teologiske Studier 7; Århus: Aros; Göttingen: Vandenhoeck & Ruprecht, 1980), 103–8. Cf. also Mogens Müller, "The Hidden Context: Some Observations to the Concept of the New Covenant in the New Testament," in *Texts and Contexts: Biblical Texts in Their Textual and Situational Contexts. Essays in Honor of Lars Hartman* (ed. Tord Fornberg and David Hellholm; Oslo: Scandinavian University Press, 1995), 649–58.

[13] Paul only speaks of the new covenant here and in 1 Cor 11:25 in connection with the institution of the Eucharist.

[14] The oldest known Christian commentary on a whole Old Testament book is Hippolytus' on Daniel from ca. 204. With regard to New Testament scriptures, the oldest known but not surviving commentaries on a continuous text were produced by Gnostics; see Hans-Friedrich Weiss, *Frühes Christentum und Gnosis* (WUNT 225; Tübingen: Mohr Siebeck, 2008), 208.

attitude towards Scripture: the first Bible of the Church (the "Hebrew Bible") now became the first part of a Christian Bible (the "Old Testament"), which also contained specifically Christian writings. This means that the Gospels in all probability were composed to function in Christian settings alongside what was then in process of becoming the "Old" Testament.

Whereas the challenge in the beginning had been to show that the Christ-event was wholly in accordance with the scriptures, Scripture being the unquestioned authority, in the second century the problem became how to best maintain Jewish Holy Writ as a Christian text as well. And whereas allegorical interpretation could seem to be neglecting the text's face value, and pesher commentary obviously did the same, the "proof from Scripture" model was thought capable of delivering evidence for Christ as being the exact fulfilment of prophecy and therefore the culmination of God's salvific enterprise rooted in his eternal decision. Confronted with Marcion's and the Gnostics' denial of the identity of the Creator with the father of Jesus Christ, the "proof from Scripture" argument was meant to secure the continuity of salvation history by taking its beginning in creation itself. This understanding, however, was only possible if the content of Scripture was supposed to be clear and plain to any benevolent reader.

The crucial difference between, on the one side, the use of Scripture in Paul's letters, the Gospels of Mark, Matthew and John, and on the other side the Lucan writings, in my view, should not be considered as two more or less contemporaneous traditions of interpretation, but as steps in an ongoing development. However, traditional scholarship's understanding of the Synoptic Problem, with the two later Gospels being virtually contemporary and therefore independent of each other, has also caused a more or less unconscious harmonization with regard to the understanding of their use of Scripture.

However, in my opinion there is much evidence for considering the Gospel of Matthew to be among the sources of the Gospel of Luke, that Gospel being rather late and probably to be dated in the second or third decade of the second century.[15] Once the improper harmonization of the use of Scripture in the Gospels is given up, and the special

---

[15] For an accumulative argument see Mogens Müller, "Lukasevangeliets iscenesættelse af en historisk Jesus," in Mogens Müller and Thomas L. Thompson (eds.), *Historie og konstruktion. FS Niels Peter Lemche* (Copenhagen: Museum Tusculanum, 2005), 286–305.

character of the use of Scripture in the Lucan writings is seen, the way is free to see in the earlier parts of the New Testament the afterlife of the pesher-like *method* of interpretation known from some of the Dead Sea Scrolls.[16] Intriguingly, however, just as the *form* of the continuous pesharim belongs to a late stage in the life of the community that engaged in this type of interpretation, so running commentaries on the books of the Old Testament are also clearly a feature of the interpretations of Christians of the second century and later.

---

[16] Without postulating any literary or other direct dependence, it is interesting to observe that we find a pesher-like way of interpretation in Gnostic sources from the second century. Here a saying of gnostic content is often followed by a New Testament quotation, introduced by the formula τουτέστιν or τοῦτ' ἔστιν, to indicate what was really meant by the New Testament author. Just as pesher and its derivates introduce a surprising meaning, the Greek formula does the same although in the reverse order. Cf. Weiss, *Frühes Christentum und Gnosis*, 207–485, passim.

INDEX OF BIBLICAL REFERENCES

Targum

Apocrypha And Pseudepigrapha

NEW TESTAMENT

INDEX OF SCROLLS AND OTHER CLASSICAL SOURCES

RABBINIC TEXTS

OTHER CLASSICAL SOURCES

INDEX OF MODERN AUTHORS